Nicole S. Colaianni
Bad for Business

Nicole S. Colaianni

Bad for Business

—

Sexual Harassment in the American Workplace,
1975–2017

DE GRUYTER

This book was written as part of the Research Training Group Authority and Trust in American Culture, Society, History and Politics (GRK 2244), funded by the German Research Foundation (DFG).
The Open Access publication of this book was funded by the Open Access Monograph Fund of the University Library of Heidelberg University (Ruprecht-Karls-Universität Heidelberg).

ISBN 978-3-11-914752-1
e-ISBN (PDF) 978-3-11-220732-1
e-ISBN (EPUB) 978-3-11-220738-3
DOI https://doi.org/10.1515/9783112207321

Library of Congress Control Number: 2025944294

Bibliographic information published by the Deutsche Nationalbibliothek
The Deutsche Nationalbibliothek lists this publication in the Deutsche Nationalbibliografie; detailed bibliographic data are available on the Internet at http://dnb.dnb.de.

www.degruyter.com
Questions about General Product Safety Regulation:
productsafety@degruyterbrill.com

For my mother, Christa Walter.

Contents

Introduction

On August 19th, 1981, Vice President George H. W. Bush received a letter from Karen Sauvigné, director of the Working Women's Institute, claiming that "obviously sexual harassment is bad for business."[1] The letter, while signed by Sauvigné, was a team-effort and had undergone several rounds of review before the women of the Institute deemed it ready to be sent to the White House.[2] The Working Women's Institute had been founded in 1975 as a single-issue organization dedicated to fighting sexual harassment in the US-American workplace. The organization had coined the term 'sexual harassment,' provided services to women affected, and by 1981, had spent six years fighting for acknowledgment of the phenomenon by the public, the private sector, and the federal government. They had made significant headway in their quest for recognition during President Jimmy Carter's tenure, but with the change in administration in 1981 the organization's successes seemed at threat. Within his first year in office, President Ronald Reagan tasked Vice President George H. W. Bush with revising the guidelines on sexual harassment published by the Equal Employment Opportunity Commission (EEOC) – the agency responsible for enforcing the Civil Rights Act both in the public and private sector.

Rather than expanding on the plight of individual victims or explaining the systemic discriminatory dynamics at play in the workplace, Sauvigné's letter focused on an argument bound to draw the administrations attention:

> The fact is that the prevention of sexual harassment is in the best interest of the business community. If the Reagan administration is serious about getting the economy moving, you will be interested in eliminating sexual harassment [...] because the fact is that productivity begins where harassment ends. [...] sexual harassment has a serious impact on employers. When productive energies are diverted by sexual by-play, the company suffers.[3]

The women of the Institute argued that the eradication of sexual harassment, did not hinder an organization's success, but much rather was a necessity for economic prosperity.

---

1 Sauvigné, Karen: Letter to Vice President Bush from Karen Sauvigné (WWI), August 19th, 1981, p. 2, BCA, Research on Women Records, Box 95, Folder Publications of American Federation of State, County and Municipal Employees.
2 Several Revisions and Comments at: Barnard Center for Research on Women Records, Box: 95, Folder: Publications of American Federation of State, County and Municipal Employees.
3 Ibid., pp. 1f.

By highlighting productivity and profit, Sauvigné and her cowriters were catering to the Reagan administration's support of the private sector.

This letter presents an anomaly in regard to the Institute's usual line of reasoning. Profit, professionality, and the success of a business were not regular talking points for Sauvigné and her fellow activists. Instead, their understanding of sexual harassment was distinctly feminist, focusing on systemic and gendered power discrepancies within American society and the American workplace. These views stood in stark contrast to the social conservative rhetoric of the pro-family movement. In the public discourse, the topic of sexual harassment appeared as a highly contentious, polarized issue with the feminist understanding – or framing – on the one side and the social conservative framing on the other.

The reasoning used in the letter quoted above, however, fit in neither conception of sexual harassment. I contend that what is displayed here, is the emergence of a new framing of the issue, which I have termed *the management frame*. While feminists intermittently used such arguments to interest employers and politicians in the topic in the late 1970s and early 1980s, it was corporate lawyers and management consultants who were soon the driving force behind this framing of sexual harassment. This understanding in contrast to its feminist and social conservative counterparts was not based on an ideological, political motivation of shaping societal gender relations. Instead, its conception was driven by pragmatic managerial interests within the private sector. Due to its lack of ideological drive, it did not take center stage in the polarized public discussion of the issue. Nevertheless, throughout the last four decades, this framing has undergirded public and private debates.

In this book I demonstrate the private sector's involvement in shaping American's understanding of sexual harassment. The management frame was evident in training material, policies, and procedures advertised by professional consultants and implemented by employers. In order to protect the economic interests of the organization, employers and their advocates divorced the phenomenon from any structural and gendered implications, thereby making it more manageable within the organization. Additionally, consultants' and employers' definitions of and policies regarding sexual harassment went far beyond the federal definition and covered consensual as well as coercive sexual encounters.

Further, I argue that the U.S. federal government, by encouraging private organizations to employ anti-sexual harassment policies, preventative measures, and grievance procedures, inadvertently relinquished much of their authority regarding this topic, transferring it to the organizations in question. This process began when the Equal Employment Opportunity Commission published its anti-sexual harassment guidelines in 1980 and was significantly expedited when the Supreme Court in 1998 acquiesced the use of an affirmative defense. This meant that internal policies and procedures could now isolate employers from liability in sexual harassment cases. Additionally, the Court declined to hear charges which had not first exhausted the internal company grievance procedures.[4]

Bad for Business explores how employers (or their respective human resources departments) became the first port-of-call for employees filing a complaint. I contend that by the early 2000s employers acted in the place of all three branches of government: They defined what constituted "sexual harassment" and settled on the consequences following this behavior (legislative), they held judgement over whether or not an accusation had merit (judicative), and they were the party responsible for executing procedure and policy (executive). In short, I hypothesize that employers found themselves in a position of taking over government authorities within the microcosm of their company, effectively eliminating a system of checks and balances.

As long as employers defined sexual harassment more broadly than the federal government, they were not only protected from federal intervention but also gained additional control over their employees. A broad definition of sexual harassment, coupled with the employer's discretion when executing policies and penalizing offenses, had the potential of transforming breeches of anti-sexual harassment policies into a powerful pretense for circumventing federal anti-discrimination regulations as well as other workers' rights. Additionally, broad definitions and harsh penalties stoked fears of false accusations and accidentally violating company policy among many male employees. This missing accountability and lack of due process generated deep suspicion and distrust among employees. On the one hand, anger about such policies was often aimed not at upper management but at those reporting offenses. On the other hand, the internal (mis)handling of complaints discouraged victims of harassment from coming forward. This dynamic rendered internal measures ineffective in the fight against sexual harassment.

Central sources for my arguments are policies, procedures, training materials, and articles in company newsletters conceived and published by management consultants, corporate lawyers, and employers. Unsurprisingly, access to internal company documents is extremely limited. Individual personnel records as well as paperwork chronicling internal complaints or investigations were not accessible under any condition. Some organizations, however, made available to me more general material, such as company newsletters, new employee welcome packets,

---

4 Equal Employment Opportunity Commission: "Guidelines on Sexual Harassment," 45 Federal Register 74676, November 10th, 1980; *Oncale v. Sundowner Offshore Services, Inc.* 523 U.S. 75 (1998); *Faragher v. City of Boca Raton*, 524 U.S. 775 (1998); *Burlington Industries, Inc. v. Ellerth*, 524 U.S. 742 (1998).

code of conducts, training material, or in some rare cases even communication about the establishment of new sexual harassment policies. It is important to note that material pertaining to the last one to two decades, depending on the collection, was closed to researchers.

Knowing that my search for sources could prove challenging, I did not set limits regarding sector, size, or location. After contacting roughly 200 companies – or their corporate archives – I received thirty-one responses. Half of these either immediately denied my request or followed up with their regrets after consulting their legal departments. Of the remaining fifteen, ten referred me to university or museum archives, where their records were being held. Five companies invited me to their archives, however, three withdrew their invitation citing the pandemic as a reason. After having initially anticipated that my research trip would primarily involve appointments at various corporate archives, I ultimately found myself only able to visit two: the U.S. division of the Hongkong and Shanghai Banking Corporation and the Michigan based, furniture company Herman Miller, Inc.

Nevertheless, the acquisition of company records from merely two corporate archives should not be misconstrued as an exhaustive endeavor. Upon receiving referrals to university archives from multiple human resources departments, it became apparent that numerous enterprises actively contribute their archival materials to universities or museums. My research led me to sixteen archives in eleven cities across the continental United States. I conducted an examination of archival collections from a total of twenty companies, including the Digital Equipment Corporation, Apple, Lehman Brothers Holdings, and Pan Am Airlines. Furthermore, many of these collections referenced or held copied material from other industry leaders, supplying me with additional information. The Digital Equipment Corporation, for instance, repeatedly referenced Microsoft's policies.[5]

My sample contains employers in tech, manufacturing, mining, banking, broadcasting, and hospitality. Some of these companies were regional and employed only several hundred workers, while others operated nationwide (and globally) and are listed as Fortune 500 companies. Various studies have found that factors, such as size, turnover, region, white/blue collar environment, corporate structure, or growth rate significantly affected the rate and handling of sexual harassment experienced by employees.[6] Thus, I expected these factors to be of

---

5 The same dynamic can be observed regarding university policies, e. g. UC Davis, Martha West Papers, Box 6, Folder 18 Sexual Harassment Program at UCD.

6 Goldstein, Morris and Robert Smith: The Estimated Impact of Anti-Discrimination Laws Aimed at Federal Contractors, in: Industrial and Labor Relations Review 29 (1976), pp. 523–543; Leonard, Jonathan: Employment and Occupational Advance under Affirmative Action, in: Review of Economics and Statistics 66 (1984), pp. 377–385; Kallev, Alexandra et al.: Enforcement of Civil Rights

significance in my own research. However, contrary to my original hypothesis, I found that they did not substantially impact internal written policies and procedures. Instead, policies from the early to mid-1980s onwards were relatively standardized within the American private sector. Therefore, I feel confident making general statements based on the sources available to me.[7]

In addition to company internal documents, I make use of a multitude of sources which include but are not limited to articles published in the mainstream and alternative press, private letters, government documents, survey data, theoretical deliberations, and research material collected by feminist groups. For further insight into the business world, I turned to pamphlets and short films produced by management consultants; to business magazines which published excerpts of companies' policies and procedures, and updated readers on the newest developments; and to opinion pieces, letters to the editor, and interviews. These revealed not only the hard facts but the perception of the issue in the business community. Furthermore, court decisions, *amicus curiae* briefs, Equal Employment Opportunity Commission statements, and transcripts of congressional hearings have provided valuable insights.

It is important to highlight that the sources available to me gave me little insight into individual cases, especially if these were resolved without litigation. By analyzing a policy or a grievance procedure, I cannot gather whether a company implemented the steps advertised in the written document. By watching a training video, I cannot gauge the employees' reactions. Nor can I make assumptions about the individual context in which the video was shown to employees. Where possible, I fill these gaps with existing social science research and often turn to survey data. However, my intent is not to highlight individual cases, nor even to make claims about the numerical extent of sexual harassment within the four decades analyzed. Instead, I argue on a conceptual basis. I demonstrate that the definitions of sexual harassment have shifted significantly over time and that the private sector has gained considerable discursive authority over the topic.

I wish to highlight, that this is a study primarily focusing on the for-profit private sector. While the management frame permeated the public sector as well, the government has distinct ideological goals. While productivity and professionalism are vital in public sector jobs, federal, and state governments are also concerned with shaping social values and relations. Therefore, depending on the administration, ideological, and political concepts of anti-discrimination, diversity, or the

---

Law in Private Workplaces: The Effects of Compliance Reviews and Lawsuits Over Time, in: Law and Social Inquiry 31/4 (2006), pp. 855–903.

7 Nevertheless, it is prudent to remind the reader that this is a qualitative, not a quantitative study and as such, hypotheses will have to be confirmed with further research.

protection of traditional family values shaped the conceptualization of workplace policy and procedure.

Naturally, there are also for-profit organizations, whose shareholders and CEO's hold distinct ideological and political views, which permeate their business practices. The fast-food chain Chick-fil-A, for instance, has long since been committed to conservative Christian views, closing the business on Sundays so that employees may go to church, and donating to anti-LGBTQ+ organizations.[8] On the other end of the political spectrum, Bumble, an internet dating site, exemplifies a for-profit business devoted to feminist values, which is evident both in the set-up of the product itself, as well as the company's dedication to affirmative action.[9] More broadly speaking, however, the private sector does not show the same interest in societal values as does its public counterpart. A separation of the two is therefore of significance.

At times this distinction proves difficult. Surveys and statistics often do not differentiate between the two, but prove helpful, nevertheless. Similarly, there are institutions which present borderline cases. Private universities, for instance, must be seen as a separate category. While for-profit private educational institutions can be included in the private sector without any hesitation, the non-profit variety warrants more consideration. In most cases, these universities receive some public funds and are, therefore, bound by governmental restrictions. Nevertheless, because the biggest portion of their funding stems from donations and tuition fees, these universities are, similarly to private sector for-profit businesses, reliant on the influx of clients (students) and concerned with their reputation. As university records are available in much more detail than corporate documents, I sporadically make use of these sources. However, I use these sources with caution and make explicit the instances in which they are included.

In the context of investigating a subject matter that remains contentious to this day, I wish to clarify my use of terminology. First, while the provision of a definitive definition for sexual harassment would undoubtedly enhance clarity, I regret to inform the reader that such precision remains elusive in this discourse. My argument hinges entirely upon the analysis of various definitions, which I contend are subject to change over time. However, when not specifying a definition, I refer to instances that constitute illegal sexual harassment. The current judicial interpretation of sexual harassment as a form of sex discrimination and therefore as a violation of the Civil Rights Act (1964) was first proposed by feminist scholar

---

8 Valinsky, Jordan: How Chick-fil-A Became a Target for Going 'Woke,' in: CNN Business (June 2nd, 2023).

9 Gingras, Abbey: 28 Companies Invested in the Success of Women at Work, in: Ripplematch (March 8th, 2021).

Catharine MacKinnon and subsequently implemented by the executive and judicial branch of the U.S. federal government. While this definition, too, has been reinterpreted by the courts over time, with the effect of including more scenarios into its fold, its legal basis in the Civil Rights Act has remained intact. According to this definition, "[u]nwelcome sexual advances, requests for sexual favors, and other verbal or physical conduct of a sexual nature constitute sexual harassment" either when the acceptance or rejection of these advances are tied to tangible changes in the employment relationship (*quid pro quo* harassment) or when the work environment becomes so hostile, that the victim of the harassment can no longer perform their job to the best of their ability (hostile work environment harassment).[10] Therefore, contrary to common perception, unwelcome sexual advances legally do not constitute sexual harassment unless they are coercive in nature or become so "severe and pervasive" that they have a negative effect on the victim's performance or ability to do their job.[11]

Second, when referring to individuals affected by sexual harassment, I routinely use the terms 'target' or 'victim.' The latter has been criticized in recent years for allegedly implying weakness and a lack of agency in those to whom it referred.[12] I wish to make exceedingly clear that I do not use the term in this way. Instead, 'victim' is the terminology most often used within the criminal justice system and describes a person "who has been subject to a crime." According to the federally funded Sexual Assault Kit Initiative, "the word serves [...] as a status that provides certain rights under the law. However, the word does not imply weakness, assume guilt or assign blame."[13] It is in this context that I employ the term 'victim.'

Third, there is no denying that sexual harassment affects men and women disproportionately. A multitude of studies and surveys over the last four decades have shown that women are harassed more often than men and that harassers are much more frequently male than female.[14] This is not to deny that women

---

10 Equal Employment Opportunity Commission: Guidelines on Sexual Harassment, 45 Federal Register 74676, November 10th, 1980.

11 *Meritor Savings Bank, FSB v. Vinson*, 477 U.S. 57 (1986).

12 Cf. Gilson, Erinn Cunniff: Vulnerability and Victimization: Rethinking Key Concepts in Feminist Discourse on Sexual Violence, in: Journal of Women in Culture and Society 42/1 (2024), pp. 71–98.

13 For a discussion on the terms 'victim' and 'survivor' see: Sexual Assault Kit Initiative: Victim or Survivor. Terminology from Investigation Through Prosecution.

14 Most recently: U.S. Merit Systems Protection Board, Sexual Harassment in Federal Workplaces: Understanding and Addressing the Problem. A Report to the President and the Congress of the United States, December 2022; Feldblum, Chai R. and Victoria A. Lipnic: EEOC Report by the Select Task Force on the Study of Harassment in the Workplace, June 2016.

can take on the role of harasser, nor do I wish to minimize the fact that men were – and are – victimized by sexual harassment.[15] Nonetheless, I contend that the gendered nature of the phenomenon is significant for this analysis and therefore I have decided against using strictly gender-neutral language and at times, refer to the prototype victim as "she" and the harasser as "he."

Last, as has become apparent in these first few pages, the terms *narrative* and *frame* are elementary for the analysis of the various concepts of sexual harassment. I use the term *narrative* to refer to a common belief system, composed of shared experiences and collective goals within a specific discourse space.[16] This discourse space may vary in size and organizational complexity, ranging from small grassroots groups or a single company to an entire social movement or industry.[17] The discourse spaces analyzed in *Bad for Business* are broad, comprised of many organizations and individuals. The analysis of large discourse spaces risks neglecting nuances but allows for the recognition and comparison of dominant narratives within society.

Within these discourse spaces, individuals examine, evaluate, and adapt topics and issues to match their larger narrative. Accordingly, a topic will be charged with different norms, ideologies, and meanings, depending on the narrative in which it is incorporated. Within social movement theory, this process has been termed *framing*, and the resulting variations of the topic are referred to as *frames* or *frameworks*.[18] This terminology shall be adopted within this book. As frames

---

15 For a discussion on the importance of increased scholarly attention to sexual harassment directed at men see: Dziech, Billie Wright and Michael W. Hawkins: Sexual Harassment in Higher Education. Reflections and New Perspectives, Abington [2]2011, pp. 85–102.

16 This paper makes use of Michel Foucault's theories on discourse and discourse spaces. Foucault, Michel: Archäologie des Wissens, Frankfurt [15]2011, pp. 33–60; cf. Strüver, Anke: Grundlagen und Zentrale Begriffe der Foucault'schen Diskurstheorie, in: Handbuch Diskurs und Raum. Theorien und Methoden für die Humangeographie sowie die Sozial- und Kulturwissenschaftliche Raumforschung, ed. by Georg Glasze and Annika Mattissek, Bielefeld [2]2005, pp. 65 f.; Landwehr, Achim: Historische Diskursanalyse, New York – Frankfurt [2]2009, pp. 65–78.

17 For further reading on definitions and theory regarding social movements, see: Opp, Karl-Dieter: Die Perspektive der Ressourcenmobilisierung und die Theorie Kollektiven Handelns, in: Paradigmen der Bewegungsforschung. Entstehung und Entwicklung von Neuen Sozialen Bewegungen und Rechtsextremismus, ed. by Kai-Uwe Hellmann and Ruud Koopmans, Wiesbaden 1998, pp. 96 f.; Olofsson, Gunnar: From the Working-Class Movement to the New Social Movements, in: Social Movements. Transformative Shifts and Turning Points, ed. by Ravi Kumar Savyasaachi, New Delhi 2014, pp. 34 f.

18 For a thorough discussion on the theory of frames, see: Hellmann, Kai-Uwe: Paradigmen der Bewegungsforschung, in: Paradigmen der Bewegungsforschung. Entstehung und Entwicklung von Neuen Sozialen Bewegungen und Rechtsextremismus, ed. by Kai-Uwe Hellmann and Ruud Koopmans, Wiesbaden 1998, pp. 70–72; Koopmans, Ruud: Konkurrierende Paradigmen oder

convey not only an isolated opinion on one topic but are carriers for various and often contradicting world views, their advocates consciously present, promote, and defend them beyond the discourse space in which they were developed.

The further a frame is pushed into mainstream thought, the more its corresponding narrative will find acknowledgment and legitimization in society at large. Likewise, a frame will find it easier to be broadly accepted if its related narrative is already dominant. Hence, for social movements, in particular, the creation and promotion of their respective frame was a conscious strategy in achieving social change.[19] Since governmental institutions, public policies as well as media outlets shaped and reflected public discourse, these were the main areas worth influencing.[20] Their acceptance and rejection of certain frames is indicative for the success of the individual movements and the development of broader societal notions.

The identification of larger narratives within US-American society has been the subject of several scholarly works. I argue that the dominant frames of sexual harassment found in the mainstream discourse since the late 1970s are largely consistent with the three preeminent narratives (feminist, social conservative, and laissez-faire) identified by historian Rebecca Klatch.[21] These frames are compiled of a multitude of voices and therefore are not wholly homogeneous. Overall, however, despite including many different tones and variations, each of these frames is rooted in an identifiable narrative and is led by consistent values and intentions. Thus, the feminist and social conservative frames, presented in Part I, are developed within the Women's Liberation and the Pro-family Movement respectively. The management frame, presented in Part II and further explicated upon in Part III, was conceived of within the for-profit private sector.

Friedlich Ko-Existierende Komplemente? in: Paradigmen der Bewegungsforschung. Entstehung und Entwicklung von Neuen Sozialen Bewegungen und Rechtsextremismus, ed. by Kai-Uwe Hellmann and Ruud Koopmans, Wiesbaden 1998, pp. 216–231; Ryan, Charlotte: Prime Time Activism. Media Strategies for Grassroot Organizing, Boston 1991, pp. 220 f.

19 Zippel: Politics, p. 80.

20 Geise, Ann L: The Female Role in Middle Class Women's Magazines from 1955 to 1976. A Content Analysis of Nonfiction Selections, in: Sex Roles 5/1 (1979), p. 52; Ryan, Barbara: Feminism, pp. 6 f.; Zippel: Politics, pp. 7, 10; For further reading on the influence of media on the public discourse, see: Ryan, Charlotte: Prime Time Activism, pp. 17 f., 23, 27; McDonald, Paula and Sara Charlesworth: Framing Sexual Harassment through Media Representation, in: Women's Studies International Forum 37 (2013), p. 97.

21 Klatch, Rebecca E.: Women of the New Right, Philadelphia 1987, pp. 4–12. In Klatch's work the feminist narrative merely appears as a comparison to the social and economic conservative narratives. For a brief summery on world views and goals of Second-Wave Feminists, see: Ryan, Barbara: Feminism, pp. 89 f.

Part I (Chapters 1–3) covers the early movement against sexual harassment and its opponents. Feminists had named the phenomenon in 1975 and began conceptualizing it as a social and political problem. Until the early 1980s, feminist organizations developed a body of research and theory on the issue and struggled for recognition of sexual harassment as a violation of women's civil rights. Publicly, they were strongly opposed by social conservative groups. In Chapter One, I set a foundation by comparing and contrasting the feminist and the social conservative theoretical frameworks. Only by thoroughly comprehending the reasonings behind these positions can the later development of the management frame be discerned.

In Chapter Two, I turn to feminists' relationship to private sector employers. As feminists initially addressed sexual harassment in the workplace as opposed to housing or education, employers were naturally drawn into the conflict. Early on, feminists stood in an antagonistic relationship with employers. Victims of sexual harassment complained of employers' inaction and indifference to or even worse their endorsement of and participation in sexual misconduct. Additionally, following feminists' conceptualization of sexual harassment as a civil rights issue, feminist lawyers, and their clients stood opposed to employers and their legal representation rather than the individual harasser, when pursuing a case in the judiciary.

In Chapter Three I relate how, despite this adversarial relationship, feminists soon found that employers could prove powerful allies. Employers concerned with increased litigation and the resulting high legal costs, in the late 1970s and early 1980s sought out experts for advice. At the time, these experts were feminists organized in groups such as the Working Women's Institute. These groups, in turn, began developing training and counseling material specifically targeted at employers. Unsurprisingly, early definitions and policies written by employers for use in their organizations, included distinct instances of the feminist understanding of sexual harassment.

Part II (Chapters 4 and 5) examines the period from 1980 to 1998, in which feminist organizations lost much of their influence over the subject matter. In Chapter Four, I discuss how victims of sexual harassment gained institutionalized avenues for filing complaints. The federal Equal Employment Opportunity Commission, in 1980, began acting on complaints regarding sexual harassment; the Supreme Court, in 1986, confirmed that sexual harassment constituted sex discrimination and thereby, explicitly enabled victims to seek resolutions through litigation; and several unions began including clauses specifically forbidding sexual harassment within their contracts.

In the early and mid-1980s it had become clear that sexual harassment in the workplace was a significant issue and warranted employers' attention. In Chapter

Five, I highlight how management consultants and corporate lawyers began professionalizing on the topic. With new experts available, employers no longer needed assistance from feminist groups. Instead, they got their advice from personnel professionals, who were motivated neither by feminist nor social conservative goals but instead sought to protect the employer from financial losses. An analysis of training material developed by management consultants and corporate lawyers reveals the understanding of sexual harassment which I have termed the 'management frame.'

Part III (Chapters 6 and 7) examines the period from 1998 to 2017. The Supreme Court's twin decision in *Faragher v. City of Boca Raton* and *Burlington Industries v. Ellerth* (1998) encouraged employers to handle sexual harassment complaints internally. In Chapter Six, I contend that by writing policies, investigating complaints, and adjudicating over merit and disciplinary action, employers gained significant control over the issue. They effectively performed functions normally reserved for the legislative, executive, and judiciary branch of a states' government. In doing so, employers further perpetuated and enshrined the management framework of sexual harassment.

Lastly, in Chapter Seven, I address the consequences of binding arbitration and non-disclosure agreements and draw historical parallels to the early 1970s. With over half of American private-sector employees bound by pre-dispute arbitration agreements, many targets of harassment did not have the option of taking issues to court. Additionally, confidentiality and non-disclosure agreements often precluded victims of sexual harassment from speaking about their experiences. I argue that such agreements created a situation which resembled dynamics in the 1970s. The silence surrounding the issue and the lack of legal options resulted in patterns of harassment and discrimination going unnoticed, the severity and extent of the phenomenon being underestimated, and victims feeling isolated. In 1975, activists took to the streets and coined the term sexual harassment. In 2017, they took to their laptops and tweeted #MeToo.

The Reagan administration had argued that the Equal Employment Opportunity Commission's standards unfairly burdened employers and threatened profits. Nevertheless, public protest led the administration to abandon any formal changes to the EEOC policy on sexual harassment. Instead it opted for quieter forms of obstruction: Cutting budgets and reshuffling staff to reduce the agency's effectiveness. Nevertheless, over 40 years later, principles of merit and an alleged negative economic impact are again cited as arguments to challenge the EEOC and its anti-discrimination policies.

As I write this introduction, it is day 112 of President Trump's second term, which has already been marked by unprecedented cuts to federal agencies. Among the hardest-hit have been programs centered on diversity, equity, and inclusion (DEI), which President Trump dismissed as "nonsense,"[22] and which he claimed constituted "a pernicious identity-based spoils system" that undermined merit, burdened employers, and damaged the broader economy.[23] Consequently, within days of taking office, the President issued various executive orders mandating all federal agencies to immediately halt any and all DEI initiatives.[24] Unsurprisingly, the EEOC has undergone financial cuts, loss of staff, change in leadership, and a shift in enforcement priorities.[25] While Trump's rhetoric and actions are undeniably extreme, he is not the first president to cite economic arguments to challenge the EEOC. In doing so, the President relies on arguments that form the core of the management framework, which I will uncover in this book.

---

22 Trump, Donald J.: Remarks by President Trump at the World Economic Forum, January 23rd, 2025; cf. The White House: Fact Sheet: President Donald J. Trump Removes DEI from the Foreign Service, March 18th, 2025; High, Tracey et al.: President Trump Acts to Roll Back DEI Initiatives, in: Harvard Law School Forum on Corporate Governance, February 10th, 2025.
23 Trump, Donald: Executive Order 14151: Ending Illegal Discrimination and Restoring Merit-Based Opportunity, January 21st, 2025.
24 Trump, Donald J.: Executive Order 14173: Ending Radical and Wasteful Government DEI Programs and Preferencing, January 20th 2025; Trump, Donald J.: Executive Order 14168: Defending Women from Gender ideology Extremism and Restoring Biological Truth to the Federal Government, 20th January, 2025; Trump, Donald J.: Executive Order 14151: Ending Illegal Discrimination and Restoring Merit-Based Opportunity, January 21st, 2025.
25 EEOC: The State of the EEOC: Frequently Asked Questions; EEOC: Fiscal Year 2025 Congressional Budget Justification, March 11th, 2024; Anonymous: EEOC Continues Operations Amid Leadership Changes and New Executive Orders, in: Thomson Reuters Tax & Accounting, February 6th, 2025; Anonymous: DEI Dead at Revamped EEOC: EEOC Enforcement Priorities after Trump Administration Makeover, in: Epstein Becker Green Workforce Bulletin, February 5th, 2025.

Part I
Naming and Politicizing the Issue

> The boss from the shop was always fresh with the girls. He liked to see us blush [...]. But we
> was afraid of him, and so we couldn't help each other. Once he touched me, very fresh like,
> and I cried, and he said 'Lets be good friends, Rosie [...].' I was trembling so I couldn't nearly
> do my work. [...] so the next day I went to another shop, and I told the first lie I ever told
> in my life. I told the boss I come from another city. I liked this new boss; he was not so
> fresh [...]. [T]hen the next day the boss he come to me and he says, 'I'm sorry, Rosie, we like
> your work, but your other boss he telephoned [...] so we can't keep you here.[1]

Rosie was a seventeen-year-old woman working as a seamstress in the early 20th century. In 1914, she did not conceive of her experience as "sexual harassment." The term would not be coined until 1975. Nevertheless, Rosie was neither the first nor the only woman to experience sexual pressures which interfered with her livelihood. Despite being aware of their shared plight, fear, and economic dependence kept Rosie and her colleagues from organizing and from confronting their boss. Instead, Rosie left her job, only to find that she could not escape his reach.

The sexual exploitation and coercion of working women goes back centuries before even Rosie's time. No matter in which context or era, enslaved, indentured, and working-class women have always been vulnerable to sexual pressures and assaults by the men they worked with and for.[2] In Rosie's time, sexual advances towards women on the job were so prominent that working women were often compared to "working girls," establishing a direct link between wage-labor and prostitution. Pursuing employment outside of the home was considered "unlady-like" and, thus, a life-style reserved for those lacking virtue.[3]

When, in the course of the World Wars, women, and specifically middle-class women, increasingly entered the labor market, this narrative faded but nevertheless continued to permeate attitudes towards working women. Sexual exploitation and sexuality more generally, was seldom spoken of and did not often appear in the mainstream press. When it did, the phenomenon of sex in the workplace was conceived of in the form of jokes,[4] sex scandals involving prominent individuals,[5]

---

1 Life and Labor, 4/8 (August 1914), p. 242, cited in: Bularzik, Mary: Sexual Harassment at the Workplace. Historical Notes, in: Workers' Struggles, Past and Present. A 'Radical America' Reader, ed. By James Green, Philadelphia 1983, p. 123.
2 Bularzik: Sexual Harassment at the Workplace, p. 119.
3 Ibid., pp. 119 f.
4 Farley, Lin: Sexual Shakedown. The Sexual Harassment of Women on the Job, New York 1978, pp. 12–14.

or romantic advice. Coinciding with the dawn of the sexual revolution, articles and full-length books, such as Helen Gurley Brown's *Sex and the Single Girl* encouraged women to romantically pursue their boss.[6]

By 1970, female workers made up 37.5% of the U.S. labor force. In 1980, this number had risen to 42.2%. By then, for the first time, over half of American Women were employed outside of the home.[7] In addition to cultural changes and technological developments, economic necessity prompted many women to seek out wage labor. The economic boom of the 1950s had long since subsided and the 1970s saw a period of economic stagnation. Well-paid manufacturing jobs became scarcer, while the number of lower paid jobs in the service industry increased.[8] Women were clustered in what would later be known as 'pink collar jobs.' The most common job by far for a woman to hold in the 1970s was that of secretary. This was followed by teaching, retail work, and nursing.[9] Furthermore, the increase of divorced or never-married mothers, led to a rise of families headed by women in the 1960s and 1970s.[10] Contrary to the common perception of the time, many women were not working only for "pin money" or to supplement the family income but depended on the wages they earned.[11] Nevertheless, women's work was often undervalued and underpaid. Sex segregation and sex discrimination in the workplace led to a gender pay gap of 40%.[12]

Beginning in the second half of the 1960s, second-wave feminists took on the issues of sex discrimination at work. The National Organization for Women (NOW) was founded in 1966 as an interest group fighting against sex discrimina-

---

5 Baker, Carrie N.: He Said, She Said. Popular Representation of Sexual Harassment in Second-Wave Feminism, in: Disco Divas. Women and Popular Culture in the 1970s, ed. by Sherrie A. Innes, Philadelphia 2003, p. 48; Baxandall, Rosalyn and Linda Gordon: Second-Wave Feminism, in: A Companion to American Women's History (Blackwell Companions to American History), ed. by Nancy A. Hewitt, Malden, MA 2002, p. 422.

6 E.g. 1962 New York Times bestseller: Brown, Helen Gurley: Sex and the Single Girl, New York ²2003, pp. 33–37; Jo Foxworth on "nine commandments for women in business" reported on in: Carlson, Walter: Advertising. Feminist Mystique under Fire, in: The New York Times (Jun 30, 1965), p. 46.

7 U.S. Department of Labor, Women's Bureau: Occupations of Women in the Labor Force Since 1920, 2021.

8 Baker: Women's Movement, p. 47.

9 U.S. Department of Labor, Women's Bureau: Occupations of Women in the Labor Force Since 1920, 2021.

10 Garfinkel, Irwin et al.: The Growth of Families Headed by Women. 1950–1980, in: Demography 27/1 (1990), pp. 19–30.

11 Baker: Women's Movement, p. 47.

12 U.S. Department of Labor, Women's Bureau: Occupations of Women in the Labor Force Since 1920, 2021.

tion, which had only recently been outlawed by the Civil Rights Act of 1964.[13] Employers were now legally prohibited from differentiating between (prospective) employees on the basis of their sex. The prohibition of sex discrimination in the workplace was established, *de jure*, but was still lacking in practice.[14] Feminist groups, such as NOW, 9to5, and Women Employed demanded equal pay, training, opportunities for promotion, and an end to sex-segregation in the workplace. Throughout the following years acceptable behavior in the workplace began to change and violations were increasingly publicly discussed and brought to court.[15]

In addition to their fight against workplace discrimination, second-wave feminists also took up the issue of sexual violence. Feminists across the country established rape crisis centers, women's shelters, and offered self-defense classes. Additionally, they developed a body of theory regarding sexual violence. In 1975, Susann Brownmiller published her monograph *Against Our Will*, which was the first extensive feminist work on rape. While the book was criticized for its representation of homosexuality and its lack of quantitative data, it was extremely relevant in developing a feminist understanding of rape as a widespread, gendered, systemic problem as opposed to the abnormal and abhorrent act perpetrated by an individual sexual deviant.[16]

Despite much attention diverted to sex discrimination and sexual violence both within and outside of the feminist movement, a discussion on inappropriate sexual conduct at work only emerged in 1975.[17] The issue of sexual harassment was a relative late-comer to second-wave feminism. When feminists did address the issue, they based much of their understanding on previously developed feminist theories on sex discrimination in the workplace and sexual violence.

The 1960's and 1970's have often been described as decades of substantial social change. Considering the increasing number of women in the labor force, changing sexual mores, a growing feminist consciousness, and the establishment of civil rights legislation, it is no surprise that the topic of gender relations and the

---

13 Baxandall: Second-Wave Feminism, p. 415; Boris, Eileen and Allison Louise Elias: Workplace Discrimination, Equal Pay, and Sexual Harassment. An Intersectional Approach, in: The Oxford Handbook of U.S. Women's Social Movement Activism (Oxford Handbooks), New York 2017, p. 195.
14 Zippel: Politics, p. 23.
15 Geise: The Female Role, p. 59; Arriola, Elvia R.: 'What's the Big Deal?' Women in the New York City Construction Industry and Sexual Harassment Law. 1970–1985, in: Columbia Human Rights Law Review 22/1 (1990), p. 34.
16 Brownmiller, Susan: Against Our Will. Men, Women and Rape, New York – Toronto 1981.
17 Arriola: Construction Industry, p. 33; For a well-researched summary of mainstream media attention to sexual harassment in the 1970's, see: Baker: Popular Representation, pp. 39, 42.

treatment of women in the workplace entered public discourse.[18] The major American dailies, such as *The New York Times, The Chicago Tribune*, and *The Washington Post*, many magazines, including *Esquire, Redbook* and *Good House-keeping*, and radio and television broadcasts kept the public informed about the on-goings in "women's lib."[19]

Changes in gender roles and norms coupled with increasing feminist activity and the spreading of a feminist consciousness provoked the establishment of a social conservative pro-family movement.[20] The groups and individuals of this movement explicitly self-identified as "anti-feminist" and acted against what they perceived as "the moral decay" of America.[21] Concretely, this translated into a push for the protection of established gender roles and the preservation of traditional family structures.[22] Organizations, such as the Eagle Forum (found-

18 Aronson, Pamela: The Dynamics and Causes of Gender and Feminist Consciousness and Feminist Identities, in: The Oxford Handbook of U.S. Women's Social Movement Activism, ed. by McCammon et al., New York 2017, pp. 338–340; Sowerwine, Charles and Patricia Grimshaw: Equality and Difference in the Twentieth-Century West. North America, Western Europe, Australia, and New Zealand, in: A Companion to Gender History (Blackwell Companions to History), Malden, MA – Oxford – Victoria ²2006, pp. 586–610; Arriola: Construction Industry, p. 65; For further reading on social movements and the mainstream press, see: McDonald, Framing Sexual Harassment, p. 97; Ryan, Charlotte: Prime Time Activism, pp. 165–188. While presenting a thorough analysis of the dynamics between social movements and the media, Ryan self-identifies as an activist of the New Left. The possible bias resulting from the positioning of the author necessitates the reader to exercise adequate caution when making use of her work.
19 E.g.: Dienstag, Eleanor: Women's Lib for Boys and Girls, in: The New York Times (May 7, 1972), p. BRA3; Bradford, Beverly: Women's Lib Comes to Suburbs, in: The Washington Post (Aug 6, 1970), p. H1; Baker: Popular Representation, p. 42.
20 Ryan, Barbara: Feminism, p. 103; Sutton, Matthew Avery: Reagan, Religion, and the Culture Wars of the 1980's, in: A Companion to Ronald Reagan (Wiley Blackwell Companions to History), ed. by Andrew L. Johns, Chichester et al. 2015, p. 207.
21 Klatch: Women, pp. 5, 133; Brocker, Manfred: Protest – Anpassung – Etablierung. Die Christliche Rechte im politischen System der USA, Frankfurt 2004, p. 55; Critchlow, Donald T.: Phyllis Schlafly and Grassroots Conservatism. A Woman's Crusade (Politics and Society in Twentieth-Century America), Princeton – Oxford 2005, p. 222; Schreiber, Ronnee: Righting Feminism. Conservative Women and American Politics, Oxford, NY 2011, p. 5; Howard, Angela: Series Introduction, in: Reaction to the Modern Women's Movement. 1963 to the Present (Antifeminism in America. A Collection of Readings from the Literature of the Opponents to U.S. Feminism. 1848 to the Present 3), ed. by Angela Howard and Sasha Ranaé Adams Tarrant, New York – London 1997, p. ix.
22 Nickerson, Michelle M.: Mothers of Conservatism. Women and the Postwar Right (Politics and Society in Twentieth-Century America), Princeton, NJ 2012, p. 137; Rymph, Catherine E.: Republican Women. Feminism and Conservatism from Suffrage through the Rise of the New Right, Chapel Hill, NC 2006, pp. 213f.

ed in 1972),[23] and Concerned Women of America (CWA, 1979), considered themselves direct counter-parts to NOW. It is in this context that I begin my exploration of the development of sexual harassment as a political concept.

1 Feminist and Social Conservative Action and Theory

"Damn it, that's enough! I'm a human being and I will no longer tolerate these indignities."[24] Carmita Wood resigned her position as an administrative assistant at the nuclear studies lab at Cornell University in the summer of 1974.[25] She had decided that the severe anxiety she associated with the harassment at her job was no longer tolerable. Despite repeatedly having rejected her boss' advances, she continued to be subjected to his crude remarks and sexual gestures. A single mother, now no longer earning a steady wage, she filed for unemployment benefits. Despite her presenting witnesses who testified to her boss' behavior, the New York State Department of Labor did not recognize her supervisor's coercive sexual advances as "good cause" for her resignation and denied her unemployment benefits.[26] Wood, like so many women before her was forced out of a job and denied any assistance because of the unwelcome sexual advances made to her by her boss. However, unlike the many women before her, she decided to publicly speak out. Wood was well aware that her ordeal was not unique. In 1975, she is quoted in the Ithaca Journal, stating that "women must be judged on their ability to perform their job – not on whether we maintain a sexual rapport with our bosses [...]. [It] constitutes a pattern [...] that is degrading, demeaning, and causes a steady erosion of our self-respect and personal dignity."[27] In line with the motto of the feminist movement, she recognized that although her experiences were deeply personal, they were also political.

This chapter explores early definitions and competing feminist and social conservative framings of sexual harassment. The feminist understanding was developed to a large part by two single-issue organizations: the Women's Workers In-

---

23 Founded under the name STOP ERA, renamed Eagle Forum in 1975.
24 Wood, Camita: Woman Alone, in: Labor Pains, 1/1 (Aug. 1975), p. 5.
25 Campbell, Jessica: The First Brave Woman Who Alleged 'sexual Harassment,' in: Legacy.com (Dec 7th, 2017).
26 Working Women's Institute Annual Program Report 1978, BCA, Research on Women Records, Box 96, Folder Working Women's Institute General Program Proposals, Annual Program Report, Audited Financial Statements 1978–1981; cf. Baker: Women's Movement, p. 28.
27 Anonymous: Don't 'Reach Out and Touch Them.' Opinion, in: Ithaca Journal, Apr. 24th, 1975, p. 13.

stitute and the Alliance Against Sexual Coercion. In direct opposition stood the social conservative pro-family movement, headed by Phyllis Schlafly and her Eagle
Forum. After I present these groups in more detail and explore how they approached the subject matter on a practical level, I will turn to the groups differing
and in part contradicting theoretical conceptions of sexual harassment. Following
an in-depth analysis of the feminist and social conservative frame, I will briefly
draw attention to how the term was often used colloquially.

1.1 Feminist and Social Conservative Activists

When Carmita Wood made the decision to speak out against the treatment she experienced at the hands of her boss, she had neither the fitting terminology nor
any institutionalized support. Thus, as a first step, Wood searched for allies.
She found them in Lin Farley, Karen Sauvigné, and Susan Meyer, who were at
the time working at Cornell's Human Affairs Program. Sauvigné had previously
taught classes on women in the workplace and after discussions with her – mostly
female – students, she had come to the conclusion that almost everyone in that
room had at one point quit or been fired because of unwelcome sexual advances
on the job.[28] For Sauvigné and her colleagues, Wood's dilemma was the final push
which led them to found the organization Working Women United; later renamed
the Working Women's Institute (WWI).[29]

Naming the issue "sexual harassment" was a conscious decision. Drawing on
the concept of racial harassment, which had already been acknowledged both by
the legal system as well as the wider public, the founding members of WWI settled
on the term "sexual harassment."[30] The first action organized by WWI was a
speak-out in Ithaca, New York, in which local women were invited to share
their stories. During the speak-out the organization distributed a survey to the
270 women in attendance, inquiring about their experiences with sexual harass-

28 Baker, Carrie N.: The Emergence of Organized Feminist Resistance to Sexual Harassment in the
United States in the 1970s, in: Journal of Women's History 19/3 (2007), pp. 164 f.
29 The organization was initially named Working Women United (WWU). In 1978 the Working
Women's Institute (WWI) was founded in addition to WWU, as a home for the research project
and the legal brief bank. A decision was made in 1979 to move all action to the WWI and disband
the WWU. These changes had little practical consequences for the group and were mostly on
paper. Hence, I will not be differentiating between Working Women United and the Working
Women's Institute and refer to both as the WWI.
30 Baker: The Emergence, pp. 163 f.

ment. This document was the first time the phrase 'sexual harassment' was defined publicly. According to this very first definition, sexual harassment consisted of "any repeated and unwanted sexual comments, looks, suggestions or physical contact that you find objectionable or offensive and causes you discomfort on the job."[31]

The definition was kept broad and the stories told were equally varied. One woman recounted her boss repeatedly making sexual advances towards her. She reported his behavior to the company and nothing was done. Ultimately, she was forced out of the job because after she "reacted angrily [...] he responded by putting a permanent letter in her personnel file denouncing her as a poor worker." Another woman "spoke of the humiliation and anger she felt at being judged by physical appearance rather than job performance." "[Falling] short of the arbitrary sexual standards" she felt resentful towards the women who "measured up" and was angry that these imposed standards had the power of "dividing working women against one another." A third speaker explained that she gave up her plans to go to law school when her professor "refused to give her a recommendation after she turned him down." On the stories went, twenty in all. Each one recounted an incident of sexual harassment and each one was different or at the very least, emphasized a different aspect of the experience: the retribution and jokes after complaining, the stress and fear resulting from facing the harasser every day, the difficulty of finding a new job after receiving negative performance reviews, the trauma of sexual assault, and the humiliation of being treated as a sex object rather than a competent worker.[32] However, despite their differences, each situation recounted at the speak-out corresponded WWI's preliminary definition of sexual harassment.

Based on this definition and inspired by the speak-out, WWI decided on a three-part strategy to face the issue of sexual harassment head on: First, offer assistance to individual women, second, organize outreach and raise public consciousness on the issue, and third, research the phenomenon. These three strategies, while conceived of as different projects within the organization, often went hand in hand. The information individual women provided, for instance, was anonymized and used for a study identifying common reactions to harassing behavior as well as prevalent consequences for the victims. Similarly, the studies, surveys, and research done was the basis of the informational material provided to interested parties for public consciousness raising.

---

31 Working Women Definition from 1975 is cited in: Farley: Sexual Shakedown, p. 20; and in: Alliance Against Sexual Coercion: Fighting Sexual Harassment. An Advocacy Handbook, 1979, p. 43, BCA Feminist Ephemeral Collection, Box 1, Folder Alliance Against Sexual Coercion.
32 Anonymous: Speak Out Draws Tears and Anger, in: Labor Pains 1/1 (1975), p. 1.

Upon the organization's founding and even more so after its introduction to the public by The New York Times, Redbook, and even the Wallstreet Journal in 1975, WWI received "a tidal wave of response from women across the country," many of which were requests for help.[33] Hence, the first step was providing women with immediate assistance in order to address their individual situations.[34] At times this help was of a psychological nature, other times women sought legal assistance, and more often than not, victims either wanted to simply be heard or gather general information. Since the organization itself operated principally on a voluntary basis and did not have the resources to provide doctors or lawyers on a regular basis, WWI soon established a network of allies to complement their own counseling and self-help groups. By 1980, this network had expanded nationally and included lawyers specializing on civil rights issues, medical professionals including therapists, and a multitude of organizations eager to provide services to sexual harassment victims. In order to avoid further victimization of those seeking help, WWI confirmed with each member of this network that they had all the pertinent information on sexual harassment, were trained on how to interact with targets of harassment, and were ideologically in line with the organization's view on gender relations.[35]

The second part of WWI's strategy was concerned with providing information to working women and to the public at large. Among others, this included writing and distributing various pamphlets, actively engaging with the media both by initiating contact as well as being a source of information for reporters, sending representatives as expert witnesses both in court and at congressional hearings, and providing workshops and giving lectures to working women as well as sympathet-

---

33 Nemy, End: Women Begin to Speak Out Against Sexual Harassment at Work, in: The New York Times (Aug 19, 1975), p. 38; Anonymous: How Do You Handle Sex On the Job? in: Redbook (Jan 1976); Bralove, Mary: A Cold Shoulder. Career Women Decry Sexual Harassment by Bosses and Clients, in: The Wall Street Journal (Jan 29, 1976), p. 1; Brownmiller, Susan and Dolores Alexander: How We Got Here, From Carmita Wood to Anita Hill, in: Ms. The New Magazine for Women (Jan/ Feb 1992), pp. 70 f.; Baker: Popular Representation, p. 48; Zippel, Katharin: The Politics of Sexual Harassment. A Comparative Study of the United States, the European Union, and Germany, New York et al. 2006, p. 71.
34 Crull, Peggy: The Stress Effects of Sexual Harassment in the Office. Presented at: Conference on Occupational Health Issues Affecting Clerical/Secretarial Personnel. National Institute for Occupational Safety and Health, 21st July 1981, p.10, BCA, Research on Women Records, Box 97, Working Women's Institute Sexual Harassment Information.
35 Working Women's Institute: National Sexual Harassment Legal Back-Up Center. Final Report, May 15th, 1981, p. 1, BCA, Research on Women Records, Box 96, Folder Working Women Institute Report on National Sexual Harassment, Legal Back-Up Center, Litigation; Working Women's Institute: Services Available to Legal Practitioners, BCA, Research on Women Records, Box 96, Folder Bell Laboratories Corporate Study.

ic organizations. As we shall see in chapter three, after WWI established their core material and had expanded their resources, the organization also offered information and counseling to employers who were committed to eradicating sexual harassment as well as providing workshops to their employees on the company premises. In the late 1970s, this aspect of WWI's work was still given a relatively low priority, but by 1982 an organized effort was made to provide employers with information on preventative measures as well as advice on the manner of response to allegations. Workshops and seminars were developed with the intent of training supervisors and managers to prevent and to react constructively to sexual harassment in their workplace.[36]

As the third part of their strategy, WWI conducted research on the issue. Even in its infancy WWI considered research on sexual harassment of utmost importance. The group realized that understanding the problem was a necessary step to succeed in their goals of protecting individual women, gaining institutional recognition of the issue, and long-term elimination of the problem.[37] Defining sexual harassment was merely the first step in unveiling a larger pattern. Now questions about the extent and exact nature of the problem needed answering. How many workers were affected? What were common reactions to harassment? What were the most common forms of harassment? Who were the harassers? And perhaps most importantly, what were effective ways to stop harassment?[38] WWI conducted studies and surveys, researched legal precedent, and kept track of all legal proceedings concerning the issue. This last effort resulted in the establishment of an extensive brief bank, designed to assist future legal counsel to build their case.[39]

One subscriber to the organizations regular legal updates and fervent user of the brief bank was Catharine MacKinnon. She was not associated with WWI but had an enormous influence on how sexual harassment was conceived, by WWI, by the larger feminist community, and later on, by the U.S. judiciary. As a feminist and civil rights attorney, she would in 1986 argue Michelle Vinson's case in the

---

36 E. g.: Working Women's Institute: Summary Sheet about the National Sexual Harassment Legal Back-Up Center and Litigation Manual, 1981, pp. 6 f, BCA, Research on Women Records, Box 96, Folder working Women Institute Report on National Sexual Harassment, Legal Back-Up Center, Litigation Manual; Sauvigné, Karen: Sexual Harassment is Against the Law, 1982, p. 4, BCA, Research on Women Records, Box 97, Folder Working Women's Institute Sexual Harassment Information.
37 WWI: Litigation Manual, 1981, pp. 1–6.
38 Cf. Crull: The Stress Effects, p. 10.
39 WWI: Litigation Manual, 1981, p. 1.

first Supreme Court case on sexual harassment, *Meritor Savings Bank v. Vinson.*[40] MacKinnon became enthralled with sexual harassment as a subject matter and made it her mission to develop a legal understanding. Her book, *Sexual Harassment of Working Women: A Case of Discrimination* was published in 1979 and most of her arguments were soon confirmed by the courts and the federal government. Shortly after the release of her book, MacKinnon wrote a note to Karen Sauvigné, "concerning the invaluable role of the Institute [WWI] in my research." She goes on to write:

> My attention was originally drawn to the issue of sexual coercion of women on the job by your long-ago one page flier about Carmita Wood's situation. As we both continued our work with the issue of sexual harassment, your brief bank and periodically updated citation sheets proved immensely helpful in alerting me to some developments I might otherwise have overlooked and in providing ready access to many documents I might otherwise have procured only at considerably greater difficulty. It is clear to me not only that your work is of central importance to women faced with sexual harassment on the job, but is also crucial for researchers, lawyers and others working with victims to fight back. My book is a better book for your many contributions. I only hope that the added exposure it gives the issue will benefit the Institute's work in some small measure.[41]

As highlighted in this quote, the network on which so much of WWI's work was based relied on the principle of reciprocity. Even though the WWI was the first and – at least in the late 1970s – the largest group concerned with sexual harassment in the workplace, other feminists gravitated toward the issue and contributed to, built on, and learned from WWI's developing body of research.

Another organization which warrants an introduction at this point is the only other single-issue organization on sexual harassment of the mid 1970s: The Boston-based Alliance Against Sexual Coercion (AASC), founded in 1976. Contrary to WWI, which approached the problem as a workers' rights issue, AASC focused on sexual harassment as a form of sexual violence. AASC's founding members had been volunteers at the Washington DC Rape Crisis Center. They encountered working women seeking assistance after being coerced into sexually cooperating with persons of authority at their place of work. These women's plight, however, did not fit the Centers definition of rape and not having the resources or adequate information to help, these women were turned away. Upon recognizing this pattern, a group of volunteers founded the AASC and made it their mission to provide train-

---

40 *Meritor Savings Bank v. Vinson,* 477 U.S. 57 (1986).
41 Letter from Catherine A. MacKinnon to Karen Sauvigné regarding her book, 14th September 1979, BCA, Research on Women Records, Box 96, Folder Working Women's Institute Proposals to Various Organizations/People for Funding.

ing to organizations who came in touch with victims of sexual harassment – starting with the Cambridge Rape Crisis Center and the local women's shelter.[42]

The WWI and the AASC came to many similar conclusions and developed similar ideas. There were, however, some crucial differences between the two organizations, ideologically, structurally, and regarding practical action. As a much smaller operation, compared to WWI, the AASC focused on training other organizations on how to productively assist individual victims.[43] After some initial hesitation and denunciation of sexual harassment as "not a bread and butter issue," many women's organizations, most notably the National Organization for Women, incorporated the issue of sexual harassment into their programs.[44] In order to teach others, the AASC developed a body of research and published several informational pamphlets.[45] This focus on assisting community organizations and on including sexual harassment as a form of sexual violence and thus, prioritizing trauma counseling and practical strategies for victims rather than legal help, reflected the AASC's ideological convictions.

While WWI placed significant expectations on the legal system to address the issue of sexual harassment, the AASC adopted a more critical perspective regarding the potential of legal remedies.[46] They believed that because the legal system was itself part of patriarchy and capitalism, it inherently discriminated against women, less affluent individuals, and people of color.[47] Therefore, it could not be trusted to bring relief to all women but would instead benefit mostly upper and middle class White women, while minority women and those without the means to pursue their case in court would continue to fall through the cracks of the legal system.[48] An additional concern was that the legal system limited women's agency, because they appeared as victims and as individuals seeking protection by government institutions.[49] This did not mean that the AASC rejected all

---

42 Baker: The Emergence, p. 171.
43 Crull: The Stress Effects, p. 10.
44 Baker: The Emergence, pp. 169 f.
45 See for instance: Alliance Against Sexual Coercion: Organizing Against Sexual Harassment, in: Worker's Struggles Past and Present. A 'Radical America' Reader, ed. by James Green, Philadelphia 1983, pp. 234–248; Alliance Against Sexual Coercion: Sexual Harassment at the Workplace, Boston 1977.
46 Crull: The Stress Effects, pp. 10 f.
47 Ibid., pp. 16, 69, 71; cf. Hilson, Christopher J.: New Social Movements. The Role of Legal Opportunity, in: Social Movements. Transformative Shifts and Turning Points, ed. by Ravi Kumar Savyasaachi, New Delhi 2014, p. 307.
48 Reuben, Carol: CRC Plans South's 1st Institute to Fight Sexual Harassment, in: The Atlanta Constitution (February 26th, 1981), p. 1E; Zippel: Politics, p. 16.
49 Zippel: Politics, pp. 20, 57.

legal action, but their focus lay on raising awareness for sexual harassment outside of the legal system. WWI, on the other hand, as exemplified by Farley's statement, saw their protests, research, and networking primarily as a means to an end. They hoped that the development of a factual foundation and increased public awareness would influence court rulings and sufficiently pressure policy makers into acting on sexual harassment.[50] The organizations' diverging opinions on the usefulness of the legal system in the fight against sexual harassment is only one of many examples which speak to a characterization of WWI as part of a liberal, and AASC of a radical feminist movement.

The WWI, in regard to its members' racial and socio-economic make-up, fell in line with liberal feminism throughout the second-wave feminist movement. As bell hooks lamented, in the preface to her widely read work on black feminism *Ain't I a Woman? Black Women and Feminism*, race was not a welcome topic in many liberal feminist groups:

> In general black folks were far more likely to denounce women's liberation, seeing it as a white women's thing. As a consequence, black female individuals, who eagerly embraced the movement were often isolated and estranged from other black folks. We were usually the only black person in predominantly white circles. And any talk of race was viewed as shifting the attention away from the politics of gender.[51]

The observation that feminist spaces, while not purposefully excluding black women, were predominantly white and underemphasized the importance of race in gendered power dynamics, matches what we know of WWI's membership. The very first publication of the organization's newsletter *Labor Pains* in 1975 calls out to potential members:

> We need as many women as possible to get involved. What kind of women do we need? All kinds – literally! Already Working Women United includes women from grandmothers to granddaughters, college professors to factory workers, radicals to conservatives. What unites us is our common bond of being women who have worked, who presently work, or who hope to work, and our common desire to eliminate the overt and subtle discrimination which affects all of us at work because we happen to be women.[52]

The group seeks to be diverse, in age, class, and even in terms of political positioning. Interestingly though, the category of race is not mentioned. One can only speculate, whether this was an oversight or an intentional attempt to retain the focus

50 Ibid., p. 56.
51 hooks, bell: Ain't I a Woman? Black Women and Feminism, ²2015, p. 12.
52 Anonymous: Why Working Women United, in: Labor Pains 1/1 (1975), p. 3.

on, as hooks put it, "the politics of gender." In either case, the omission speaks to the group's roots in the mostly White, liberal feminist movement of the 1970s.

It seems that by 1980, the group increased their appreciation for new perspectives. In a report dated July 1980, the organization updated their members that a full-day workshop was the "first opportunity to work in a team with Kendall Franklin, a new member of the Institute's Speakers Bureau, who is also acting as a part-time organizer of speaking requests." The report continues: "While Kendall needs to become more familiar and comfortable with the content of our workshops, she is an important asset. Being a Black woman, Kendall also brings a perspective that enables us to better reach minority women about the issue."[53] Here, an explicit attempt is made to broaden the organization's reach to including "minority women." At the same time, the highlighting of Franklin as a Black woman and her unique positioning because of her race leads to the assumption that she is the first or at the very least one of few women of color involved in leadership roles of the organization.

While I want to emphasize that several of the women seeking assistance from the organization were minority women and I am not implying that WWI did not strive to aid all working women,[54] I do contend that there was an implicit bias which drew the organization's focus to situations more closely related to their members own life experiences. An organization led by White, middle class women with an academic background may be familiar with the plight of a clerical worker dependent on the good favor of her boss or of a young student in need of a good recommendation from her professor.[55] The hardships of a woman working on an assembly line or a domestic worker invariably finding herself in isolation at her employer's house and in his bedroom, seemed further removed. In addition, the public image of sex at work, usually presented as comedic instances in film and literature, was not that of a factory worker facing the hostility of her male coworkers, but instead a boss chasing the secretary around his desk.[56] Considering that these types of jobs were also racially coded with White women being far more likely to work white-collar jobs,[57] it is not surprising that race did not

---

53 Working Women Institute: Institute Six Month Report, July 1980, p. 2, BCA, Research on Women Records, Box 96, Folder Working Women Institute General Program Proposals, Annual Program Report, Audited Financial Statements 1978–1981.
54 Crull, Peggy: The Stress Effects, p. 7.
55 Ibid., pp. 2f.
56 Cf. Berebitsky: Sex and the Office, pp. 117–140.
57 Anonymous: Clerical Work. A Manual for Change. Report of the Permanent Commission on the Status of Women on Sex Discrimination in Clerical Work, February 1978, pp. 32f., BCA, Feminist ephemera Collection, Box 59, Folder Permanent Commission on the Status of Women;

play a large role in conceptualizing and defining sexual harassment by WWI. In fact, the perceived importance of race and class in addition to gender in instances of sexual harassment was the most conspicuous of the ideological splits between the WWI and the AASC. The importance of systemic power discrepancies other than gender and the two distinct viewpoints of these organizations will be explored throughout the next section in the context of a discussion on the systemic nature of sexual harassment.

Although these ideological differences are of importance on an analytical level when attempting to categorize various understandings of sexual harassment, in practice they were not divisive. Immediately after their founding, WWI and AASC attempted several joint projects, agreed to aid rather than to compete (for instance in regard to financing or media attention), and readily exchanged information. Their main operations, however, remained independent of each other.[58]

The organizations' research efforts, the publication of MacKinnon's book, and the plentiful data pool collected from the hundreds of women seeking assistance in their personal struggles culminated in a distinct feminist theoretical understanding of sexual harassment. This framing was to a large part built upon the already existing feminist theories on sex discrimination in the workplace and sexual violence against women.[59] By the time single-issue organizations on sexual harassment were founded, the second-wave feminist movement had already successfully instigated considerable legal and policy changes, including the Equal Pay Act, a ban on sex discrimination in educational facilities, legal access to birth control for unmarried women, and the nation-wide legalization of abortion.[60] By 1975,

U.S. Department of Labor Women's Bureau: Facts on Women Workers, March 15th, 1982, p. 1, BCA, Feminist Ephemera Collection, Box 80, Folder U.S. Department of Labor; Southeast Women's Employment Coalition: Women of the Rural South. Economic Status and Prospects, 1986, p. 29, BCA, Feminist Ephemera Collection, Box 70, Folder Southeast Women's Employment Coalition.
58 Baker: Women's Movement, p. 86.
59 For an overview on feminist action against sex discrimination in the workplace, see: Boris, Eileen and Allison Louise Elias: Workplace Discrimination, Equal Pay, and Sexual Harassment. An Intersectional Approach, in: The Oxford Handbook of U.S. Women's Social Movement Activism (Oxford Handbooks), New York 2017, pp. 193–213; On action against sexual violence, see: Arnold, Gretchen: U.S. Women's Movements to End Violence Against Women, Domestic Abuse, and Rape, in: The Oxford Handbook of U.S. Women's Social Movement Activism (Oxford Handbooks), New York 2017, pp. 270–290.
60 McCammon, Holly J. and Brittany N. Hearne: U.S. Women's Legal Activism in the Judicial Arena, in: The Oxford Handbook of U.S. Women's Social Movement Activism, ed. by McCammon et al., New York 2017, pp. 528f.; Brocker: Protest, p. 42; For information on advances by second-wave feminism in the early 1970's, see: Inness, Sherrie A.: 'strange Feverish Years'. The 1970s and Women's Changing Roles, in: Disco Divas. Women and Popular Culture in the 1970s, ed. by Sherrie A. Innes, Philadelphia 2003, pp. 1–12.

this feminist activism had brought on considerable change in both public policy and opinion.

Recognizing these developments and fearing an outright rejection of the former *status quo*, a pro-family movement emerged. This movement, as part of the Christian Right,[61] grew in the late 1970's as a reaction to what the political analyst Yuval Levin describes as the "cultural chaos" of the 1960's and 1970's.[62] This social conservative movement condemned societal changes, such as the greater number of women in the workplace, a heightened divorce rate, and increased sexual freedom,[63] as the "moral decay [...] of contemporary America."[64] Increasingly gaining strength in the late 1970's and early 1980's, this social conservative pro-family movement was composed of and led by social conservative women,[65] who saw themselves as a direct "alternative to women's lib."[66] One of the core motivations of this movement was to protect the traditional family from "anti-familial feminist ideology" and ensure the upholding of conventional gender roles,[67] which contrary to the feminist interpretation, did not oppress but actually benefit women.[68] Gender inequalities were not seen as sex discrimination but as natural differences elementary to the preservation of a morally sound society.[69]

---

61 McAllister, Ted V.: Reagan and the Transformation of American Conservatism, in: The Reagan Presidency. Pragmatic Conservatism and Its Legacies, ed. by W. Elliot Brownlee and Hugh Davis Graham, Lawrence, KS 2003, p. 46; Busch, Andrew E.: Reagan and the Evolution of American Politics. 1981–1989, in: A Companion to Ronald Reagan (Wiley Blackwell Companions to History), ed. by Andrew L. Johns, Chichester et al. 2015, pp. 98–100; Sutton: Culture Wars, pp. 204, 206–209.
62 Levin, Yuval: The Fractured Republic. Renewing America's Social Contract in the Age of Individualism, New York 2016, pp. 59f., 69. Levin self-identifies as a conservative and aligns himself with the American Right. According to the author his writing is influenced by "[his] most basic political views" and must be considered in this context; Critchlow, Donald T.: Mobilizing Women. The 'social' Issue, in: The Reagan Presidency. Pragmatic Conservatism and its Legacies, ed. by W. Elliot Brownlee and Hugh Davis Graham, Lawrence, KS 2003, p. 294; Schreiber: Righting Feminism, pp. 5, 17, 118; Brocker: Protest, pp. 47, 53, 55, 57; Moser, Richard: Was It the End or Just a Beginning? American Storytelling and the History of the Sixties, in: The World the Sixties Made. Politics and Culture in Recent America (Critical Perspectives on the Past), ed. by Van Gosse and Richard Moser, Philadelphia 2003, p. 38.
63 Klatch: Women, p. 26; Levin: Fractured Republic, pp. 67f.
64 Klatch: Women, p. 5.
65 Schreiber: Righting Feminism, p. 5; Critchlow: Grassroots Conservatism, p. 301.
66 Phyllis Schlafly on the founding of the Eagle Forum, cited in: Critchlow: Grassroots Conservatism, p. 221.
67 Elshtain, Jean Bethke: Feminists Against the Family, in: The Nation (Nov 17, 1979) pp. 1, 497–500.
68 Klatch: Women, pp. 10, 49, 50.
69 For exemplary social conservative discussions on gender roles, see: Schlafly, Phyllis: The Power of the Positive Woman, New Rochelle, NY 1977, pp. 101–113; Connaught, Marshner: Who is

Due to a commitment to a narrative in which sex discrimination did not exist and sexual harassment was viewed as a minor individual predicament, no equivalent of the feminist single-issue organizations on sexual harassment would form within the social conservative pro-family movement. However, pro-family organizations such as the Eagle Forum and Concerned Women for America, promoted the traditional family as the ideal life style and advocated for the division of labor.[70] As feminists promoted job integration and the eradication of traditional gender roles as the main solution regarding sexual harassment, they faced strong opposition from social conservative organizations.[71] Both movements endeavored to bring about a change in gender norms and relations within society. Feminist and social conservative groups acted to challenge the established order, which they perceived to be controlled by the respective other.

The driving individuals on both sides of the dispute were women, speaking as women to women.[72] Both feminist and conservative activists believed in the existence of a gendered division within society. Despite this division bearing a distinctly contrasting normative coloration within the opposing movements and despite being accredited to a different cause, either structural conditions or God-given truths, both sides used their gender identity to their advantage in practical action.[73] They argued that female actors were better equipped to speak on and mobilize for women's issues because of their belonging to and distinct experiences as members of the group of women.[74] This applied to feminist organizations and was visible in the way sexual harassment was framed within this narrative, namely as a problem affecting women as a collective. Similarly, this was exemplified in the social conservative framing of sexual harassment in which women, as a group,

---

the New Traditional Woman? (1982), in: Reaction to the Modern Women's Movement. 1963 to the Present (Antifeminism in America. A Collection of Readings from the Literature of the Opponents to U.S. Feminism. 1848 to the Present 3), ed. by Angela Howard and Sasha Ranaé Adams Tarrant, New York – London 1997, pp. 161–165.

70 Cf. Critchlow: Grassroots Conservatism; Schreiber: Righting Feminism.

71 Cf. Klatch: Women, p. 10.

72 E.g. Schlafly: Positive Woman, p. 101; Klatch: Women, p. 152; Ryan, Barbara: Feminism and the Women's Movement. Dynamics of Change in social Movement Ideology and Activism, New York 1992, p. 94; Schreiber: Righting Feminism, pp. 8, 13, 42; Schreiber, Ronnee: Anti-Feminist, Pro-Life, and Anti-Era Women, in: The Oxford Handbook of U.S. Women's Social Movement Activist, ed. by McCammon et al., New York 2017, p. 315.

73 Schreiber: Righting Feminism, p. 43; For more information on the use of identity politics by women's movements, see: Whittier, Nancy: Identity Politics, Consciousness-Raising, and Visibility Politics, in: The Oxford Handbook of U.S. Women's Social Movement Activism, ed. by McCammon et al., New York 2017, pp. 376–397.

74 Schreiber: Righting Feminism, p. 5.

were said to be protected from the immoral behavior awaiting them in the public sphere by the division of labor.

By appearing as the representatives of women as a group, activists lent their demands considerable power and legitimacy.[75] Social conservative women, simply by stating their traditionalist views as women, seriously impeded feminists' assumed discursive hegemony regarding women's issues and provided male conservatives with a legitimization for the rejection of feminist ideas.[76] Thus, the struggle between feminists and social conservatives could no longer publicly be simplified as a dispute between women fighting for liberation on the one side and men denying women their freedom, on the other.[77] Social conservative women were therefore crucial actors within the New Right not only because of their indispensable volunteer work, but also due to their targeted use of gendered identity politics.[78]

1.2 Feminist and Social Conservative Theoretical Frameworks

The feminist theoretical framework on sexual harassment was developed, at times implicitly and at times explicitly, to contrast the social conservative narrative on gender relations which, although declining in influence, still dominated public thought. For instance, highlighting sexual harassment as a problem was only necessary in an environment in which it was perceived as trivial. Similarly, stressing the issue's systemic nature was only important to contrast its perception as a personal disagreement between two individuals. Hence, exploring the feminist framing of sexual harassment is most productive when directly contrasting it with its social conservative counterpart. The following analysis will show the differences of these two competing framings by exploring three vital questions: Is sexual harassment seen as a problem? Is the issue systemic? And is the issue gendered? The analysis will conclude with an examination of the colloquial confusion surrounding the term 'sexual harassment' in the second half of the 1970s.

Throughout this discussion the feminist perspective is based on the theoretical work done by the AASC, the WWI, and Catharine MacKinnon. Their theoretical framework was presented in court hearings and *amicus curiae* briefs, was expounded upon in two major congressional hearings, one in 1979 and the other in 1981, and published in several pamphlets and more in-detail monographs. Be-

---

75 Ibid., p. 53; Klatch: Women, p. 10.
76 Schreiber: Anti-Feminists, p. 316.
77 Critchlow: Mobilizing Women, p. 312; Busch: American Politics, pp. 103 f.
78 Klatch: Women, p. 8; Schreiber: Righting Feminism, pp. 13, 17 f., 40, 47; Critchlow: Mobilizing Women, p. 296; Nickerson: Mothers of Conservatism, p. 137.

sides MacKinnon's 1979 publication, two monographs by cofounders of the WWI and the AASC, respectively, warrant mentioning: Lin Farley's work *Sexual Shake-down*,[79] and Leah Cohen's book *The Secret Oppression*.[80]

The conservative perception of sexual harassment is not as easily discernible as is the feminist, because the topic of sexual harassment was seldom explicitly sought out within social conservative groups. Phyllis Schlafly's testimony in the 1981 hearings before the Senate Committee on Labor and Human Resources called by Republican Senator Orrin Hatch with the intention of weakening the Equal Employment Opportunity Commission guidelines is one of the few examples in which sexual harassment was explicitly and extensively discussed by a representative of the social conservative narrative.[81] Schlafly is well-known for her endorsement of Barry Goldwater in 1964,[82] her activism in the pro-family movement, and most prominent of all, her successful campaign against the ratification of the Equal Rights Amendment. As a directing member in several conservative women's organizations, including the Eagle Forum of which she was the founding director, she continually focused on upholding traditional gender roles.[83] Her spoken and written testimony before the congressional committee was exemplary for the social conservative frame of sexual harassment and shall be used extensively in the following analysis.

1.2.1 Problem or Triviality?

There was no doubt in the feminist frame that sexual harassment constituted a problem warranting serious consideration and political action. This postulation was based on the quantitative extent of the problem, the harasser's motivations, and the extensive consequences suffered by women both on an individual and collective level. The social conservative view could not have been more different: Schlafly, despite stating within the first sentences of her testimony that sexual harassment is a "serious issue," took the position that "a woman being squeezed on her

---

79 Although Lin Farley, a founding member of WWI, had left the organization by 1977, her resignation was due to personal rather than ideological reasons, and her book is based upon WWI data and reflects the views of the organization.
80 Cohen, Leah and Constance Backhouse: The Secret Oppression. Sexual Harassment of Working Women, Toronto 1978.
81 Baker: Women's Movement, p. 136.
82 Schlafly, Phyllis: A Choice Not an Echo, Alton, IL 1964; Schreiber: Anti-Feminists, p. 318.
83 Critchlow: Grassroots Conservatism, p. 7.

skirt [...] is simply not a federal case."[84] Schlafly followed the historically established argument that while sexual advances towards women in the workplace
were undesirable,[85] this was the case not because they constituted a legal offense
but because they were morally questionable. The perception of sexual harassment
as a moral question and matter of manners is echoed in the societal discourse.[86]
For instance, in an editorial published by *The New York Times* in 1977 commenting
on *Alexander v. Yale*, the first court case on sexual harassment in an educational
setting, the pundit, Russell Baker, laments that a "robust father" or a "large brother or boyfriend" was sufficient to "make the faculty behave itself." He contended
that the riddance of such "nuisances" did not require the "expensive machinery of
the courthouse."[87] Social conservatives criticized government intrusion into such
private matters and voiced the fear that if the courts were to engage with the issue
an unmanageable amount of futile litigation would ensue.[88] This opposition to
government involvement is consistent with the social conservative narrative, described by historian Rebecca Klatch, which characterizes "Big Government" as
an extension of "human secularism" and is therefore viewed as an ally to the "left-
ist opponent."[89]

For feminists, the very first step to recognizing sexual harassment as a problem was naming and defining the phenomenon. As shown above, the Institute
published the very first definition in 1975. This definition, for the purposes of making visible a greater pattern of societal behavior was broad, ranging "from clearly
suggestive looks and/or remarks, [...] to outright sexual assault."[90] Feminists argued that only by including this spectrum of behavior was it possible to recognize

---

84 Committee on Labor and Human Resources, United States Senate: Hearings on Sex Discrimination in the Workplace. Examination of Issues Affecting Women in Our Nation's Labor Force.
97th Congress. First Session. Apr 21, 1981, Washington 1981, p. 401.
85 Zippel: Politics, p. 11; Baker: Women's Movement, p. 145.
86 Further examples: In response to a multitude of harassment allegations the Los Angeles
Screen Actors Guild established a "Moral Complaints Bureau". Reported on in: Bralove: Cold
Shoulder, p. 1; In *Miller v. Bank of America* (1976) the court confirmed the defendant's insistence
that sexual harassment was covered by the bank's "moral misconduct" policy. *Miller v. Bank of
America*, 418 F. Supp. 233 (1976); cf. Baker: Women's Movement, pp. 25, 149.
87 Baker, Russell: The Court of First Resorts, in: The New York Times (Jul 26, 1977), p. L29.
88 Ibid., p. 53.
89 Williams, Daniel K.: Reagan's Religious Right. The Unlikely Alliance between Southern
Evangelicals and a California Conservative, in: Ronald Reagan and the 1980s. Receptions, Policies,
Legacies (Studies of the Americas), ed. by Cheryl Hudson and Gareth Davies, New York 2008,
pp. 138 f.; Klatch: Women, pp. 5, 133.
90 Dierdre Silverman, who developed the survey with Susan Meyer, presents its findings and
cites the group's definition of sexual harassment in: Anonymous: Sexual Harassment. Working
Women's Dilemma, in: Quest, 3/3 (1976), pp. 15–24.

a pattern. By promoting such an open definition, however, WWI inadvertently aided the trivialization of the issue. Keeping the definition of sexual harassment broad led critics to focus on 'lesser' offences. It was much easier to curtail inappropriate verbal comments as mere misbehavior than it was to do so with coerced intercourse or even rape. Schlafly in her testimony purposefully excludes any "criminal acts" which she declares "should be punished to the full extent of the law."[91] Therefore, when she spoke of sexual harassment, she spoke 'only' of "bosses pinching secretaries," which had a trivializing effect.[92]

In order to gain a sense of the scope of the issue, feminist organizations initiated surveys and began collecting data.[93] These early surveys drew criticism for specifically targeting respondents and therefore yielding very high numbers of harassment incidences. For instance, in surveys conducted by the women's magazine *Redbook* as well as the Federal Department of Housing and Urban Development up to 90% of female respondents asserted that they had been sexually harassed in the workplace.[94] Despite these surveys not following the scientific method, they for the first time drew attention to the extent of the problem and thus were effective tools for consciousness-raising, were a basis for successful arguments in courts and before congressional hearings, and sparked interest within the media.[95] On the grounds of these surveys, James Hanley, the chair of the first congressional hearings on sexual harassment, in 1979, declared that the issue was "not only epidemic" but "pandemic, an everyday, everywhere occurrence."[96] The committee subsequently arranged for the Merit System Protection Board Survey,[97] which Freada Klein, co-founder of the AASC, would later describe as "the first decent methodological study" on sexual harassment,[98] and which would be used in

---

91 Committee on Labor: Hearings on Sex Discrimination, p. 400.
92 Ibid., p. 397.
93 Baker: Women's Movement, pp. 33 f.
94 Anonymous: How Do You Handle Sex, p. 149.
95 Baker: The Emergence, p. 175; Baker: Women's Movement, p. 113; Dobbin, Frank: Inventing Equal Opportunity, Princeton, NJ et al. 2009, p. 197.
96 James Hanley's opening Statement. Subcommittee on Investigations of the Committee on Post Office and Civil Service, United States House of Representatives: Hearings on Sexual Harassment in the Federal government. 96th Congress. First Session. October 23rd, November 1st, 13th, 1979, p. 1; cf. Baker: Women's Movement, pp. 88, 112 f.; Baker: The Emergence, p. 168; Arriola: Construction Industry, p. 39.
97 Mathis, Patricia A., and Ruth T. Prokop with the U.S. Merit System Protection Board: Sexual Harassment in the Federal Workplace. Is It a Problem? A Report of the U.S. Merit Systems Protection Board Office of Merit Systems Review and Studies, Washington, D.C. 1981.
98 Brownmiller: From Wood to Hill, p. 71; Baker: Women's Movement, p. 124.

reports, information material, and testimony for the next decade.[99] It found that 42% of the 10,648 female respondents, all of them federal employees, reported having been sexually harassed within the two years prior to the survey.[100] Recognizing that a vast number of working women encountered sexual harassment was essential for recognizing this behavior as a problem.

These numbers, however, did little to convince social conservatives of the gravity of the issue. According to Schlafly, women not only voluntarily engaged and purposefully provoked advances of a sexual nature, they also frequently lied about having experienced unwelcome conduct. These "mischievous" claims were uttered with the intention of obtaining financial advantages, attracting attention, or were "applied in hate or revenge when one party wants out" of a consensual relationship.[101] Allegations of sexual harassment were, therefore, to be treated with extreme caution as they had the power to unduly damage the accused's reputation. The ensuing damages of "frivolous complaint[s]" were a prominent point of discussion in the first congressional hearings on the subject of sexual harassment in 1979.[102] The perception that the overwhelming number of reported incidents were either induced and welcomed by female dress and conduct, or were false accusations altogether, led social conservatives to the conclusion that "real" sexual harassment was very rare.[103]

In the feminist framing, establishing the exertion of power as the offender's motivation further solidified the perception of sexual harassment as a problem. The core assumption adopted from the anti-rape and battered women's movements,[104] was that sexual harassment, analogous to rape, was an expression of

---

99 Sauvigné, Karen and Joan Vermeulen: Testimony of Working Women's Institute before U.S. Senate Labor and Human Resources Committee, April 21st, 1981, p. 2; Atwell, Robert: American Council on Education. Sexual Harassment on Campus: Suggestions for Reviewing Campus Policy and Educational Programs, December 1986, pp. 1, 3, BCA, Research on Women Records, Box 95, Folder Cornell University's Reports, Articles, Information etc.; Burns, Sarah E. speaking on behalf of WWI and Georgetown University Law Center: Testimony of Sexual Harassment before the Subcommittee on Employment Opportunities of the House Committee on Education and Labor, September 30th, 1986, p. 4, BCA, Research on Women Records, Box 96.
100 Sexual Harassment in the Federal Workplace. Is It a Problem? A Report of the U.S. Merit Systems Protection Board Office of Merit Systems Review and Studies, March 1981, pp. 33–35; Baker, Carrie N.: Sexual Extortion. Criminalizing Quid Pro Quo Sexual Harassment, in: Law and Inequality: A Journal of Theory and Practice 13/1 (1994), p. 215.
101 Committee on Labor: Hearings on Sex Discrimination 1981, p. 402.
102 Subcommittee on Investigations: Hearings on Sexual Harassment 1979, p. 11; cf. Baker: Women's Movement, pp. 116 f., 144.
103 Committee on Labor: Hearings on Sex Discrimination 1981, p. 400.
104 E.g.: AASC: Sexual Harassment at the Workplace, p. 42; Zippel: Politics, p. 43.

power.[105] As MacKinnon formulated it, "economic power is to sexual harassment as physical force is to rape."[106] Denoting sexual harassment as an issue based on expressions of power rather than misplaced sexual urges or even bilateral attraction contributed largely to declaring sexual harassment as a serious issue.[107]

Regarding the issue of consent, legal scholar Vicki Schultz in her influential essay "Sanitizing the Workplace" argues that feminists in the late 1970s and early 1980s were in favor of banning consensual relationships along with coerced sexual behavior in the workplace. Thus, according to Schultz, they were a driving force for what she calls the "sanitization of the workplace."[108] To make her point, Schultz cites feminist anthropologist Margaret Mead who in an essay in 1978 called for "a taboo on sex at work."[109] I concede that this position found some traction within wider feminist circles, especially those focusing on sexual violence. Interestingly, however, when specifically discussing sexual harassment the essay, in the early 1980s, is repeatedly cited by management consultants but is largely disregarded by feminist single issue organizations.[110] Therefore, I vehemently disagree with Schultz' assessment that feminist groups defining sexual harassment are responsible for 21st century bans on consensual sexual relationships in the workplace.

The call for a general ban (or taboo) on sexual and romantic relationships in the workplace was not a majority opinion within feminist circles. More importantly, this position was never one espoused by either of the large single-issue organizations working on preventing sexual harassment. Both the Working Women's Institute and the Alliance Against Sexual Coercion, as well as Lin Farley, Leah Cohen, and Catharine MacKinnon, the feminist authors of the early monographs on the issue, were committed to an understanding of sexual harassment which was defined as "unwanted" conduct. I argue contrary to Schultz, that Mead's appeal had little bearing on the development of the feminist understanding of sexual harassment. Instead, the feminist framework put great emphasis on separating

---

105 Brownmiller, Susan: Against Our Will. Men, Women and Rape, New York – Toronto 1981, p. 256; Farley: Sexual Shakedown, pp. 16, 103; Cohen: The Secret Oppression, p. 90; cf. Zippel: Politics, pp. 14, 56, 207.

106 MacKinnon, Catharine: Sexual Harassment of Working Women. A Case of Sex Discrimination, New Haven et al. 1979, pp. 217f.

107 Baker: Women's Movement, p. 94; Boris: Workplace Discrimination, p. 203.

108 Schultz, Vicki: The Sanitized Workplace, in: The Yale Law Journal 112/8 (2003), p. 2080.

109 Mead, Margaret: A Proposal: We Need Taboos on Sex at Work, in: Redbook, 150 (April 1978), pp. 31, 33, 38.

110 This argument will be made in detail in Chapter Six.

consensual sexual behavior from sexual harassment, which was seen as "unwelcome" and coerced behavior, and, thus, a form of sexual violence.[111]

The social conservative framing did not make this clear distinction between coerced and consensual sexual conduct. Schlafly emphasized that when men and women worked together a "chemistry [...] naturally occurs" which inescapably led to sex at work. In her testimony, she spoke of the problems of sexual behavior in the workplace which, apart from dividing families and causing an increased divorce rate, "create[d] real problems of morals, morale, discipline [and] work efficiency." Schlafly interchangeably spoke of sexual harassment and "extra-marital liaisons between consenting adults," thereby melding ideas of voluntary and coerced sexual behavior.[112] A discussion on sexual harassment, for Schlafly, presented as a battleground over acceptable sexual behavior in general. In her 21-page written testimony, she did not once acknowledge the coercive element sexual harassment held. Many authors of the various newspaper articles, editorials or letters to the editor criticizing legal and policy changes concerning sexual harassment echoed Schlafly's understanding of the subject matter by not differentiating between consensual sexual interactions and sexual harassment.[113]

In line with denying the coercive nature of sexual harassment, Schlafly went one step further, and placed the burden of responsibility on the targeted woman:

> Non-criminal sexual harassment on the job is not a problem for the virtuous woman except in the rarest of cases. When a woman walks across the room, she speaks with a universal body language that most men intuitively understand. Men hardly ever seek sexual favors of women from whom the certain answer is 'no' [...].[114]

In this quote, Schlafly identifies the "body language" of a woman as the factor inducing a man to make inappropriate advances. This, according to Schlafly, happened frequently, as many women had "abandoned the commandments against adultery and fornication" and thoughtlessly engaged "in any sexual activity."[115] Sexual harassment proved to be a matter of female responsibility, easily remedied by a change in female conduct and dress. Consequently, by choosing to exhibit a

---

111 AASC: Sexual Harassment at the Workplace, p. 401.
112 Ibid., pp. 401–403.
113 E. g. Baker, Russell: The Court, p. L29; Anonymous: Executive Sweet: Many Office Romeos Are Really Juliets, in: Time Magazine (October 8th, 1979), p. 76; cf. Baker: Women's Movement, p. 101.
114 Committee on Labor: Hearings on Sex Discrimination 1981, p. 400.
115 Ibid., p. 401.

certain behavior, a woman invited male advances, which must then be classified as 'welcomed.' Placing the core responsibility for sexual harassment with the female target permeated the public debate on the topic.[116] It was also a tactic utilized by several defense attorneys who routinely questioned plaintiffs about their dress, conduct, and sexual history.[117]

In addition to the expression of power as the harasser's motivation, the feminist frame emphasized the consequences faced by targets of sexual harassment. These extended far into the victim's life, influencing their health, reputation, finances, and career advancement. The feminist frame highlighted the increased stress victims of sexual harassment experienced, which often lead to both physical and psychological symptoms. Headaches, tiredness, nausea, drastic weight changes, as well as an increase of "alcohol and tranquillizer [sic]" intake were the most common physical effects observed in WWI's clients. Psychologically, these women often felt fear, anger, excessive tension, a loss of self-confidence, and a decrease in morale and motivation.[118] Affected women often found themselves in, what Farley describes as a "submit-or-quit dynamic."[119] The targets' options were reduced to either tolerating and/or engaging in coerced sexual activity or resigning their position. The loss of income was therefore the most obvious result of sexual harassment. However, even in cases in which the target of harassment promptly found a new position, they suffered economic consequences. A change of jobs was commonly connected with entry at a lower level, loss of seniority and often an extended time period before being considered for a promotion. Career advances were therefore impeded and financial benefits linked with these advances were lost for the time being.[120] The woman's resulting lower status in the workplace in turn aggravated the problem as it intensified the already existing power discrepancy and heightened the likelihood of a renewed victimization.[121] Individual harm regarding economic and social status was seen to be directly transferable to the collective level where these shortcomings were said to result in a further perpetuation of existing conditions.

Schlafly did not share the feminist concern that women, both as individuals as well as a collective, faced economic hardship as a direct result of sexual harass-

---

116 E. g. Cawthon, Frances: Danger! Curves Ahead Driving Harassed Worker off his Track, in: The Atlanta Constitution (January 4th, 1881), p. 3F; Furgurson, Pat: The Women at Work, in: The Atlanta Constitution (August 29th, 1975), p. 4 A; cf. Baker: Women's Movement, pp. 48, 134, 144.
117 Baker: Women's Movement, p. 144.
118 Crull: The Stress Effects, pp. 3–5.
119 Farley: Sexual Shakedown, p. 22.
120 Ibid., pp. 22, 48, 80; cf. Baker: Women's Movement, p. 177; Baker: Sexual Extortion, p. 232.
121 Farley: Sexual Shakedown, p. 48; cf. Zippel: Politics, p. 14.

ment. Following her commitment to maintaining traditional family structures based on a gendered division of labor, she did not acknowledge a woman's economic necessity to engage in wage labor. As a consequence, Schlafly only viewed sexual harassment as a problem "in the armed services where women do not have the freedom to resign."[122] Leaving a job in any other situation was considered a valid and even desirable solution to eradicate sexual harassment. Her concern was reserved for those women she considered "virtuous" and for those men falling victim to false allegations. Additionally, she criticized all sexual relationships within the workplace, declaring that they prompted a rise in divorce rates which in turn destabilized the American family and proved detrimental to the affected housewives.[123]

According to Schlafly, sexual relationships at work also bore another problem, namely that of sexual favoritism.

> [Sexual interactions at work] result in substantial discrimination against the virtuous woman. She doesn't have a sex problem, but she may have a job problem; she will end up being discriminated against because the job or raise or promotion may go to the female who uses her sex to get ahead. [...] Such women create real problems of morals, morale, discipline, work efficiency, and discrimination against virtuous women.[124]

Fears related to sexual favoritism do not focus on those women who have submitted to the bosses' sexual requests – whether these were unwelcome is irrelevant here – but instead are concerned with those colleagues who were *not* targeted for sexual favors. It is assumed that those employees who are not asked to engage in sexual interaction with their supervisor are denied preferential treatment.[125] As becomes evident in this quote, the person made responsible by Schlafly is not the supervisor who solicits sexual favors or deals out preferential treatment, but the "female who uses her sex to get ahead." As argued by historian Julie Berebitsky, the fear that women would "sleep their way up" has proven a persistent worry with very little factual corroboration since the early 20th century.[126]

As discrimination laws in the United States are built on the principle of equality and are heavily linked with the idea of fairness, the idea of sexual favoritism as sexual harassment resonated with many in the public discourse.[127] However, as legal scholar Vicki Schultz points out in her analysis, it is of note that other

---

122 Committee on Labor: Hearings on Sex Discrimination 1981, p. 398.
123 Ibid., p. 409.
124 Committee on Labor: Hearings on Sex Discrimination 1981, p. 403.
125 Schultz, Vicki: The Sanitized Workplace, in: The Yale Law Journal 112/8 (2003), p. 2091.
126 Berebitsky: Sex and the Office, pp. 17 f.
127 Ibid., p. 143.

forms of favoritism garner much less attention and scrutiny even though "[g]oing out to a sports bar together may be just as likely to lead to gender-based forms of exclusion as going out on a date together."[128] Critics also note that identifying instances of sexual favoritism as sexual harassment allows for introducing into the sexual harassment definition a scenario in which a fully consensual relationship and welcomed behavior may be classified as harassment. Thus, the line between consensual and coerced behavior is blurred. Another objection to equating sexual favoritism and sexual harassment, bemoans the implication that victims of both sets of behavior are aggrieved on the same scale.[129] These voices argue that while being passed over may be unfair, it does not compare to the emotional, in addition to the economic, distress experienced by those navigating unwanted attention, advances, and even assault.

While critique of the classification of sexual favoritism as sexual harassment came predominantly from the feminist camp, it is noteworthy that in a feminist narrative, one too can find an understanding of sexual harassment, which strikes a similar chord as that of sexual favoritism. I am speaking of the characterization of ageism as sexual harassment. Lin Farley, in her 1978 book *Sexual Shakedown*, devotes several pages to "Older Working Women." In these pages, she argues that due to the persistent sex stereotyping and sexualization women face in society, their value in the workplace was often attached to their attractiveness and youth rather than their experience and skill. This made it harder for women past the age of thirty to obtain a new job or keep, never mind advance, in their current job. Farley states that "[t]he repercussions of this kind of sexual harassment of the older woman worker are serious and far-reaching."[130] In Farley's view then, this discrimination of older women is a "kind of sexual harassment."

While it is conceivable that age discrimination of women is most often a form of sex discrimination and that there is a multitude of incidences in which middle aged and older women are subjected to gender harassment and/or sexualized harassment, I caution against outright accepting Farley's assumption that ageism may automatically be classified as sexual harassment. Her examples focus on the discrimination women over thirty faced during the job search. According to an employment-agency job counselor in 1975 "[e]mployers want to have young, cute things around them."[131] In Farley's examples, women are denied a job not because they rejected a bosses' sexual advances but because the boss did not consider

---

128 Schultz, Vicki: The Sanitized Workplace, p. 2189.
129 Berebitsky: Sex and the Office, p. 284.
130 Farley: Sexual Shakedown, p. 98.
131 WOW study on "discrimination against older women" cited in: Farley, Sexual Shakedown, p. 98.

them desirable on a sexual level in the first place. This feminist line of argument approaches the social conservative contention for the inclusion of sexual favoritism in the definition of sexual harassment. While the former blames society and the employer for perpetuating a sexualized view of women and applying conditions such as youth and attractiveness, the latter chides individual women for using their "sexual wiles" to advance in their career.[132] I suggest that this feminist understanding of ageism and the social conservative understanding of sexual favoritism are two sides of the same coin.

1.2.2 A Systemic Condition?

Similar to many other issues which had long been considered private, individual matters, second-wave feminists linked sexual harassment to systemic conditions which affected women as a group.[133] According to their narrative, behavior such as sexual harassment (like other forms of sexual violence) affected the relationship between men and women in general as it was symptomatic for and conducive to systemic power discrepancies within society.[134] The uneven power dynamics expressed by sexual harassment were seen to extend far beyond the individual situation. Hence, feminist criticism of sexual harassment entailed an unmitigated objection to systemic power discrepancies between the sexes.

Second-wave feminists varied in how much importance they allotted power discrepancies based on factors other than gender in respect to sexual harassment. While some feminists sought to keep the focus on changing gender dynamics, other groups openly addressed the heightened vulnerability faced by non-white and low-income women. Women of color, unproportionally found themselves targeted by sexual harassment. Not only was their economic dependency statistically speaking higher than that of white women,[135] making them more vulnerable to

---

132 Committee on Labor: Hearings on Sex Discrimination 1981, p. 400.
133 Farley: Sexual Shakedown, pp. 45 f., 112; Enke, Anne: Taking Over Domestic Space. The Battered Women's Movement and Public Protest, in: The World the Sixties Made. Politics and Culture in Recent America (Critical Perspectives on the Past), ed. by Van Gosse and Richard Moser, Philadelphia 2003, p. 164; Zippel: Politics, p. 14.
134 E. g.: Alliance Against Sexual Coercion: Sexual Harassment and Coercion. Violence Against Women, in: Aegis (Jul/Aug 1978), p. 28; cf. Arnold: Violence Against Women, p. 271.
135 U.S. Department of Labor cited in: Alliance Against Sexual Coercion: Advocacy Handbook, 1979, p. 15 f.; Strum, Philippa: Affirmative Action for Women and Non-Black Racial Minorities. A Paper Prepared for Discussion at Plenary Meeting at the Biennial Conference at Mount Vernon College in Washington D.C., June 1979, pp. 3 f., BCA, Feminist Ephemera Collection, Box 3, Folder American Civil Liberties Union; Business and Professional Women's Foundation: Women in the Workplace, May 1986, p. 3, BCA, Feminist Ephemera Collection, Box 9, Folder Business and Professional Women's Foundation.

economic pressures but sexual harassment was often an explicit expression of racism. In a 1981-article, Judy Trent Ellis, a lawyer specializing in discrimination cases, explained that sexual harassment was often "due to both race and sex, either implicitly, so that the woman is unsure whether the harassment is racially or sexually motivated or explicitly, where the harasser expressed his sexual interest in terms of her race."[136] One can hardly imagine a more explicit example than Willie Ruth Hawkins' case from 1980. She was told by a white coworker that he "wished slavery days would return so that he could sexually train her and she would be his bitch."[137] In this case, the intersectionality of race and sex becomes particularly obvious. The harassment described here was not accumulative sexual and racial, but inexplicably linked; one informed the other.

Whereas WWI accepted race as one catalyst for sexual harassment, the AASC went further and consciously promoted an intersectional understanding in regard to sexual harassment.[138] They named sexism as well as "capitalism, [...] racism, heterosexism, and ageism" as the parameters of the unequal power dynamics at play.[139] Capitalism, in comparison to the other factors named, held a unique position: It "feeds [...] on" the other factors for power discrepancies, such as sexism and racism and was considered the root cause of sexual harassment. The "power structures" in a capitalist system, according to their line of reasoning, inevitably led to women's subordination as these structures deprived workers of autonomy and created economic pressures, therefore, leaving female workers with a "double liability" due to their vulnerability to sexual harassment.[140] They concluded that the eradication of sexual harassment necessitated the abolition of capitalism and the establishment of "an egalitarian and democratic work structure."[141]

This opinion was not shared by Farley or the WWI and in 1979, Farley and Klein publicly voiced their disagreement in an exchange mediated by *Aegis* mag-

---

136 Ellis, Judy Trent: Sexual Harassment and Race: A Legal Analysis of Discrimination, in: Journal of Legislation 8/1 (1981), pp. 40, 42.

137 *Continental Can Company v. Minnesota*, 297 N.W.2d 241, 1980, p. 246; cf. Baker: Race, Class, and Sexual Harassment in the 1970s, in: Study of Women and Gender. Faculty Publications, Smith College, Spring 2004, pp. 16 f.

138 Intersectional aspects of sexual harassment are explained further by Zippel: Politics, p. 56; and Baker: Race, Class, and Sexual Harassment.

139 AASC: Organizing Against Sexual Harassment, p. 239; cf. Baker, Women's Movement, p. 96.

140 Alliance Against Sexual Coercion: Sexual Harassment and Coercion, p. 29; AASC: Organizing Against Sexual Harassment, pp. 238–239; Hooven, Martha and Nancy McDonald: "The Role of Capitalism: Understanding Sexual Harassment," in: Aegis (November/December 1978), p. 33. Hooven and McDonald were long-time members of the AASC; cf. Baker: Women's Movement, p. 96.

141 AASC: Sexual Harassment at the Workplace, p. 11; cf. Baker: Women's Movement, p. 44.

azine. Klein, when reviewing Farley's book, accused her of "ignor[ing] the complexities of sexual harassment" by neglecting the "dichotomy between patriarchy [...] and capitalism" and focusing on patriarchy as the "ultimate source of sexual harassment."[142] Farley, in the next issue, exclaimed that "the idea of capitalism itself somehow com[ing] up with the idea of sexual harassment is absurd." She defended her argument, intending to "set the record straight," stating that capitalism in its raw form would have helped women escape their subordinate position in society as it "created a 'free market' in labor" in which women could compete with men.[143] According to her it was patriarchy, not capitalism, which allowed male control over the labor force and therefore fostered an ideal environment for sexual harassment.[144] Farley continued to say that sexual harassment reinforced male dominance and therefore was an instrument for safeguarding these patriarchal structures.

This difference in opinion took place within the feminist discourse space and did not further attract attention beyond feminist groups and alternative media. The version of the feminist frame, which made its way into mainstream discourse, focused almost exclusively on sexual harassment as a result of and a condition for gendered power discrepancies.[145] However, when discussing sexual harassment in the context of the workplace and more specifically in the for-profit private sector, a nuanced understanding of these groups' positionings on capitalism becomes relevant.

The systemic structures enforcing a gendered division of labor in society were denounced in the feminist frame as the root cause of sexual harassment. In the social conservative frame, they were portrayed in a much different light. Schlafly explains that far from causing sexual harassment, the division of labor actually counteracted the phenomenon. Sexual harassment only came to be a problem as a result of "irrational feminist demands for the elimination of 'sex discrimination.'"[146] By diverging from the established system, the "many more women in the workplace," according to Schlafly, had provoked the increase of sexual behavior at work.[147] In regard to sex integration in the armed forces, she declares that "[n]othing in the world would create more sexual harassment than the drafting of 18 to

---

142 Klein, Freada: Book Review of Sexual Shakedown: The Sexual Harassment of Women on the Job, by Lin Farley, in: Aegis (November/December 1978), pp. 34f.
143 Farley, Lin: Response to Sexual Shakedown Review, in: Aegis (January/February 1979), pp. 24–26; cf. Baker: Women's Movement, pp. 96f.
144 Cf. Baker: Women's Movement, pp. 96f.
145 Zippel: Politics, p. 14.
146 Ibid., p. 409.
147 Ibid., p. 401.

20-year-old girls into the Army. We already have a major problem of sexual harassment that has accompanied the assignment of women aboard ships and in other nontraditional jobs in the armed services."[148] It became clear that Schlafly did not make the men who engaged in harassing behavior responsible, but instead blamed the new practice of allowing a close working relationship between men and women.

Schlafly underscored her support for a system in which a gendered division of labor was the societal norm by arguing against political initiatives promoting sex integration such as affirmative action and demands for equal pay.

> We certainly do not want a society in which the average wage paid to all women equals the average wage paid to all men, [...]. We want a society in which the average man earns more than the average woman so that his earnings can fulfill his provider role in providing a home and support for his wife, who is nurturing and mothering their children.[149]

Despite not being the primary object of discussion, topics such as sex integration and equal pay were nevertheless addressed in a hearing concerning sexual harassment, because they, according to the feminist frame, counteracted sexual harassment. The emphasis on such issues, within this setting, exemplified that the topic of sexual harassment had become an arena in which contrasting ideals of societal gender roles and relations clashed.

1.2.3 Gendered Behavior?

Despite the recognition of intersectional factors influencing sexual harassment within the feminist frame, the topic was first and foremost considered a women's issue and comprised a large gender component.[150] Gender, within the feminist narrative, was shaped by and closely linked to systemic conditions. Sexual harassment, defined as *male* behavior aimed towards *women*, was considered inseparable from structural parameters anchored in society.[151]

The feminist frame identified sexual harassment as an instrument used to preserve male control over the labor market. Women quitting their jobs, losing promotions, and earning lower wages were all results of sexual harassment and

---

148 Ibid., p. 397.
149 Ibid., p. 398.
150 Baker: Women's Movement, p. 50; Zippel: Politics, pp. 7, 14.
151 Same-sex sexual harassment was rarely considered in the feminist analysis of the topic and was not a prominent aspect of the larger discussion on sexual harassment during the time period analyzed. It is later addressed by the Supreme Court in the case of *Oncale v. Sundowner Offshore Services, Inc.* in 1998.

had significant consequences, not only for the affected victims but also for women as a group. Farley explicitly stated that sexual harassment served to "keep women out" and "keep women down."[152] Women employed in or training for jobs in traditionally male dominated fields often reported hostile work environment sexual harassment, in which the harassment had the clear intention of inducing women to resign their positions – hence, "keeping [them] out" of the respective fields.[153]

Similarly, in sectors in which a female labor force had become the norm, sexual harassment served as an instrument to deny women career advancement. Continued objectification and sexualization of women at work legitimized an understanding of female employees as less competent.[154] In combination with the lack of seniority due to heightened job mobility, this meant that women were often passed over for promotions – hence, women were "[kept] down."[155] Within the feminist frame, sexual harassment was charged with perpetuating gendered job segregation as well as the notion that women had no place in the public sphere.[156] Therefore, it bore tremendous consequences for women's economic and social status.

The lack of women in these jobs and in management positions, in turn, made for ideal circumstances for continued sexual harassment. Nadine Taub, the plaintiff's council in *Tomkins v. Public Service Electricity and Gas Co.* (1977), summed this up in her appellant brief, stating that "female employees are more frequently in positions where they can be subjected to the sexual demands of male supervisors."[157] Taub in her argument underscored how gendered behavior was the result of systemic circumstances. Additionally, individual action against sexual harassment was made exceedingly difficult by the gendered nature of the power structure. Farley, pursuing the same reasoning, argued that when there were no women higher up on the chain of command, male supervisors felt more secure in exhibiting sexually harassing behavior towards an employee. If they reported to a female supervisor, harassment would be less likely as their potential victims

---

152 Farley: Sexual Shakedown, p. 90.
153 Ibid., pp. 65, 90; cf. Baker: Women's Movement, pp. 67 f., 80; Zippel: Politics, p. 11.
154 Farley: Sexual Shakedown, pp. 16 f.
155 Ibid., p. 46.
156 E. g. Connie Korbel, one of the women speaking at the Ithaca speak-out, laments whether maybe she "should've stayed home and had babies". Transcript of the Speak-Out on Sexual Harassment of Women at Work, Ithaca, NY, May 4th, 1975, Karen Sauvigné Papers, Brooklyn, NY, Private Collection, p. 12, cited in: Baker: Women's Movement, pp. 32 f.
157 Taub, Nadine: Plaintiff-Appellant's Appeal Brief, *Tomkins v. Public Service Electric and Gas Company*, 568 F. 2d 1044, pp. 18 f.

would presumably find it easier to engage a higher positioned ally.[158] Judge Swygert, in his ruling of *Bundy v. Jackson* (1981), was one of very few judges accepting sexual harassment as a result of systemic dynamics resulting in sex discrimination. He stated that "so long as women remain inferiors in the employment hierarchy, they may have little recourse against harassment beyond the legal recourse [the plaintiff] seeks in this case."[159]

The feminist narrative indicated that societally condoned demonstrations of power towards members of the same sex did not include a sexual component. Feminist author Susan Brownmiller whose book *Against Our Will* (1975) was vastly influential in recognizing rape as an expression of power and provided a basis for Farley's work on sexual harassment, goes into detail about one prominent exception, "[p]rison rape is generally seen today for what it is: an acting out of power roles within an all-male, authoritarian environment in which the younger, weaker inmate [...] is forced to play the role that in the outside world is assigned to women."[160] In Brownmiller's interpretation of this sexualized same-sex power demonstration, gender roles are allocated. The argument made is that sexualized power is invariably gendered. By extension, sexual harassment, as a form of sexual violence, was viewed as an expression and a manifestation of maladjusted gendered power dynamics and was always exhibited unidirectionally by a man towards a woman.[161] Wider acknowledgment and inclusion of same-sex harassment in the broader feminist frame did not occur until the late 1980s.

The sexualization of women and therefore also the sexualization of the behavior aimed at women, was partially explained to be a result of social conditioning. Women were ascribed a social and cultural role as sex objects, which was prioritized over their ability as workers.[162] This common perception of women was

---

158 Farley: Sexual Shakedown, p. 182; This argument is based on the presumption that women were commonly inclined to support each other. This assumption, even though it is supported by survey data showing that women, in comparison to men, were more likely to consider sexual harassment a problem, is, nevertheless, a precarious generalization. A discussion on sexual harassment often induced a high amount of competition, rather than encouragement, among women. For data on the differing perceptions of sexual harassment by women and men, see: Baker: Women's Movement, p. 158.

159 *Bundy v. Jackson*, 641 F.2d 934 (1981), United States Court of Appeals, District of Columbia; cf. Baker: Women's Movement, p. 120.

160 Brownmiller: Against our Will, p. 258.

161 Cf. Baker: Women's Movement, p. 43; Zippel: Politics, p. 15.

162 Farley: Sexual Shakedown, pp. 14 f.; Wehrli, Lynn: Sexual Harassment at the Workplace. A Feminist Analysis and Strategy for Social Change. Master's Thesis, Massachusetts Institute of Technology, 1976, p. 70. Wehrli's master thesis was one of the first in-depth feminist analysis of sexual harassment as injustice towards women; cf. Craig, Steve: Madison Avenue versus The

used to legitimize sexual harassment and suggested that women unconditionally welcomed any sexual attention.[163] Feminist lawyers argued that women, in contrast to men, were uniquely affected by sexual harassment, because this practice was so heavily entwined with a cultural bias against women. Thus, they declared sexual harassment as inherently gendered behavior.[164] This argument resonated with public policy makers. When opening a congressional hearing concerning sexual harassment in the U.S. Postal Service, in 1979, representative George Thomas Leland clarified that there were many "misconceptions" about women which were "not based on fact, but rather due to cultural biases" and which were "no excuse whatsoever for women to be relegated to the role of sex objects."[165]

The feminist and the social conservative frame showed some overlap in accepting sexual harassment as gendered behavior. Within the social conservative frame, the idea that sexual harassment was based on the sex of those involved was taken for granted, necessitating no further elaboration. However, their concept of gender differed significantly from the feminist understanding. Whereas "gender" in the feminist narrative was clearly linked to social structures and socialization, in the conservative narrative it referred to rudimentary sex roles which were a biological given.[166] Schlafly clearly states that men and women naturally have contrasting "gender identit[ies]" and, therefore, assumed different roles in society.[167] Only when these differences were ignored, as was done by "feminist efforts" to create "a gender-free society," sexual harassment occurred.[168] Due to the "sexual attraction men and women have for each other, [...] sexual interaction at work" became inevitable after women entered the workforce in larger numbers. In her testimony, Schlafly ascribed the heightened numbers of sexual harassment cases to increased numbers of women in the workplace and strongly urged against any government action promoting sex integration in the public sphere, appealing to Congress to "keep women out of places where they don't be-

---

Feminine Mystique. The Advertising Industry's Response to the Women's Movement, in: Disco Divas. Women and Popular Culture in the 1970s, ed. by Sherrie A. Inness, Philadelphia 2003, pp. 14, 22.

163 Farley: Sexual Shakedown, p. 13; cf. Zippel: Politics, p. 15.

164 E. g. Taub: Brief, *Tomkins v. Public Service Electric*, pp. 20 f.; Same argument used by the plaintiff in Barnes v. Costle, 561 F.2d 983 (D.C. Cir. 1977), cf. Baker: Women's Movement, pp. 50 f.

165 Subcommittee on Postal Personnel and Modernization of the Committee on Post Office and Civil Service, United States House of Representatives: Hearings on Racial Discrimination and Sexual Harassment in the U.S. Postal Service. 97th Congress. First Session, July 1st, 1981, cited in: Baker: Women's Movement, p. 125.

166 Schlafly: Positive Woman, p. 103.

167 Committee on Labor: Hearings on Sex Discrimination, p. 418.

168 Ibid., p. 417.

long."[169] In Schlafly's social conservative narrative sexual harassment was framed as a natural interaction between men and women, precisely *because* they were men and women.

In conclusion, the feminist frame characterized sexual harassment as a serious political issue conceived by and resulting in the further perpetuation of systemic gender inequalities. The social conservative frame, too, saw sexual harassment as a phenomenon closely linked to gender, but viewed traditional gender structures as protective rather than harmful to women. The message presented in the social conservative frame harshly contrasted that of the feminist frame; sexual harassment was not recognized as a wide-spread or serious problem and therefore warranted no societal and much less legal action. In contrast, the insight that sexual harassment needed to be stopped by political action accompanied the feminist frame as a constant undercurrent. Feminists had a strong interest in clearly formulating their thoughts and ideas about sexual harassment, because the theory developed was deliberately used as the basis for legal work, consciousness-raising, and further activism.

1.2.4 Colloquial Confusion

In the public discourse, these different frames of sexual harassment were not as clearly distinguishable as presented in this chapter. Contemporaries, especially those who did not consider themselves either feminist or social conservative, did not analyze and categorize their stances regarding sexual harassment even while using the term. The term itself was accepted into the public discourse relatively soon after its inception, however, it was not always accompanied by a definition. In fact, 'sexual harassment' was a term everybody seemed to know and at the same time, one that generated widespread bewilderment. It was not uncommon for parties to a conversation to refer to different concepts, while using the same terminology.[170] This confusion, no doubt added to the contentiousness of the issue.

One common public perception of sexual harassment was (and is) an understanding of sexual harassment as part of a sexual violence spectrum. Taking its lead from the feminist frame, this model assumes sexual harassment to be a form of sexual violence. However, diverging from the feminist frame, as presented

---

169 Ibid., p. 402.
170 Examples include: Anonymous: Executive Sweet, p. 76; Anonymous: Just When are Passes Harassing? in: The Atlanta Constitution (August 4th, 1978), p. 1B; Anonymous: The Law and Threats to Virtue, in: The Wall Street Journal (April 27th, 1976), p. 22; Berns, Walter: Terms of Endearment, in: Harper's Weekly (October 1st, 1980), pp. 14–20.

by single issue organizations working on sexual harassment, in this model, sexual harassment was often considered as one step of several on a ladder leading to rape. This understanding of sexual harassment was common in the rhetoric of organizations, often feminist themselves, who were dedicated to fighting sexual violence. The group Men Stopping Rape, for instance, spoke of a "rape-spectrum," which included "sexual innuendo, rape 'jokes', objectification, [...] sexual harassment, rape imagery in pornography, [...]" as pre-stages of rape.[171] Similarly, a brochure by the African Women's Committee for Community Education defined sexual harassment as "the use of words, gestures, bodily actions and other means of verbal and non-verbal communication to insult, degrade, humiliate and otherwise dehumanize women." According to this brochure, such harassment had the purpose of "rape-testing," a practice in which the harasser "measures the response of a potential victim, to his harassment, to determine if she would make an easy target for rape."[172] In both examples, sexual harassment was considered a form of sexual violence, which could prelude but was in itself not as severe as rape. This did not coincide with the WWI or the AASC definition, which covered any unwanted sexual advances, ranging from looks and verbal comments to rape, as long as the conduct was coercive and took place in an institutionalized context, most commonly the workplace.

Another public understanding hinged on the connection between the concepts of sexual harassment and sex discrimination. As we shall see shortly, feminists developed a legal understanding in which sexual harassment was to be legally treated as sex discrimination under the Civil Rights Act. This equation was not two-directional. Hence, all sexual harassment constituted sex discrimination, but not all sex discrimination was considered sexual harassment. This, however, did not stop members of the public from using the terms interchangeably.

Adding another layer of confusion, the term sex discrimination colloquially took on a much broader meaning than the legal concept intended and was regularly used to refer to any unequal treatment of men and women. A column in *The Atlanta Constitution* written by Ron Hudspeth pushed this point to an almost comical extent. In the article Hudspeth argues "It's men, not women, who are [sexually] harassed," and provides the following example:

---

171 Biernbaum, Michael and Joseph Weinberg: Men Unlearning Rape, in: WREE-View of Women. Newsmagazine of women for Racial and Economic Equality, 16/3,4 (Fall/Winter 1991), p. 12, BCA, Feminist Ephemera Collection, Box 80, Folder U.S. Department of Labor.
172 Coalition for a Hassle Free Zone: Fact Sheet on Street Harassment, 1992, BCA, Feminist Ephemera Collection, Box 14, Folder Coalition for a Hassle Free Zone.

There is seemingly no end to the sexual harassment of males. For instance, when a woman has a flat tire on the expressway, all she has to do is step outside her car and stand. Within minutes, some male will stop and politely change her tire. Let a male with a flat tire try that. My hope is he has rations for a log stay. A female wouldn't stop to change Robert Redford's tire.[173]

In his column, Hudspeth draws attention to several instances of differential treatment between the sexes, which, in his opinion, negatively affect men. This differential treatment is then described as "sexual harassment." One may question whether Hudspeth was genuinely confused about the terminology, the more likely scenario being that this was a strategic substitution. After all, the ambiguity here allowed him to criticize not the persistent existence of gender roles, but instead the movement against sexual harassment.

As was the case in the examples above, the term 'sexual harassment' is seldom defined in primary source material outside of the feminist single-issue groups specifically working on the phenomenon. In social conservative circles as well as in the wider feminist context, the term sexual harassment was fluid in its meaning. Publicly, depending on the context, the term alluded to a step on a sexual violence spectrum or it included any sexualized behavior in the workplace. It denoted a specific legal concept or it simply related to differential treatment of the sexes. All in all, the continued research and public consciousness raising done by single-issue feminist organizations pushed the issue further into the public discourse. While the term was used in various ways, these organizations increasingly provided background information and clear definitions. These definitions were aimed at contradicting social conservative arguments in regard to gender relations and would become more precise and more public as they became part of the feminist legal strategy.

2 A New Adversary: Feminist Action Against Employers

While researching the issue and developing a theoretical framework, the adversary feminists faced were those promulgating social conservative thought patterns. However, upon closer examination of feminist action in practice during the early fight against sexual harassment, it becomes apparent that feminists encountered a second antagonist: the employer. Identifying the employer and the representatives of the social conservative framework as two separate entities is

---

173 Hudspeth, Ron: It's Men Not Women Who Are Harassed, in: The Atlanta Constitution (April 4th, 1981), p. 1B.

possible only with the benefit of hindsight. Contemporary feminists seldom made this distinction. Instead, they often amassed employers with those they saw as representatives of the social conservative framing. Typically judges, politicians, and employers were listed and referred to as one entity.[174]

Similarly, social conservative activists saw employers as their natural allies. This is demonstrated most acutely by Phyllis Schlafly in her 1981 congressional testimony. On the subject of new federal regulations on sexual harassment she refers to "the employer" as an "innocent bystander" who is "unjust[ly] [...] penalize[ed] [...] for acts over which he has no control." Immediately following this, she declares that "the role of motherhood and the role of the dependent wife" are suffering "harassment" by "feminists and their federal government allies."[175] Schlafly identifies core social conservative values as well as the employer as victims of feminist rhetoric on sexual harassment. By doing so, she establishes an affinity between the two groups.

In this chapter, I strive to show that feminists considered the employer an opponent in the fight against sexual harassment. As a consequence, they directed a great part of their activism specifically at employers and their organizations. This is visible in the feminist single-issue organizations' direct-action campaigns, in the development of a legal strategy focusing on Title VII of the Civil Rights Act, and in the support for and influence on the wording of the sexual harassment guidelines published by the Equal Employment Opportunity Commission (EEOC).

2.1 Feminist Direct Action

The feminist conceptualization of sexual harassment as a systemic and political problem indicated that any action would involve women organizing as a group. Organizations, such as the Working Women's Institute (WWI) and the Alliance Against Sexual Coercion (AASC), emphasized women's agency and the importance of victims to "regain a sense of their own power."[176] Many women had felt left alone with their experiences. They often were too ashamed to speak of their victimization, fearing that they had somehow invited the harassing behavior.[177] Communicating with one another, educating themselves, and participating in the orga-

---

174 E.g.: Crull, Peggy and Marilyn Cohen: Expanding the Definition of Sexual Harassment, Research Series Report No. 4, Winter 1982, p. 3, BCA, Research on Women Records, Box 97, Folder Working Women's Institute Sexual Harassment Information.

175 Committee on Labor: Hearings on Sex Discrimination 1981, p. 397.

176 AASC: Organizing Against Sexual Harassment, p. 240; cf. Zippel: Politics, p. 57.

177 E.g. AASC: Sexual Harassment and Coercion, pp. 28f.

nizations' activities created a sense of belonging, defined a common goal, and enabled women across the country to collectively fight sexual harassment.[178]

Much of the feminist educational material relied on the theoretical framework discussed in Chapter One. It focused on societally accepted gender roles and overarching issues of patriarchy. Using strategies of direct action targeted at lawmakers, individual men, as well as the public at large, feminist organizations drew attention to these power discrepancies. Feminist activism was also oftentimes aimed directly at where sexual harassment took place, the workplace. Employers were seen by feminists as actors who had an innate potential to initiate immediate change but deliberately chose not to do so. Feminist activists spoke out against this inertia through protests, the media, and individual counseling. Thus, employers had become a prime target for direct feminist action.

2.1.1 Speak-Outs and Protests

Speak-outs and protests held by feminist organizations were one concrete strategy of drawing attention to the topic. They served, as Karen Sauvigné cofounder of WWI explained, as a "mechanism for public consciousness raising."[179] Considering that sexual harassment in the workplace, as opposed to sexual harassment in education or in housing, was the focus of this early feminist activism, the topic was understood as a worker's rights issue. Therefore, making working women conscious of the problem and informing them of their rights could directly impact their relationship with their employer. In some cases, in an effort to turn out as many working women as possible, organizers advertised an upcoming event on the premises of local businesses. This was the case in 1975, when the budding WWI invited women workers to the first ever speak-out on sexual harassment. "Hop[ing] for wide community participation,"[180] the group distributed pamphlets and hung posters in common areas of the three largest factories in the area: Ithaca Gun, Morse Chain, and National Cash Register. This was done without the permission of the businesses in question and can therefore be classified as an obstructive and maybe even contentious move against these employers.[181]

---

178 Zippel: Politics, pp. 54 f.; Baker: Women's Movement, p. 35; cf. Roth, Roland: Kollektive Identitäten Neuer Sozialer Bewegungen, in: Paradigmen der Bewegungsforschung. Entstehung und Entwicklung von Neuen Sozialen Bewegungen und Rechtsextremismus, ed. by Kai-Uwe Hellmann and Ruud Koopmans, Wiesbaden 1998, pp. 52–56.
179 Ryan: Feminism, p. 73; Whittier: Identity Politics, p. 385; Sauvigné, Karen: Letter to 'Mauri,' dated March 28th, 1975, cited in: Baker: Women's Movement, p. 31.
180 Baker: Women's Movement, pp. 31 f.
181 Ibid., p. 32.

More antagonistic were protests, picket lines, or even union organizing directed specifically at individual organizations and business.[182] As early as 1972, sixty
flight attendants held the first meeting of their organization Stewardesses for
Women's Rights. The group was founded to protest their employers' sexist advertising campaigns and the humiliation of "underwear inspections" in which their
supervisors – both male and female – "checked whether stewardesses were wearing bras, as required."[183] Two years later, in 1974, the group had joined the efforts
of the 20,000-member strong Association of Flight Attendants to protest National
Airlines' and Continental Airlines' advertising campaigns. The latter was promising potential customers that "we'll really move our tail for you." The prior had
published portraits of women in their uniforms with the caption "I'm Linda,
Fly Me!"[184] Additionally, the company was requiring their flight attendants to
wear name tags with this message.[185] The Association's threats of a "spontaneous
lack of enthusiasm," if such adds were not discontinued were followed by a strike
in 1975 which led to a "four month shutdown" of National Airlines.[186]

Similarly, in 1979, the New York organization Women In The Trades organized
a walk-out, calling upon female employees of a local textile factory to abandon
their tasks in the middle of the workday in order to protest the sexual coercion
that had run rampant on the factory floor.[187] In yet another example, the California based organization Women Organized Against Sexual Harassment in 1981 initiated a letter writing campaign. The organization encouraged students, staff, and
the wider public to write letters, addressed to the dean of the University of California, Berkeley, protesting the continued employment of a professor who had

---

182 Bularzik, Mary: Sexual Harassment at the Workplace. Historical Notes, in: Worker's Struggles, Past and Present: A 'Radical America' Reader, ed. by James Green, Philadelphia 1983, p. 123;
cf. Action throughout the 1990s: NOW and Women's Action Coalition protest letter against the
restaurant chains Bazookas and Hooters, NYPL, Women's Action Coalition Records, Box 5, Select
Letter Campaigns, 1992.
183 Johnston, Laurie: Airlines Assailed by Stewardesses: 'sexism' of Employers and Flying Public
Is Scored, in: New York Times, N.Y. (December 13th, 1972), p. 21.
184 Anonymous: Stewardesses Protest Suggestive Airline Ads, in: New York Times, N.Y. (June 30th,
1974), p. 33; Baker: The Emergence, p. 164.
185 Mutari, Ellen: Women on the Move. Creating Job Satisfaction. Career Development of Flight
Attendants, in: Business and Professional Women's Foundation, no date, p. 6, BCA, Feminist
Ephemera Collection, Box 9.
186 Rattner, Steven: National Airlines Shutdown is Nearing Four Months, in: New York Times,
N.Y. (December 29th, 1975), pp. 43 f.
187 Nontraditional Employment for Women: NEW – Nontraditional Employment for Women.
Training, placing and supporting women in the trades since 1978, no date, p. 1, BCA, Feminist
Ephemera Collection Box 57, Folder Non-traditional Employment for Women.

been accused of sexual coercion by female faculty and students alike.[188] All of these cases were prompted not solely by the existence of harassment in these workplaces, but by the employers' subsequent inaction.

2.1.2 Publicity and Media

Soon after coining the term 'sexual harassment,' feminist single-issue organizations had established themselves as experts on the topic. Consequently, the media turned to these groups for information.[189] Additionally, these organizations proactively attempted to influence the press in their reporting, making this a conscious strategy.[190] By writing press releases and holding press conferences, activists reached out to the media asking for coverage of the issue. This approach proved successful and the term 'sexual harassment' was rapidly adopted by the mainstream press.[191] This relationship with the press allowed feminist single-issue organizations to effectively promote their framing of sexual harassment as a reasonable, factual understanding of the issue.[192]

The first articles on the subject published in the major American dailies explained the phenomenon to their readers and in doing so, often portrayed the feminist framing of the matter. This included the understanding of sexual harassment as a workers' rights issue. Feminist spokeswomen continuously emphasized the employers' responsibility to act – a perspective that could readily be found in the press coverage in the late 1970s. This held true for mainstream newspapers such as the *New York Times*, the *Chicago Tribue*, and the *Washington Post*, as well as for more specialized business magazines.[193] Mary Bralove, writing for *The Wall Street Journal*, commented that "[t]hese days the wall of silence surrounding the issue of sexual harassment is gradually crumbling" and warned em-

---

188 Kurita, Shari: The Status of Berkeley's Title IX Compliance, in: the Daily Californian, no date, no page; Finkel, Lynn: Sexual Harassment, in: The Daily Californian, no date, pp. 20–22.

189 Baker: Popular Representation, p. 40; Baker: Women's Movement, p. 100.

190 Zippel: Politics, p. 56.

191 Arriola: Construction Industry, p. 45.

192 Zippel: Politics, p. 166.

193 E. g. Crittenden, Ann: Women Tell of Sexual Harassment at Work, in: The New York Times (October 25th, 1977), p. 60; Brenner, Elizabeth: Sexual Harassment: Hard to Define, Harder to Fight. Sex Harassment Hits Women's Self-Respect, in: Chicago Tribue (May 30th, 1979), p. B1; Bralove, Mary: Women Give Gate to Career "Advances" by Wolves, in: Chicago Tribue (February 4th, 1976), p. B1; White, Jane See: Sexual Harassment. A Pivotal Issue, in: The Washington Post (August 15th, 1978), p. E10; Baker, Donald P.: Proving Sexual Harassment Is a Struggle, in: The Washington Post (October 24th, 1979), p. A7.

ployers that they "best pay more attention to the safety of their female staff."[194] By publicly introducing employers as part of the equation, this press coverage served to apply pressure on employers.

Despite the appearance and acceptance of the term 'sexual harassment' in the mainstream media from 1975 onwards, it would be misleading to suggest the immediate rise of the topic to the forefront of the public attention. In 1991, in a piece appearing in the feminist publication *Ms. Magazine*, Freada Klein is quoted stating that "[w]e felt so alone out there [...]. There was a *Redbook* survey in 1976 and a *Ms.* Speak-out and cover story in 1977. That was all."[195] Additionally, it must be emphasized that, although the feminist frame of sexual harassment slowly gained acceptance in mainstream papers, it was by no means the only representation of the topic. Alongside articles reflecting sexual harassment as a gendered structural injustice, there were many published voices trivializing and firmly criticizing the feminist perspective on the subject matter.[196] Nevertheless, by the late 1970s the issue of sexual harassment was sufficiently public and contentious to cause significant damage to a company's reputation, which in turn could prove costly to repair. Therefore, utilizing their influence with the press or simply threatening to do so, proved to be an effective strategic tool feminists employed against their chosen adversaries.[197]

2.1.3 Pamphlets and Counseling Services

Both WWI and AASC emphasized the importance of disseminating information among working women. Only when women were aware of their options could they bring about both individual and systemic change. As discussed in Chapter One, the counseling program for working women in the wider New York Metropolitan Area was an important pillar for WWI's activism. Moreover, the AASC made it one of their primary objectives to supply other women's organizations, rape crisis centers, and community outreach programs with information on the issue.[198] Instead of extending their counseling services for individual women,

---

194 Nemy: Speak Out, p. 38. For an expanded interpretation and contextualization of this article, see: Baker: Popular Representation, p. 48; Bralove: Cold Shoulder, p. 1. For an expanded interpretation and contextualization of this article, see: Baker: Popular Representation, p. 43.
195 Brownmiller: From Wood to Hill, p. 71.
196 Hudspeth: Men Not Women. p. 1B; Baker, Russell: The Court, p. L29; cf. Arriola: Construction Industry, p. 45; For an overview on press coverage of sexual harassment 1975–1980 see Baker: Women's Movement, pp. 100–106.
197 Baker: Women's Movement, p. 106.
198 Ibid., p. 86.

they hoped to amplify their impact by training and informing other organizations so that they, too, could aid women seeking help.[199]

In addition to individual counseling, significant methods for reaching those seeking information were workshops, leaflets, and newsletters. WWI started their newsletter, *Labor Pains*, as early as August 1975, and the AASC joined with the National Communication Network and the Feminist Alliance Against Rape in Boston in publishing their monthly paper *Aegis* in 1978.[200] Regular newsletters updated interested individuals regarding recent developments on the subject, defined collective goals, advertised upcoming events, and gave specific advice on how best to react to instances of sexual harassment.[201] Due to their newsletters, information packets, workshops, and counseling sessions, WWI and the AASC became nationally known as the contact points for anyone seeking information or assistance regarding sexual harassment.[202]

As illustrated by a pamphlet entitled "How and Why to Document a Case" published by WWI in 1982, much of the advice given to working women by these organizations assumes the employer as the opposition. As the title suggests, the pamphlet encourages harassment victims to "document what occurs as carefully as possible," even if they "do not intend to make a complaint." A "personal statement" should be corroborated with "as much back-up material as you can collect." The latter piece of advice was given because when filing a sexual harassment complaint "it often becomes one word against the other" and the employer would "more often than not seek the easy way out!"

The pamphlet goes on to recommend:

> It would be safest to follow-up the meeting by sending them [the employer, supervisor or HR department] a memo (and keeping a copy for yourself) reiterating what was said at the meeting. If you chose to do this, do not be naïve – they are doubtless more sophisticated than you in dealing with personnel problems and smoothing ruffled feathers. Try to protect yourself by making a record and being careful about what you say. Also be sure to make notes in your log about any contacts with anyone in the company about the problem. [...] it will make it more difficult for the employer to come back at a later date and say that your version of the meeting is incorrect.[203]

199 E.g.: Backhouse, Connie et al.: Fighting Sexual Harassment. An Advocacy Handbook, Boston 1981. This Handbook, published by the AASC, addressed organizations wishing to aid harassed women; Baker: Women's Movement, p. 43.
200 Hurwitz, Heather McKee: From Ink to Web and Beyond. U.S. Women's Activism Using Traditional and New Social Media, in: The Oxford Handbook of U.S. Women's Social Movement Activism (Oxford Handbooks), New York 2017, p. 468; Baker: Women's Movement, pp. 34f.
201 Ryan: Feminism, p. 94; Baker: Women's Movement, pp. 35, 43.
202 Baker: Women's Movement, pp. 40, 82, 104.
203 Working Women's Institute: How and Why to Document a Case, New York 1982, p. 3.

The message is clear: the employer was not to be trusted. This is underlined by the use of phrases such as "safest" and "protect yourself." WWI tells complainants not to be "naïve" when interacting with representatives of the company. Working women should be aware that the company, if given the chance, would "come back at a later date" to deny "your version" of events. The pamphlet also cautions the reader to "<u>never</u> leave your log at work," the implication being that it could (and would) be stolen by the harasser or the employer. The underlining of the word "never" implies that this was considered probable.

Beyond keeping a personal log, the pamphlet directs the reader to "show, that you objected to the behavior as soon as possible after it happened. If you don't complain, your employer may claim that you really did not mind it [or] were encouraging it [...]." For the purpose of keeping a record, WWI suggested these complaints be made in written form. They were to be made continually until the harassment stopped, lest the employer claim that "you accepted the harassment as one of your terms and conditions of employment." It is notable that the pamphlet did not include the possibility of the harasser contending that his actions were consensual, but instead focused on the employer arguing this case.

According to the same pamphlet, a sexual harassment complaint may provoke managerial retaliation.

> Frequently, after a worker [...] makes a complaint, someone begins to find fault with her work. [...] Protect yourself against such charges by your employer as incompetence, lateness, absenteeism, or an inability to get along with other employees. [...] you should not give the company any excuse to fire you.[204]

Again, the victim is not warned of the likely retaliation by her harasser but instead by that of her employer. Instead of advising victims to use their employer as a possible ally and resource, WWI suggested complainants find "leverage" against the company. One way of accomplishing this was by taping the perpetrator in the act. According to the pamphlet, even just "indicating you have a tape is strong medicine." Likewise, finding other women within the organization "with similar or related complaints," would increase the likelihood of "persuad[ing] the employer to remedy the situation."[205]

In conclusion, much of the advice dispersed by the WWI and the Alliance Against Sexual Coercion to those seeking immediate relief was centered around the employer rather than the harasser. While the advice was effective on the internal company level and could help resolve a situation before an EEOC complaint

---

204 Ibid.
205 WWI: How and Why to Document a Case, p. 3.

became necessary, it was *de facto* advice on how to build a solid case for court. The stronger the basis for a legal suit, the more likely it was that the employer would react to resolve or settle the issue prior to litigation. Hence, even if the complainant never intended to take their case to court, establishing the basis for a strong suit could convince the employer to react promptly.

Without legal remedies steeped in the Civil Rights Act, this advice would have been much less effective. The legal understanding of sexual harassment as sex discrimination, which was widely accepted by the time this pamphlet was written in 1982, was far from established in 1975. Thus, the inclusion of sexual harassment in the Civil Rights Act was a great success of the feminist legal strategy, which shall be discussed on the following pages.

2.2 Developing a Legal Strategy

Due to the precedent-setting nature of the U.S. court system, a decision made in one case could have lasting consequences for future verdicts.[206] By extending and reinterpreting the bounds of the Civil Rights Act, the judiciary had an immense impact on the handling of sexual harassment.[207] In the United States, government interference in business or American's private lives was often met with extreme skepticism by the general public. Consequently, feminist activists assumed that lawmakers who depended on ongoing support for their re-election would be hesitant to implement new legislation regarding sexual harassment.[208] Instead, feminists, following lawyer Catharine MacKinnon's lead, fought for the issue's inclusion into existing Civil Rights legislation via the judiciary. Judges, compared to legislators, came into direct contact with victims and had direct exposure to the feminist framing imminently before reaching a decision. Feminist lawyers presented their arguments, organizations wrote *amicus curiae* briefs, and individuals such as Karen Sauvigné, Lin Farley, and Freada Klein appeared as expert witnesses.[209] Thus, the judiciary became an important focus of feminist attempts to influence federal law and policy.

Before the term sexual harassment was coined, affected women had very few legal options. They could file criminal charges for rape or assault, if the harassment they experienced encompassed such behavior, but they had few options

---

206 Zippel: Politics, pp. 4, 43, 44, 71, 159.
207 Dobbin: Equal Opportunity, p. 8.
208 McCammon: Women's Legal Activism, pp. 528, 533.
209 Zippel: Politics, pp. 3 f., 26, 44, 67, 69.

in cases in which the coercing force was economic, not physical. There was one exception: the charge of solicitation. In her book *Sexual Shakedown*, Farley relays one such situation. She recounts the story of the owner of a fast food restaurant who, in the early 1970s, was known for announcing to young female applicants interested in a job as a waitress, that he expected them to "go to bed with him [once a week]."[210] The prosecutor later argued that the owner of the store was essentially seeking to pay for sexual services and that this behavior amounted to the charge of solicitation. A criminal court agreed and the defendant was convicted for solicitation.[211] This case, however, was an outlier rather than the norm.

In addition to criminal charges, depending on the state and on the case, affected women could make use of tort laws. Most common was the charge of breach of contract.[212] An employment contract which specified a length of service and/or required a notice period before termination could leave the employer open to litigation. However, in the 1970s, most working women did not find themselves on the career ladder where such contracts were most common. Instead, the great majority was in at-will employment relationships,[213] unable to sue for breach of contract if they were terminated. To a much lesser extent, however worth mentioning, husbands of affected women were sometimes known to file alienation-of-affection charges, in those states in which such laws still existed. This charge, however, could cut both ways, and a number of women who had been coerced into sexual relationships found themselves being sued by their harassers' wives.[214]

Despite the limitations, in the 1970s, criminal and tort laws were many women's best option for justice.[215] Throughout the decade and continuing into the 1980s, organizations, such as the Working Women's Institute, and feminist lawyers continued to make their clients aware that in some instances tort or criminal laws might apply. However, by the close of the 1970s, feminist organizations and lawyers advising victims on possible legal action mentioned these strategies only as a side note. Instead, their legal action aimed at winning legal precedents

---

210 Farley: Sexual Shakedown, p. 9.
211 Ibid., pp. 10 f.
212 Sauvigné, Karen: Digest of Leading Sexual Harassment Cases, September 1981, p. 5, BCA, Research on Women Records, Box 97, Folder Testimonies of Working Women's Institute.
213 Autor, David H. et al.: Does Employment Protection Reduce Productivity? Evidence From US States, in: The Economic Journal 117 (June 2007), p. 191.
214 Berebitsky: Sex and the Office, pp. 56 f.
215 Women Employed Institute: Conference Workshops Explore Political and Economic Issues, in: Women Employed News (1982), p. 5, BCA, Feminist Ephemera Collection, Box 89, Folder Women and Philanthropy.

in the realm of civil rights litigation and by doing so bringing about an expansion of the law.

Many organizations, focusing on legal avenues of action, including WWI, believed in the power of the law to change public opinion. They concluded that a change of the legal landscape served as an official acknowledgment of sexual harassment as a social problem. Politicians, reporters, and the public at large would, so was their hope, cease trivializing the issue. There exists, of course, substantial research on legal action as a catalyst of social change, in the context of second-wave feminism and beyond.[216] I contend, however, that there was a second aspect to this feminist legal fight.

A civil rights lawsuit named the employer as the defendant and thus legal action was a way of pressuring employers into responding to the culture of sexual harassment. I believe this motivation has appeared so self-evident that the existing historiography has somewhat neglected it. Similarly, the influence a civil rights case could have on an employer often only appeared in the form of an implicit undercurrent in much of the contemporary source material. Nevertheless, there were instances where this motivation is made explicit. Take for example this internal publication by the WWI's Legal Back-Up Center from 1981:

> Unfortunately, experience has shown that many employers will not begin developing procedures to prevent and eradicate sexual harassment in the workplace until they are under serious legal pressure. Thus, it is WWI's expectation that the Back-Up Center will provide the basis for change in women's working experience by increasing the pressure on employers through a rapid increase in the volume and sophistication of legal challenges.[217]

Feminist legal action succeeded in putting "serious legal pressure" on employers, including those who were not themselves the subject of judicial action. A high-profile suit or a substantial settlement, did not go unnoticed by industry leaders and small businesses alike.[218] Litigation, therefore, was a very effective strategy to motivate the involvement of the private sector in the discussion on sexual harassment.

---

216 E. g. Baker: Women's Movement; Zippel: Politics.

217 WWI: Litigation Manual, pp. 6 f.

218 Cf. Stinson: Sexual Harassment. A Risky Proposition, in: Bell Laboratories Newsletter, pp. 6–11, BCA, Research on Women Records, Box 96, Folder Bell Laboratories Corporate Study; Prudential Insurance Company of America: Sexual Harassment Program (October 1980), p. 5, BCA, Research on Women Records, Box 96, Folder Bell Laboratories Corporate Study; Dobbin: Equal Opportunity, p. 202.

Legally, feminists argued that sexual harassment was a form of sex discrimination and thus was a breach of Title VII of the Civil Rights Act of 1964. The section of the law in question reads:

> It shall be an unlawful employment practice for an employer to fail or refuse to hire or to discharge any individual, or otherwise to discriminate against any individual with respect to his compensation, terms, conditions, or privileges of employment, because of such individual's race, color, religion, sex, or national origin.[219]

Using the Civil Rights Act, second-wave feminists had already been successful in addressing sex discrimination issues in employment. Sex-segregated help-wanted ads had been ruled unlawful, marriage bars had been lifted, and women had broken into traditionally male jobs.

These successes were in many ways preceded and made possible by the decade long effort to achieve racial equality in the courts. It was no coincidence that four out of five of the early sexual harassment cases were filed by African American women.[220] These plaintiffs drew on the same vein as racial discrimination suits to argue against sexual harassment. This was both an ideological as well as a strategic move. Portraying sexual harassment as a sex discrimination issue was in line with the feminist theoretical framework. At the same time, leaning on American ideals of fairness and the importance of merit bore the potential of garnering support even from conservative judges.

The feminist focus on sexual harassment as a civil rights issue, greatly influenced the phenomenon's conceptualization. Immediately after the term's inception, the phenomenon had been understood primarily as an issue of sexual violence. However, with the first successful court rulings and the publication of MacKinnon's legal arguments, it was increasingly accepted as a worker's rights issue. Title VII of the Civil Rights Act was directed at the employer, not the harasser, unless, of course, they were one and the same. By turning to the Civil Rights Act for relief, feminists turned their focus to employers as their adversaries.

In order to convince a judge that sexual harassment should be considered a civil rights violation, feminist lawyers argued three points: first, they asserted that their clients were harassed, because they were women, and thus part of a protected class; second, they defined what actions constituted sexual harassment and categorized different forms of harassment; third, they insisted that employers needed to be held responsible for their supervisors' and employees' actions.

---

219 Civil Rights Act of 1964. 42 U.S.C. § 2000e-2. 2018, article a.
220 Baker: Race, p. 8; Lareau: Historical Development, pp. 207f.

2.2.1 Discrimination Based on Sex

In the mid-1970s, unwelcome sexual advances or demands were legally viewed as private and individual incidences rather than discriminatory acts. Judges in early cases may have accepted testimony of the harassing behavior as true, but they characterized it as a "personal proclivity" and suggested that it was not a matter for federal courts.[221] To counter this assumption, the plaintiff had to establish, not only that they had experienced unwelcome behavior, but also that they had been targeted *because* of their gender.[222] In other words, for a claim to be covered by the Civil Rights Act, the plaintiff had to show that they belonged to a protected class.

For women of color this raised a separate issue. The Civil Rights Act did not allow for an intersectional element in discriminatory action and required a plaintiff to state outright whether they were suing for sex or race discrimination. Often the two forms of discrimination were interlinked and impossible to separate. The case *Barnes v. Costle* is a prime example for this dilemma. After losing her job, Paulette Barnes, a Black woman, was encouraged by her EEOC case worker not to file for sex but rather for race discrimination. In her complaint she alleged that her boss had begun a campaign to "belittle her," "strip her of her job duties," and eventually abolished her position "in retaliation for [her] refusal to grant him sexual favors."[223] Two months after Barnes was let go, her position was reestablished and a White woman was hired in her place. The EEOC agent advising Barnes had little confidence in the success of a sexual harassment case and felt that a complaint for racial discrimination offered better chances for a favorable outcome. Nevertheless, Barnes filed for sex discrimination in 1975, and in 1977 won her appeal, making her case, *Barnes v. Costle,* the first appeals court win for a victim of sexual harassment.

Plaintiffs alleging sexual harassment were overwhelmingly, if not exclusively, female. In their argument, they dedicated themselves to the feminist frame, which assumed gender to be a condition for sexual harassment. As shown above, the feminist theoretical framework unequivocally stated that sexual harassment was not only gendered but was unidirectional: emanating from men and targeting women. The decision in *Williams v. Saxbe* (1976) marked the first time a plaintiff convinced a judge,[224] that if the gender line had not been crossed, the behavior

---

221 *Corne v. Bausch and Lomb, Inc.,* 390 F. Supp. 161 (1975), United States District Court, District of Arizona.
222 MacKinnon: Sexual Harassment of Working Women, pp. 192–200; cf. Zippel: Politics, pp. 10, 42; Dobbin: Equal Opportunity, pp. 192, 217.
223 *Barnes v. Costle,* p. 985.
224 *William v. Saxbe.*

they had been subjected to would not have been sexualized. Judge Richey, a D.C. district court judge, held that the gender of the victim had been deciding for the supervisor's display of sexualized behavior. Therefore, the sexual harassment experienced by the plaintiff constituted sex discrimination in the workplace.

The *Williams* case was one of five district court cases in 1976 in which the plaintiff argued for the recognition of sexual harassment as sex discrimination. Of these five cases Judge Richey was the only judge to rule in favor of the plaintiff. *Williams v. Saxbe* being the outlier and only a district court case was not precedent setting. However, after the appeals court confirmed the decision and overturned the other four cases between 1976 and 1978, the law was settled; Sexual harassment was legally recognized as a form of sex discrimination. Although final confirmation did not come until the Supreme Court ruled on *Vinson v. Meritor Savings* in 1986,[225] the courts in the late 1970s and early 1980s no longer questioned the correlation between sexual harassment and the plaintiff's gender. Now courts were asking different questions: What kind of conduct constituted harassment? And should the employer be held liable?

2.2.2 Quid Pro Quo and Hostile Work Environment Sexual Harassment

As discussed in the previous chapter, WWI's definition for sexual harassment was exceedingly broad. While this was helpful in the feminist attempt to recognize patterns and aided many women in recognizing discriminatory structures in their workplace, in the legal arena it was ineffective. No judge, whether this be in the 1970s or 2010s, would be convinced that a single sexist comment by a boss or co-worker constituted sex discrimination under the Civil Rights Act. Nor did the feminist authors behind these definitions expect such 'mild' cases to be tried. Catharine MacKinnon saw the need for a more concrete definition and began writing a legal argument which could be used in court.

MacKinnon conceded that, in order for conduct to be classified as sexual harassment in the legal arena, there needed to be an element of institutionally backed coercion. Most feminist single-issue groups focusing on sexual harassment agreed with this assessment in their definitions. Take for example a statement by the group Women Organized Against Sexual Harassment:

> The term [sexual harassment] has also been used to refer to any imposition of unwanted sexual advances on women–for example, by men on the street. But situations where the man has institutional power over the woman have become the focus of concern for

---

225 *Vinson v. Meritor.*

women students and workers because a refusal on their part can be met with reprisals affecting their careers.[226]

According to a feminist understanding it was precisely these "reprisals," that transformed unwanted sexual conduct into sexual harassment. These reprisals were of an institutional nature and therefore lay directly or indirectly in the control of the employer. MacKinnon in her analysis clarified that reprisals could be both tangible and less concrete. Following this argument, she established two broad categories of sexual harassment: *quid pro quo* and hostile work environment. These categories became essential for the legal conceptualization of the phenomenon and shall be given further deliberation in the following paragraphs.

As courts began recognizing sexual harassment as sex discrimination, they did so on the basis of *quid pro quo* cases. In these cases, job benefits as well as unfavorable employment action were subject to the employee's submission or rejection of sexual requests. In a *quid pro quo* case, the target's submission or rejection may have made the difference between a promotion awarded or denied, a demotion averted or passed, a job offered or lost. Consider the example involving the fast-food restaurant owner charged for solicitation, in 1975. During a job interview, he asked the twenty-year-old informant who was posing as an applicant:

> What would you say if I'll give you the job if you go to bed with me? [...] I wouldn't say every day or anything like that. I say once a week.[227]

This is a textbook case of *quid pro quo* sexual harassment; the condition of employment is linked to the applicant agreeing to having regular intercourse with the owner.

Quid pro quo sexual harassment recognizes that in institutional settings such as the workplace or educational facilities, "[those] in positions of authority [may] try to use their power in making coercive sexual advances [...]."[228] Thus, imposing, as MacKinnon described it, "sexual requirements in the context of a relationship of unequal power."[229] In *quid pro quo* cases, these requests most often came from the employer or from persons who had been given direct authority over the employee by the employer. Hence, *quid pro quo sexual* harassment by an employer,

---

226 Women Organized Against Sexual Harassment: Sexual Harassment, What It Is, What to Do About It, 1980, p. 2, BCA, Feminist Ephemera Collection, Box 90, Folder Women Office Workers.
227 Farley: Sexual Shakedown, p. 9.
228 Women Organized Against Sexual Harassment: What it is, p. 2.
229 Cohen: Regulating Intimacy, p. 131.

supervisor, or manager was most easily recognizable as a manifestation of abusive power dynamics.

In contrast, sexual harassment by co-workers was most common in the second category: hostile work environment sexual harassment. Distinguishing this category from *quid pro quo* harassment is the absence of "tangible consequences," meaning a lack of officially sanctioned changes in working conditions, such as a demotion or changes in pay. It has, however, the same potential for harming a woman's health and career. Political scientist Kathrin Zippel describes this form of sexual harassment as "psycho terror at work."[230] She explains that it relied, not on distinct threats endangering the victim's employment, but instead created an intolerable atmosphere. "Sexual bullying," or hostile environment sexual harassment, interfered with the target's health, safety, and job performance. For many women it made work intolerable and induced them to resign their positions.

In the context of hostile work environment, it is also prudent to introduce the concept of gender harassment. When coining the term 'sexual harassment,' Sauvigné and her peers alluded to the legally and publicly accepted concept of 'racial harassment.' 'Sexual' harassment then became the pendant, when the harassment was directed toward someone not because of their skin color but because of their gender. The term 'sexual' in this understanding was simply the adjective for the term 'sex,' referring to a person's biological sex rather than a sexual act. The early intention of the phrasing was to include both sexualized and non-sexualized (or gender) harassment.

However, because many judges as well as the public at large viewed sexuality as an individual matter,[231] the feminist movement against sexual harassment in the late 1970s focused much of their energy and resources on proving that unwanted sexual conduct was to be included in an understanding of sexual harassment. Consequently, WWI, in particular, highlighted stories in which working women encountered unwelcome sexualized conduct.[232] The organization's goal was to emphasize that, although the behavior may be sexualized, it had little to do with sexual urges and everything to do with unequal power dynamics. This reasoning cou-

---

230 Zippel: Politics, p. 9.
231 *Corne v. Bausch and Lomb, Inc.*; For a summary of the early sexual harassment cases, see: Lareau: Historical Development, pp. 208 f.; Dobbin: Equal Opportunity, pp. 194 f.
232 E.g.: Working Women's Institute: Sample Agenda. Sexual Harassment Committee Training, 1987, BCA, Research on Women Records, Box 95, Folder Cornell University's Reports, Articles, Information; Vermeulen, Joan: WWI. Preparing a Title VII Sexual Harassment Case, no date, CA, Research on Women Records, Box 95, Folder How to Prepare a Sexual Harassment Case; Testimony before the Subcommittee on Employment Opportunities 1986; cf. Berebitsky: Sex and the Office, p. 221.

pled with the double meaning of the term sex, and the organization's initial focus on white and pink color jobs led to an underestimation of the relevance of gender harassment.[233]

Gender harassment and sexualized harassment were often combined when creating a hostile work environment. This was a problem often faced by women in traditionally male jobs, although the phenomenon was not exclusive to these jobs. A female aircraft welder in New Jersey recounted that a male coworker had "cut the chain holding up a big motor mount I was welding. It fell down on me and burned my arm to the bone."[234] Female miners in Utah found semen in their lockers and feces smeared on the wall of their changing room spelling out the word "sluts."[235] A police woman in San Francisco was driven to a secluded area and had a gun pointed at her by a male colleague who explained "I just want to see how fast you women cops can run."[236] These are all instances of hostile work environment sexual harassment and present examples for both sexualized and non-sexualized harassment. As feminist theorist Lin Farley explained in her book, *Sexual Shakedown* such behavior was meant to "keep women out" of traditionally male jobs.[237]

Despite the severe forms hostile work environment harassment could take, judges initially rejected the argument that such harassment should be considered sex discrimination. The element of institutionalized coercion was less obvious compared to *quid pro quo* sexual harassment where tangible changes in employment were more readily observed and documented. It was not until 1981, in *Bundy v. Jackson*, that an appeals court for the first time recognized hostile work environment sexual harassment as a form of sex discrimination.

Sandra Bundy, who had been working at the Columbia Department of Corrections as a Vocational Rehabilitation Specialist, filed a sexual harassment complaint in 1976. Bundy alleged that she had been repeatedly propositioned by several supervisors and fellow employees. In her testimony, she described frequently being asked about her "sexual proclivities" by both colleagues and supervisors. On multiple occasions, she was asked by one supervisor, Arthur Burton, to spend the workday afternoon "with him in his apartment," and by another, James Gainey, to "join him at a motel and on a trip to the Bahamas." When Bundy complained to

---

233 Berebitsky: Sex and the Office, p. 222; Baker: Women's Movement, pp. 84 f.
234 Cited in: Baker: Woman's Movement, p. 68.
235 *Jenson v. Eveleth Taconite Co.*, 130 F.3d 1287 (8th Cir. 1997), p. 663.
236 Cited in: Baker: Woman's Movement, p. 67.
237 Farley: Sexual Shakedown, p. 90.

Lawrence Swain, Burton and Gainey's supervisor, Swain allegedly replied that "any man in his right mind would want to rape you."[238]

The District Court accepted Bundy's account of the facts as true and acknowledged that "sexual intimidation was a normal condition of employment in Bundy's agency."[239] However, despite the Court's recognition of these facts, Bundy lost her case. The judge argued that the sexual misconduct did not prompt tangible changes in Bundy's working conditions. The behavior, according to the Court, was neither coercive nor did Bundy suffer any damages. Therefore, Bundy's claims of sexual harassment were, in the District Court's opinion, rendered moot.

The Appeals Court did not agree and *Bundy v. Jackson* (1981) became a landmark decision regarding hostile work environment sexual harassment. Bundy had filed for appeal, asking the Court to hold that "an employer violates Title VII merely by subjecting female employees to sexual harassment even if the employee's resistance to the harassment does not cause the employer to deprive her of any tangible job benefits."[240] The court agreed and a new precedent was set. Hostile work environment sexual harassment constituted a violation of the Civil Rights Act.

As was the case in *Bundy v. Jackson*, the perpetrators of this type of harassment could be both the victims' peers and/or superiors. The key difference to the *quid pro quo* model was that the harassment did not threaten and was not followed by tangible changes in the victim's employment status. A target of hostile work environment sexual harassment was not fired or demoted, because they would not engage in sexual activity. Instead, victims often lost their professional motivation and left their position because of the stress, fear, health issues, safety concerns, and humiliation resulting from the harassment.[241]

2.2.3 Employer Liability

After establishing that the complainant had indeed been targeted because of her gender and demonstrating that the behavior she had been subjected to qualified as sexual harassment, feminist counsel was left with one more hurdle: convincing the court that the employer was to be held liable for their employees' harassing behavior. Civil rights litigation was not directed at the individual who initiated the discrimination, but at the employer, who under Title VII was responsible for providing a work environment free of discrimination.

---

238 *Bundy v. Jackson*, p. 939.
239 Ibid.
240 Ibid.
241 Arriola: Construction Industry, p. 24.

Judges, lawyers, and legal scholars were heavily divided on the extent of an employer's responsibility. Questions regarding the limits of employer liability dominated the legal discourse on sexual harassment for decades. Should employers be held liable for the unsanctioned actions of their employees? What if the employer did not know about the harassment? What if they had specifically forbidden harassing behavior? Legal arguments varied on either upholding a strict liability standard or insisting on a notice requirement standard. The former left no leeway for employers. It disregarded any preventative or corrective action taken by the employer and assumed employers responsible for any harassment within their organizations, no matter whether or not they knew of the discrimination. The latter afforded the employer some room for a legal defense by insisting that liability was not a forgone conclusion if the employer had no (constructive) knowledge of the harassment.

In feminist legal arguments, the employer was to be held strictly liable for the action of their employees, whether or not the employer knew of the harassment. Strict employer liability in other instances of sex or race discrimination was already a settled precedent by 1975.[242] The courts however did not automatically transfer this to sexual harassment cases.[243] One early example, *Miller v. Bank of America*, illustrates this point. Margaret Miller, a bank teller at Bank of America, filed suit against her employer in 1976, claiming that "her operations supervisor, a white male, promised her a better job if she would [sic!] be sexually 'cooperative,' and caused her dismissal when she refused." The court posed the question at hand as follows, "[t]he issue before the Court is whether Title VII was intended to hold an employer liable for what is essentially the isolated and unauthorized sex misconduct of one employee to another."[244] Contrary to other early decisions, the judge in *Miller* did not focus on whether the sexual misconduct was correlated to the gender of the target. It did not matter to the judge if the harasser had discriminatory motives. Instead, the focus was placed on whether the employer should be held accountable. The interpretation of the conduct as "isolated" and "unauthorized" led the District Court to absolve Bank of America from liability. This judgement was reversed in its appeal.

Nevertheless, several years after Miller first pled her case, when judges no longer considered sexual harassment a private matter, the extent of employer liability continued to be a highly contentious issue. Decisions were made on a case-by-case basis. Even in 1986, when the issue of sexual harassment for the first time

---

242 Vermeulen: Preparing a Title VII Sexual Harassment Case, p. 2.
243 Ibid.
244 *Miller v. Bank of America* (1976).

reached the U.S. Supreme Court, the justices opted for a narrow ruling and left open the question of employer liability. Legally, this question would not be settled until 1997. As shall be shown, this ambiguity kept employers and feminists in limbo, affording a liminal space in which questions of responsibility were negotiated.

In accepting sexual harassment as sex discrimination, the appeals judges in the first five cases, including *Miller v. Bank of America,* simultaneously declared employers liable for the conduct exhibited within their organizations.[245] These early cases, however, were all *quid pro quo* sexual harassment cases. Judges were much more inclined to hold employers responsible for an employee's termination or demotion than for a hostile atmosphere. In cases in which a supervisor was trading employment perks for sexual favors, his authority stemmed directly from the employer. As a part of management, the harasser was acting as an agent of the company and as such, he was the employer's responsibility.[246] Hostile work environment cases were a different story but here too the agency principle was significant: The first cases of hostile work environment harassment in which the courts held employers responsible were instances in which the plaintiff showed that supervisors and managers either sanctioned and/or actively took part in the harassing behavior.[247]

Regarding employer liability, both in *quid pro quo* as well as in hostile work environment cases, the central legal question splitting the courts was that of notice. Should an employer be held liable even if he had not been notified of the problem? On one side of the debate stood the decision on *Miller v. Bank of America,* in which the 9th Circuit Appeals Court held that "the employer will be absolutely liable for sexual harassment by its agents and supervisory employees, regardless of whether the employer knew of the harassment."[248] This verdict, as well as decisions by some lower courts, ran parallel to the feminist argument which contended that the employer should be held liable, not only if he knew about the harassment but also in cases where he "should have known."[249] Joan Vermeulen of the WWI legal backup center praised the *Miller* decision stating that "[s]uch an approach constitutes a recognition that little if any progress will be made toward eradicating employment discrimination if the employer is able

---

245 *Corne v. Bausch and Lomb* (1975); *Miller v. Bank of America* (1976); *Tomkins v. Public Service Elec. and Gas Co.* **(1976)**; *Williams v. Saxbe,* 413 F. Supp. 654 (1976), United States District Court, District of Columbia; Barnes v. Costle, (1977).

246 E.g.: *Barnes v. Costle,* p. 995.

247 E.g.: *Williams v. Saxbe,* 413 F. Supp. 654 (1976); *Garber v. Saxon* Business Prods., Inc., 552 F.2d 1032 (4th Cir. 1977).

248 *Miller v. Bank of America* (1976), cf. Vermeulen: Preparing a Title VII Case, p. 4.

249 Vermeulen: Preparing a Title VII Case, p. 4.

to hide behind the shield of individual employee action." According to Vermeulen, employers provided the workspace and, thus, were responsible for the treatment of their employees in it. When employers were not aware of what happened in this space, they had neglected their responsibility to ensure an environment free of discrimination for all their employees.[250] This negligence, according to this line of argument, was just as damning as active involvement or sanctioning of harassing behavior.

However, judges in agreement with this 9th circuit decision were in the minority. Many still dismissed cases in which there was no proof that the employer knew of the misconduct and thus established a "notice requirement."[251] In these cases, the courts ruled that the employer must have received "actual or constructive notice" about the harassment to be considered liable.[252] As Vermeulen points out, this requirement posed almost as many questions as it answered:

> Those courts which have found a prerequisite to liability have yet to provide any indication as to what would be considered constructive notice. Thus it is unclear whether it must be knowledge of the specific allegations or whether knowledge of such things as the supervisor's character or the economic power relationships between the sexes at the particular workplace would be sufficient to constitute constructive knowledge.[253]

Like the larger query on liability, questions on what exactly "constructive knowledge" entailed were answered only on a case-by-case basis. This left a cloud of uncertainty among employers, lawyers, and management consultants.

In addition to the question of notice, courts were split on the importance of a written company policy forbidding sexual harassment. Was a supervisor who abused his position of authority to be seen as representing the company, if he acted against an explicitly formulated company policy? Could an employer be held liable for the group of employees who created a hostile work environment for their coworkers even if they were clearly disobeying company rules? This, too, was acquiesced by the 9th Circuit in *Miller v. Bank of America*. The employer, in this case Bank of America, was to be held "absolutely liable for sexual harassment by its agents and supervisory employees, [...] regardless of whether the harasser violated company policy."[254]

---

250 Ibid.
251 Ibid., p. 5.
252 *Tomkins v. Public Service Elec. and Gas Co.*, 422 F. Supp. 553 (1976), United States District Court, District of New Jersey.
253 Vermeulen: Preparing a Title VII Case, p. 5.
254 Ibid., p. 4.

Again, judges in later cases disagreed. Many concluded that the existence of an explicit written policy forbidding sexual harassment within the organization absolved the employer from liability. In *Continental Can v. State of Minnesota*, for instance, the judges ruled that because the company had a written policy forbidding sexual harassment on record, they could "not possibly be held responsible" for the harassment perpetrated by one of their employees.[255] According to this decision, the employee in question broke with company policy, indicating that his actions were not condoned by Continental Can.

There were, however, also some cases in which judges opted for the middle ground. They accepted a policy as a shield against liability only when said policy had been widely distributed among employees and reflected the employer's intent and action. In *EEOC v. Sage Realty Corporation*, the plaintiff convinced the district court that the management and the staff at Sage Realty Corporation ignored an existing written policy and instead operated under an unofficial policy which accepted and was conducive to sexual misconduct. In this case, Judge Ward ruled that the mere existence of a written policy was not enough to protect the employer from legal consequences.[256]

Regardless of whether an individual adjudication ultimately accepted a policy as an adequate defense or not, judges, lawyers, and feminists alike encouraged employers to adopt written policies. In *Kyriazi v. Western Electric*, the final court decision included a mandate for the defendant to adopt a written policy and to provide employees with information on how to report incidences of harassment.[257] These court decisions were a strong motivation for employers to pay attention to the issue and to publish more detailed policies.[258]

Oftentimes these policies were simply a revision of the company's already existing Equal Employment Opportunity (EEO) policies or Affirmative Action (AA) Plans to explicitly include sexual harassment as a form of sex discrimination. Other organizations created new policies, in addition to their EEO and AA statements, solely dedicated to forbidding sexual harassment. In some cases, these policies also included an internal grievance procedure which provided complainants with a specific set of steps when filing their allegations. For employers, grievance procedures were a means to react to and solve issues before they were put before a judge. If it did come to a suit, the existence of a procedure could show the court

---

255 Sauvigné: Digest 1981, p. 4.
256 Ibid.; *EEOC v. Sage Realty. Corp.*, 507 F. Supp. 599 (S.D.N.Y. 1981).
257 Sauvigné: Digest 1981, p. 4.
258 Cf. Stinson: Sexual Harassment. A Risky Proposition, in: Bell Laboratories Newsletter, pp. 6 – 11; Prudential Insurance Company of America: Sexual Harassment Program (October 1980), p. 5; Dobbin: Equal Opportunity, p. 202.

that the policy was not only theoretical but was followed up by practical steps. Additionally, if a company had a procedure in place but it had not been utilized by the plaintiff, the employer in question was in an advantageous position when claiming that he was not given notice of the situation.

Again, the courts were divided on whether a plaintiff's neglecting to make use of an internal grievance procedure should affect their case in court. However, with little to lose and much to gain, it is not surprising that grievance procedures as well as written policies became increasingly popular in both the public and the private sector.[259] Feminists considered internal grievance procedures as highly desirable, postulating that when well-conceived, such procedures significantly heightened the trust female employees put in the sincerity of the policy and thus increased the likelihood that incidents would be reported.[260] In fact, convincing employers to adopt an anti-sexual harassment policy and a correlating procedure, was one major goal of the feminist legal effort.[261]

2.3 The EEOC's Sexual Harassment Guidelines, 1980

As shown above, feminist groups made an effort to influence court decisions and fought against sexual harassment in the judiciary. However, one of the arguably most cogent developments occurred within the executive branch. In 1980, the Equal Employment Opportunity Commission (EEOC) revised its sex discrimination guidelines and by doing so became the first government agency to codify sexual harassment as sex discrimination. This development was fundamentally influenced by feminist theory, rhetoric, and direct action. Analogous to feminist action in the courts, feminists' fight for the acknowledgment of sexual harassment as a systemic problem by the executive branch had the goal of expanding the law, changing public opinion, and directly influencing employers.

The federal government was involved in the debate on sexual harassment both in its capacity as representative of the people with the responsibility of creating and enforcing legislation, and as one of the largest employers in the country. In this latter role, the federal government itself faced repeated allegations of sex-

---

259 Dobbin: Equal Opportunity, p. 202.
260 Working Women's Institute: How Working Women's Institute Can Help Your Company, [not dated; based on the attached list of training and consulting staff this must be from 1981/1982], BCA, Research on Women Records, Box 97, Folder Working Women's Institute Sexual Harassment Information; WWI: How and Why to Document a Case.
261 Sauvigné: Letter to Vice President Bush.

ual harassment by and towards federal employees.[262] In fact, *Williams v. Saxbe* (1976), the first case on sexual harassment to have a result favorable to the plaintiff, was brought against the Justice Department of the United States federal government. Throughout the decades, agencies and individuals directly associated with the federal government continued to face sexual harassment charges, indicating that the problem has not been eradicated on the federal level.[263] At the time of this writing several high-level government officials, not to mention the President himself, have been either accused or convicted of sexual harassment and/or assault.[264]

Nevertheless, by 1979, influenced by several court rulings and feminist activism, the Carter-administration was pro-actively taking on the issue. Necessary action was first discussed in a congressional hearing in 1979 headed by Congressman James Hanley, Chairman of the Subcommittee on Investigations of the House Post Office and Civil Service Committee.[265] While the congressional hearing did not result in new legislation explicitly forbidding sexual harassment, it did bring on several changes in federal policy.

First, the Office of Personnel Management (OPM) was instructed to issue guidelines to all federal agencies condemning sexual harassment. Further, the OPM was to provide an effective grievance procedure for federal employees experiencing sexual harassment.[266] Lastly, the EEOC conceived of guidelines, acknowledging sexual harassment as sex discrimination. Contrary to the OPM policy and procedure, the EEOC guidelines were meant to advise both the public and private sector on the rules regarding sex discrimination. The final version of the guidelines, which have not been meaningfully changed since, was published in November 1980.[267]

The EEOC guidelines were just that, guidelines. Neither judges, legislators, nor employers were bound by them. Nevertheless, the EEOC's definition of sexual harassment were deeply influential. Its publication signaled the acknowledgment of sexual harassment as a problem by the federal government. It is not to be underestimated how important it was for judges, reporters, and employers to have a definition to rely on which was provided by a seemingly neutral source, rather than a

---

262 Zippel: Politics, pp. 62, 217.

263 Ibid., p. 217.

264 Sherman, Carter: Sexual Assault Allegations Seem to be a Badge of Honor in Trump's America. Was #Metoo an Epic Failure? In: The Guardian (March 30th, 2025).

265 Baker: Women's Movement, p. 107.

266 Ibid., p. 120.

267 Zippel: Politics, pp. 58 f.

feminist interest group with clear ideological goals. Hence, this definition was used as a reference point by many judges, finally leading the Supreme Court to confirm it in 1986. Additionally, the guidelines put employers on notice and served as a template for many internal company policies throughout the 1980s.

The Equal Employment Opportunity Commission was established in the wake of the Civil Rights Act and was charged with its enforcement in 1965. In its beginning stages, the agency was reluctant to include the elimination of sex discrimination into its concrete aims.[268] This famously led to the establishment of the National Organization for Women (NOW) in 1966.[269] A decade after opening its doors, in 1975, the EEOC's stance on the newly surfaced problem of sexual harassment was ambiguous. On the one hand, the EEOC, in an *amicus curiae* in 1975, positioned itself in favor of the feminist argument on sexual harassment. In the brief the agency stated that "the choice between frequent unsolicited sexual advances and being unemployed has a significant and clearly unwarranted effect on employment opportunities."[270] On the other hand, in 1976 *The Washington Post* relayed accounts from "female personnel" inside the agency complaining "of coercion by their bosses to engage in sexual games."[271] Additionally, the newspaper described the agency as "deeply troubled" and "demonstrably ineffective."[272]

After taking on its leadership in 1977, Eleanor Norton substantially transformed the agency. Norton, a feminist and former civil rights activist, had learned about the topic of sexual harassment in her capacity as the Chair of the New York City's Commission on Human Rights and had briefly served on the board of the Working Women's Institute.[273] With Norton at its head, the EEOC committed to fighting sexual harassment and succeeded in curbing the "scandalous backlog" by almost half within two years.[274] Although the EEOC had no judicial authority, it was authorized to conduct investigations, could initiate voluntary settlements between the parties involved, and was empowered to bring lawsuits on behalf of individuals targeted by discriminatory behavior. During Norton's leadership the agency often proved to be a valuable ally for targets of sexual harassment.[275]

---

268 Ibid., pp. 34, 60, 160; Lareau: Historical Development, p. 213; Boris: Workplace Discrimination, pp. 198, 200.
269 Baxandall: Second-Wave Feminism, p. 415; Boris: Workplace Discrimination, p. 195.
270 *Corne v. Bausch and Lomb, Inc*; cf. Baker: Women's Movement, p. 19; Dobbin: Equal Opportunity, p. 193.
271 Anonymous: The Mess at EEOC, in: The Washington Post (April 28th, 1976), p. A12.
272 Ibid., p. A12; Baker: Women's Movement, p. 116.
273 Zippel: Politics, p. 57; Baker: Women's Movement, p. 116.
274 Anonymous: The Mess at EEOC, A12; Baker: Women's Movement, p. 116.
275 Lublin, Joann S.: Guideline-Happy at the EEOC? in: The Wall Street Journal (August 28th, 1980), p. 18; Zippel: Politics, pp. 52, 59; Dobbin: Equal Opportunity, pp. 15, 80; Herzog, Ulrich: Sexuelle

Norton, as the head of the EEOC, was acting as an agent of the federal government. However, the feminist framing on issues of sex discrimination, including but not limited to sexual harassment, are distinctly recognizable in the agency's rhetoric during Norton's governance. Therefore, I argue, that action on sexual harassment taken by the EEOC during Norton's tenure, for the purposes of this book, may be considered "feminist." This is particularly true for the reform of the agency's sex discrimination guidelines which generated a high level of support from feminist organizations.

Norton believed in the exemplary function of the government and called on all federal agencies to "set the tone for other employers in trying to rid the workplace of this manifestation of the culture's bias against women [referring to sexual harassment]."[276] Given Norton's awareness of the importance of corporate involvement in eliminating sexual harassment, it is a feasible presumption that the guidelines were written with the intent of influencing employers directly. This is substantiated by the EEOC's pronounced effort of distributing the sexual harassment guidelines. The agency proactively reached out to employers in order to notify them of their responsibility of introducing preventive measures and prohibiting harassing conduct in their organizations.[277] Due to the guidelines, great importance and regular recurrence in internal company policies,[278] the fol-

Belästigung am Arbeitsplatz (Abhandlungen zum Arbeits- und Wirtschaftsrecht 76), Heidelberg 1997, pp. 85–87.

276 Subcommittee on Investigations: Hearings on Sexual 1979, p. 91; cf. Baker: Women's Movement, 115; Zippel: Politics, p. 58.

277 Anonymous: The Mess at EEOC, p. A12; Baker: Women's Movement, p. 16.

278 See for instance: Ross Systems, Inc.: Policy Regarding Sexual Harassment, October 28th, 1982, CHM, Information Technology Corporate Histories Collection, Ross Systems Box 1, Folder Ross Systems Personnel Policies Memos 1980–1988; Resorts International Hotel Casino: Sexual Harassment Inter Office Correspondence, August 21st, 1981, BCA, Research on Women Records, Box 96, Folder Bell Laboratories Corporate Study; Hoffman – La Roche Inc.: Equal Opportunity Policy, March 1st, 1982, BCA, Research on Women Records, Box 96, Folder Bell Laboratories Corporate Study; Becton Dickinson and Company: Equal Employment Handbook, in or before 1982, BCA, Research on women Records, Box 96, Folder Bell Laboratories Corporate Study; Cesar's Boardwalk Regency Hotel Casino: Human Resources Notice. Sexual harassment Policy and Procedure, September 15th, 1981, BCA, Research on women Records, Box 96, Folder Bell Laboratories Corporate Study; Pyonzeck, Otto (President of Universal Manufacturing Corporation): Statement of Policy, pre-1983, BCA, Research on Women Records, Box 96, Folder Bell Laboratories Corporate Study; Harrah's Marina: Fact Sheet on Sexual Harassment, pre-1983, BCA, Research on women Records, Box 96, Folder Bell Laboratories Corporate Study; The Prudential Insurance Company of America: Memorandum for all employees of the prudential its subsidiary companies, and special agents in the U.S. Subject: Sexual Harassment, October 8th, 1980, BCA, Research on Women Records, Box 96, Folder Bell Laboratories Corporate Study.

lowing paragraphs are dedicated to a deeper analysis of the EEOC's sexual harassment guidelines.

The presence of the feminist frame is particularly striking in section *a* of the EEOC guidelines. Here, a definition based on the subcategorizations suggested by Catharine MacKinnon is codified:

> a) Unwelcome sexual advances, requests for sexual favors, and other verbal or physical conduct of a sexual nature constitute sexual harassment when (1) submission to such conduct is made either explicitly or implicitly a term or condition of an individual's employment, (2) submission to or rejection of such conduct by an individual is used as the basis for employment decisions affecting such individual, or (3) such conduct has the purpose or effect of substantially interfering with an individual's work performance or creating an intimidating, hostile, or offensive working environment. [...][279]

MacKinnon's categorization of *quid pro quo* harassment is evident in conditions (1) and (2). The EEOC's explanation of hostile work environment sexual harassment in (3) stems directly from MacKinnon's 1979 publication.[280]

As has been discussed on previous pages, the feminist frame made a very clear distinction between coerced and consensual sexual acts, condemning only the former. This sentiment is made evident in section *a* by the use of the term "unwelcome."[281] Unfortunately, in practice, the difference between coerced and consensual may be strikingly obvious in some situations and hardly recognizable in others. In addition to the circumstances of the situation, one's viewpoint may drastically influence this assessment. Regarding the importance of perspective, Marry Rowe, an ombudsperson at Cornell University, described the "eerie experience [...] of having two people who disagree profoundly, stipulate to exactly the same facts."[282] As is alluded to in this quote, the victim, the harasser, and bystanders may have different interpretations of whether the conduct in question was coerced.

By using the term "unwelcome," the EEOC allows an assessment of the situation from the victim's perspective. The guidelines give the victim space to challenge behavior which they considered inappropriate. This is in alignment with the feminist conceptualization of sexual harassment in which the consequences for those targeted are foregrounded. This focus on the victim's perception of the situation is not to be taken for granted. To compare, German law requires sex-

---

279 EEOC: Guidelines.
280 MacKinnon: Sexual Harassment of Working Women, pp. 32–47.
281 EEOC: Guidelines; cf. Herzog: Sexuelle Belästigung, pp. 47 f.
282 Rowe, Mary P.: Dealing with Harassment Concerns. A Talk, p. 3, BCA, Research on Women Records, Box 95.

ualized behavior to be "recognizably rejected" before it is legally classified as sexual harassment.[283] In the German case, the law emphasizes the perspective of a bystander in evaluating sexual harassment situations. In contrast, the EEOC guidelines did not consider the harasser's intentions or an outsider's perspective. Instead, the target's point of view was pivotal.

Uncompromisingly taking the perspective of the alleged victim, however, came with its own set of problems. One social conservative newsletter proclaimed: "the feminists are trying to force the U.S. Senate and the country to accept the feminist definition of 'sexual harassment,' i.e., any words, as well as actions, that any women claims it is [...]."[284] The implication here was that the definition of sexual harassment was so broad and so focused on the target's perspective, there was no way for the accused to counter a woman's allegations. Thus, claims of sexual harassment could be, and according to social conservatives were, routinely weaponized.

Critics argued that in addition to the possibility of malicious accusations, there was always the possibility of the target misunderstanding or overreacting to a benign interaction. The subjectivity of perception, combined with increased sexual freedom after the 1960s, led many, both within social conservative circles and beyond, to assume that some men may be confused as to which women they were permitted to give sexual attention. An early management consultant handbook posed the question, "[i]s this a woman who is going to ask you to bed or is this a woman who does not do those kinds of things?"[285] Sexual harassment in this view could happen accidently and be the result of a genuine misunderstanding.

Despite these difficulties, however, the use of the term "unwelcome" in the EEOC guidelines and the acceptance of hostile work environment sexual harassment in addition to *quid pro quo* cases reflect the great influence the feminist theoretical framework had on the definition propagated by the EEOC. The guideline's articles *c*, *d*, and *e* moved away from theoretical conceptions and specifically addressed employers. They explained the employer's responsibility and called for internal disciplinary and preventative action.

Regarding the controversial aspects of employer liability, the guidelines, much more so than the judiciary, took a clear position in favor of the feminist framing. Article *c* of the guidelines reads:

---

283 Zippel: Politics, pp. 18f.
284 Schlafly, Phyllis: Feminism Falls on its Face, in: Phyllis Schlafly Report, November 1991.
285 Meyer, Coeli Mary et al.: Sexual Harassment, New York – Princeton 1981, p. 64.

c) Applying general Title VII principles, an employer [...] is responsible for its acts and those of its agents and supervisory employees with respect to sexual harassment regardless of whether the specific acts complained of were authorized or even forbidden by the employer and regardless of whether the employer knew or should have known of their occurrence [...].[286]

The EEOC advocated for strict employer liability. They specified that an employer was not absolved from this responsibility, even when a written policy existed and the harasser was engaging in behavior "forbidden by the employer." Similarly, the agency did not impose a notice requirement, stating that the employer was to be held accountable "regardless" of whether they "knew or *should have* known [emphasis added]" about the harassment.

The reader may have doubts about the relevance of the EEOC's insistence on strict liability, considering the diverging opinions in the judiciary and knowing that the guidelines were not legally binding. However, many employers were unaware of the weak legal backing articles *c*, *d*, and *e* enjoyed and management consultants were quick to overemphasize their importance. Consultants knew that article *a* had readily been confirmed by the judiciary and predicted that the guidelines in their entirety would soon sway the courts to rule in favor of strict liability.

Employers were increasingly concerned, and many, for the first time, paid attention to the issue. In a survey covering roughly 300 large U.S. corporations, sociologists Frank Dobbin and Erin Kelly found a significant spike regarding the introduction of internal policies covering sexual harassment in 1980.[287] My own research, while not a quantitative study, leads to the same conclusions; of the 16 policies I have collected which were published before the year 1985, only two were published before 1980 and 11 were published between 1980 and 1982. Employers had perked up and sought to prepare themselves.

"Employers Act to Curb sex Harassing on Job; Lawsuits, Fines Feared. Formal Policies are Issued, training Sessions Held: But Policing is Difficult;"[288] in 1980 and 1981, the sentiment of this headline was echoed repeatedly in various business journals. The courts, partially due to the ambiguity surrounding the issue of employer liability, had remained vague on how an organization may take action against sexual harassment. The EEOC attempted to fill that gap and offer guidance

---

286 EEOC: Guidelines.

287 Dobbin: How to Stop Sexual Harassment, pp. 1203–1243.

288 Lublin, Joann S.: Resisting Advances: Employers Act Curb Sex Harassing on the Job; Lawsuits, Fines Feared. Formal Policies Are Issued. Training Sessions Held. But Policing Is Difficult, in: The Wall Street Journal (April 24th, 1981), p. 1.

on concrete measures. The call for strict liability evident in article *c* was mitigated by paragraphs *d* and *e*. Article *d* served as a motivation to engage the employer immediately after the fact, while article *e* emphasized the importance of preventative action.

Article *d* reads:

> d) [...] an employer may rebut apparent liability for such acts [referring to hostile work environment sexual harassment] by showing that it took immediate and appropriate corrective action.[289]

Following this article, grievance procedures became increasingly popular. This was a trend which emerged in the immediate aftermath of the guidelines' publication and which held strong throughout the 1980s and beyond.[290] Grievance procedures served to inform the employer of any potentially legally problematic situations, thus allowing rapid "appropriate corrective action."

Besides motivating employers to act immediately after becoming aware of any harassment, the EEOC laid out strategies for prevention:

> e) Prevention is the best tool for the elimination of sexual harassment. An employer should take all steps necessary to prevent sexual harassment from occurring, such as affirmatively raising the subject, expressing strong disapproval, developing appropriate sanctions, informing employees of their right to raise, and how to raise the issue of harassment under Title VII, and developing methods to sensitize all concerned. [291]

In this context, punitive action ("developing appropriate sanctions") was seen as a deterrent and therefore useful as a preventative measure against sexual harassment. Similarly, having the internal infrastructure to effectively field complaints was meant to dissuade potential perpetrators from engaging in any inappropriate behavior.

The agency's encouragement for employers to issue assurances that complaints would be taken seriously and would be followed by action, aligned with the feminist framing of sexual harassment as a serious structural problem. Furthermore, the guidelines reflected the high priority feminist groups gave to circulating information about the issue by instructing employers to "affirmatively rais[e] the subject" and "developing methods to sensitize all concerned." Interestingly, article *e* did not claim that employers could avoid or even limit their legal responsibility by employing strong preventative programs. Instead, the agency as-

---

289 EEOC: Guidelines.
290 Dobbin: Equal Opportunity, p. 75.
291 EEOC: Guidelines.

sumed that, if the measures in place were successful in preventing sexual harassment, there would be no reason to sue the company. In a courtroom setting, however, the EEOC did not intend for such (failed) proactive action to protect employers from liability.

To review, the EEOC guidelines employed the feminist framework on sexual harassment in several instances. They acknowledged that sexual harassment constituted sex discrimination under the Civil Rights Act, accepted MacKinnon's categorization of *quid pro quo* and hostile work environment sexual harassment, and argued for strict employer liability.[292] Addressing the employer directly, the guidelines, encouraged organizations to set up mechanisms allowing for quick action after receiving a complaint, and outlined several preventative measures which employers "should" take.

Nevertheless, there was one section in the guidelines which ran counter to the feminist frame. Following the guidelines' publication in their preliminary form in the spring of 1980, the public was invited to issue comments and criticism, so that adjustments could be made. While many praised the guidelines as presenting a clear statement against sexual harassment,[293] others harshly criticized them as "less than satisfactory,"[294] "go[ing] far beyond the intent of courts and Congress," and "invit[ing] an avalanche of questionable charges."[295] In an attempt to dissuade the critics, the final guidelines were published in November 1980 with the addition of article *f.*[296]

This addition concerned the inclusion of the concept of sexual favoritism as a form of sexual harassment.

> f) [W]here employment opportunities or benefits are granted because of an individual's submission to the employer's sexual advances or requests for sexual favors, the employer may

---

292 Zippel: Politics, p. 65; Baker: Sexual Extortion, p. 219.
293 E. g. Vermuelen, Joan: Comments on the Equal Employment Opportunity Commission's Proposed Amendment Adding Section 1604.11, Sexual Harassment, to Its Guidelines on Sexual Discrimination, in: Women's Rights Law Reporter, 6/4 (1980), pp. 285–294; Blumenthal, Susan K: EEOC Guidelines. Comments and Analysis, Model Policies for the Office, June 10th, 1980, Files of the Equal Employment Opportunity Commission, Washington D.C.; Wells, Denise: Alliance Against Sexual Coercion to Equal Employment Opportunity Commission, June 6th, 1980, Files of the Equal Employment Opportunity Commission, Washington D.C., HSL, Cambridge Women's Center Records, Box 7, Folder Crimes Against Women. Alliance Against Sexual Coercion, 1976–1988; cf. Baker: Women's Movement, p. 117.
294 Seligman, David: Sex in the Office, in: Fortune (April 7th, 1980), p. 42.
295 Lublin: Guideline-Happy, p. 18.
296 Zippel: Politics, p. 9.

be held liable for unlawful sex discrimination against other persons who were qualified for but were denied that employment opportunity or benefit.[297]

As discussed elsewhere,[298] feminists argued that the notion of sexual favoritism cast a shadow on voluntary sexual relations, equivocated the harm done by these relationships with that induced by coercive behavior, and nourished the widespread belief that women – on a majority basis – used their sexuality to gain advantages in the workplace. As such, this amendment has been deemed by historians and contemporary legal experts alike as a major concession to social conservative criticism and demands. Despite this compromise, the establishment of a federal policy against sexual harassment in this form was widely considered a feminist success.[299]

In summary, throughout Eleanor Norton's tenure at the agency, the EEOC overwhelmingly accepted the feminist framing of sexual harassment. The institutionalization of a feminist anti-sexual harassment policy in and by the executive branch of the federal government led to wider public recognition of the issue as a genuine concern.[300] It was also the catalyst for many employers in the private sector to pay attention and act upon the issue. Based on the guidelines' inclusion of a feminist definition, on the involvement of feminist actors in their conception, and on the organized effort by feminists to endorse their final publication, I read their issuance as part of an antagonistic feminist strategy directed at employers.

In this chapter, I demonstrated that feminist actors in the latter half of the 1970s and early 1980s came to view employers as their adversaries. Representatives of the social conservative framing continued to be feminists' main opponents over ideological and theoretical control of the issue. However, since sexual harassment occurred in the workplace, feminist action often targeted employers. The latter, in feminists' view, were responsible for this space and yet remained at best apathetic and at worst complicit to the plight of working women. Feminist organizations launched direct action campaigns aimed at companies' reputations, developed a legal strategy focused on sexual harassment as a workers' rights issue, and supported the Equal Employment Opportunity Commission and its guidelines which emphasized strict employer liability.

Despite this initial antagonistic tone, feminist organizations soon came to realize that although employers needed to be a part of the conversation on sexual harassment, this dialog need not necessarily be adversarial. Employers' potential

297 EEOC: Guidelines.
298 See Chapter One.
299 MacKinnon: The Logic of Experience, p. 831.
300 Zippel: Politics, p. 33; Baker: Women's Movement, pp. 134, 136f.

to aid in eradicating the problem was substantial. Thus, feminists made plans to influence employers with cooperative action. This shall be the subject matter of the following chapter.

3 Employers: Possible Feminist Allies?

Unsurprisingly, the Working Women's Institute's main clientele was composed of working women. Some additional interest came from victims' loved ones and from other organizations fervid to assist sexual harassment victims within their own organizations. However, as WWI grew both in size and in notoriety, some of the speaker invitations and requests for workshops were made by for-profit corporations. Initially, the fledging organization did not advertise such services to employers, but occasionally accepted such invitations. Speaking engagements requested and paid for by private employers begin appearing in the WWI records as early as 1978.[301] By 1980, WWI actively advertised their services to employers and in the following years relied on these services for much of their funding.[302]

I posit that as the private sector grew increasingly attentive to the issue, feminist activists began considering a less antagonistic relationship with employers. The Institute had, beginning in their very first newsletter, repeatedly ascribed employers a great scope of action concerning the issue of sexual harassment. As shown in the previous chapter, feminists' antagonism stemmed from employers' lack of action despite their unique position. Several years after their founding, the organization began to differentiate between cooperative and uncooperative employers.[303] While the latter category continued to face WWI in various adversarial settings, the organization now assumed that cooperative employers simply lacked information and were open to collaborating with the Institute.

In this chapter, I will discuss this change in strategy and will outline what action the Institute suggested employers take. I will show that feminist suggestions of implementing policies and grievance procedures fell on fertile ground because both public and private employers had already established an internal infrastruc-

---

301 WWI consulted with Hoffman-LaRouche and Bell Laboratory, see: Working Women's Institute: Annual Program Report, 1979, BCA, Research on Women Records, Box 96, Folder Working Women's Institute General Program Proposals, Annual Program Report, Audited Financial Statement 1978–1981.
302 WWI: Program Description and Proposal 1980, BCA, Research on Women Records, Box 96, Folder Working Women's Institute General Program Proposals, Annual Program Report, Audited Financial Statement 1978–1981.
303 Ibid.

ture in their pursuit of complying with other Equal Employment Opportunity and Affirmative Action regulations. Lastly, in a brief analysis of corporate sexual harassment policies and grievance procedures published in or before 1982, I demonstrate that the policies in question were heavily influenced by the feminist frame. This leads to the conclusion that the feminist effort to establish themselves as experts and to reach out to employers was successful.

3.1 Working Women's Institute's Change in Strategy

The Working Women's Institute's volunteers had spent five years producing informational material, course plans for workshops, transcripts for speeches, and guides for counseling – all aimed at working women. This work served as a foundation for WWI to branch out and address additional target groups. In a program description and proposal for 1980, the organization proclaimed that it would "double the number of speaking engagements" by reaching out to "new audiences – teenagers, women re-entering the workforce, those in non-traditional jobs, [and] the business community." The report further laid out plans to "run workshops and seminars, and do consultation work with unions, corporations, nonprofits and governmental agencies that deal with working women."[304] WWI indeed managed to double their speaking engagements and began to affirmatively cater to larger organizations, including private companies. Following this report, WWI volunteers developed a new set of pamphlets and a more specialized training manual aimed specifically at advising employers, managers, and supervisors on how to eradicate sexual harassment from their workplaces.

On a logistical level, reaching out to employers made financial sense for WWI. Thus far the organization had kept afloat mainly by relying on individual donations and grants from various congenial non-profit organizations.[305] However, as the topic became more widely known, requests for aid increased,[306] leaving the volunteer-based organization stretched thin. Invitations for consultations

---

304 Ibid.
305 WWI: 1982 Dual Proposal (Including 1982 Corporate Pilot Project), BCA, Research on Women Records, Box 96, Working Women's Institute General Program Proposals, Annual Program Report, Audited Financial Statement 1978–1981.
306 WWI: Working Women's Institute Six Month Report, July 1980; Working Women's Institute General Program, 1981, BCA, Research on Women Records, Box 96, Folder Working Women's Institute General Program Proposals, Annual Program Report, Audited Financial Statement 1978–1981.

and speaking engagements from for-profit organizations, which had trickled in for years, began pouring in as the EEOC released their anti-sexual harassment guidelines in 1980. Those employers paying attention now found themselves scrambling for information on the issue. The demand for consultations by employers, willing to pay for services rendered, was an opportunity for WWI to gain financial stability. With the turn of the decade, the Institute systematically responded to incoming requests by employers, and even began actively advertising their services to for-profit organizations.[307] Thus, by 1980 WWI had added another pillar to their funding structure.

This pragmatic acceptance of for-profit organizations as clients was accompanied by an ideological shift concerning the role of employers. Rather than mainly engaging with them as adversaries in the arena of the court room, WWI had now opened direct lines of communication. The Institute never completely relinquished their antagonistic stance towards employers and a pronounced skepticism remained palpable in the organization's general rhetoric.[308] On a more practical basis, however, employers were now considered a conversation partner. This marked a change in the Institute's perception of the role the employer played in the fight against sexual harassment.

WWI argued that employers' reaction to and handling of sexual harassment mattered. Employers were in control of the workplace and thus had the power to make positive changes. Thus, influencing their understanding of sexual harassment could have a far-reaching effect. The Institute's corporate workshops, consultations, and example policies had the "purpose [...] to sensitize staff and assist in devising new procedures for responding appropriately to the problem."[309] WWI had acknowledged that employers were not necessarily all antagonists and could have a mediating function or even be powerful allies.

Albeit timidly, the Institute was embracing employers as cooperative partners. This shift in strategy was criticized by more radical feminist groups, among them the Alliance Against Sexual Coercion (AASC). As shown elsewhere,[310] the AASC considered capitalism to be a core cause for sexual harassment. Therefore, a general skepticism towards the private sector is not surprising. Feminist critics (both within and outside of the AASC) implied that an alliance with the private sector would cloud the Institute's values. Additionally, they argued that such

---

307 WWI: Six Month Report, July 1980; WWI: General Program, 1981; WWI: 1982 Dual Proposal; Working Women's Institute: Proposal to Rubin Foundation, 1982, p. 3, BCA, Research on Women Records, Box 96, Folder Bell Laboratories Corporate Study.
308 WWI: Help Your Company, p. 1.
309 WWI: Program Description and Proposal 1980.
310 Refer to Chapter One.

collaboration could allow corporations to coopt the issue and lead feminist activists to lose their discursive authority on the subject matter.[311] As shall become
apparent in the following chapters, the latter would prove to be a valid concern.[312]

The implication that WWI was abandoning their values by approaching employers for cooperation, however, cannot be substantiated. The Institute's program
description from 1980 gives some insight into the organization's intentions for collaborating with employers:

> WWI feels the time is ripe to pass on what we have learned and build the foundation for
> concrete **institutional changes.** The goal is to encourage those who deal with working
> women to be more responsive to this problem. To accomplish this, Working Women's Insti-
> tute intends to [...] help governmental agencies, businesses, unions and other organizations
> to **incorporate into their structures** a new awareness of and a new way of dealing with
> sexual harassment. Through this new effort, we will be able to touch the lives of millions
> of working women who will be treated with more **understanding at each point in the pro-
> cess** when sexual harassment becomes a problem. [emphasis added][313]

The key phrase in this paragraph is "institutional changes." Far from abandoning
the feminist theoretical framework from the early years, WWI reaffirmed it. As
the reader will remember, a vital element of the feminist framework is the assertion that sexual harassment is a systemic issue. By influencing lawmakers, judges,
and those in control of the workplace, WWI took concrete steps to reform the system. Acting in line with their theoretical framework, WWI was now increasingly
focused on transforming institutional structures within the workplace. Concretely,
this institutional change was to be brought about, first, by "sensitiz[ing] staff," at
all levels of the respective company, and second, by "assist[ing] in devising new
procedures for responding appropriately to the problem."[314] Instead of simply
blaming employers for sexual harassment in their organizations, WWI was now
offering concrete advice on how to change the situation.

This advice was only of value if employers decided to act on it. WWI was not a
governmental agency, it was not associated with a university, and it had an obvious ideological leaning. Nevertheless, in order to be considered, WWI had to

---

311 Alliance Against Sexual Coercion: Sexual Harassment. Emotional Rape, 1980, HSL Cambridge
Women's Center Records, Box 15, Folder Women and Violence. Sexual Harassment.
312 For the professionalization of personnel professionals on sexual harassment, turn to Chapter
Five. For the internalization of anti-sexual harassment measures within a company turn to
Chapter Six.
313 WWI: Program Description and Proposal 1980, p. 9.
314 Ibid.

establish their authority on the subject matter among representatives of the private sector. They did so by using rhetoric highlighting the group's institutional nature while at the same time minimizing its activist intentions. Therefore, WWI pamphlets targeted at employers used language associated with governmental, legal, and academic contexts.[315]

When introducing the Institute to the reader, the pamphlet "How Working Women's Institute Can Help Your Company," contends that "the Institute is a nationally recognized organization."[316] There is no further explanation by whom or in what form "the Institute," a term in itself indicating reputability, might be "recognized." Furthermore, the authors of this pamphlet put significant emphasis on their organization's geographical sphere of action as "national." The first sentence of this same pamphlet reads: "Working Women's Institute leads the national effort to explore the [...] issue of sexual harassment on the job."[317] This choice of wording implied government backing for WWI. After all, the most likely entity to undertake a "national effort" was the federal government. This wording, combined with WWI regularly including a copy of the EEOC guidelines when contacting employers may well have given the (false) impression that the Institute was affiliated in some way with the federal government.

In addition to these latent implications of government affiliation, WWI highlighted their function as a research institute to their corporate clientele. Despite research being a large part of the organization's action, it is important to remember that the Institute was not affiliated with a university, had little to no government funding, and had in no way curtailed their activism or their ideological goals. Nevertheless, when presenting themselves to their potential corporate clientele, the group used language that implied the kind of scientific objectivity one might expect in a university context. In their pamphlets, WWI ensures the reader that the advice given is based on their six years-worth of "direct experience" which provided data points for "scientific research" and "resource cataloguing." Here, the Institute's counseling services, their direct-aid, and their networking to provide victims with recourses – all major pillars of the Institute's work – are significantly downplayed. At the same time the use of the terms "science" and "research" evokes a sense of academic neutrality.

This is not meant to invalidate the WWI's research or to imply that the organization was hiding their agenda. It is true that around the turn of the decade,

315 Cf. WWI: Help Your Company; Sauvigné: SH is Against the Law; Sauvigné, Karen: What's A Supervisor to Do? Handling Sexual Harassment Complaints, BCA, Research on Women Records, Box 97, Folder Working Women's Institute Sexual Harassment Information.
316 WWI: Help Your Company, p. 1.
317 Ibid.

feminist organizations were the key actors exploring causes, symptoms, extent, and solutions in regard to sexual harassment. No other entity was as invested or as consistent in their research and their actions. Thus, their reputation as an expert on the topic was well founded. It is notable, however, that terms such as "systemic," "feminist," or "institutional change," which are so prevalent in most of WWI's publications, are absent from pamphlets directed at employers and supervisors.[318] Clearly, the Institute softened their activist side when presenting themselves to employers. It is feasible that the WWI worried that their political leanings had the potential to alienate corporate clients and impugn the credibility of their research.

Compared to the tone of the pamphlets and counseling provided to employees on how to handle sexual harassment,[319] the language in the brochures for employers is much more amicable towards management. In the pamphlet *How Working Women's Institute Can Help Your Company*, the authors sympathize with the employer by "recogniz[ing] that the problem [...] literally had no name seven years ago" and that it is a "complex" and at times "confusing" issue.[320] In contrast to the message in many news stories, however, WWI was clear that confusion over the subject matter did not justify inaction. Instead, this and other pamphlets clarified that employers needed to bestir themselves.

In order to motivate employer action, the institute highlighted the employer's legal obligation and the cost of sexual harassment to the company. By repeatedly referencing court cases, civil rights law, and the EEOC guidelines, WWI cast itself in the light of a legal authority.[321] In communication with employers, WWI was unequivocal in their assertion that sexual harassment constituted sex discrimination and that the employer was liable for any such conduct in their organization. As we have seen in earlier chapters both of these claims were still contested in the courts in the late 1970s and early 1980s. Thus, when WWI contended that "[t]he EEOC and the federal courts hold the employer (including all supervisory personnel) responsible for maintaining a working environment free from sexual harassment, intimidation or hostility of any sort,"[322] they were excluding vital legal information. In their publications, WWI created the impression that strict employer liability had a solid legal foundation. By doing so, internal corporate action was presented as the only way for employers to protect themselves.

---

318 Ibid.; Sauvigné: SH is Against the Law; Sauvigné: What's A Supervisor to Do?
319 As discussed in Chapter Two.
320 WWI: Help Your Company, p. 1.
321 Sauvigné: SH is Against the Law.
322 Sauvigné: What's A Supervisor to Do? p. 1.

WWI emphasized that "sexual harassment is expensive." Costs arising from lawsuits and settlements were not to be underestimated. One WWI pamphlet advised the reader that "reported settlements in sexual harassment cases have been as high as $52,000 and unofficial speculation of undisclosed cases suggests some settlements are well in excess of $100,000."[323] Additionally, the Institute argued that even when disregarding the legal costs, employers would benefit financially from eliminating sexual harassment. Using the Merit System Protection Board Survey as its source, WWI showed that the costs of heightened absenteeism, sick leave, low morale, and a lack of productivity were considerable.

On an analytical level, it is notable that WWI in its pamphlets, directed at employers and supervisors, highlighted this economic argument. Concern for an employers' economic interest was originally not part of the feminist frame. Factors, such as low productivity or absences at work, were discussed only in the context of a victim's experience. Whether the Institute's activists were aware that they were adding a new argument or whether they unconsciously shifted their rhetoric cannot be verified. In either case, the focus on the economic risk was a highly successful strategy to increase employers' interest. As shall be shown in later chapters, the financial costs associated with sexual harassment complaints became a core argument for action within the business community.

The Institute recommended company action consist of three steps: first, conceive of and publish a written policy, second, provide a complaint procedure, and third, educate the staff as a preventative measure. These three measures interplayed with each other; none could be effective in isolation. As one pamphlet explains:

> Being aware of sexual harassment and knowing that company policy prohibits it is critical to correcting and preventing future problems. If prevention fails, a quick and fair response to any incident is the next best strategy.[324]

Thus, a policy not backed up by a grievance procedure was ill-fated. Similarly, the Institute argued that without wide distribution of the policy and without training for employees on all levels, sexual harassment would continue to be underestimated, trivialized, and made a non-issue in the workplace.

---

323 Sauvigné: SH is Against the Law, p. 3.
324 Ibid., p. 8.

3.1.1 The Policy

In their pamphlets, training, and other consultation with employers, WWI emphasized the importance of a written policy statement specifically against sexual harassment. According to the Institute, such a policy should be made up by two elements: a clear definition of the subject matter and an unequivocal statement of
non-tolerance. In the pamphlet *Sexual Harassment is Against the Law* WWI explicitly advises the use of the EEOC guidelines' definition as a model for internal company policy.

Interestingly, in that same pamphlet, the organization does not follow its own
advice. The definition presented to the reader in the introduction does not contradict its EEOC counterpart but is much more concrete.

> Sexual harassment includes a wide range of behaviors that can be manifested by looks,
> touches, jokes, innuendoes, gestures epithet or direct propositions. At one extreme it is a di-
> rect demand for sexual favors coupled with an explicit or implicit threat of firing for refusal.
> At the other, it's being forced to work in an environment in which, through various means
> such as sexual slurs and/or the public display of degrading sexual images the victim (usually
> women) is made to feel humiliated because of her sex.[325]

Rather than broadly defining possible harassing behavior as "unwelcome sexual
advances, requests for sexual favors, and other verbal or physical conduct of a
sexual nature,"[326] in their own definition WWI is much more descriptive in
what such behavior might look like.

This gives rise to the question of why, in this instance, the Institute would
defer to the EEOC. It is feasible that an overly concrete definition, although
more memorable and much clearer to the employee, may also lead to the inadver-
tent exclusion of thus far unconceived scenarios. The use of the EEOC definition
on the other hand "assure[s] a sufficiently broad definition of sexual harassment
and [...] demonstrate[s] commitment to acting within the law."[327]

It is notable that throughout the pamphlet, the authors focus on article *a* of
the EEOC guidelines.[328] Article *f*, dealing with sexual favoritism, is only briefly
mentioned, not quoted, and immediately followed by a brief explanation of the
validity of consensual relationships:

---

325 Sauvigné: SH is Against the Law, p. 1.
326 EEOC guidelines 1980, article a.
327 Sauvigné: SH is Against the Law, p. 7.
328 Ibid., p. 1.

> There is then the matter of the office romance. Mutual relationships or harmless flirting are not sexual harassment, so long as neither party finds it offensive. Remember, the key word in any definition of sexual harassment is 'unwelcome.' [329]

This distinction becomes exceedingly relevant in the following decades. As personnel professionals became the primary source of advice for employers, romantic relationships between coworkers fell into disrepute.

In all their advice to employers, the Institute emphasized that a policy could only be effective when its enforcement was assured. WWI warned against written policies merely existing on paper while a *de facto* oral policy accepted or even encouraged sexual harassment. In the pamphlet, *Sexual Harassment is Against the Law,* Sauvigné states that once sexual harassment was defined, the "CEO of the organization" must resolutely prohibit such behavior. She explains that one important strategy to ensure that a written policy is adhered to is its wide distribution. The step of dissemination to "every employee at every level" is deemed by the WWI "equally important" as the prohibition of sexual harassment in the first place. The Institute suggests that the written policy be "includ[ed] [...] with paychecks," "post[ed] permanently on all bulletin boards, "publish[ed] in the employee newsletter," and discussed "in all orientation sessions."[330] The Institute argued that knowledge of the existence of such a policy was the precondition for its implementation.

3.1.2 Complaint Procedure

The Institute explained that in order for a policy to be effective, it had to be implemented in conjunction with a grievance procedure. Without explicit instructions on how and with whom to file a complaint, the policy lacked any substance. Thus, WWI proclaimed that as a prerequisite for effectiveness the "complaint procedure should be as widely known within the company as the policy itself." With regard to its content, the Institute ascertained that such a procedure must be "fair" and "impartial" to ensure "the confidence of employees."[331] Without this trust, the procedure and the policy itself was considered futile. Additionally, the procedure should be designed to include "safeguards that protect both the accused and the accuser," while at the same time taking care not to be "intimidating or seem stacked against the complainant."[332]

---

329 Ibid., p. 4.
330 Ibid., p. 7.
331 Ibid.
332 Ibid.

In theory, these aspects were sensible and straightforward. They were reminiscent of the ideal court room; those evaluating the situation were committed to fairness and impartiality. The accused was considered innocent until proven guilty. And the accuser was not intimidated or discouraged from bringing a complaint. In practice, however, the brochures were vague on how exactly a company could fulfill these requirements.

Exemplary for the discord between theory and practice is the issue of impartiality. On the one hand, the Institute's pamphlets highlighted the danger of personal bias to the impartiality of the process. According to WWI, supervisors in charge of executing the grievance procedure had to be "effectively trained" in order to "know what biases they may have that could impede their acting effectively."[333] On the other hand, the negative effects a hierarchical, non-democratic power structure could have on the neutrality of employees and supervisors were not discussed. The fact that the person or persons "implementing the procedure" were beholden to a CEO and/or an executive board and therefore were neither unbiased, nor in complete control of their decisions was not addressed. Therefore, in a corporate setting impartiality was a promise that could only partially be upheld. Despite this constituting a glaring flaw, which would continue to haunt corporate procedures for decades, the Institute proposed this idealized criterion for an internal corporate procedure.

A vital part of any grievance procedure was an institutionalized investigation. The Institute stressed that complainants needed to be taken seriously and potential harassers should be made aware that forbidden conduct would be disciplined. Thus, every formal complaint was to be followed by a "thorough" and "quick" investigation.[334] In such a case, the company's respective personnel management, human resources, or equal employment opportunity office was made responsible for leading the investigation.

Naturally, the Institute was aware that not all complaints were formal. Many targets of harassment resorted to an "informal request for assistance" from their boss, human resources or other trusted supervisor. WWI stated that while such an informal complaint should not immediately trigger an official investigation, it should nevertheless be taken seriously. In the brochure *What's a Supervisor to Do?*, Sauvigné addresses managers directly and explains that "[the complainant] may want your advice on how informally to resolve the situation herself, or she may want you to intervene on her behalf."[335]

---

333 Ibid.
334 Ibid.
335 Sauvigné: What's a Supervisor to Do? p. 1.

Irrespective of whether the complaint was issued formally or informally, in the procedure conceived by WWI, the complainant was always given a choice on how to proceed. This reflects feminist theory developed in the anti-rape movement. Reporting the crime, aiding the investigation, and testifying at trial was a grueling experience for many. WWI transferred this knowledge to the concept of internal corporate investigations of sexual harassment allegations. The organization intended to ensure targets of harassment felt in control of their situation by letting them choose their preferred recourse.

At the same time, the pamphlet made clear that even if the complainant addressed the situation on their own, the company could not simply ignore the situation: "Once you [manager] know about the problem you have a duty to monitor it and act to stop the pattern if her own actions do not bring the desired result."[336] In fact, according to WWI, supervisors had to be "alert to any appearance of impropriety," and thus an investigation could become necessary, even when no complaint had been made. This is especially true for "occupations where women are integrating traditionally male fields."

> [...] This is because sexual harassment is statistically more likely to occur in such environments and it is assumed that you [manager] should be aware of its potential. You are therefore expected to be vigilant in looking for and rooting out sexual harassing behavior.[337]

Hence, by involving the complainant in decisions about the process instead of launching a full investigation, the Institute by no means absolved the employer from responsibility.

WWI's intention for complaint procedures, investigations, and disciplinary action was not punishment or retribution but ridding the workplace of sexual harassment. According to WWI's studies, most women did not seek vengeance or justice – inside or outside of court – but simply wanted the matter "resolved and taken care of" so that they could "continue to work."[338] Hence, in their pamphlets, WWI asserted that "[a]ll parties are best served if the problem is resolved at the lowest possible level in the company hierarchy – you [manager] now have an opportunity to resolve it within your group or department."[339]

Various pamphlets prepare the managers for the victim's likely emotional state saying that "she will probably feel a combination of anger-rage-bitterness, and at the same time, fear-shame-guilt-timidity." They remind managers that "it

336 Ibid.
337 Ibid.
338 Yount, Katherine: Interview 120, 1983, HSL, Kristen Yount Papers, Folder 3.11.
339 Sauvigné: What's A Supervisor to do? p. 1.

was difficult for the complainant to bring the problem to your attention at all; she has decided to talk to you about it because either she trusts you, or it has gotten to be more than she can handle."[340] This reflects a core element of the feminist framing: sexual harassment is a problem, because of the consequences faced by those victimized. The legal and economic consequences were used as an argument to draw the employer's attention, but the concrete advice and instructions were driven by the victims' needs.

Despite this focus, alleged harassers were not villainized by WWI. When conducting an investigation and interviewing the person against whom a complaint has been launched, managers were advised to be as "non-inflammatory" as possible. One pamphlet suggested that this may be accomplished by talking "to the accused harasser about [...] the seriousness of sexual harassment," "remind[ing] him of the company policy," and "referenc[ing your] belief that he would not deliberately hurt a co-worker." Made explicit in the context of awareness training, the employers were to provide employees with "non-threatening" opportunities to "examine their own attitudes."[341]

According to WWI, much of these "attitudes" were linked with the employees' gender socialization.

> Traditional concepts of sex roles tell us it is perfectly natural for men to make sexual overtures. However, these concepts fail to distinguish between behavior that is appropriate in a social setting and that which is appropriate in the work setting. Behaviors that might be acceptable in another context, when carried into the workplace, can become problematic. The man may be simply playing out his own accustomed sex role and relating to female workers in a way that is comfortable to him. But because most positions of authority are held by men and women are less established in the workplace, the woman must be cautious about rebuffing his sexual advances. [...] This puts her in a situation where her job security is tied to her sexuality, when the only standard that should apply is her ability and performance on her job.[342]

In this quote, WWI allows for the possibility of sexual harassment occurring without malicious intent, if the perpetrator was simply performing his internalized gender role. Therefore, WWI proposed several "possible actions to consider [...] before initiating serious disciplinary action."[343] These suggestions ranged from having a conversation with the harasser, requesting the harasser privately or publicly apologize to the complainant, "insist[ing] [the] harasser get counseling," or

---

340 Ibid.
341 Ibid.
342 Ibid., p. 3.
343 Sauvigné: What's a Supervisor to do?

"issuing a warning." More drastic steps included the transfer of the harasser, "withhold[ing] work assignments" and/or noting the incidences in the harasser's performance evaluation and personnel file. Suspension or dismissal of the harasser, according to WWI, were to be considered only in repeat or particularly serious cases.[344] This endorsement of lenient rather than drastic measures reflects WWI's commitment to a systemic approach in the fight against sexual harassment. Not the individuals but the larger circumstances were made responsible for the problem. In order to provoke systemic change, individuals had to be educated rather than intimidated and punished.

3.1.3 Prevention

Besides resolving individual situations, prohibiting, and disciplining sexually harassing conduct by means of a policy and complaint procedure could also prevent future cases. However, as Sauvigné stated rather bluntly in one brochure: "Policies and procedures are not worth the paper they are printed on and can be expected to have little impact on the problem if they are not backed with education and training." In line with previous statements that sexual harassment could be "complex and confusing," she explained that "much of the sexual harassment that occurs at work is excused or ignored because people fail to understand what sexual harassment is and why it is wrong."[345] According to Sauvigné, employees at all levels had to be educated on the issue.

WWI's proposed training included teaching employees "basic coping strategies, like saying 'stop' to the harasser, even if he's the boss," as well as "recogniz[ing] its subtle manifestations, to see when their own behavior might be harassing." The training was designed to teach potential harassers and potential victims alike what they could do against sexual harassment without villainizing individual employees. The goal was to "learn to work together without sexual intimidation of any kind."[346]

Awareness training, according to the Institute, was particularly necessary because of the gendered dynamics of the problem at hand. In line with their theoretical understanding of the issue, WWI repeatedly and explicitly stated that harassment was a problem mostly affecting women. Although the Institute stipulated that "men too can be sexually harassed," it highlighted that "male to female" harassment was "most common" and that the number of incidences victimizing men was "considerably lower." This gendered understanding of sexual harassment was

344 Ibid.
345 Sauvigné: Sexual Harassment Is Against the Law, p. 8.
346 Ibid.

also present in the Institute's pronoun usage; the harasser was continually re-ferred to as "he," while the complainant was introduced as "she/he" or "she."

When in 1981 the Harvard Business Review published a study on what it coined "the perception gap," WWI incorporated the article into their training pro-gram. The concept itself had already been explored in feminist texts and was ad-dressed in the 1980 Merit System Protection Board survey.[347] Even though the idea itself was not new, for the Institute, it was strategic not to present the concept as one developed by feminists. Rather, credit was given to the business journal, which was already familiar to and considered trustworthy by many employers. In the article, the Harvard Business Review explained that "top managers are largely unaware that sexual harassment occurs within their organizations." It con-cluded that this was "due to a wide gap between male and female perceptions of the problem."[348] Due to "most managerial and supervisory positions [being] held by men,"[349] those best positioned to instigate change were also most likely to un-derestimate the extent and severity of the problem. To rectify this issue, WWI highlighted the importance of training on "all levels," making sure to include a suggestion for specialized supervisor training.[350]

WWI recommended employers apply a combination of a well-known policy, an accessible complaint procedure, and carefully conceived awareness training for eliminating sexual harassment within their organizations. The Institute prom-ised that by following this simple recipe "any company can achieve a working cli-mate that is conducive to doing business [and] that is flexible enough to accommo-date human needs."[351] WWI promoted this formula of action on several occasions, including the first congressional hearings on sexual harassment. The federal government as the largest employer in the country took heed and implemented these steps in their workforce.

3.2 The Federal Government as an Employer

In September and November 1979, the committee on Post Office and Civil Service held the first congressional hearings on sexual harassment. Congressman James

---

347 MSPB: Sexual Harassment in the Federal Workplace, 1981.
348 Collins, Eliza G. C. and Timothy B. Blodgett: Sexual Harassment...Some See I...Some Won't, in: Harvard Business Review (March 1981).
349 Sauvigné: SH is Against the Law, p. 4.
350 Ibid., p. 8.
351 Ibid., p. 4.

M. Hanley, who chaired the hearings, in his introductory remarks, declared the issue of sexual harassment to be "not only epidemic" but "a pandemic, an everyday, everywhere occurrence."[352] These hearings led the Merit Systems Protection Board and the Office of Personnel Management (OPM) to initiate three distinct measures to combat sexual harassment within the federal government: an unambiguous policy statement was issued, a prevention and training program initiated, and a comprehensive survey conducted. The implementation of these measures signaled that the federal government in its role of an employer accepted responsibility in eradicating sexual harassment from the federal workplace. Employing these measures reflected an acceptance of the feminist theoretical framing and practical feminist advice.

According to WWI, the first step for an employer to take was the implementation of a clear policy statement. Alan K. Campbell, director of the OPM, had found in his preliminary investigations that some agencies, such as the General Service Administration, the Department of Commerce, and the Department of Health, Education and Welfare, had already implemented policies and procedures specifically addressing sexual harassment. While commending these agencies and departments for their initiative, Campbell noted that many agencies had as of yet avoided the issue and that even where definitions and policies were provided, these differed from agency to agency.[353] Hence, the OPM devised a policy which became binding across the federal government within the year.

The definition of sexual harassment used in the policy in many ways paralleled the definition issued by the EEOC a year later. Although the terminology varied, conceptually the OPM policy forbid both *quid pro quo* and hostile work environment sexual harassment. Additionally, this policy referred to sexual harassment as "unsolicited and unwelcome sexual overtures,"[354] thereby highlighting the non-consensual aspect of sexual harassment.

Besides its scope, there was one other key difference between the OPM definition of 1979 and the EEOC guidelines of 1980. The latter focused on a definition

---

352 James Hanley's Opening Statement. Subcommittee on Investigations: Hearings on Sexual Harassment, p. 1; cf. Baker: Women's Movement, pp. 88, 112f.; Baker: Organized Feminist Resistance, p. 168; Arriola: Construction Industry, p. 39.

353 Campbell, Alan K. (Director, Office of Personnel Management) Before U.S. House of Representatives Committee on Post Office and Civil Service Subcommittee on Investigation. James M. Hanley, Chairman, November 13th, 1979, pp. 1f., BCA, Research of Women Records, box 96, Folder U.S. Office of Personnel management Sexual Harassment.

354 OPM: Policy Statement and Definition of Sexual Harassment, 1979, p. 1, BCA, Research on Women Records, Box 95, Folder U.S. Office of Personnel Management Memorandum on Sexual Harassment.

based on discrimination, while the former relied on "the principle of merit."[355] The OPM's policy did not reference that a number of courts had recognized sexual harassment as a form of sex discrimination. Instead, eliminating sexual harassment was portrayed as a matter of "ethics," and was necessary because the U.S. government had to hold itself to "high standards" as to preserve the "confidence of the American people."[356] Invoking a "code of ethics" which included "integrity" and "impartiality," as well as repeated references to "merit principles," was emblematic within the pre-1980, federal government discourse on sexual harassment.

With the publication of the final EEOC guidelines in November 1980, which replaced the OPM policy for federal employees as well as including all non-federal employer-employee relationships, the federal narrative shifted to include sexual harassment as a breach of civil rights law. Rhetoric concerning discrimination and a focus on merit were not mutually exclusive and they were both compatible with the feminist framework. Nevertheless, feminist organizations strategically focused on an understanding of sexual harassment as a civil rights violation. Thus, the federal shift from a merit-based understanding to one focusing on discrimination was in line with feminist action and advice.

Concurring with feminist advice, OPM director Alan Campbell declared that a policy would not suffice to rid the workplace of sexual harassment.[357] In addition to a policy and a grievance procedure, all federal employees needed to be educated on the issue. To this end, a training program was implemented almost immediately after the hearings in 1979. The original training program was "made available for all employees in both supervisory and non-supervisory positions."[358]

Rather than providing one comprehensive course on sexual harassment, the OPM proposed to include "coverage [of sexual harassment] in existing courses."

[R]ather than develop a separate course, a more constructive approach would be to emphasize coverage in existing courses. [...] Courses on performance and conduct deficiencies, grievance handling, employee relations and code of conduct, supervisory skills, merit principles [...] are among our courses that provide an excellent opportunity to emphasize the Government's commitment to protect employees from sexual harassment and institutionalizing systems and behaviors to eliminate these practices.[359]

The inclusion of sexual harassment as a "high priority topic" in various agency's training sessions was a major first step to demonstrating the government's com-

355 Ibid.
356 Ibid.
357 Campbell, Subcommittee on Investigation 1979, p. 6.
358 OPM: Policy Statement 1979, p. 1.
359 Campbell, Subcommittee on Investigation 1979, p. 8.

mitment to abolishing the practice. However, discussing sexual harassment in the context of seminars on "merit principles" and "conduct deficiencies" focused the federal narrative regarding sexual harassment on these themes. These incorporated classes did not allow for a multi-facetted analysis of the issue. An employee could leave a training session having understood that sexual harassment was unseemly conduct or that it was a breach of merit principles, but fail to understand that it was a civil rights issue.

Less than a year later, the OPM changed course and initiated a training program solely focused on the topic of sexual harassment. Rather than discussing only one aspect of the issue, the new course encouraged participants to "think about some aspects of sexual harassment that you might not have thought of before."[360] The curriculum involved educating participants on the definition of sexual harassment, making employees "aware of differing perceptions of sexually harassing behavior," promoting an understanding of "the impact of sexual harassment on employee morale and productivity," and empowering participants to take action "if sexual harassment is experienced or observed."[361]

The new training was based on the original OPM policy rather than the EEOC policy, which went into effect shortly after the development of this training program. Therefore, the course had as its basis the governmental merit policy rather than civil rights legislation. However, in contrast to any of the previous course additions, this comprehensive course highlighted the gendered power dynamics often in play in sexual harassment situations,[362] and described the issue not only in the context of prohibited personnel practices but also as an issue of sexual violence.[363]

In addition to the implementation of policy, procedure, and training by the Office of Personnel Management, the Merit System Protection Board (MSPB) commenced a large-scale effort to document the pervasiveness of sexual harassment within the federal government. The MSPB was established with the passing of the Civil Service Reform Act of 1978, which went into effect in January 1979. As the

---

360 OPM: Workshop on Sexual Harassment, Trainers Manual, 1980, Appendix Handout #1, BCA, Research on Women Records, Box 96, Folder U.S. Office of Personnel Management Sexual Harassment.

361 Ibid., p. 2.

362 Ibid., pp. 2f.

363 One example question reads: "Like rape, sexual harassment has been a hidden problem, treated as a joke, or blamed on the victim. Because of a long history of silence on the subject, many (people) feel uncomfortable or embarrassed when they talk about personal incidents of harassment. Do you feel this way? Do you have any idea why?" OPM: Workshop 1980, Appendix Handout #1.

"guardian of the federal merits system," the MSPB's main objective was to ensure that federal employees be judged only based on their skill and performance.[364] On the one hand, the agency served as a port-of-call for federal employees who experienced prohibited personnel practices due to their race, ethnicity, sex, or political affiliation. On the other hand, the MSPB conducted research and organized surveys in order to pinpoint employment related issues within the federal government.

As Alan Campbell rightly stated in the 1979 hearings,[365] there was "as yet no reliable data to determine the extent of the problem [sexual harassment] in the Federal sector." Subsequently, the MSPB conducted a survey of the federal workforce specifically regarding their experiences with sexual harassment. Described by Freada Klein, co-founder of the Alliance Against Sexual Coercion, as "the first decent methodological study,"[366] the survey was highly respected by journalists, activists, employers, politicians, and judges alike.[367] In May of 1980, the survey was sent out to 23,000 men and women in the federal workforce. Within the next three months 20,100 surveys were returned. At 85%, this was an unusually high response rate.[368] While previous studies had succeeded in gathering some information and highlighting the fact that sexual harassment was a problem,[369] they were not conducted following a scientific method and thus the resulting data was inaccurate. The systematic distribution and the high return rate in the MSPB study, in contrast, laid the foundation for reliable, unbiased data.

The results confirmed what had been suggested in the hearings. Sexual harassment was widespread and it was underreported. Indeed, 42% of female and 15% of male employees reported having experienced sexual harassment at their job within the last two years of taking the survey. When asked to specify, 30% of female and 9% of male respondents indicated that the behavior to which they had been subjected fell into one of the following two categories: "severe – such as pressure for sexual favors," or "most severe – actual or attempted rape or sexual assault." Despite these high numbers, only 50% of female respondents "knew of the discrimination complaint system" and of that group only 20% be-

---

364 Merit Systems Protection Board: About MSPB, 2024.
365 Campbell, Subcommittee on Investigation 1979.
366 Brownmiller: From Wood to Hill, p. 71; Baker: Women's Movement, p. 124.
367 Sauvigné: Letter to Bush, p. 2.
368 Merit System Protection Board: Summary of The MSPB Special Study of Sexual Harassment in the Federal Workplace, September 1980, p. 2, BCA, Research on Women Records, Box 95, Folder Publications of American Federation of State, County and Municipal Employees.
369 Anonymous: How Do You Handle Sex; cf. Baker: The Emergence, p. 175; Baker, Women's Movement, p. 113; Dobbin, Equal Opportunity, p. 197.

lieved that "the system would work for them." This lack of information about the available "formal remedies," and "a lack of trust" in the formal channels led to chronic underreporting of sexual harassment. Of those who had identified themselves as victims of sexual harassment, only a total of 3% indicated having filed a formal complaint.[370]

Additionally, the survey substantiated Catharine MacKinnon's claims that *quid pro quo* was not the only form of harassment and that a hostile work environment could be just as damning. The summary report of the MSPB survey reads:

> Surprisingly, the problem of sexual harassment does not emanate from supervisors alone, but occurs even more frequently among coworkers. Fully 65% of the female victims and 76% of the male victims reported being harassed by a coworker or other employee, while only 37% of the female victims and only 14% of the male victims said that they had been sexually harassed by a supervisor.[371]

This data became instrumental to convincing judges that a hostile work environment could amount to sexual harassment.

The survey also drew attention to the "perception gap." Men and women acquiesced the statement "uninvited sexual attention constitutes harassment and should not be tolerated in the Federal workplace" at the same rate. Despite this general consensus, male respondents were almost double as likely (44%) as their female counterparts (23%) to believe that the "issue of sexual harassment has been exaggerated." According to the MSPB's summary report this was likely due to the much lower rates of sexual harassment directed against men, therefore decreasing the likelihood that a male worker had experienced sexual harassment first-hand. The report also warned that this "perception gap" could prove to be a serious problem in the federal fight against sexual harassment. Due to men "comprise[ing] the majority of all supervisors," the group of supervisors as a whole was more likely to underestimate the issue of sexual harassment and thus "undermine the authority [...] of agency policy statements" and "have the effect of thwarting their implementation."[372]

A lack of engagement in the fight against sexual harassment was concerning, because the survey not only shed light on how widespread the problem was but also revealed that "[s]exual harassment has a real price tag for the taxpayer." Karen Sauvigné, in a letter to Vice President Bush dated August 19th, 1981, summa-

---

370 MSPB: Summary of The MSPB Special Study 1980, pp. 3–5.
371 Ibid., p. 3.
372 Ibid., pp. 3–5.

rized the MSPB's findings on the financial costs of sexual harassment to the federal government as follows:

> The Merit Systems Protection Board, by considering such costs as turnover, lost productivity, medical bills and sick leave conservatively estimates the direct costs of sexual harassment to the federal government alone in the period May 1978 to May 1980 to be $189 million. Moreover, the indirect costs of sexual harassment – costs related to defending suits brought by its victims – can be staggering.

Sauvigné went on to state that "obviously sexual harassment is bad for business" and that it has "a serious impact on employers."[373]

In these statements, Sauvigné did not differentiate between the federal government and private employers. The MSPB survey justified such a generalization. Although the Board in its summary report explicitly lamented the lack of more comparative data, it nevertheless inquired about participants' previous work experience. A great majority of those respondents who had worked elsewhere (88% of women, and 90% of men) "felt that sexual harassment is no worse in the Federal workplace than in the private sector or in state or local government."[374] These last two findings, first that sexual harassment was expensive and second that the data found in this study was likely comparable to the situation in the private sector, garnered attention from many employers. Indeed, over the next two decades this and various follow up surveys by the MSPB were incorporated and cited in numerous company policies and corporate training materials.[375]

In conclusion, while the congressional hearing in 1979 did not result in new legislation explicitly forbidding sexual harassment, it did bring on several changes in federal policy. The Office of Personnel Management issued a policy and a grievance procedure, to all federal agencies condemning sexual harassment. Additionally, the agency initiated training programs with the aim of spreading awareness of the problem and thereby hoping to prevent it from occurring altogether.[376] The Merit System Protection Board oversaw a large-scale survey of federal employees

---

373 Sauvigné: Letter to Bush, p. 2.
374 MSPB: Summary of The MSPB Special Study 1980, p. 4.
375 E.g.: Atana: Sexual Harassment Prevention Training – Once and For All: Stopping Sexual Harassment at Work, 2021, Cordua Training Videos: Sexual Harassment – Awareness, Perception and Prevention: An Employee's Responsibility, [no date, late 1990s]; Digital Electronics Corporation: Addressing Sexual Harassment in the Work Environment, in: Personnel Perspectives Digital Newsletter, 1991, p. 12, CHM, Digital Equipment Corporation Records, Box 150, Folder Personnel Perspectives, 1984–1992.
376 Baker: Women's Movement, p. 120.

regarding the subject matter. Although the initial governmental focus was weight-ed more towards a definition of sexual harassment as a violation of merit princi-ples rather than civil rights law, the measures implemented were in accordance with both feminist practical advice and theoretical understanding regarding sex-ual harassment.

3.3 Feminist Frame in Early Corporate Policies

The federal government promoted "high standards" among its employees as it wished to fulfill a model function for the general population. In its role as an em-ployer, it intended to promote exemplary employer-employee relationships. Thus, the federal government hoped to inspire private employers to emulate its initia-tives. Before the federal government acknowledged sexual harassment as a prob-lem, there was little to no action on the issue in the private sector. As a result of a dialogue with feminist organizations, a handful of employers implemented inter-nal policies and grievance procedures in the late 1970's.[377] However, these efforts were sporadic and isolated. Hence, the federal initiatives of 1979 were the first major steps any employer, private or public, had taken against sexual harassment. Nevertheless, most corporations had policies and personnel infrastructure in place which served as a base for internal anti-sexual harassment measures.

The decades preceding 1980 had brought with them a bureaucratization and logistical changes in most companies. The rise of personnel management offices, later rebranded as human resources departments, came about as early as the 1930s. The National Labor Relations Act (1935), often referred to as the Wagner Act, enshrined the right of (most) American workers to organize and join labor unions.[378] Consequently, employers were not permitted to terminate, demote, or in any other way discriminate against employees on the basis of their union affil-iation. As union membership surged in the 1940s and collective bargaining be-came a norm, employers had to manage new labor regulations and union con-tracts.

Sociologist Frank Dobbin argues for a causation between this shift in employ-er-employee dynamics, and the establishment or extension of personnel manage-ment departments in the private sector. A survey by the National Industrial Con-ference Board found that by 1946, 66% of the companies participating had a

---

377 WWI: Six Month Report, July 1980; WWI: General Program, 1981; cf. Baker: Women's Movement, pp. 163 f., 174.
378 National Labor Relations Act of 1935. Public Law No. 74–198, 49 Stat.449, 1935.

personnel department in place. This number had nearly doubled since the Board's last survey in 1939.[379] In order to avoid allegations of discrimination against union members, personnel departments all over the country issued various new policies. In many companies, promotions, demotions, and termination of employment now had to be justified by written performance reviews. Available jobs had to be posted publicly and be accompanied by a description of what tasks and responsibilities the position entailed. Internal grievance procedures, often involving union representatives, had become common place. In the early 1950s these measures were advertised as the "modern personnel system."[380] However, as union membership waned after peaking in the 1940s, so did employers' commitment to these policies, making them merely notional.

A decade later, the Civil Rights Act (1964) gave the "modern personnel system" a new breath of life. During debates on the bill and after the immediate passage of the Act, few employers would have imagined that the new law would impact them meaningfully.[381] Congress did not specifically define the term "discrimination" and so it fell to personnel experts to devise equal employment opportunity programs to demonstrate compliance of the law. Additionally, from 1961 onwards, many companies were influenced by President Kennedy's executive order obliging federal contractors to "take affirmative action" measures. While both the equal employment opportunity (EEO) and the affirmative action programs (AA) were at first aimed at eliminating racial discrimination, by the turn of the decade, they also addressed sex discrimination. When employers began acting on the issue of sexual harassment, many delegated this newest civil rights issue to their personnel departments, who were already in charge of employee relations and anti-discrimination policy. Taking up the mantle of yet another discrimination issue, personnel managers simply added to already existing EEO and/or AA policies.

Some companies attached a brief paragraph specifically addressing sexual harassment in the internal EEO policy.[382] Others decided to include a document on "employee harassment," in the EEO material. For instance, one insurance company issued a policy as part of their EEO files, forbidding "harassment of employ-

---

379 Dobbin: Equal Opportunity, p. 43 f.

380 Ibid., p. 5.

381 Ibid., pp. 2 f.

382 E. g.: Universal Manufacturing Corporation: Personnel Policy Procedure. Equal Opportunity Employment Policy, May 20th, 1981, BCA, Research on Women Records, Box 96, Folder Bell Laboratories Corporate Study.

ees for sexual, racial, religious or any other reason."[383] The file explicitly mentioned "concerns [about] sexual overtures of a supervisory employee toward his/her subordinates" as a "chief concern encompassed in this policy."[384] Still others implied or outright argued that the issue was covered by their policies even though they never explicitly used the phrase "sexual harassment."

In 1982, W. O. Amann, Employee Relations Manager at Lockheed Electronics Company, Inc. made this explicit when they expressed the company's refusal to participate in a study on sexual harassment policies by the New Jersey Department of Community Affairs. In their letter they write:

> Like many other companies, we have attempted to incorporate policies on sexual harassment into our overall rules and regulations with regard to Equal Employment Opportunity and Affirmative Action. Because of this approach, we have not identified sexual harassment as a separate issue within our overall EEO/AAP efforts, except, of course, to make our management personnel aware of the parameters of the problems of sexual harassment and how instances of sexual harassment may be handled within our overall policies and procedures.[385]

Sexual harassment, according to Lockheed Electronics Company, was simply one presentation of a larger problem: discrimination. As this was already covered by their existing policies, there was no need for any alterations. Due to the lack of further information, it is impossible to assess how detailed Lockheed's EEO and AA policies were and whether the coverage of sexual harassment was argued in good faith.

For reference, other companies' EEO policies varied significantly in regard to their specificity. Some policies simply consisted of a statement that declared "we are an equal opportunity workplace" and that "discrimination on the basis of

---

383 The company took part in the 1982 New Jersey Department of Community Affairs survey on sexual harassment but chose to remain anonymous. Included information on size (3,554 employees) and sector (insurance). Anonymous Insurance Company: Policy Statement on Employee Harassment, File 007 in the New Jersey Department of Community Affairs survey on sexual harassment, undated [pre-1982], BCA Research on Women Records, Box 96, Folder Bell Laboratories Corporate Study; cf. Monsanto Human Rights Policy, Employee Guidebook, p.15, St. Louis Washington University Archive, Monsanto Company, Series 05 Company Publications (Internal Use), Box 1, Employee Guidebook for Monsanto Human Rights Policy.

384 Anonymous Insurance Company: Policy Statement on Employee Harassment, pre-1983.

385 Amann, W. O.: Letter from Amann as a representative of Lockheed Electronics Company, Inc. to Barbara Wicklund of the New Jersey Department of Community Affairs Division on Women regarding their survey on sexual harassment, October 27th, 1982, BCA Research Women Records, Box 96, Folder Bell Laboratories Corporate Study.

race, sex, ethnicity [...] will not be tolerated."[386] Others had a detailed outline of offenses. The Universal Manufacturing Corporation, for instance, listed infractions such as "obscene abusive language," "malicious gossip," "immoral conduct," or "threatening, intimidating, and/or coercing fellow employees on the premises at any time for any purpose."[387] As these are behaviors often aligned and associated with sexual harassment, such a policy would have been significantly more beneficial to targets of sexual harassment than the prior example.

Another and by far the most common form in which personnel managers integrated the issue into existing policies was adding a document solely focusing on sexual harassment.[388] In their memo distributing their new sexual harassment policy, the Prudential Insurance Company of America explained their reasoning for singling out this issue: "Remember, it's just one more part of our overall EEO policy, we don't mean to exaggerate it, but since it is new and since it is receiving a lot of attention, we'd like to set the record straight."[389]

When employers heeded feminist and governmental advice to institute internal policy and procedures, their material was often colored by feminist theory. Throughout my research, I obtained sexual harassment policies of eighteen corporations published in or before 1982. Of these, only three were circulated before the release of the EEOC guidelines in 1980.[390] The policies assembled here vary in size and come from organizations representing various sectors, including but not limited to manufacturing, print media, tourism and the insurance sector. Neither the sector nor the organization's size, however, seem to have factored into the content or form of the policy or procedure. All but one of these policies – Caesar's Board-

---

386 Amann: Letter from Amann as a representative of Lockheed Electronics Company; cf. HSBC Equal Employment Opportunity, June 1ˢᵗ, 1987, HBSC Archives, Folder 6-NA0078001 Human Resources Guidelines and Procedures.

387 Universal Manufacturing Corporation: Rules We Live By. Pamphlet, 1981. In addition, to this code of rules, Universal Manufacturing Corporation enacted a policy specifically addressing sexual harassment in July of 1981.

388 Playboy: Sexual Harassment Policy Statement, File 012 in the New Jersey Department of Community Affairs survey on sexual harassment, March 1982, BCA, Research on Women Records, Box 96, Folder Bell Laboratories Corporate Study; Becton Dickinson and Company: Sexual Harassment on the Job, in: Equal Opportunity Manual Procedures, File 009 in the New Jersey Department of Community Affairs survey on sexual harassment, undated [pre-1982]; AIRCO. Inc: Sexual Harassment Policy (January 1ˢᵗ, 1981, in: Personnel Manual, p. 17; BCA Research on Women Records, Box 96, Folder Bell Laboratories Corporate Study.

389 Prudential Insurance Company: Memorandum Sexual Harassment.

390 Cruise & Faster Corporation: Sexual Harassment, in: Employee Manual, 1981/1982, BCA, Research on Women Records, Box 96, Folder Bell Laboratories Corporate Study.

walk Regency Hotel Casino – show some form of feminist influence in their approach.[391]

I do not argue that these policies are themselves feminist, but that they were in some form inspired by the feminist framing of this issue. Whether this is due to the feminist leadership of the EEOC, to the extensive feminist media campaigns on the issue, or due to WWI's advice and information packets targeted at employers is not discernable in most cases. Nevertheless, the influence is palpable. The following paragraphs shall highlight feminist elements in these very early corporate policies.

Despite the differences in size and sector, the established policies in many cases are similar. However, when defining sexual harassment, clear differences between the policies devised pre-1980 and post-1980 can be observed. While the latter relied on the EEOC guidelines as a template, the former had no such guidance. Cruise & Faster Corporation proclaimed in their policy statement from 1980 that "it is not easy to define precisely what harassment is." They continued to explain that sexual harassment "certainly includes unwelcome sexual advances, requests for sexual favors and other verbal or physical conduct of a sexual nature such as uninvited touching or sexually-related comments."[392] Strikingly, Playboy Inc., another employer with a policy preceding the guidelines, used this identical wording.[393] The third employer with such an early policy, an insurance company which provided its information anonymously, was the same in content, if not in wording.

The definition of these three companies may ring familiar to the attentive reader who will be reminded of the definition provided by the Working Women's Institute in 1975. As with that early definition, these policies interpreted any unwelcome sexual behavior as sexual harassment. Neither definition specified that in order to amount to sexual harassment the questionable behavior had to negatively affect the target's working conditions. WWI amended their definition just months after their initial publication at the speak-out in Ithaca in 1975. Nevertheless, the similarity between this first WWI definition and the Cruise & Faster, Playboy, and the anonymous insurance company's policies are noteworthy. It seems likely that these corporations used the same source for information when devising their policies. However, even if this resemblance was purely coin-

---

391 Caesar's Boardwalk Regency Hotel Casino
392 Ibid.; Playboy: Sexual Harassment Policy Statement, 1982.
393 Identical wording in Playboy and Cruise & Faster Corporation Policies; Same approach in Anonymous Insurance Company: Policy Statement on Employee Harassment, pre-1983; Amann: Letter from Amann as a representative of Lockheed Electronics Company, Inc.

cidental the inclusion of the terms "unwelcome" and "uninvited" relate to the feminist framing of the issue centered around the targets experience.

Sexual harassment policies devised after 1980 were heavily influenced by the EEOC guidelines. In my sample, thirteen of the fifteen policies published after the release of the preliminary guidelines were shaped by the EEOC guidelines. The New York City Health and Hospital Corporation sent out a copy of the guidelines in their entirety to all its employees. Many more organizations opted to quote or paraphrase the EEOC in their policy statements. Some gave credit to the EEOC by citing the agency,[394] others wrote statements clearly inspired by the policy, paraphrasing or simplifying the text and at times adding more concrete examples.[395]

In most policies in my sample, article *a* of the guidelines was highlighted. Article *f* covering sexual favoritism, or "discrimination against non-submitters," only appears in the script for employee training by the Prudential Insurance Company of America and is not mentioned in their policy document.[396] As shown elsewhere, the majority of the EEOC guidelines were heavily influenced by the feminist frame. However, article *f* was added as a concession to social conservatives. Thus, the citation or paraphrasing of article *a*, and the general omission of article *f* in internal company policies transferred a feminist understanding of sexual harassment into the corporate world.

While most company policies in this analysis relied heavily on the EEOC guidelines, the definitions were often supplemented with further explanations. In most cases, these additions indicated feminist information sources and a feminist understanding of the issue. Harrah's Marina, for instance, classified sexual harassment as a "power issue" in which "the victim cannot stop the behavior."[397] The assertion that sexual harassment was tied to power relations is a strong indicator of a feminist understanding of the issue. Additionally, the company proclaimed in their policy that sexual harassment was a widespread, serious prob-

---

394 Anonymous Service Industry Business: Company Policy on Sexual Harassment, File 011 in the New Jersey Department of Community Affairs survey on sexual harassment no date post-1980/pre-1983, BCA, Research on Women Records, Box 96, Folder Bell Laboratories Corporate study; Prudential Insurance Company: Memorandum Sexual Harassment; Harrah's Marina: Harrah's Guide to Preventing Sexual Harassment, pre-1983, BCA, Research on Women Records, Box 96, Folder Bell Laboratories Corporate Study.

395 Resorts International Hotel Casino: Sexual Harassment Inter Office Correspondence, 1981; Hoffman – La Roche Inc.: Equal Opportunity Policy, 1982; Becton Dickinson and Company: Equal Employment Handbook, pre-1982; Universal Manufacturing Corporation: Personnel Policy Procedure, 1981.

396 Prudential Insurance Company: Memorandum Sexual Harassment.

397 Harrah's Marina: Fact Sheet on Sexual Harassment, pre-1983.

lem, warranting the company's attention.[398] Likewise, two separate businesses in the service industry, wishing to remain anonymous, emphasize in their respective policies that "complaints of sexual harassment are not merely personal matters."[399] Again an insistence on a systemic rather than personal nature of the problem was inherently a feminist understanding of the issue.

Additionally, the feminist understanding of sexual harassment hinged on the behavior being one-sided and unwelcome. Thus, per definition, consensual relationships were not classified as sexual harassment. This contradicted social conservative voices who often equated sexual harassment with changing sexual attitudes, "a lack of morality,"[400] and consensual workplace relationships. Thus, by explicitly stating that "the purpose of this policy is not to regulate our employee's personal morality" Playboy and Cruise & Faster Corporation explicitly reject the social conservative call to vilify any extra-marital sexual relationships. Harrah's Marina, too, agrees with this, stating that "the company does not wish to dictate morals or become involved in the personal lives of its employees [but] recognizes its responsibility to provide an atmosphere which is free from [sexual harassment]." This "responsibility" according to the Harrah's Marina policy was both an ethical and a legal one.[401]

In 1982, there was still an ongoing legal debate on what instances could be considered sexual harassment, to what extent sexual harassment was an employer's responsibility, and even, if sexual harassment should be understood as sex discrimination. Despite this controversy, Harrah's Marina was not alone in recognizing a legal responsibility to eliminate sexual harassment from their workplace. The majority of businesses in my sample accepted feminist assertions that sexual harassment was "against the law."[402] Policies implemented at Ross Systems Inc. and Hoffman-La Roche Inc. quote from the EEOC guidelines but instead of citing the agency, present this definition as "the law."[403] Most other policies use the term

---

398 Ibid.

399 Anonymous Service Industry Business: Company Policy on Sexual Harassment, pre-1983.

400 Schlafly: Positive Woman.

401 Harrah's Marina: Guide to Preventing Sexual Harassment, pre-1983.

402 Examples include but are not limited to: Ross Systems, Inc.: Policy Regarding sexual Harassment, 1982; Resorts International Hotel Casino: Sexual Harassment Inter Office Correspondence, 1981; Hoffman – La Roche Inc.: Equal Opportunity Policy, 1982; Becton Dickinson and Company: Equal Employment Handbook, pre-1983; Cesar's Boardwalk Regency Hotel Casino: Human Resources Notice, 1981; Pyonzeck: Statement of Policy, pre-1983; Harrah's Marina: Fact Sheet on Sexual Harassment, pre-1983; The Prudential Insurance Company: Memorandum Sexual Harassment, 1980.

403 Ross Systems, Inc.: Policy Regarding sexual Harassment, 1982.

"illegal" in connection with sexual harassment,[404] or refer their reader to Title VII of the Civil Rights Act. The Universal Manufacturing Corporation, in their information packet specifically addressed to management and supervisors on how to handle sexual harassment complaints, is the most detailed of the policies analyzed.

> When President Lyndon B. Johnson signed into law the Title VII of the Civil Rights Act – Equal Employment Opportunity Act in 1964, a series of laws and regulations evolved that have created a substantial impact on our operating personnel policies and upon you as a manager or supervisor. You are likely to be involved in every aspect of personnel from recruitment to discharge, promotion to discipline, or assignment to transfer, etc. Your decision must be consistently fair, impartial and non-discriminatory to comply with both the intent and letter of the law regarding EEO.[405]

Universal's emphasis on the importance of complying with both the "letter" and the "intent" of the law implies the company's commitment to eradicating sexual harassment rather than attempting to avoid liability. In general, the companies' readiness to accept sexual harassment as illegal conduct in their respective statements can be interpreted both as an effort to convince their employees of the legitimacy of their policy and/or to be a result of their reliance on feminist legal consultations.

Such feminist consultations seem to have played a significant role in these companies' acceptance of employer liability. Three of these early policies explicitly acknowledge both their "moral and legal obligation to provide a work environment free of sexual harassment."[406] The Prudential Insurance Company of America in particular is explicit about the company's legal responsibility for sexual harassing behavior of their employees:

> [The company has] Employer Liability [...] with respect to sexual harassment regardless of whether the specific acts complained of were authorized or even forbidden by the employer and regardless of whether the employer knew or should have known of their occurrence. Why is the employer held strictly liable for supervisors? Because supervisors have the au-

---

404 E.g.: Anonymous Service Industry Business: Company Policy on Sexual Harassment, pre-1983; Becton Dickinson and Company: Equal Employment Handbook, pre-1983; Cesar's Boardwalk Regency Hotel Casino: Human Resources notice, 1981; Playboy: Sexual Harassment Policy Statement, 1982.
405 Universal Manufacturing Corporation: Personnel Policy Procedure, 1981.
406 Anonymous Service Industry Business: Company Policy on Sexual Harassment, pre-1983; Similar in Hoffman – La Roche Inc.: Equal Opportunity Policy, 1982, Ross Systems, Inc.: Policy Regarding sexual Harassment, 1982.

thority to make or influence personnel decision and thus, have the ability to make sexual favors a term or condition of their subordinates' employment. [...][407]

Here Prudential partially paraphrases and partially repeats verbatim the 1979 ruling of *Miller v. Bank of America*. In feminist consulting brochures this case was often used as the example of the judiciary ruling in favor of strict employer liability, when in fact this was only one case, which was not precedent setting. Thus, Prudential's reference to this specific case in a policy published three years after the *Miller* judgment was delivered,[408] indicates that the company relied on feminist legal advice.

In general, the readiness of most of these early policies to accept legal responsibility speaks to feminist influence on these policies. It is no surprise that there exists a large overlap of companies convinced of their legal responsibility to avoid sexual harassment and organizations implementing policies and procedures at a time when this was not yet the norm in corporate America. Internal policies and procedures after all were said to have a preventative effect and would give employers the chance to "ensure that a known situation does not recur."[409] Companies, convinced that they would be held responsible in a court of law, saw the immediate benefit of addressing complaints internally and preventing sexual harassment in the first place.

As WWI stressed in each of their pamphlets directed at employers: Accessibility of the policy is the first step to prevention.[410] By having written rather than oral policies, the companies in this sample have already taken the first step in making their respective policies serviceable. Most policies in the sample addressed "all employees."[411] Of course, the policy statements themselves are not an adequate source to judge their actual dissemination among the staff. However, there are some references in the policy statements that indicate the intent of a company to truly make the document accessible. Several companies affirmed within their policy that there was a need for "every member of staff [to] read

---

407 Prudential Insurance Company: Memorandum Sexual Harassment.
408 Ibid.
409 Hoffman – La Roche Inc.: Equal Opportunity Policy, 1982.
410 Meyer: Sexual Harassment, p. 74.
411 E. g. Resorts International Hotel Casino: Sexual Harassment Inter Office Correspondence, 1981; Anonymous Service Industry Business: Company Policy on Sexual Harassment, pre-1983; Bell Laboratories: Policy on Sexual Harassment, pre-1980, BCA, Research on Women Records, Box 96, Folder Bell Laboratories Corporate Study; Becton Dickinson and Company: Equal Employment Handbook, pre-1983; Universal Manufacturing Corporation: Personnel Policy Procedure, 1981.

and understand this policy."[412] To accomplish this, Resorts International Hotel Casino, a company with a high proportion of Spanish speaking employees, provided their policy statement in both English and Spanish.[413] Similarly, a midsized business in the service industry (which wished to remain anonymous), specified that "this statement shall be published on every bulletin board."[414] Lastly, Becton Dickinson and Company insisted, within their policy, that the document be discussed in the company's established Equal Opportunity training.

The inclusion of the issue in existing employee seminars is especially interesting as I have found very few references to in-house training on sexual harassment within the material collected. The two major exceptions to this are the Prudential Insurance Company of America and Bell Laboratories. The latter was one of the first companies WWI collaborated with and much of WWI's advice to corporations was based on their work with Bell Laboratories.[415] Thus, it comes as no surprise that when Bell Laboratories began in-house seminars early in the decade, this training was closely modeled after WWI workshops and seminars. For their workshops and more general education on sexual harassment within their company, Bell Laboratories developed their own company specific material, including pamphlets, and even a thirty-minute film entitled "sexual harassment: it's not a part of the job."[416] This material was devised throughout WWI's year-long consultation with the company and thus its content overlaps significantly with that printed by WWI.

The Prudential Insurance Company also devised their own internal workshops but rather than developing their own material, the company made use of external resources. Specifically, Prudential included the short film *The Workplace Hustle* into their in-house seminar.[417] In the script for the workshop, the teacher is advised to introduce the film as follows:

> Since it wasn't produced by Prudential, by definition it's not perfect, but we think it does a good job of presenting the problem of sexual harassment. It addresses the subject through a series of vignettes, the case study of a female vice president of a Financial Institution who

412 Anonymous Service Industry Business: Company Policy on Sexual Harassment, pre-1983.
413 Resorts International Hotel Casino: Sexual Harassment Inter Office Correspondence, 1981.
414 Anonymous Service Industry Business: Company Policy on Sexual Harassment, pre-1983.
415 WWI: Institute Six Month Report, July 1980; Working Women's Institute General Program, 1981.
416 Bell Laboratories: Policy on Sexual Harassment, pre-1980.
417 Asner, Edward et al.: The Workplace Hustle: A Film About Sexual Harassment of Working Women, 1980.

was the victim of sexual harassment, and several interviews with Lin Farley who is the author of 'sexual shakedown:' She also coined the Phrase 'sexual harassment.'[418]

The film, produced by Clark Communications Inc., in 1980, was one of the first of the genre: A short film to be sold to companies to use as part of their anti-sexual harassment seminars. Lin Farley at this point in time, was no longer affiliated with the Working Women's Institute and as such the film was not a project connected to the Institute, but rather a for-profit production. However, Lin Farley, a founding member of WWI, author of one of the first books on sexual harassment, and regular expert witness in court, did not abandon her feminist understanding of the subject matter. Thus, this film, which heavily relies on Farley's expertise and explanations, teaches a feminist framing of sexual harassment. As the film is a large part of Prudential's seminar, Prudential, despite relying on internal training rather than working with WWI, taught sexual harassment from a predominantly feminist perspective. As is exemplified by Bell Laboratories and the Prudential Insurance Company, in 1982 the devising of internal corporate training on sexual harassment did not yet mean a rejection of the feminist framing.

As was made abundantly clear by WWI, a policy could not be effective, if it was not accompanied by a "consistent," "fair," and "well-known" grievance procedure.[419] While few policies in this sample have an additional document outlining the exact steps of a grievance, most policies at the very least promise an investigation of any charges and dedicate an internal contact person responsible for receiving complaints.[420] Most companies, including Playboy, the Universal Manufacturing Corporation, and Hoffman-LaRoche, specified not an individual person by name but the office they hold.[421] This was always an office associated with the

---

418 The Prudential Insurance Company: Memorandum Sexual Harassment, 1980.
419 Sauvigné: Sexual Harassment is Against the Law, p. 2.
420 E. g. Resorts International Hotel Casino: Sexual Harassment Inter Office Correspondence, 1981; Anonymous Service Industry Business: Company Policy on Sexual Harassment, pre-1983; Hoffman – La Roche Inc.: Equal Opportunity Policy, 1982; Bell Laboratories: Policy on Sexual Harassment, pre-1980; Anonymous Insurance Company: Policy Statement on Employee Harassment, 1982; Becton Dickinson and Company: Equal Employment Handbook, pre-1983; Playboy: Sexual Harassment Policy Statement, 1982; Universal Manufacturing Corporation: Personnel Policy Procedure, 1981; The Prudential Insurance Company: Memorandum Sexual Harassment, 1980.
421 Hoffman – La Roche Inc.: Equal Opportunity Policy, 1982; Bell Laboratories: Policy on Sexual Harassment, pre-1980; Anonymous Insurance Company: Policy Statement on Employee Harassment, 1982; Becton Dickinson and Company: Equal Employment Handbook, pre-1983, Playboy: Sexual Harassment Policy Statement, 1982; Universal Manufacturing Corporation: Personnel

personnel department, such as the Affirmative Action Coordinator or the Equal Employment Officer. The intent here was to provide a contact person knowledgeable about the legal situation and the company policy while at the same time being removed from the day-to-day company hierarchy, thus limiting conflicts of interest. In addition to complainants being sent to the companies' respective personnel offices to file official grievances, the majority of the policies analyzed, explicitly makes all managers and supervisors responsible for the proper enforcement of the policy.[422] In many of these cases, managers and supervisors are reminded "to apply in a fair and consistent manner the policies."[423]

For the sake of fairness, every single policy in this sample promises a "complete" and "timely" investigation of complaints.[424] Due to the limitations of these sources, it is impossible to know whether complaints were indeed always followed by such an investigation. The sources do show that those policies specifying how to initiate an investigation follow feminist advice.

First, Bell Laboratories and the Prudential Insurance Company of America included in their grievance procedure that "a complainant should be asked for permission to investigate."[425] Bell Laboratories states that if the allegations are against someone with previous complaints, the "counselor" should "seek permission" to go forward with an investigation.[426] In this case, it is unclear who has the final say on whether an investigation will be initiated. In most cases, however, these companies agreed that a complaint must not necessarily lead to an investigation, if this went against the target's explicit wishes. Retaining the victims' agency rather than forcing them through an investigation was the course of action recommended by WWI in their consultations.

Policy Procedure, 1981; The Prudential Insurance Company: Memorandum Sexual Harassment, 1980.
422 See for example: Anonymous Insurance Company: Policy Statement on Employee Harassment, Universal Manufacturing Corporation: Personnel Policy Procedure, 1981; The Prudential Insurance Company: Memorandum Sexual Harassment, 1980; Harrah's Marina: Fact Sheet on Sexual Harassment, pre-1983; Harrah's Marina: Harrah's Guide to Preventing Sexual Harassment, pre-1983; Anonymous Service Industry Business: Company Policy on Sexual Harassment, pre-1983.
423 Hoffman – La Roche Inc.: Equal Opportunity Policy, 1982; also: Universal Manufacturing Corporation: Personnel Policy Procedure, 1981.
424 AIRCO. Inc: Sexual Harassment Policy, 1981; also: Anonymous Insurance Company: Policy Statement on Employee Harassment, Universal Manufacturing Corporation: Personnel Policy Procedure, 1981; The Prudential Insurance Company: Memorandum Sexual Harassment, 1980; Harrah's Marina: Fact Sheet on Sexual Harassment, pre-1983; Harrah's Marina: Harrah's Guide to Preventing Sexual Harassment, pre-1983; Bell Laboratories: Policy on Sexual Harassment, pre-1980; Resorts International Hotel Casino: Sexual Harassment Inter Office Correspondence, 1981.
425 Prudential Insurance Company: Memorandum Sexual Harassment, 1980.
426 Bell Laboratories: Policy on Sexual Harassment, pre-1980.

Second, the WWI advised that an investigation could be initiated without a complaint. Thus, two companies in this sample, the Universal Manufacturing Corporation and Harrah's Marina, emphasized that action should be taken, even if there was no official complaint by the victim. A manager was not absolved from acting simply because the victim had not filed an official complaint. This mirrored WWI's assertion that the lack of a complaint did not relieve the company from its legal responsibility.

In order to secure their respective policy's effectiveness, every business in this sample promised that the confirmation of allegations would be followed by "disciplinary action, up to and including dismissal."[427] In regards to disciplinary action, WWI encouraged "non-confrontational conversations," "self-reflection," and education over punishment. Additionally, according to WWI, conflicts were best resolved at the lowest level possible. Harrah's Marina in its policy follows this advice to the letter, stating that:

> The purpose of the law is not vengeance, but to stop the offensive behavior. [...] The company also recognizes that the use of preventative measures is the best method of dealing with the issue of sexual harassment. [...] The vast majority of people don't really want to hurt each other. Once a harasser knows that what he/she is doing really hurts another person, he/she will normally stop performing the offensive behavior. [...] If the individual exhibiting such behavior is one of your employees, you [as the manager] should stop any such behavior and hold a counselling session with the individual committing the act. [...] Assess your own behavior to make sure you are not committing any act which could be considered sexual harassment.[428]

It is assumed that the individual harasser is unaware of the consequences of "his/her" behavior. Although phrased in a gender-neutral way, the acceptance of accidental harassment alludes to feminist assertions of gender specific socialization as one cause of sexual harassment. The policy holds the individual responsible for their actions but acknowledges that he/she is not culpable for the entire systemic problem of sexual harassment. The policy argues that everybody, managers included, needs to educate themselves on the matter and root out the problem.[429]

---

427 Resorts International Hotel Casino: Sexual Harassment Inter Office Correspondence, 1981; also: Anonymous Insurance Company: Policy Statement on Employee Harassment, 1982; Anonymous Service Industry Business: Company Policy on Sexual Harassment, pre-1983; Hoffman – La Roche Inc.: Equal Opportunity Policy, 1982.

428 Harrah's Marina: Fact Sheet on Sexual Harassment, pre-1983; Harrah's Marina: Harrah's Guide to Preventing Sexual Harassment, pre-1983; see also: Universal Manufacturing Corporation: Personnel Policy Procedure, 1981.

429 See similar argumentation at Universal Manufacturing Corporation: Personnel Policy Procedure, 1981: "Most employment discrimination is not caused by outright or flagrant bias. It is

Moreover, Harrah's Marina proclaims their dedication as an institution to "taking corrective action,"[430] in order to "ensure that the work environment is free of this form of discrimination."[431]

It seems that, when, in the early 1980s, an employer decided to implement a written policy on sexual harassment, they incorporated feminist advice – either intentionally or simply because this advice was the most readily available. Thus, I conclude that the policies analyzed are proof that WWI successfully influenced and worked with employers. However, in addition to the numerous acknowledgments of the feminist framing and the clear rejection of the social conservative frame, these policies already showed isolated instances of a new understanding of sexual harassment. Declaring sexual harassment "not appropriate in a professional environment," repeatedly referencing lower productivity and higher costs as a result of harassment and using non-gendered language when referring to both victim and harasser are all elements present in these early policies. They are also core elements of a new framing of sexual harassment which would emerge and solidify in the following two decades: the management frame.

usually the result of attitudes of which we are not fully aware. Managers and supervisors must learn to detect discriminatory attitudes in themselves and their subordinates. When these attitudes effect on the job behavior, a positive effort must be taken to change behavior. All employees must understand that discrimination or harassment cannot be tolerated in the workplace."

430 Anonymous Insurance Company: Policy Statement on Employee Harassment, 1982; AIRCO. Inc: Sexual Harassment Policy, 1981.

431 Becton Dickinson and Company: Equal Employment Handbook, pre-1983.

Part II
Institutionalization and Professionalization, 1980–1998

Digital's definition is clear –
[sexual] harassment refers to conduct or behavior which is personally offensive, threatening or impairs morale or work effectiveness of employees.[1]

This definition was not that of feminist organizations or that of the Equal Employment Opportunity Commission. "Digital's definition," published in 1991 in Digital Equipment Corporation's (DEC) employee newsletter portrayed a new understanding of sexual harassment. Contrary to social conservative spokespersons, the main-stream press, and many employers a decade prior, the company did not underestimate or trivialize the issue. The discussion of sexual harassment in the context of a private organization shows that DEC considered the issue worth addressing and regulating internally. However, this definition did not rely on the Civil Rights Act or the concept of sex discrimination. Instead, it indicated the personal nature of the issue and highlighted the importance of "work effectiveness." "Digital's definition" is a prime example of what I call the "management framework" of sexual harassment, which developed from 1980 onwards and was established by 1998.

In Part II, I discuss the institutionalization of external and internal policies and grievance procedures, the professionalization of the staff involved, and the specifics of the newly developing management frame from 1980 until 1998. Due to the legal uncertainty in the years between the release of the EEOC guidelines in 1980 and the first Supreme Court decision regarding the issue in 1986, it would be counterproductive to designate a clear-cut caesura. Instead, the early 1980s must be seen as a transitionary phase in which feminist activists were still heavily involved but the government, unions, and employers had already begun a process of professionalization regarding sexual harassment compliance. Therefore, chronologically speaking, Part I and Part II of this book overlap slightly. In contrast, 1998 marks a clear caesura ending Part II. The Supreme Court decisions in *Bulington Industries, Inc. v. Ellerth* and *Faragher v. City of Boca Raton* significantly influenced the dynamics between the state, employers, and employees.

---

1 Digital Electronics Corporation: Addressing Sexual Harassment in the Work Environment, in: Personnel Perspectives Digital Newsletter, 1991, p. 12.

During his tenure, President Jimmy Carter had staffed several agencies with personnel committed to civil rights and affirmative action programs,[2] and had appointed 262 federal judges with lifetime tenure. These appointments ensured that the federal courts remained relatively liberal during the otherwise conservative 1980s.[3] Eleanor Holms Norton would head the EEOC until the close of 1981 at which point the change in presidential administration made itself noticeable with several adjustments to the agency. President Ronald Reagan had been elected on a platform of deregulation and in his inaugural address he famously proclaimed that government was the problem rather than the solution to America's economic woes.[4]

Mainstream press had adopted the term *sexual harassment* by the late 1970s.[5] In the early 1980s, editors no longer presumed the necessity of defining the term to ensure their readers' comprehension. According to Working Women's Institute's founding member Peggy Crull, by the close of the 1970s "every women's magazine had run a piece [on sexual harassment]." Mary Bralove, writing for *The Wall Street Journal* in 1976, commented that "[t]hese days the wall of silence surrounding the issue of sexual harassment is gradually crumbling."[6] It was not, however, until the early 1990s that both specialized and mainstream media repeatedly discussed sexual harassment.[7]

In the fall of 1991, Anita Hill's allegations against Clarence Thomas shifted the issue from the sidelines into the national spotlight.[8] The public became riveted by what *The New York Times* described as a "Theater of Pain."[9] The Senate Judiciary Committee Hearings were televised and drew unprecedented attention from the

2 Baker: Women's Movement, p. 138; Aberbach, Joel D.: Transforming the Presidency. The Administration of Ronald Reagan, in: Ronald Reagan and the 1980s. Receptions, Policies, Legacies (Studies of the Americas), ed. by Cheryl Hudson and Gareth Davies, New York 2008, pp. 197–201.
3 Federal Judicial Center: Biographical Directory of Article III Federal Judges 1789-Present, Judges appointed by Jimy Carter.
4 Levin: Fractured Republic, p. 73; Heclo, Hugh: Ronald Reagan and the American Public Philosophy, in: The Reagan Residency. Pragmatic Conservatism and its Legacies, ed. by W. Elliot Brownlee and Hugh Davis Graham, Lawrence, KS 2003, pp. 27–29; Adamson, Machael R.: Reagan and the Economy. Business and Labor. Deregulation and Regulation, in: A Companion to Ronald Reagan (Wiley Blackwell Companions to History), ed. by Andrew L. Johns, Chichester et al. 2015, p. 149.
5 Arriola: Construction Industry, p. 45.
6 Nemy: Speak Out, p. 38; Bralove: Cold Shoulder, p. 1.
7 Arriola: Construction Industry, p. 45.
8 For Hill's opening statement, see: Committee on the Judiciary, Nomination of Judge Clarence Thomas, pp. 36–40.
9 Rosenthal, Andrew: Theater of Pain. A Terrible Wrong Has Been Done, but to whom? in: The New York Times (Oct 13, 1991), p. E1.

American public. Roughly a decade prior to Thomas' confirmation hearings, Hill had been a lawyer working under Thomas both at the U.S. Department of Education and at the Equal Employment Opportunity Commission.

Hill alleged that during the time she worked for Thomas, she was continually confronted with his sexually harassing behavior. She explained that after she had repeatedly rejected his invitations to "go out socially," Thomas began to speak graphically about sexual matters during work hours. According to her testimony, topics included "his own sexual prowess," "descriptions of his anatomy," as well as pornographic material he had viewed. Thomas vehemently denied the accusations, referring to his happy marriage and alluding that Hill had propositioned him rather than vice versa. In the course of a three-day hearing, from October 11th to 13th, 1991, Anita Hill, Clarence Thomas and several witnesses answered the Committee's questioning.[10] Thomas was confirmed by the Senate as Supreme Court justice on October 15th, 1991, with a narrow vote of 52–48.

In an interview in 2021 – thirty years after the hearings – Hill asserted, "that even though Clarence Thomas was confirmed, I do believe that what I did was effective because it opened the conversation publicly in a way that had never been done before."[11] This was an accurate assessment. The hearings were aired live on cable, network TV, and the radio, reaching an estimated audience of 27 million homes.[12] For many Americans this was the closest they had ever concerned themselves with the matter of sexual harassment. The vague opinions they had previously formed, were now intensely discussed, examined, and cemented in the wake of national press coverage on the hearings.

In order to substantiate this point, I conducted a brief quantitative analysis of articles mentioning the term sexual harassment in the several mainstream American daily newspapers. *The New York Times* published 46 articles in 1981 and remained in this range, never exceeding 62 articles a year until 1991, the year of Anita Hill's testimony, when a total of 314 articles mark a clear caesura in the amount of media attention given to the topic. These numbers remain high (over 250 articles), even after the initial focus on the Thomas confirmation hearings subsided throughout the decade. Similar numbers can be found for other American newspapers. While more conservative papers, such as the *Wallstreet Journal*

---

10 Committee on the Judiciary: Nomination of Judge Clarence Thomas.

11 Gross, Terry: Anita Hill Started a Conversation About Sexual Harassment. She's Not Done Yet, in: NPR, September 28th, 2021.

12 Rucinski, Dianne: The Polls – A Review. Rush to Judgment? Fast Reaction Polls in the Anita Hill-Clarence Thomas Controversy, in: The Public Opinion Quarterly 57/4 (Winter 1993), p. 575.

and *The Chicago Tribune* generally published less on sexual harassment, the number of articles nevertheless increased significantly in and after 1991.[13]

By 1991, the notion that an individual suspected of sexual harassment could be appointed to the U.S. Supreme Court incited considerable public outrage.[14] The *Hill-Thomas Hearings*, as they became known, went down in many history books as a, if not *the*, defining moment in the fight against sexual harassment. For many historians, they present a break so significant that the hearings mark either the beginning or the end point in their works.[15] While I have consciously chosen not to follow in these footsteps, this should not be read as a denial of the gravity of the event. Several developments, such as the passing of the revised Civil Rights Act in 1991, the rising number of complaints with the EEOC in the following year, and the increase in employers' interest in the topic can indeed be connected to the highly influential hearings. I contend, however, that the Hill-Thomas Hearings, rather than instigating change, served as a catalyst for developments that were already under way.

This holds true for the public perception of sexual harassment. While the hearings significantly increased awareness of the issue, they did not change the frameworks that were already in place. The hearings had a definitive quantitative effect in increasing the number of Americans who had heard and thought about the phrase but did not directly provoke a change in the definition of sexual harassment. Due to the polarizing nature of the hearings, sexual harassment was considered either through the social conservative or the feminist lens.

Beyond the public spotlight, however, a new framing of sexual harassment had been developing. Feminists had succeeded in involving the federal government and had encouraged employers to act on the issue of sexual harassment. In doing so, feminists advocated for internal policies, training, and grievance procedures, which they assumed would spread their narrative to employers and employees alike. However, as employers took an interest in the topic of sexual har-

---

13 Using the ProQuest Historical Newspapers I searched for the keywords "sexual harassment" in titles and lead paragraphs of articles, letters to the editor, editorials: The Washington Post (1975: 6, 1976: 6, 1979: 23, 1980: 54, 1990: 109, 1991: 272). The Chicago Tribune (1975: 2, 1976: 1, 1979: 17, 1980: 48, 1990: 107, 1991: 652) Wallstreet Journal (1976: 2, 1979: 2, 1980: 10, 1990: 12, 1991: 111).
14 Wilkins, David B.: Presumed Crazy. The Structure of Argument in Hill/Thomas Hearings, Southern California Law Review 65/3 (1992), p. 1518; Wicker, Tom: Blaming Anita Hill, in: The New York Times (Oct 10, 1991), p. A27.
15 See for instance: McDonald: Framing Sexual Harassment, pp. 95–103; Modleski, Tania: Breaking Silence, or an Old Wives' Tale. Sexual Harassment and the Legitimation Crisis, in: Mass Culture and Everyday Life, ed. by Peter Gibian, New York – London 1997, pp. 219–232; Skaine, Rosemarie: Power and Gender. Issues in Sexual Dominance and Harassment, Jefferson, NC – London 1996.

assment, they increasingly assumed discursive authority on the subject matter. This gradual process led to the establishment of the management framework and shall be the overarching theme for Part II.

In the following chapter, I will discuss union and federal action which led to the establishment of institutionalized grievance procedures for victims of sexual harassment. By providing a port-of-call to targets, these institutions, to varying degrees, encouraged employees to report harassing behavior. As the opportunities to register complaints increased, so did the risk of financial damages to a business. Additionally, these institutions established direct channels of communication with employers and appealed to a company's responsibility to employ internal policies and procedures. These outside pressures made many employers acutely aware of the subject matter.

In their quest for low-risk solutions, employers began turning to professionals rather than to feminist activists for advice. As I shall demonstrate in Chapter Five, both corporate lawyers and management consultants began specializing in the issue of sexual harassment. However, the two professions underwent separate training, diverged in their *modi operandi*, and drew legitimacy for their expertise from different sources. Lawyers advised employers to fight in the courts. Management consultants, on the other hand, argued that an internal policy with an attached grievance procedure would allow employers to intercept complaints before they turned into lawsuits.[16] Despite lacking any statistical foundation or judicial approval, businesses gravitated towards the latter.

Encouraged by the establishment of external complaint procedures, as well as by the professionalization of experts on the topic, employers instituted internal grievance systems. These procedures, along with policies, training programs, and informational material were devised by management consultants. Instead of following either the feminist or social conservative framing of sexual harassment, the profession reconceptualized sexual harassment and developed a new framework. In the second part of Chapter Five, I examine the 'management frame' by analyzing several handbooks, articles in business magazines, and training videos. Contrary to its counterparts, the management frame lacked a strong ideological component, and instead highlighted the economic risk sexual harassment posed for an organization.

---

16 Dobbin: Equal Opportunity, p. 192.

4 A Port-Of-Call:
The Institutionalization of Complaint Procedures in Unions and the Federal Government

When Carmita Wood in 1975 decided to fight against the harassment she experienced, she turned to feminist colleagues.[17] The women she enlisted formed an organization, invented terminology, and planned protests. Wood took these measures, not because she was unhappy with the standardized process in the government or her place of work, but because there was no such process.[18] This changed within the time period discussed in the following pages. In this chapter, I will present how unions, the EEOC, and the judiciary began offering institutionalized processes for filing complaints. I posit that by offering grievance procedures outside of the workplace, unions, and the federal government increased the pressure for employers to instate policies and procedures on a company level. By doing so, these institutions inadvertently created fertile conditions for the development of the management frame.

The institutionalization and subsequent publicization of complaint procedures through institutions other than the victims' place of work, was, in some instances, immediate. Other times, especially in the context of unions, it was a long and cumbersome development. This process was shaped both by the institutions themselves and by the individuals attempting to file complaints. One such individual was Interviewee 120. Her story was recorded by sociologist, Kristen R. Yount, who in the years between 1980 and 1983, interviewed male and female miners about working conditions and gender relations in the nation's coal mines.[19]

These interviews prove to be an especially valuable source as the mining industry repeatedly found itself entangled with accusations of sexual harassment. "Initiation rites, in which a new miner must be stripped and greased before entering the mines" were reawakened after lying dormant for at least a generation; cigarette searches were often said to be "overly thorough" when they involved a female miner; and in 1983 alone, there were "three cases pending against miners who drilled 'peepholes' in women's showers."[20] In the 1970s, mining, even compared to industries such as construction or manufacturing was heavily male dom-

---

17 The reader was familiarized with Carmita Wood's story in Part I.
18 At the time it was still named Working Women United, refer to Chapter One for more information.
19 Kristen R. Yount Papers, 1980–2004, Harvard Schlesinger Library.
20 Churchman, Deborah: Sexual Harassment a Continuing Employment Challenge, in: Mountain Life and Work. The Magazine of the Appalachian South (July/August 1984), p. 10.

inated. According to the United Mine Workers of America, until 1973 "not a single woman" was employed as a miner.[21] Due to the distinct lack of female miners, mines had been targeted by federal affirmative action policies in the mid-1970s. Nevertheless, the number of female miners remained low and sex discrimination in the hiring process as well as during employment persisted.[22] Yount's interviews give a unique insight into the every-day life of female miners.

Interviewee 120's story, told in 1983, illustrates several aspects I will discuss in the following chapter. Note, however, that her account does not present an anomaly. In fact, she makes a fitting example precisely because her story is representative of many others recorded in these interviews.[23] At the time of the interview, Interviewee 120 was one of twenty women working at Deer Creek Mine in the state of Utah. Initially, she had trouble getting hired, not because she lacked qualifications, but because, as the company asserted, "there wasn't room in the bathhouse." She explained "they didn't have room for another woman [even though] there was very few working there when I started."[24]

When Interviewee 120 was hired a year later she was elated. She enjoyed the physical labor and her pay was significantly higher compared to any of her former jobs.[25] However, four years into working at Deer Creek, she experienced an attempted rape.

> After I was hired [...] I never had any problem. And things went really well. And then over a year ago I had an attempted rape on my person there by one of their new bosses. [...] He forced me up against the wall. [...] And he did it in front of the, uh like I say these other people were there. [...] if he would do this in front of other people, what would he ever do if he caught me alone. And I was terrified of him. I was flat terrified. And j [sic], almost quit my job because of it.[26]

Quitting was not an option for the mother of four. She decided to take immediate steps.

On that same day, she made three official reports. First, she went directly to the mine's superintendent, Jimmy Atwood:

21 Karwoski, Susan Anne: Women Miners Show Strength at Annual Conference, in: Mountain Life and Work. The Magazine of the Appalachian South (July/August 1984), p. 6.
22 White, Connie et al.: Sexual Harassment in the Coal Industry. A Survey of Women Miners. The Coal Employment Project, Tennessee 1981, HSL, Feminist Ephemera Collection, Box 8, Folder 12 Sexual Harassment 1980.
23 Yount: Interview 120, 1983.
24 Ibid., p. 1.
25 Ibid.
26 Ibid., pp. 2f.

[H]e asked me what happened and I told him and he went out and interviewed the two witnesses, the dispatcher and a parts runner who saw it. And they told him almost word for word what I had [...]. And he told me he would get back with me.[27]

Second, she handed her union representative and acting president, Mel Larson, a written grievance to file on her behalf.

I asked him to read it and say now is this all right. And he said that was just fine. And he took it in and he handed it in [...].[28]

Her third and last stop that day was the police station. She filed charges against her attacker and was told that she "did the right thing [in coming to the station]."[29] Her intention in making these complaints was straight forward: "to make sure that that would never happen again."[30]

When the police did not arrest the man in question and nothing came of the criminal investigation, she was not surprised.[31] Her disappointment was much more pronounced when she did not receive the support she had expected from her employer. After her superintendent, Jimmy Atwood, had told her, "he would get back to [her]," she "thought it would be resolved and taken care of." She was wrong. In fact, in her interview, she described the company's attitude as "the worst part of [it]." Shortly after making her complaint, Atwood called her into a meeting and "threatened to sue [her] with the company lawyers if [she] pursued it."[32] Yount asked her for more details, yielding the following exchange:

120: And that [company's threat to sue], I mean to me was just even more degrading and humiliating. Not, not only did it happen and not only did they know it and talked to witnesses who seen it, then I was threatened, if I tried to do anything to protect myself that I would be sued.

PO: On what grounds did they say they were going to sue you?

120: I don't know. [...] He [alleged attacker] denied it and he said that he was pushed into me.

[...]

120: I should have probably went [sic] and got a lawyer right away. [...] I mean I never expected Jimmy Atwood to talk to me, to me like that [...]. I mean [...] when they sit right there and try to call you a liar and act like this never happened and tell you that if you pursue it,

---

27 Ibid., p. 4.
28 Ibid., p. 9.
29 Ibid., p. 8.
30 Ibid., p. 4.
31 Ibid., p. 8.
32 Ibid., pp. 2–4.

> you're fighting company lawyers, [...] it's just overwhelming. I mean the first place you're, you're scared, you're still not over the shock of what's, uh happened to you, and I mean, I mean [...] you're alone in a room full of men who don't seem to understand what rape is. I mean, it's not a joke, it's not funny [...].[33]

Interviewee 120 had not announced a lawsuit; she had not asked for money; she had not even insisted on her attacker's termination. She wanted the mine to "put him on opposite shift of me so I could continue to work."[34] Despite being presented with a relatively low-stakes solution, her employer escalated the situation by attempting to silence her with the threat of a lawsuit.

Realizing that she was now in a conflict, not just with the harasser, but with her employer, she was all the more dependent on support from her union. When enquiring about the status of her grievance, she discovered that her union representative, Mel Larson, had taken matters into his own hands.

> [L]ater I found out, that he [Larson] walked in and he gave it [the grievance] to Kelly Alvin, the personnel man at the time, and walked out in the hallway and [...] stood outside for a couple of minutes and turned right back in got it and said I wasn't covered. But they never told me, so I could – You have a time limit where you have to file until that time, and they never told me until the time was up that I couldn't refile.[35]

Not only did her grievance not yield any action, but her representative never filed it. Additionally, he had intentionally given her the impression that it was being processed, depriving her of the opportunity to resubmit it while still within the notice period.

When Interviewee 120 discovered that her grievance was never acted upon, she pressed Larson for an explanation:

> 120: He told me that I was not covered. The union didn't cover me like that. [...] they didn't protect me and have to because they accept my money. They have to protect me. But they felt they didn't have to.
>
> PO: Why, why did they say they didn't have to? [...]
>
> 120: They said the contract did not cover that. I was not covered in the contract.
>
> PO: As far as Attempted Rape, that wasn't part of – ?
>
> 120: Yeah. [36]

---

33 Ibid., pp. 3, 12.
34 Ibid., p. 4.
35 Ibid., p. 9.
36 Ibid., p. 6.

The union did not have a written policy explicitly committing themselves to protecting their members from sexual harassment or incidences of physical sexual violence. Nevertheless, interviewee 120 had assumed the union to be her ally.

4.1 Union (In-)Action on Sexual Harassment

Union membership in the USA had gone down consistently for decades and by the early 1980s only 20 % of the workforce was unionized.[37] The rate for women was even lower with only 11 % of working women having joined a union.[38] Despite this diminishing membership, unions continued to serve as the most powerful advocate for working Americans and as such, their stance on workplace issues had a considerable impact on employers. This influence went beyond only affecting union employees. Union contracts, especially clauses referring to anti-discrimination policy, were often used as a template for employment agreements with non-union employees. Thus, demands made by unions had the potential of becoming best practices in the company or industry at large.[39]

Collective bargaining by unions aims at creating a more even power dynamic between workers and their employers. As discussed, feminists attributed many sex discrimination issues in the workplace specifically to such power discrepancies. Hence, organized labor was a potential forum through which to fight sex discrimination in the workplace. In 1984, Richard L. Trumka, the president of the United Mine Workers of America (UMWA) emphatically proclaimed that "an injury to one is an injury to all, and that applies to the problems that women have experienced in the mines, such as job discrimination and sexual harassment." In fact, by the 1980s, multiple labor leaders expressed "support for our union sisters" and were calling for "solidarity" between their female and male members.[40]

37 Data for 1983 in: Dunn, Megan and James Walker: U.S. Bureau of Labor Statistics. Union Membership in the United States, (September 2016).
38 Clarke, Elissa: Stopping Sexual Harassment. A Handbook by the Labor Education and Research Project, June 1980, p. 19, BCA, Research on Women Records, Box 97, Folder Congress-House Fair Employment Practices Committee Correspondence with WWI.
39 Avendano, Ana: Sexual Harassment in the Workplace: Where Were the Unions? In: Labor Studies Journal, 43/4 (2018), p. 1.
40 Karwoski: Women Miners, pp. 6f.

Despite these calls for solidarity, union women, like Interviewee 120, had cause to question whether they could rely on the full support of their union. Women had traditionally not been part of unions.[41] In 1983, women made up 42.2 % of the U.S. workforce, but held only 14.3 % of union jobs. This underrepresentation was particularly pronounced in the UMWA, where women made up less than 1% of the union membership.[42] Thus, women's concerns often had little weight in the union context.

Additionally, union history in the United States was steeped in race and sex discrimination. In the nascent stages of the American labor movement instances of racial discrimination were pervasive. Several labor unions, especially those representing blue collar workers, implemented exclusionary measures that systematically marginalized African American, Hispanic, and other minority laborers. These exclusionary practices were often manifested through stringent membership criteria that were explicitly founded upon racial or ethnic considerations.[43] Analogously, in their formative years, numerous labor unions exhibited a male hegemony, wherein women encountered impediments in securing representation and opportunities. Women were frequently consigned to occupations characterized by lower status and diminished skill requirements, reflecting a manifestation of occupational segregation.[44]

Furthermore, certain unions exhibited a lack of commitment to, or even resistance against, the principle of gender equality, thereby perpetuating systemic gender-based disparities.[45] In the 1950s, union leaders had supported 'protective measures' such as weight-lifting restrictions for women workers; they had en-

---

41 Mellor, Steven and Lisa Kath: Union Revitalization: How Women and Men Officers See the Relationship between Union Size and Union Tolerance for Sexual Harassment, in: Employee Response Rights Journal 28 (2016), p. 57; Avendano: Where Were the Unions, pp. 6 f.

42 Karwoski: Women Miners, p. 6.

43 Nissen, Bruce: The Legacy of Racism. A Case Study of Continuing Racial Impediments to Union Effectiveness, in: Labor Studies Journal 33/4 (December 2008), pp. 349 f. cf. Frymer, Paul: Black and Blue. African Americans, the Labor Movement, and the Decline of the Democratic Party, Princeton 2008; Draper, Alan: Conflict of Interests. Organized Labor and the Civil Rights Movement in the South:1954 – 1968, Ithaca 1994; Foner, Philip: Organized labor and the black worker. New York 1974; Korstad, Robert Rodgers: Civil Rights Unionism: Tobacco Workers and the Struggle for Democracy in the Mid-Twentieth Century South. Chapel Hill 2003.

44 Cf. Women in Unions: Gaining Power but Little Room at the Top, in: U.S. News & World Report, March 17th, 1975, p. 70, University of Miami Archive, Pan American World Airways, Inc. Records, Personnel, Policies and Procedures, Box 2.

45 Lynd, Deslippe, Denise: Whose Equality? Race and Working-Class Feminism in the United States, in: Austalasian Journal of American Studies 17/2 (December 1998), pp. 31 – 44; Boris, Eileen and Lara Vapnek: Women's Labors in Industrial and Postindustrial America, in: The Oxford Handbook of American Women's and Gender History, New York 2018, pp. 171 – 194.

dorsed limitations on working hours for women; and a decade later, as historian Ana Avendano explains, "[s]ome unions [...] strongly urged the U.S. EEOC to interpret bona fide occupational qualifications narrowly, which would allow employers and unions to continue to discriminate based on gender and race despite the antidiscrimination laws."[46]

As labor activist Bessie Hillman put it in 1961:

> I have a great bone to pick with the organized labor movement. They are the greatest offender as far as discrimination against women is concerned. Today women in every walk of life have bigger positions than they have in organized labor.[47]

The problem of sexism in unions was not eliminated by the Supreme Court decision *Vaca v. Sipes* (1967) in which the Court judged it to be a "union's duty [to] fairly represent all members," and forbade "arbitrary" and "discriminatory" action against any one member.[48] Nor was it solved by the implementation of the Civil Rights Act, which forbade sex discrimination in the workplace and in unions alike. In fact, many unions took a stand against Title VII of the Civil Rights Act, fearing discrimination lawsuits. In an attempt to "lessen liability [... for themselves]," they supported efforts "to weaken the [...] EEOC."[49] Thus, on multiple occasions unions found themselves on the same side as employers and conservative politicians when it came to anti-discrimination laws.

On the issue of sexual harassment, unions were split. Unions, like the rest of the country, were only just learning about sexual harassment in the early 1980s. Many refused to take on the issue. Several went beyond ignoring the matter by aiding the accused in their defense. *Jenson v. Eveleth Taconite Co* (1997) is one of the most prominent cases of a union supporting the accused harassers over the complainants.

Eveleth Taconite Co. was a mining company, which prior to 1975 had hired no female employees. By 1997, as a result of federally mandated affirmative action programs, 5% of workers in the company's mines were women.[50] The female miners were exposed to a hostile work environment. Several women testified to fearing for their physical safety and a young boy described to the judge how his mother "pack[ed] her lunch box for work each day: a knife, mace, rope to tie shut the

---

46 Avendano: Where Were the Unions, p. 7.
47 Cited in: Avendano: Where Were the Unions, p. 6.
48 *Vaca v. Sies*, 386 U.S. 171 (1967).
49 Avendano: Where Were the Unions, p. 7.
50 *Jenson v. Eveleth Taconite*, p. 879.

door to her work area, and food."[51] Despite the mistreatment at their place of work and although all plaintiffs were union members, the United Steelworkers Union did not come to their aid. The union president himself had blatantly participated in the harassment and a union steward claimed to have no knowledge of the union's sexual harassment procedures despite just having participated in a training regarding the issue.[52]

Instances of sexual harassment were not always easily reduced to an employer-employee conflict. By 1980, the prominent understanding of sexual harassment had expanded to include hostile-work environment sexual harassment, which more often than not involved peer-on-peer harassment. This often put the union in the midst of a conflict between two union members.[53] To circumvent this problem and to increase their chances for union support, the women miners suing Eveleth Taconite emphasized the harassment by supervisors. They avoided complaining directly about their peers, because, as one woman explained in her testimony, "to be a squealer was to betray the entire union movement, tantamount to becoming a company spy."[54] Filing a grievance against a fellow union member was entirely legal. Nevertheless, even a brochure by the feminist Labor Education and Research Project, warned against "giving management the green light to discipline a fellow union member."

The pamphlet went on to quote United Steelworker member Sarah Slaughter, who explains why such a complaint was not only considered "bad practice,"[55] but could also harm the complainant's case.

> Once you report to management, the situation is entirely out of your hands. Management may do nothing, or they may punish the employee more harshly than you had intended, firing him for instance. The union must try to protect the employee's job, and you will then be in a position of siding with management against your own union. This will be very unpleasant and it won't win you any friends. It also divides the union, man against woman, and weakens union protection for everyone.[56]

---

51 Cited in: Avendano: Where Were the Unions, p. 4.
52 Avendano: Where Were the Unions, p. 4.
53 Clarke: Stopping Sexual Harassment, p. 22.
54 Cited in: Avendano: Where Were the Unions, p. 4.
55 Clarke: Stopping Sexual Harassment, p. 22.
56 Ibid., pp. 22 f. Similar sentiment in testimony from the president of the United Steelworkers Union during *Jenson v. Eleveth*: "It's my job to represent the employees and the members of my union out there... and it's not my job to give discipline. It's my job to protect them from discipline." Cited in Avendano: Where were the Unions, p. 4.

When a union found itself navigating a dispute between union members, it often sided with the accused against the disciplinary action from the employer.[57] In fact, labor historian, Reginald Alleyne, found that "sexual harassment grievances in labor arbitration overwhelmingly involve men challenging discipline for sexually harassing conduct."[58]

In order to dissuade workers from filing a grievance against fellow members, some unions implemented procedures addressing inter-member conflict. Some union constitutions included the possibility of a "Trial by Members," or had a section describing "Conduct Unbecoming a Union Member." Penalties for violations ranged from "a reprimand, to a fine, to expulsion from the union." Such clauses in the union constitution could be applicable to complaints of sexual harassment even if the term itself was not mentioned in the document. However, a trial by members or a decision by a union representative was seldom favorable to the complainant when a hostile culture towards women persisted and the majority of members perceived sexual harassment as a triviality.[59]

This is not to say, however, that every union had such a culture, nor that all unions rejected the fight against sexual harassment. In this regard, there was a big difference between unions representing a blue-collar workforce and those with a predominantly white-collar membership.[60] The women at Taconite as well as Interviewee 120 worked in a traditionally male industry. This translated to their unions, both in regard to the extremely low female membership, and concerning the continuing male chauvinist culture and structure. Miners, construction workers, and mechanics, however, were not the only American workers organized in unions. Teachers, actors, nurses, and office workers had unions in their fields. As historian Ruth Milkman put it eloquently: "[T]he typical male union member is a private-sector, blue collar 'hardhat,' whereas the typical female union member is a public-sector, white collar or professional worker employed in education, healthcare, or public administration."[61]

Naturally, a greater number of female members in a union lead to the prioritization of women's concerns within that union. Some unions, early on, embraced the topic of sexual harassment as a workers' rights issue worthy of their attention. Unions such as the Transport Workers Union or the National Education Associa-

57 Alleyne, Reginald: Arbitrating Sexual Harassment Grievances: A Representation Dilemma for Unions, in: University of Pennsylvania Journal of Labor and Employment Law 2/1 (Spring 1999), p. 4; Avendano: Where Were the Unions, p. 4.
58 Alleyne: Arbitrating SH Grievances, p. 2.
59 Clarke: Stopping Sexual Harassment, p. 24.
60 Avendano: Where Were the Unions, p. 8.
61 Cited in Avendano: Where Were the Unions, p. 8.

tion accepted the issue of sexual harassment much sooner than their blue-collar counterparts.[62] Additionally, there were unions with second-wave feminist roots, which specifically formed with the intent of addressing women's issues. The feminist strategy to encourage organized labor, according to historians Rosalyn Baxandall and Linda Gordon, was "particularly successful with clerical workers."[63] Women Office Workers (WOW), Women Employed, and 9 to 5 are only a few examples of regional unions of office workers with feminist roots. The top concerns of these unions were "equal pay, detailed job descriptions, maternity benefits, the right to refuse to do personal errands for the employer, and the eradication of sexual harassment in the workplace."[64] Additionally, union women from various unions networked and founded the Coalition of Labor Union Women, which soon after its founding took on the issue of sexual harassment.[65]

When a union did decide to fight sexual harassment, much of the material they worked with emphasized a feminist framing of the issue.[66] Often this material was provided by feminist organizations such as the Working Women's Institute.[67] As part of the effort to fight sexual harassment, the unions in question addressed sexual harassment internally by instituting policies and grievance procedures specifically forbidding sexual harassment. They published brochures, distributed information material about the topic to their members, and began offering seminars and counseling. Even more importantly, these unions took the fight against sexual harassment to the employer using the power of collective bargaining. When a union recognized sexual harassment as a pervasive problem, the organization covered this issue in negotiations with the employer. In such cases, employment contracts for all union members included language explicitly stipulating the workplace be free of sexual harassment.[68]

The success of such negotiations was mixed. For instance, the International Union of United Automobile, Aerospace, and Agricultural Implement Workers of America (UAW), as early as 1979, led a campaign to introduce specific anti-sex-

---

62 Avendano: Where Were the Unions, p. 253; National Education Association Sexual Harassment Training Workshop, 1980, GWU, National education Association Records, Box 2807, Folder Women's Leadership Training Program – Training Workshop Sexual Harassment.
63 Baxandall, Rosalyn and Linda Gordon: Second-Wave Feminism, in: A Companion to American Women's History, ed. by Nancy A. Hewitt, 2002, p. 421.
64 9 to 5: The 9 to 5 Bill of Rights, November 1983, p. 1.
65 Avendano: Where Were the Unions, p. 253.
66 For instance: Clarke: Stopping Sexual Harassment; Coal Employment Project and Coal Mining Women's Support Team: Sexual Harassment in the Mines. Legal Rights and Legal Remedies, no date (early 1980s), HSL, Feminist Ephemera Collection, Box 8, Folder 12.
67 E. g. Working Women's Institute: Program Description and Proposal 1980.
68 Clarke: Stopping Sexual Harassment, p. 19; Alleyne: Arbitrating SH Grievances, p. 1.

ual harassment language in union contracts. General Motors strongly rejected the idea stating that "agree[ing] to any language on sexual harassment [...] would be tantamount to admitting guilt." Ford and Chrysler, on the other hand, readily consented to the union's proposition. However, the language agreed upon differed in the two contracts. The UAW-Ford contract "confirms the grievability of sexual harassment." Further, it obligates both the union and the company to follow an agreed upon investigation procedure. The UAW-Chrysler contract had an additional clause, in which Chrysler committed to issuing "a policy statement to its management informing them that sexual harassment was not to be tolerated."[69]

Any contract language acknowledging sexual harassment as a forbidden practice had the potential of bolstering a victim's case. Nevertheless, the Labor Education and Research Project advised unions to fight for effective language by insisting on the inclusion of three elements.[70] The contract agreed upon by the UAW and Boston University is an excellent example for successful language.[71]

> The University recognizes that no employee shall be subject to sexual harassment. In this spirit it agrees to post in all work areas **a statement of its commitment to this principle.** Reference to sexual harassment includes any sexual attention that is unwanted. In the case of such harassment, **an employee may pursue the grievance procedure for redress.** Grievances under this Article will be **processed in an expedited manner.** If, after the grievance is settled, the employee feels unable to return to his/her job, the employee shall be **entitled to transfer** to an equivalent position at the same salary and grade [...].[72]

First, this contract reiterates a general policy within the workplace that forbids sexual harassment. In the case of Boston University, such a policy already existed and was now distributed more widely. In other cases, such as in the contract with Chrysler, however, the employer agreed to implement a new policy, which would be applicable to all employees, not only union members. Second, it establishes that sexual harassment is an offence which may be addressed through the union grievance procedure. Third, the process is set up in a way that allows for immediate relief. The grievance procedure is "processed in an expedited manner" and the victim is given the option of transferring to a different but equivalent job.[73]

While contract language specifically forbidding sexual harassment heightened a target's chances for a successful outcome, its existence was not a necessary

---

69 Clarke: Stopping Sexual Harassment, p. 19.
70 Ibid.
71 See Introduction for a discussion on the partial inclusion of private universities in my analysis of the private sector.
72 UAW-Boston University contract cited in: Clarke: Stopping Sexual Harassment, p. 19.
73 Clarke: Stopping Sexual Harassment, p. 19.

condition for the union to effectively assist a victim of harassment. Interviewee 120 was correct in assuming her union could provide relief, even though neither her employer nor the union had any explicit policy regarding sexual harassment. As most courts agreed that sexual harassment was a violation of employment law, a union member could follow the procedure with the union as they would with any other complaint.

Such a complaint would usually be initiated by filing a union grievance against the employer. This is the route Interviewee 120 attempted to take. Her union was in violation of the law because Mel Larson, her union representative, refused to file her grievance.[74] In fact, Interviewee 120 was advised by both Utah's Equal Rights Commission and the federal Mine Safety and Health Administration to sue her union for its inaction. The union, as well, acknowledged their mistake and, a year after her ordeal, officially apologized to Interviewee 120.[75] Had Larson complied with the law, the union would have initiated an investigation and negotiations with the employer. Only after initial negotiations failed, could the union have legally abandoned the grievance. Alternatively, the union could have decided to fight the sexual discrimination alongside Interviewee 120 by presenting the matter in arbitration.[76]

In conclusion, not all unions were dependable allies to working women in the fight against sexual harassment. Unions could be found on both sides of the battle line. They could either "contribute to women's economic disempowerment by addressing sexual harassment in a manner that discourages women from acting collectively;"[77] Or they could act as powerful and effective allies forcing employers to take on the issue of sexual harassment and providing victims of harassment with a union grievance procedure. By choosing the latter, unions, such as the United Auto Workers, Women Office Workers, or the Transport Workers Union contributed significantly to the protection of female union members and the wider institutionalization of anti-sexual harassment policies and procedures within private corporations.

---

74 Yount: Interview 120, 1983, p. 6; Similar example in Alleyne: Arbitrating Sexual Harassment, pp. 4f.

75 Yount: Interview 120, 1983, pp. 5f.

76 Karwoski: Women Miners, p. 7; cf. Alleyne: Arbitrating SH Grievances, p. 10; Arbitration through union contracts is not to be confused with mandatory arbitration. Turn to Chapter Seven for a closer analysis of these differences.

77 Crain, Marion: Women, Labor Unions, and Hostile Work Environment Sexual Harassment: The Untold Story, in: Texas Journal of Women and the Law 4/9 (1995), p. 44.

4.2 The EEOC As First Point of Contact

Interviewee 120 was met with silence or resistance at all three places she initially brought forth a complaint. While her situation seemed bleak, she, at this time, was in a better position than women wishing to file a complaint only a few years earlier. Despite the inaction from the police, her employer, and her union, she had a place to complain: the federal government.

The Equal Employment Opportunity Commission had taken up the fight against sexual harassment as early as 1975.[78] As discussed in previous chapters, the agency's biggest step towards eradicating sexual harassment from the workplace was the publication of the sexual harassment guidelines in 1980. It is necessary to make explicit that by acknowledging sexual harassment as an equal employment opportunity issue, the EEOC brought these cases under its purview. In practice, this meant that the agency was now open to receiving and acting upon complaints regarding sexual harassment. This meant that women like Interviewee 120, from 1980 onwards, had an institutionalized path to file their grievances. Additionally, all other government agencies had been put on notice regarding the issue.

Thus, when Interviewee 120 went to both the EEOC and to the Mine Safety and Health Administration (MSHA), she found the allies she had been seeking. When asking Interviewee 120 about her reasoning behind contacting MSHA, an agency primarily concerned with miners' safety, Yount is provided with the following explanation:

> Well, you can't work safely if you, if you keep, I mean (chuckle). If you don't know who's coming up behind you or if you're, what you're involved with and you can't keep your mind on what you're doing, you certainly can't be safe. And that's the grounds I went on. [...]

> They [the other women workers] wanted me to do everything I could [including going to MSHA] because they felt if that happened to me and nothing happened, it could happen to them too. [...] they all offered to help me.[79]

She and her female coworkers recognized that what had happened was not a private, individual incident, but a problem that needed to be acknowledged and dealt with by the federal government. By turning to the EEOC and the federal Mine Safety and Health Administration, Interviewee 120 demonstrated her understand-

78 EEOC *amicus curiae* in *Corne v. Bausch and Lomb*, cited in: Baker: Women's Movement, p. 19; cf. Dobbin: Equal Opportunity, p. 193.
79 Yount: Interview 120, 1983, pp. 6 f.

ing of sexual harassment as both a matter of discrimination as well as a workplace hazard.

I have explained in Part I the feminist conceptualization of sexual harassment as a matter of discrimination under the Civil Rights Act and the EEOC's acceptance of this definition by 1980. It is striking that neither feminists nor the federal government seriously pursued conceiving of sexual harassment as a workplace health and safety issue. Both feminist organizations, as well as the federal government, had found in surveys and studies that the stress triggered by sexual harassment could cause serious physical and mental health issues. These included but were not limited to "headaches," "weight changes," "skin rashes," as well as "nervousness," and depression.[80]

Additionally, sexual harassment often brought violence or the threat thereof. Interviewee 120 was not the first nor the last working women to experience (attempted) sexual assault. In other instances, particularly common in hostile-work environment cases, female employees' safety was violated in a non-sexualized manner.[81] Withholding of information, tampering with safety equipment, or refusal to properly train female workers could quickly lead to serious injuries.[82]

For Susan Taraskiewicz, the first female baggage ramp supervisor at Northwest Airlines, a campaign of sexualized bullying against her may have ended in tragedy. Taraskiewicz had documented the repeated sexualized graffiti, insults, phone calls to her home, and even the vandalism of her sister's car in Taraskiewicz's driveway. She took the collection of pictures, notes, and even voice recordings to an employment lawyer, who believed she had a "strong case." Just a few weeks later, the 27-year-old woman was found beaten and stabbed to death in the trunk of her Toyota Tercel. Before her passing she had told "friends [...] that she was afraid for her life and asked them to pray for her." Taraskiewicz's murder went unsolved. Her parents, however, were "thoroughly convinced the sexual harassment led to her death."[83]

According to the Center for Disease Control (CDC), in the years from 1980 to 1985, "42 percent of the deaths of American women resulting from on-the-job in-

---

80 Alliance Against Sexual Coercion: Advocacy Handbook 1979, p. 52.
81 E.g. In: *Mammano/Guzette v. Stauffer Chemical Corporation*, see: Crull, Peggy: Working Women's Institute Expert's Report in: *Mammo/Guyette v. Stuffer Chemical Co*, BCA, Research on Women Records, Box 95, Folder Working Women's Institute Sexual Harassment Case Summaries, Experts Testimony Originals.
82 Baker: Woman's Movement, p. 68.
83 Brown, Laura: Sex Harassment Killed Our Daughter. Parents: Job Abuse Led to Murder, in: Sun Herald (November 17th, 1994), pp. 88 f.; Carton, Barbara: An Unsolved Slaying of an Airline Worker Stirs Family to Action, in: Wall Street Journal (June 20th, 1995), p. A1.

jury [...] were homicides." Thus, for female workers, homicide was the leading cause of on-the-job death. Male workers, although much more likely to die while working, mostly fell victim to accidents rather than premeditated violence.[84] The first National Census of Fatal Occupational Injuries conducted by the federal Bureau of Labor Statistics (BLS) confirmed that for the year 1992 "homicides were, by far, the most frequent manner in which women workers were fatally injured."[85] No causation or correlation with sexual harassment incidents was indicated by either the CDC or the BLS. However, after hearing stories like Susan Taraskiewicz's, it seems reasonable to infer, at least a partial link between the violence associated with sexual harassment and the high rate of female homicides on the job.

Interestingly, in 1979, in their Advocacy Handbook, the Alliance Against Sexual Harassment, proclaimed that "sexual harassment at the workplace can be interpreted as an occupational health hazard."[86] The organization appealed to the Occupational Health and Safety Administration (OSHA) and the Division of Industrial Accidents to "become more aware and feel responsible for the issue."[87] Similarly, Working Women's Institute, in 1981, listed OSHA as an alternative way for finding possible legal relief when victims experienced physical symptoms due to, or were put in danger by sexual harassment.[88] This approach, however, was hardly ever tested,[89] and never became feminists' main strategy in fighting sexual harassment. Rather than turning to OSHA and framing their complaints as a health and safety violation, feminist groups encouraged women to turn to the EEOC and seek relief for sex discrimination under the Civil Rights Act.

In 1980, the EEOC opened their already existing complaint procedure to the issue of sexual harassment. Anybody who was being sexually harassed was encouraged by the agency itself, by feminist organizations, and even by multiple news outlets to find their local EEOC office.[90] A victim of sexual harassment contacting the EEOC usually had two options. The first was to receive informal counseling on how to handle a situation on her own and to collect information on how

---

84 Anonymous: Homicide Is Top Cause of Death from On-Job Injury for Women, in: The New York Times (August 18th, 1990), p. 8.
85 Bureau of Labor Statistics: First National Census of Fatal Occupational Injuries. Press Release, October 1st, 1993, BCA, Feminist Ephemera Collection, Box 80, Folder U.S. Department of Labor.
86 AASC: Advocacy Handbook 1979, p. 51.
87 Ibid., p. 42.
88 Sauvigné: Digest, p. 5.
89 AASC: Advocacy Handbook 1979, p. 52.
90 E.g.: Women Organized Against Sexual Harassment: Sexual Harassment, 1980; Sauvigné: Sexual Harassment is Against the Law; Bailey, Morris: Sexual Harassment is a Valid Grievance, in: The Boston Globe (April 27th, 1980), p. C5.

a more formal complaint procedure worked. The second was to formally file a complaint against her employer. This latter option was only a possibility, if the last incident had occurred within 180 days of her filing the complaint.[91] If she chose this route, she was asked to submit a written statement and to make herself available for an initial on-record interview. As a next step, the case agent contacted the complainant's employer and informed them about the allegations. The agent asked the employer for both a written statement and an on-record interview in which the charges were either accepted or – much more commonly – refuted.[92] On paper, the role of the case agent was not that of a counselor to a complainant, but that of an unbiased investigator and mediator between the two parties. In practice, however, a case agents allegiance depended on personal perception as well as informal, unwritten policy within the agency – usually depending on the current administration.[93]

Interviewee 120 remained vague in her description of the legal proceedings, leaving open how exactly the agencies assisted her. The order of events is also somewhat confusing. Nevertheless, it is evident from the interview that the case agent in charge of her case at the Equal Employment Opportunity Commission "called in" to Deer Creek Mine promptly after receiving the official complaint.[94] Considering that almost a year passed between the case agents initial contact with Deer Creek Mine and the resulting settlement,[95] it is reasonable to assume that her employer continued to refute Interviewee 120's allegations throughout the negotiations.

In these cases, EEOC protocol indicated that the assigned case agent launch an investigation. Such an investigation could range from a few phone calls to multiple site visits including the inspection of any records pertaining to the case and interviews with those involved. Depending on the outcome of the investigation, the case agent could decide on a course of action. If they found no evidence to substantiate the claims, they informed the complainant that the case had been closed. If, however, the case agent was convinced by the investigation that a complaint

---

91 AASC: Advocacy Handbook 1979, p. 48; NOW Legal Defense and Education Fund: Civil Rights Laws and Welfare, 1998, p. 5, BCA, Feminist Ephemera Collection, Box 50, Folder National Organization for Women Legal Defense and Education Fund; Working Women's Institute: Going Outside the Company. How to File A Sex Discrimination Complaint, 1983, BCA, Research on Women Records, Box 97, Folder Working Women's Institute Sexual Harassment Information.
92 NOW Legal Defense and Education Fund: Civil Rights Laws and Welfare, p. 5; Dessler, Gary: Human Resource Management, Harlow [13]2013, p. 69.
93 Cf. AASC: Advocacy Handbook 1979, p. 48; Baker: Women's Movement, pp. 116 f.
94 Yount: Interview 120, 1983, p. 4.
95 Ibid., p. 1.

had merit, the agent, in most cases, attempted to negotiate a settlement between the employer and the complainant.[96]

In Interviewee 120's case, a settlement was agreed upon. Additionally, roughly six months after the incident, while the negotiations were still ongoing, the alleged attacker was let go. The official reason given for his termination was "reduction in force." Interviewee 120, however, was certain that his departure from the company was a consequence of her complaint.[97] Not long after his termination, Deer Creek conceded to paying her "for the lost time at work cause [she] had to go to take time off to go to the union, to go to the Mesa [sic!], to go to the police department [...]." Additionally, the company agreed to implementing a policy which would "protect women miners" in the future.[98] Although Deer Creek, at the time of the interview, had still not paid Interviewee 120 the amount settled upon, she considered her fight a success. Her attacker's termination, allowed her to work without being "on edge, [feeling] so uneasy constantly." In her opinion, involving the EEOC and MSHA was the leverage she had needed to force her employer to hear her complaint.[99]

EEOC mediated settlement negotiations did not always succeed. If an agent believed a complaint was valid, but assumed the case was not strong enough to win in court, the EEOC would issue a "right to sue" letter to the complainant.[100] While no governmental agency could legally forbid anyone from filing suit in the U.S. judiciary, such a right to sue letter was a necessary document to convince a judge to let the case proceed to trial.[101] In these independent cases, the EEOC occasionally partook by writing *amici curiae* briefs. The EEOC was now known to have expertise on the topic of sexual harassment and, thus the agency's opinion was of value to a judge or jury.[102]

However, individual lawsuits were cost and time intensive. This was particularly true when victims of harassment faced large corporations in court, as there existed a high discrepancy in available resources.[103] For many women, such as In-

96 Lublin: Guideline-Happy, p. 18; Zippel: Politics, pp. 52, 59; Dobbin: Equal Opportunity, pp. 15, 80; Herzog: Sexuelle Belästigung, pp. 85–87; Dessler: Human Resource Management, p. 69.
97 Yount: Interview 120, 1983, p. 4.
98 Ibid., pp. 3f.
99 Ibid., pp. 11f.
100 AASC: Advocacy Handbook 1979, p. 50.
101 NOW Legal Defense and Education Fund: Civil Rights Laws and Welfare, p. 5.
102 EEOC Amicus Curiae briefs footnotes *Corne v. Bausch and Lomb*, cited in: Baker: Women's Movement, p. 19; Dobbin: Equal Opportunity, p. 193; Baker: Sexual Extortion, p. 220.
103 See for instance: Women Suing Bell Communications Research for Sexual Harassment, Letter Asking for Support, 1992, NYPL, Women's Action Coalition Records, Box 5, Sexual Harassment Suit 1992.

terviewee 120 who had avoided quitting her job precisely because of her economic worries, pursuing a lawsuit would not have been feasible.[104] In numerous cases, complainants relied on the EEOC to bring a lawsuit. When the case agent believed that the case could be won in court, the agency could sue the employer directly. As the agency itself was part of the executive branch, it had no judicial power. Bringing a lawsuit was the only option the agency had to enforce the Civil Rights Act. For a victim of harassment, having the EEOC lead the lawsuit against one's employer was often the best-case scenario, as legal costs, if they were not recovered from the defendant, remained with the agency.[105]

The EEOC's grievance procedure offered victims of sexual harassment an institutionalized route for their complaints. There was, however, a glaring flaw in the process: the enormous backlog of cases. Regarding the fast response time of her case agent, Interviewee 120 could count herself very lucky. There were simply too few agents for the number of complaints.[106] Consequently, if the agency had not concluded its process 180 days after the complaint was filed, the complainant, upon request, was given a right to sue letter enabling them to independently pursue litigation.[107]

To help combat the backlog of cases, the head of the EEOC, Eleanor Holmes Norton, in 1980, implemented "Rapid Charge Processing, a new system for handling individual discrimination complaints."[108] Women Employed Institute deemed this procedure as one of Norton's "major accomplishments" and explained it as follows:

> The Rapid Charge Processing System provided a mechanism for expeditious handling of individual charges. Complainants and employers were brought together in a face-to-face factfinding conference, usually scheduled within one to two months after a charge was filed. The goal of these fact-finding conferences was to facilitate prompt settlements and avoid extended investigations which are burdensome for charging parties, employers and the agency.[109]

104 Hilson: New Social Movements, p. 307.

105 NOW Legal Defense and Education Fund: Civil Rights Laws and Welfare, p. 5.

106 Women Employed Institute: WE Report Criticizes Enforcement Agency Performance, in: Women Employed News, 1982, BCA, Feminist Ephemera Collection, Box 89, Folder Women and Philanthropy.

107 AASC: Advocacy Handbook 1979, p. 50.

108 Women Employed Institute Damage Report, in: Bulletin. Women Employed Advocates. December 1982, Vol III NB 4, p. 5, BCA, Feminist Ephemera Collection, Folder Women and Philanthropy.

109 Women Employed Institute: Damage Report, p. 5.

The existence of such a semi-formal procedure reduced the average processing time of a complaint from two years to six months.[110] As was indicated by the agency's commitment to limiting the backlog of cases, the amount of *amici curiae* written in support plaintiffs, as well as the implementation of sexual harassment guidelines in the first place, the EEOC, under Eleanor Norton, often acted as an ally to victims of sexual harassment.

However, as part of the executive branch, a change in presidential administration could bring about a significant transformation of the agency. President Reagan's inauguration in 1981 heralded a conservative turn in US politics.[111] In light of this change feminist lobbyists lost much of the influence they had commanded during the Carter administration.[112] President Reagan, despite focusing on economic issues, instrumentalized social conservative rhetoric to mobilize the Christian Right of which the Pro-Family Movement was a part.[113] As a leading figure of this movement, Phyllis Schlafly had direct access to the newly elected president and was influential in shaping the Republican Party's stance on women's issues.[114]

Regarding equal opportunity, Reagan stated that: "We must not allow the noble concept of equal opportunity to be distorted into federal guidelines or quotas which require race, ethnicity, or sex – rather than ability and qualifications – to be the principal factor in hiring or education."[115] By highlighting individual potential and merit, Reagan disregarded structural inequalities as a relevant factor in success.[116] Furthermore, state involvement in the private sector was seen as a

---

110 Women Employed Institute: Enforcement Agency Performance, p. 3.
111 Critchlow: Mobilizing Women, p. 96.
112 Zippel: Politics, p. 53.
113 Geppert, Dominik: Konservative Revolutionen? Thatcher, Reagan und das Feindbild des Consensus Liberalism, in: Liberalismus im 20. Jahrhundert (Stiftung Bundespräsident-Theodor-Heuss-Haus Wissenschaftliche Reihe 12), ed. by Anselm Doering-Manteuffel and Jörn Leonhard, Stuttgart 2015, pp. 282f.; McAllister, American Conservatism, pp. 53f.; Sutton: Culture Wars, pp. 213f.; Williams: Reagan's Religious Right, p. 135; see for instance: Women Employed Institute: Reagan and Women: Policies Cause Widening "Gender Gap", in: Bulletin. Women Employed Advocates 3/2 (May, 1982), p. 1, BCA, Feminist Ephemera Collection, Box 89, Folder Women and Philanthropy.
114 Rymph: Republican Women, pp. 231f.
115 Ronald Reagan in a speech when campaigning against Jimmy Carter in 1980. Cited in: Graham, Hugh Davis: Civil Rights Policy in: The Reagan Presidency. Pragmatic Conservatism and Its Legacies, ed. by W. Elliot Brownlee and Hugh Davis Graham, Lawrence, KS 2003, p. 286.
116 Fernandez, Lilia: Ronald Reagan, Race, Civil Rights, and Immigration, in: A Companion to Ronald Reagan (Wiley Blackwell Companions to History), ed. by Andrew L. Johns, Chichester et al. 2015, p. 188.

misuse of public funds. Consequently, the review and reduction of affirmative action and equal employment opportunity programs followed.[117]

The change in administration deeply affected the EEOC. In 1982, the Taskforce on Regulatory Relief, headed by Vice President George H. W. Bush, intended to curtail the EEOC guidelines. According to the administration, the guidelines "relied greatly on individual perception" and were too harsh on employers and their businesses.[118] However, due to a letter writing campaign led by the Working Women's Institute in cooperation with WE,[119] the guidelines garnered considerable public support.[120] By March 1983, this public approval combined with the guidelines' repeated affirmation by federal courts, led Bush to abandon any attempts to change the guidelines.[121] The EEOC's official policy as well as their complaint procedure regarding sexual harassment remained intact.

The continued existence of the guidelines was tremendously consequential for the internal institutionalization of anti-sexual harassment policies and procedures within private corporations. Karen Sauvigné, in her role as director of the

---

117 Pasztor, Andy: Dozens of U.S. Regulations are Targeted for Review, Probable Easing, Bush Says, in: The Wall Street Journal (Aug 13, 1981), p. 5; cf. McAllister: American Conservatism, p. 54; Graham, Civil Rights Policy, p. 285; Tuck, Stephen: African American Protest during the Reagan Years. Forging New Agendas, Defending Old Victories, in: Ronald Reagan and the 1980's. Receptions, Policies, Legacies (Studies of the Americas), ed. by Cheryl Hudson and Gareth Davies, New York 2008, p. 127. See also: Women Employed Institute: Reagan and Women, p. 1.

118 Pasztor: Regulations are Targeted, p. 5; Anonymous: Stockman says Dealing with Sexual Harassment is ‚Burdensome' – for Employers, in: Labor Notes (September 29th, 1981), p. 136, BCA, Research on Women Records, Box 95, Folder Publications of American Federation of State, County and Municipal Employees; Zippel: Politics, p. 61.

119 Women Employed Institute was a feminist workers' rights organization and union.

120 Working Women's Institute: Letter Writing Campaign Notice, Example letter, BCA, Research on Women Records, Box 95, Folder Publications of American Federation of State, County, and Municipal Employees; Sauvigné: Letter to Bush; Reed, Carolyn and Lynn Campbell: Letter to David Stockman Regarding Office Management and the Budget, September 21st, 1981, BCA, Research on Women Records, Box 95, Folder Publications of American Federation of State, County and Municipal Employees; Flowers, Wanda: Letter to David Stockman Regarding Possible Weakening of EEOC Guidelines, October 7th, 1981, BCA, Research on Women Records, Box 95, Folder Publications of American Federation of State, County and Municipal Employees; Slaughter, Jane: Letter to David Stockman Regarding Revision of EEOC Guidelines, October 8th, 1981, BCA, Research on Women Records, Box 95, Folder Publications of American Federation of State, County and Municipal Employees; Josephson, Sandra: Letter to George Bush, October 7th, 1981, BCA, Research on Women Records, Box 95, Folder Publications of American Federation of State, County and Municipal Employees.

121 Berry, Phyllis: Letter from EEOC acting director Phyllis Berry to Senator Bill Bradley, March 25th, 1983, BCA, Research on Women Records, Box 95, Folder Publications of the American Federation of State, Country and Municipal Employees.

Working Women's Institute, described to Vice-President Bush that the guidelines led to an "increase [in] employer responsiveness to sexual harassment complaints." In the same letter, she argued that, in some cases, the "very existence of these guidelines acts as a deterrent to companies who might otherwise not have regarded the situation as serious."[122] In other instances a complaint with the EEOC was needed to provoke a response from an employer. Indeed, even those cases caught in the slow mills of bureaucracy had the power to convince an employer to take the issue seriously. The mere act of filing a complaint with the EEOC often established enough leverage to make an employer pay attention to the incident in question.

Nevertheless, the EEOC, under the Reagan administration, grew to be much less effective in managing the problem.[123] The agency was struck particularly hard by budget cuts,[124] leaving it with a budget decrease of almost twenty percent in the financial year of 1982.[125] As Senator Edward Kennedy speculated, this reduction of funds was provoked specifically by the continued existence of the anti-sexual harassment guidelines. The Senator's claim is substantiated by the fact that the EEOC's Office of Policy Implementation, which had initially written the guidelines, bore the bulk of the financial restrictions.[126]

Additionally, personnel changes drastically affected the agency's handling of sexual harassment cases.[127] Not only did the staff decrease, but many employees with a background in civil rights, New Left, or feminist activism, who had been recruited during the Carter administration, left the agency. They were replaced with individuals who, according to historian Carrie N. Baker, "lacked a commitment to equal employment opportunity."[128] The most noteworthy staffing change was the replacement of Eleonor Holmes Norton with Clarence Thomas as head of the agency in 1981. Thomas, who would lead the EEOC until the close of the decade, had previously "expressly opposed affirmative action" and went on to per-

---

122 Sauvigné: Letter to Bush, pp. 2 f.

123 E. g.: Women Employed Institute: Reagan and Women, p. 1.

124 Women Employed Institute: Enforcement Agency Performance, p. 9.

125 Women Employed Institute: Budget Cuts Affect Civil Rights Enforcement, in: Bulletin. Women Employed Advocates, 3/3 (August 1982), p. 4, BCA, Feminist Ephemera Collection, Box 89, Folder Women and Philanthropy.

126 Baker: Women's Movement, pp. 136 f., 140.

127 Women Employed Institute: EEOC Commissioners, in: Bulletin. Women Employed Advocate 3/3 (August 1982), p. 5, BCA, Feminist Ephemera Collection, Box 89, Folder Women and Philanthropy.

128 Baker: Women's Movement, p. 138; For an analysis on targeted personnel changes within the Reagan administration as a political strategy, see: Aberbach: Transforming the Presidency, pp. 197–201.

sonally face highly publicized sexual harassment allegations in the Senate during his confirmation hearings to become a Supreme Court Justice in 1991.[129]

By imposing financial limitations and bringing on a change in staff, the Reagan administration altered the agency's course of action on sexual harassment without officially modifying its policy. The Women Employed Institute (WE) monitored this shift. Anonymized, statistical information regarding the agency's actions legally fell under the Freedom of Information Act and as such should have been part of the public record. While this information was published by the EEOC throughout the years of the Carter Administration, the agency under Thomas did not relinquish these numbers even upon request. In response, WE filed and won a legal suit forcing the agency to release this information.[130]

According to WE the "EEOC's performance in enforcing civil rights laws has [...] deteriorated markedly under the Reagan administration."[131] By the end of 1982, the EEOC's backlog in cases regarding sexual harassment had doubled. This was partially due to the Commission's "serious undermining" of Norton's Rapid Charge Processing System. Additionally, the number of allegations deemed by the agency to have "no cause" increased from 29% in 1980/1981 to 35% in 1982.[132] Training programs and campaigns for public awareness were significantly limited.[133] Moreover, the number of lawsuits the agency filed on behalf of complainants declined by 74%.[134] The EEOC no longer regularly acted as an ally to those victimized by harassment.

Furthermore, the agency now advocated against employer liability in hostile work environment cases. Most notable in this regard is the agency's *amicus curiae* filed in the first Supreme Court case discussing sexual harassment: *Meritor Savings Bank v. Vinson* (1986). The agency supported Meritor Savings Bank rather than Michelle Vinson, who had been repeatedly raped by her supervisor.[135] Arguing for a knowledge standard, the agency stated that "[s]exual attraction is a fact

---

129 Baker: Women's Movement, p. 138; Committee on the Judiciary, United States Senate: Nomination of Judge Clarence Thomas to be Associate Justice of the Supreme Court of the United States. 102nd Congress. First Session. October 11th-13th, 1991, Washington 1993.

130 Women Employed Institute: Equal Employment Opportunity Commission (EEOC) Update, in: Bulletin. Women Employed Advocates (February 1984), Volume IV, Nb2, p. 5, BCA, Feminist Ephemera Collection, Box 89, Folder Women and Philanthropy.

131 Women Employed Institute: Damage Report, p. 5.

132 Women Employed Institute: Enforcement Agency Performance.

133 Baker: Women's Movement, p. 138.

134 Women Employed Institute: Enforcement Agency Performance.

135 Zippel: Politics, p. 53; Dobbin: Equal Opportunity, p. 200; Baker: Women's Movement, p. 138.

of life" not under the purview of an employer.[136] In dissonance to its own guide-lines, the EEOC, in this brief, equated "sexual attraction" and sexual harassment. Thus, the EEOC, under Thomas' leadership effectively opposed the feminist frame-work and limited possible action for victims of sexual harassment.[137]

Nevertheless, the unofficial change of policy did not induce a decline in com-plaints filed with the agency. The Hill-Thomas Hearings, in 1991, have often been, and in my opinion rightly so, credited with invoking a steep rise of reports filed with the EEOC. Despite initial feminist fears that the Senators' treatment of Hill would have an intimidating effect on other victims of sexual harassment, the numbers of complaints filed with the EEOC skyrocketed in 1992. The agency re-ceived 9,920 harassment complaints that year, which constituted a rise of over 50 % from 1991.[138] These numbers continued to grow until 1997 after which a steady decrease in sexual harassment complaints filed with the EEOC can be ob-served.[139]

The heightened attention given to the topic throughout the hearings had raised public awareness for the agency as a port-of-call. Press coverage of the issue often included concrete steps of what to do and where to turn, if one had personally encountered sexual harassment. Some articles mentioned feminist un-ions or organizations such as 9 to 5, NOW, or the Working Women's Institute. Other publications encouraged complainants to file a grievance directly with their employer or their union. Most of the press coverage, however, named the EEOC as the first contact point for victims of sexual harassment.[140]

However, the fact remained: the EEOC was much more of an ally to victims of sexual harassment during the Carter Administration than after Reagan's and then Bush's inaugurations. While the hearings did not provoke the EEOC into changing

---

136 Brief quoted in: Anderson, Katherine S.: Employer Liability under Title VII for Sexual Har-assment after *Meritor Savings Bank v. Vinson*, in: Columbia Law Review 87/6 (October, 1987), p. 1267.
137 Zippel: Politics, p. 60.
138 Smolowe, Jill et al.: Anita Hill's Legacy, in: Time U.S. (October 1992).
139 Cauterucci, Christina: Sexual Harassment Claims Spiked After Clarence Thomas Hearings. They're Spiking Again Now, in: Slate, October 2018.
140 See for instance: Goleman, Daniel: Sexual Harassment: It's About Power, Not Lust: What looks like Lechery May Be an Attempt to Keep a Woman 'in her place.' Sexual Harassment: A Matter of Power, in: The New York Times (October 22nd, 1991), p. C1; Strom, Stephanie: Harassment Cases Can Go Unnoticed: Many Companies Are Assailed as Not Being Aggressive Sexual Harassment Policies Are Often Not Pushed Hard, in: The New York Times (October 20th, 1991), p. 1; Anonymous: Increase Predicted in Md. Sexual Harassment Cases. Human Relations Official Says New Federal Law Will Encourage Seeking of Redress, in: The Washington Post, November 19th, 1991, p. C7.

the process of filing or investigating a report,[141] they lead to the increased public awareness that there was a government agency in place, ready to accept grievances. Moreover, despite the low percentage of EEOC complaints making their way into the court system, this number was still significantly higher than it had been in the early 1980s. Employers were aware that a complaint with the EEOC could escalate to a costly lawsuit. Thus, as complaints continued to pour in and the agency's reputation as a port-of-call for victims of sexual harassment grew,[142] the agency's complaint procedure created significant pressure for employers to act.

4.3 The Judiciary: Litigation As an Avenue for Action.

By accepting sexual harassment as a violation of Title VII, the judiciary opened the state's most well-established grievance procedure – filing a lawsuit – to those making allegations regarding sexual harassment. Contrary to the court cases brought in the 1970s, plaintiffs in the 1980s seldom had to convince a judge that sexuality was linked to gender, or that sexual harassment constituted a form of sex discrimination. Instead, plaintiffs focused on proving that they had indeed been harassed and that said harassment was "severe and pervasive" enough to justify action by the court.[143]

Many cases brought to court in the 1980s expanded the understanding of what incidences might be considered sexual harassment. For this, the acknowledgment of hostile work environment sexual harassment as sex discrimination in *Bundy v. Jackson* (1981) is a critical example.[144] Moreover, harassment of employees by clients or members of the public became a point of contention in the courts.[145] This was often linked to an employer's insistence that their female staff wear sexually

---

141 Such a restructuring was initiated, in 1994 by Clinton appointed EEOC Chair Gilbert Casellas, but was severely hampered by the low budget and accumulated backlog of cases. For more information cf. Igasaki, Paul: Doing the Best with What We Had: Building a More Effective Equal Employment Opportunity Commission during the Clinton-Gore Administration, in: The Labor Lawyer 1/2 (2001), p. 264.

142 Churchman: SH a Continuing Employment Challenge, p. 10.

143 Cf. *Meritor Savings Bank v. Vinson* (1989).

144 For a summary of the case, and an analysis of hostile work environment compared to *quid pro quo* sexual harassment see Chapter Two.

145 Reich, Robert: Sexual Harassment. Know Your Rights. Women's Bureau for Working Women, U.S. Department of Labor, 1991, BCA, Feminist Ephemera Collection, Box 80, Folder U.S. Department of Labor.

revealing uniforms. Margaret Hasselman, with the assistance of the EEOC, brought the first winning case on this issue to court.

Hasselman, a lobby attendant in an office building in New York, was required by her employer, Sage Realty Corporation, to don a "short and revealing" uniform, which exposed "her thighs and portions of her buttocks,"[146] and which made visible "the side of her body above the waist [when she raised her arms]." Upon wearing this uniform, Hasselman "received [from clients] a number of sexual propositions and endured lewd comments and gestures," leading her to feel "humiliated by what occurred" and "unable to perform her duties properly." Hasselman repeatedly articulated, through both verbal and written complaints, her contention that the uniform contributed to the establishment of a hostile work environment. Despite the recurrence of her grievances, they remained unaddressed, prompting her to begin her shift without adhering to the stipulated uniform requirements. In response, her supervisor presented her with an ultimatum, delineating the choice "of wearing her uniform, or leaving the [...] floor [permanently]."[147] Subsequent to her termination, Hasselman pursued legal action against her employer, ultimately prevailing in a lawsuit that asserted wrongful termination on the grounds of sexual harassment.

It is worth emphasizing that the extension of the law in regard to sexual harassment was a process conducted almost exclusively in the judiciary. Congress, up until 2022, did not pass a single law which explicitly used the phrase "sexual harassment." Nevertheless, the revision of the Civil Rights Act and its subsequent passage in 1991, had a significant effect on the volume of sexual harassment cases in the courts. Even though it did not mention the phrase, after 1991 litigation regarding sexual harassment was the fastest growing type of discrimination suit.[148]

The implementation of the Civil Rights Act of 1991 is often accredited to the heightened publicity of the Hill-Thomas Hearings.[149] However, the bill itself was introduced to Congress before Hill's allegations had been made public. When it was first deliberated upon, the revision was controversial and its passage was uncertain. After the hearings, the vote on the bill was fast-tracked and it was confirmed by a large majority of Congress.[150] Hence, while ideas for a revision had been tempering for months, the hearings considerably expedited the process.

---

146 *EEOC v. Sage Realty. Corp* (1981), p. 604.
147 Ibid., p. 605.
148 Dobbin: Equal Opportunity, p. 210.
149 Ibid., p. 208.
150 Ibid., pp. 209–212.

The new law did not affect the definition of sexual harassment but brought about some concrete changes in the handling of litigation pertaining to the issue. The Civil Rights Act of 1991 allowed plaintiffs to opt for a judgment by jury. Additionally, it enabled victims to sue not only for equitable remedies, such as back pay, front pay, and reinstatement as it was the case thus far, but also for compensatory and punitive damages.[151] The changes in the law did not affect the conceptual basis, laid by the 1964 law and its following interpretation by the courts, but instead had the potential of dramatically increasing the financial stakes of individual proceedings. Higher monetary awards and the possibility of a jury trial, which in civil rights cases statistically swung in favor of the plaintiff,[152] enhanced employers' attention to the issue.

As a result of her lawsuit, Margaret Hasselman, the lobby attendant from New York, was granted compensation for attorney fees and a sum of $33,142 in back pay.[153] In 1981 this was a comparatively large sum for a sexual harassment case. However, with the passing of the revised Civil Rights Act in 1991 the amounts awarded in the judiciary, by either a judge or a jury, rose considerably. The most palpable change was the inclusion of punitive damages,[154] which significantly increased the sums allotted by the courts. In 1994, legal secretary, Rena Weeks sued her employer, at the time the biggest law firm in the United States, because her boss, a trademark attorney, had repeatedly verbally and physically harassed her. In *Weeks v. Baker & McKenzie*, the court awarded Weeks a record-breaking sum of $3.5 million.[155] This was the largest sum awarded to a single plaintiff in the period between 1980 and 1998.

Besides awarding equitable remedies and (after 1991) punitive damages to the victims of harassment, judges could issue injunctions. By doing so, they could obligate employers to take preventative steps such as instituting an internal policy or offering seminars on the issue. Although these cases were rare, they were repeatedly cited in personnel journals and have incentivized employers to preemptively employ such measures in their organizations.[156] Moreover, in a handful of cases,

---

151 United States. Cong. Civil Rights Act of 1991. Public Law 102–166. 1991, Section 102b; Drobac, Jennifer Ann et al.: Sexual Harassment Law. History, Cases, and Practice, Durahm 2020, pp. 284–286. See here the caps depending on the size of the employing organization.
152 Dobbin: Equal Opportunity, p. 209.
153 *EEOC v. Sage Realty Corp.*, (1981), p. 268.
154 Civil Rights Act of 1991, Section 102b; cf. Dobbin: Equal Opportunity, p. 209.
155 *Weeks v. Baker & McKenzie*, No. A068499, Court of Appeal First District, Division 1, California (1998); cf. Anonymous: The high Cost of Sex Harassment, in: The New York Times (December 12th, 1994), p. A14.
156 cf. Dobbin: Equal Opportunity, p. 197; for a thorough discussion, turn to Chapter Five.

the respective courts went as far as ordering, not only the employer but also the individual perpetrators to pay a portion of the awarded damages. Again, these cases were infrequent, but they were cited repeatedly in corporate personnel policies, undoubtedly, in order to deter employees from harassing behavior.[157]

For employers, litigation involved an enormous financial risk. There was little predictability to judges' and juries' decisions. In some instances, awards for victims were low, covering only a couple hundred or thousand dollars in back pay. Other times, as described above, the damages for an employer were in the millions. This made it impossible for employers to budget for legal costs. As the number of judges accepting sexual harassment as sex discrimination increased and a multitude of varying scenarios were included under the label of 'sexual harassment,' an ever-larger number of court cases was filed. Thus, the likelihood of court-ordered damage payments for employees rose continuously.

The escalation of damage payments and liability findings in sexual harassment cases during the 1980s and 1990s mirrored a broader trend within the U.S. legal system.[158] Changes in tort law and an increased awareness of consumer rights, patient rights, and workers' rights culminated in an increase of both individual and class-action lawsuits. [159] Legal actions spanned a spectrum of issues, including challenges related to defective products, unsafe working conditions, and medical malpractice.[160] Simultaneously, environmental concerns prompted a surge in environmental litigation. Companies found responsible for pollution or environmental harm encountered substantial liability, leading to a discernible uptick in the magnitude of damage payments.[161] Notably, the 1980s marked a period characterized by a pronounced rise in the imposition of punitive damages.

---

157 E. g. *Kyriazi v. Western Electric Co.*, 476 F. Supp. 335 (D.N.J. 1979) cited in: The Prudential Insurance Company of America's workshop "Sexual Harassment Program," 1980, BCA, Research on Women Records, Box 96, Folder Bell Laboratories Corporate Study.

158 Born, Patricia and W. Kip Viscusi: Insurance Market Response to the 1990s Liability Reforms: An Analysis of Firm-Level Data, in: The Journal of Risk and Insurance 61/2 (June 1994), pp. 192 f.

159 Burnham, William and Stephen Reed: Introduction to the Law and Legal System of the United States, St. Paul, MN ⁷2021, pp. 769–777.

160 Kessler, Daniel et al.: Effects of the Medcial Liability System in Australia, the UK, and the USA, in: Lancet 368 (2006), pp. 240 f.; Avrahm, Ronen: An Empirical Study of the Impact of Tort Reforms on Medical Malpractice Settlement Payments, in: The Journal of Legal Studies 36/2 (June 2007), pp. 183–185; McWilliams, Mike and Margaret Smith: An Overview of the Legal Standard Regarding Product Liability Design Defect Claims and a Fifty State Survey on the Applicable Law in Each Jurisdiction, in: Defense Counsel Journal (January 2015), pp. 80–82.

161 Schoenbaum, Thomas: Liability for Damages in Oil Spill Accidents: Evaluating the SA and International Law Regimes in the Light of Deepwater Horizon, in: Journal of Environmental Law 24/3 (2012), pp. 397 f.

Courts increasingly utilized punitive damages as a tool to punish defendants engaged in willful or reckless behavior. The objective extended beyond compensating victims to deterring similar misconduct in the future. In line with these developments, insurance companies responded by adjusting their financial models and raising premiums to mitigate the heightened risk associated with increased damage awards and punitive measures.[162]

In conclusion, between 1980 and 1998, victims of harassment increasingly had access to institutionalized complaint procedures outside of the workplace. Both the EEOC and the judiciary were now a port-of-call for those wishing to pursue a grievance. Unions, too, increasingly discussed the issue of sexual harassment. Here, however, a differentiation must be made. While some unions were quick to respond, others did not deem it an important concern for organized labor. The issue got even more complicated when the harasser, himself, was a union member. In these cases, unions, often protected the harasser from disciplinary action by the employer, and thus, created a situation in which victims' experiences were trivialized.

Nevertheless, as the phenomenon was increasingly recognized as a workers' rights issue, by the government, the press, and fellow labor organizations, more and more unions included the issue into their program. Organized labor had enormous potential for shaping sexual harassment policies in the American workplace. In many cases, unions provided a safe harbor for members filing a complaint, and insisted on employment contracts which specifically included the ban of sexual harassment in a workplace. These contracts had an exemplary function and made many employers aware of the importance of the issue. As such, when they joined the fight against sexual harassment, unions had an influence on employers, beyond issues pertaining only to their members.

Encouraged by the publicity surrounding Thomas' confirmation hearings, victims of sexual harassment increasingly utilized these avenues for action. Americans learned that sexual harassment was not only a personal problem, but one which could be addressed though formalized channels. They filed union grievances, sought assistance from the EEOC, and sued their employers in court. The procedures offered by institutions and agencies outside of the workplace had a direct impact on the private sector. More complaints, whether through unions, the EEOC, or the judiciary, directly translated to higher financial risks for companies tolerating or condoning sexual harassment.

Unsurprisingly, this increased pressure led to many in the private sector implementing their own measures. Deer Creek, Interviewee 120's employer, in 1982,

---

162 Born: Insurance Market Response to the 1990s Liability Reforms, pp. 192 – 194.

did not have a policy forbidding sexual harassment. This changed immediately after the Interviewee 120 initiated legal proceedings. In 1983, the company implemented both a policy and a grievance procedure specifically regarding sexual harassment.[163] Deer Creek was not an isolated case. The 1980s and 1990s saw an ever-increasing number of private corporations implementing a policy and grievance procedure.[164]

5 Establishing a New Understanding of Sexual Harassment: The Management Framework

In the late 1970s and early 1980s, interested employers attained legal advice and suggestions on how to internally handle the issue of sexual harassment from feminist organizations. Beginning in 1980, management consultants and corporate lawyers emerged as an ever-strengthening competition for these feminist groups, whose discursive hegemony on the subject matter quickly declined. By 1986, business magazines and law reviews alike reported regularly on the newest rulings, upcoming cases, large settlement agreements, and proposed solutions. Business schools began including courses on sexual harassment as an equal employment opportunity issue,[165] and law firms across the country were scrambling to educate their attorneys on the topic.[166] In this chapter, I shall demonstrate how corporate lawyers and/or management consultants expanded their sphere of responsibility and authority to include sexual harassment and how this shift led to the development of a new understanding of sexual harassment, the management frame.

5.1 Two Professions, One Goal: Advising Employers on Compliance Strategies

Management consultants and lawyers often worked alongside each other in human resources or personnel departments. Both fulfilled an advisory function for employers.[167] However, the two professions underwent separate training, diverged in their *modi operandi*, and drew their legitimacy for their expertise from different sources. This led to management consultants and lawyers developing distinct and at times competing approaches to confronting the issue of sexual

---

163 Yount: Interview 120, 1983, p. 4.
164 Dobbin: Equal Opportunity, p. 191.
165 Dobbin: Equal Opportunity, p. 193.
166 Ibid., p. 210.
167 Ibid., p. 204.

harassment. Nevertheless, when working for a business, their goal was the same: protect the employer from the negative impact of sexual harassment complaints.

From its inception, the Working Women's Institute had closely worked with civil rights attorneys.[168] These lawyers' expertise in racial discrimination and harassment suits had been a significant advantage for victims pursuing litigation in the 1970s.[169] In court these civil rights attorneys faced the respective employers represented by attorneys who were not yet specialized on the issue of sexual harassment. The topic was too new and lawsuits were, as of yet, too few to make it feasible to specialize in this area. With the turn of the decade, this changed rapidly. The implementation of the EEOC guidelines in 1980, the Supreme Court decision of *Vinson v. Meritor* in 1986, and the inclusion of the possibility of punitive damages in the Civil Rights Act of 1991 each led to enormous increases in the number EEOC complaints and court cases on the issue of sexual harassment.[170]

The Civil Rights Act of 1991, in particular, acted as an incentive for lawyers to specialize in employment law and in sexual harassment specifically. *Nation's Business* ran a front-page piece entitled "Lawsuits Gone Wild" in 1998 in which it analyzed lawsuits from the past decade. The article warned employers that "trial lawyers gained new financial incentives [to take on discrimination cases]" in 1991.[171] In his work *Inventing Equal Opportunity* (2008) sociologist Frank Dobbin quotes a New York attorney: "Trial lawyers are entrepreneurs… you give them a profit opportunity, and they're going to focus on it. Congress is giving a series of profit opportunities [by passing the Civil Rights Act of 1991]; these are not going to be ignored."[172] The new possibility for high awards to targets of harassment aided perspective plaintiffs in finding representation willing to work on a contingency basis. Previously, many victims hesitated or were outright unable to pursue legal action due to high legal costs. Thus, lawyers absorbing the financial risk by offering their services on a contingency basis, gave more victims access to the court system and consequently led to more sexual harassment lawsuits.[173]

---

168 WWI: Litigation Manual, 1981; WWI: Legal Back-Up Center. Final Report, 1981; Working Women's Institute: Annual Program Report, 1978, BCA, Research on Women Records, Box 96, Folder Working Women's Institute General Program Proposals, Annual Program Report, Audited Financial Statement 1978 – 1981.

169 WWI: Litigation Manual, 1981; WWI: Legal Back-Up Center. Final Report, 1981; Working Women's Institute: Annual Program Report, 1978.

170 Cf. Dobbin: Equal Opportunity, p. 210.

171 Barrier, Michael: Lawsuits Gone Wild, in: Nation's Business: A General Magazine for Businessmen, 1 (1998), pp. 1, 15 – 18; cf. Dobbin: Equal Opportunity, p. 210.

172 Dobbin: Equal Opportunity, p. 209.

173 Ibid., p. 210.

By the late 1990s, sexual harassment cases were the most common form of discrimination cases brought to court.[174] Not surprisingly, with the increase of cases came a surge in revenue and a rise of relevance for the field of employment law. Sexual harassment had attained a high priority with employers and now warranted the hiring of specialized and often expensive attorneys. Where there had only been a "handful" of employment lawyers before in 1991, a decade after the civil rights law changed, there were "hundreds in every major city."[175]

Cognizant of the fact that legal precedent regarding sexual harassment was not settled, attorneys responded by fighting lawsuits on a case-by-case basis. This was particularly true in reference to the issue of employer liability. As has been discussed in Chapter Three,[176] from 1980 onwards, courts used a "strict liability" standard in cases of *quid pro quo* sexual harassment.[177] In regard to hostile work environment cases, the strict liability standard was a contentious topic. While some judges adapted this standard in their decisions, others insisted on notice.[178] Even then the question remained, would the existence of a policy and grievance procedure fulfill a possible notice requirement? Most employment lawyers were wary of prescribing such a solution, when the courts had not yet offered clarification.[179]

Contrary to the judge in *Barnes v. Castle,* who explicitly advised employers to adopt a written policy, most judges abstained from providing clear instructions outlining how employers could ensure compliance with Title VII. In the first sexual harassment case to reach the Supreme Court, *Meritor v. Vinson (1986),* the justices declined both "parties' invitation to issue a definitive rule on employer liability."[180] Michelle Vinson's argument had been based on a strict liability

---

174 Ibid., p. 209.

175 Chrys Martin, Employment Law Chair at the Defense Research Institute, cited in: Dobbin: Equal Opportunity, p. 210.

176 For discussion of employer liability, strict liability, knowledge standards and relevant judicial opinions, turn to Chapter Three.

177 Lutner, Rachel: Employer Liability for Sexual Harassment: The Morass of Agency principles and Respondeat Superior, in: University of Illinois Law Review 3 (1993), p. 593.

178 E. g. On strict liability in *quid pro quo: Miller v. Bank of America* (1976); *Horn v. Duke Homes,* 755 F.2d 599 (7th Cir. 1985); *Henson v. City of Dundee* 682 F. 2d 897 (11th Cir. 1982); on strict liability of supervisory hostile work environment: *Bohen v. City of East Chicago,* 799 F.2d 1180 (7th Cir. 1986); *Vinson v. Taylor,* 753 F. 2d 141 (D.C. Cir. 1985).

179 Dobbin: Equal Opportunity, pp. 192, 204.

180 *Meritor Saving Bank v. Vinson* (1986), p. 477; for more in-depth legal interpretations refer to Ecabert, Gayle: An Employer's Guide to Understanding Liability for sexual Harassment Under Title VII: *Meritor Savings Bank v. Vinson,* in: University of Cincinnati Law Review, 55 (1986), pp. 1192–1194.

standard, while Meritor Savings Bank had argued that Vinson never filed a complaint and, thus the Bank had not received notice of the harassment. The Bank further demonstrated that it had a grievance procedure in place to facilitate employee complaints.

In the unanimous decision, the justices noted that "the mere existence of a grievance procedure and a policy against discrimination, coupled with responden-t's [Vinson's] failure to invoke that procedure," was not enough to "isolate petitioner [Meritor Savings Bank] from liability." The Court further criticized that the Bank's general grievance procedure identified Vinson's supervisor, the man harassing her, as her first point of contact for filing a complaint.[181] The justices had settled on a narrow ruling. In this case, the Bank's policy and procedure did not shield the employer from liability. At the same time, the court rejected a strict liability standard in hostile-work environment cases and implied that an employer could adopt preventative measures to convince a subsequent court to rule in their favor.[182] Thus, while not assuring employers that a policy and grievance procedure would protect them from liability, the Court suggested that this was a possibility in the future.[183]

Before the *Meritor* decision, many employers were skeptical about distributing a policy. Many feared that issuing a policy statement might be read by a court as "tantamount to admitting guilt."[184] The Court, however, removed this concern. Meritor's policy may not have been sufficient to prevent liability, but it did not damage the employer's case. In fact, the contrary seems to have been the case. Despite the lack of an explicit endorsement by the judiciary, legal scholar Lauren Edelman traced a pattern which revealed that employers with a written policy statement were found liable less often than those without such a policy.[185] One can extrapolate that while the judiciary never claimed outright that the existence and dissemination of a policy would protect the employer, judges faulted employers when they did not have such a policy. No doubt aware of this trend, corporate lawyers strongly encouraged their clients to implement a written policy and to advertise it widely "through memoranda, signs, formal or informal meetings, or through one-on-one communication."[186]

181 *Meritor Saving Bank v. Vinson* (1986), p. 477.
182 Lutner: Employer Liability, p. 600.
183 For more on Employer Liability after *Meritor v. Vinson* see: Ecabert: An Employer's Guide, pp. 1258–1279; Lutner: Employer Liability, pp. 589–628.
184 Clarke: Stopping Sexual Harassment, p. 19.
185 Edelman: Endogeneity of Legal Regulation, p. 414; Dobbin: Equal Opportunity, p. 214.
186 Ecabert: An Employer's Guide, p. 1204; see also: Phillips, Michael: Employer Sexual Harassment Liability Under Agency Principles: A Second Look at *Meritor Savings Bank, FSB v. Vinson*,

Additionally, lawyers and management consultants alike reintroduced feminists' advice to offer employee training on sexual harassment.[187] Many employers were reluctant to take this advice despite warming up to the idea of establishing internal policies. They feared that explicitly educating their employees about their rights would "open the floodgates" and encourage lawsuits against the company.[188] The American Bar Association assuaged these trepidations by explaining that making employees "familiar with the definitions and ramifications of sexual harassment" in the context of "new-employee orientation or senior management retreats," could deter harassers.[189] Moreover, lawyers argued training could teach supervisors to "quick[ly] and effective[ly]" "identify and alleviate sexual harassment."[190] Furthermore, they argued, that by rapidly and adequately reacting to complaints, an employer could significantly strengthen their case in a potential lawsuit.

Interestingly, despite encouraging the implementation of an internal policy and employee training, corporate lawyers initially advised against the employment of complaint procedures. While several out-of-court settlements included a commitment by the employer to institute a grievance procedure, court rulings rarely included mention of such a measure. Lawyers cautioned that an internal grievance procedure would ease the way for plaintiffs to fulfill the courts' notice requirement. Additionally, lawyers warned that an internal grievance procedure might allow a potential plaintiff to reveal a pattern of sexual harassment within the company. Both in the case of an individual complaint as well as after the establishment of a pattern, an internal grievance procedure would prevent employers from claiming plausible deniability during litigation.[191]

Attorneys were also concerned about the time it would take the employer to mount a thorough investigation. Such an investigation was usually part of a grievance procedure and could be a lengthy process. Thus, legal counsel worried a judge would assume the employer was delaying remedial action rather than genuinely attempting to resolve the issue.[192] Lawyers were especially perturbed about

---

in: Vanderbilt Law Review 44/6 (1991), p. 1266; Bassen, Ned: Let's Ask the Lawyers – What Can an Employer Do to Help Protect Against Sexual Harassment Lawsuits? in: Public Relations Quarterly 37/2 (1992), p. 26.

187 See for instance: Phillips: Employer Sexual Harassment, p. 1266; Bassen: Let's Ask the Lawyers, p. 26.

188 Dobbin: Equal Opportunity, p. 203.

189 American Bar Association Article, cited in Dobbin: Equal Opportunity, p. 207.

190 Ecabert: An Employer's Guide, p. 1204; cf. Dobbin: Equal Opportunity, p. 207.

191 Harvard Law Review cited in Dobbin: Equal Opportunity, pp. 205 f.; University of Cincinnati Law Review cited in Dobbin: Equal Opportunity, p. 206.

192 Dobbin: Equal Opportunity, p. 205.

how judges might interpret instances which culminated in little to no disciplinary action for the alleged harasser. In a *Howard Law Journal* article, Ronald Turner explains that "a complaint that does not end the career of the harasser would make future incidents 'foreseeable.'"[193] Thus, continuing employment of an individual accused of harassment was a considerable risk to the employer regardless of the seriousness or even the merit of the complaint. Overall, lawyers saw no upside and considerable drawbacks to internal sexual harassment grievance procedures.[194]

With little encouragement from judges to provide internal solutions, lawyers recommended a fight in the courts. Instead of attempting to predict a judge's next decision, lawyers highlighted that precedent was not set and there was still a legal fight to be won. In short, corporate lawyers, in the early 1980s, had not accepted feminists' expansion of the concept of 'sex discrimination' to include sexual harassment.[195] Even after this was confirmed by the Supreme Court, legal experts saw the lack of clarity in existing definitions both regarding the concepts of sex discrimination and sexual harassment. They were also aware of the courts' and the legislatures' refusal to indicate concrete compliance strategies. In both these points, corporate lawyers saw an opening for shaping the law to their clients' benefit.[196] Thus, they advised employers to take immediate action when hearing of sexual harassment in their corporations, but to otherwise "sit tight," leaving them – their lawyers – to closely monitor the legal situation and to fight suits as they came up, on a case-by-case basis.[197]

To many employers, this advice was unsatisfactory. Aware of the financial risks, waiting for disaster to strike and only then go to battle was not good enough for many. These doubts were especially hard to ignore while a second profession was offering more tangible solutions. From 1980 onwards management consultants, contrary to corporate lawyers, were developing strategies intended to keep employers in compliance with Title VII. This was no easy task, because the law, as Dobbin aptly describes it, was a "moving target." The courts had, over two decades, continuously expanded the definition of 'discrimination;' first only forbidding "no negro" job announcements and later making mandatory affirmative action, diversity training, and job listings. Thus, anticipating that court rulings

---

193 Cited in Dobbin: Equal Opportunity, p. 206.
194 Dobbin: Equal Opportunity, pp. 191, 205.
195 Phillips: Employer Sexual Harassment, p. 1231; Dobbin: Equal Opportunity, p. 204.
196 E.g. *Howard University v. Best*, 547 A.2d 144 (1988); *Downes v. Federal Aviation Administration*, 775 F. 2d 288 (1985); *Henson v. City of Dundee* (1982); cf. Ecabert: An Employer's Guide, pp. 1199, 1201.
197 Dobbin: Equal Opportunity, pp. 191f.

would soon be influenced by the existence of internal policies, employee education, and corporate grievance procedures, management consultants attempted
to "cover all bases" and devised a corpus of internal regulations.[198]

As a basis for all advice, personnel experts, as early as 1981, had accepted the
underlying argument made by feminists and the EEOC: Sexual harassment constituted sex discrimination and, thus was a violation of Title VII. In his book, Dobbin
explains in detail how the personnel profession as a whole benefited significantly
from their acceptance of this interpretation. By coding sexual harassment as an
equal employment opportunity issue, management consultants accepted it into
their sphere of responsibility, thereby broadening the profession's area of authority and increasing their importance to employers. Personnel experts became such
a vital part of corporate organizations that in the following decade the number of
management consultants increased ten-fold while the general workforce merely
doubled.[199]

Contrary to lawyers, management consultants argued that employers had several courses of action available to them in order to protect themselves from a financial loss in court. The implementation of a clear policy statement and employee training programs were obligatory first steps towards prevention.[200] Diversity
and anti-bias training had already become popular as the idea of cognitive bias
regarding race and gender was raised over a decade earlier. Many management
consultants first included the issue into these seminars, and later modeled separate anti-sexual harassment workshops after the already popular anti-bias training.

Citing the EEOC guidelines which called for "preventative measures,"[201] management consultants echoed feminists' calls for internal grievance procedures.
After all, businesses had been successful in convincing the courts of the validity
of internal grievance procedures to settle discrimination accusations of union
members in the 1930s. Hence, the grievance procedures for sexual harassment
complaints recommended by management consultants often paralleled union
grievance procedures.[202]

Contrary to lawyers, who saw no upside to the institution of an internal grievance procedure, management consultants argued that they had two functions.
First, by providing an institutionalized route for complaints, the company could
more easily be made aware of problems. Implied in this strategy was the specu-

198 Ibid., p. 8.
199 Ibid., pp. 10, 204.
200 Phillips: Employer Sexual Harassment, p. 126.
201 EEOC Guidelines, 1980.
202 Dobbin: Equal Opportunity, pp. 75 f.

lation that courts would eventually move away from a notice-requirement standard or that they would expand the definition of "constructive notice." Personnel experts feared that an employer could be surprised by an EEOC complaint or even a lawsuit without ever being informed of the issue. A grievance procedure allowed an employer to react to a complaint before the problem escalated to litigation.[203]

Second, personnel experts argued that grievance procedures aided the company in pursuing swift, remedial action as well as in documenting this action. If it did come to a lawsuit, the documentation of an immediate reaction, according to management consultants, had the potential of swaying a judge. Additionally, the adoption of a policy, training, and a grievance procedure may buy "good will" with the judge, potentially shielding the employer from liability.[204]

These assertions regarding judges' behavior were based largely on speculations for future rulings and only lightly relied on previous verdicts. Management consultants, like feminist activists before them, highlighted those decisions that made their point, even if they were contested in the legal arena and not yet settled law. Additionally, they focused on implicit intimations by judges rather than the explicit wording; listed grievance procedures in the same breath as their promise to provide victims with swift remedial solutions; and overemphasized the executive power of the EEOC.[205] In 1981, in one of the first handbooks on sexual harassment written by personnel experts, Meyer et al. assert that sexual harassment is against the law and claim that "the law" mandated preventative measures such as a policy and a grievance procedure.[206] Rather than citing a law or even a court decision they attempt to substantiate this information by quoting from the EEOC guidelines. As Dobbin rightly explains, a lawyer giving such legal advice would be "committing malpractice," whereas a personnel professional was merely strategizing for the future.[207]

Dobbin posits that despite the lack of assurance that personnel's strategy would bring favorable results in the court room, employers "preferred HR's promise of a bureaucratic vaccine to attorneys' case-by-case approach." The idea of preventing expensive legal proceedings by implementing a comparably low-cost grievance procedure was appealing and led many employers to disregard lawyers' objections to the strategy.[208] Additionally, fighting cases in court, even if there

---

203 Dobbin: Equal Opportunity, pp. 20, 190, 202 f.
204 Phillips: Employer Sexual Harassment, p. 1268.
205 Dobbin: Equal Opportunity, pp. 202 f.
206 Meyer: Sexual Harassment, p. 159.
207 Dobbin: Equal Opportunity, p. 77.
208 Ibid., p. 192.

was still a chance of influencing the extent of the Civil Rights Act, was unpredictable and, thus difficult to factor into a yearly budget. A grievance procedure, on the other hand, promised an overview of the pervasiveness of the problem within the company and offered the possibility to settle disagreements without court or media involvement. These settlements were consistent, manageable, and thus could more easily be considered in financial plans.

Management consultants' arguments regarding grievance procedures were so convincing that within the period discussed in this chapter, employment lawyers began adjusting their advice. According to Dobbin, even "big law firms" such as Los Angeles-based Gibson, Dunn & Crutcher "began to take personnel's advice" and implemented harassment grievance procedures.[209] While it is nearly impossible to find a corporate lawyer in support of an internal grievance procedure in the early 1980s, only a few years later, grievance procedures were listed by management consultants and lawyers alike as reasonable preventative action for employers to take.[210] In 1992, for instance, Ned Bassen, a partner at the New York-based law firm Kelley, Drye & Warren composed a ten-point program to "help protect your organization against a lawsuit." Step five encourages employers to "set up a grievance procedure for complaints of sexual harassment" and to "encourage your employees to utilize the procedure."[211] Despite the absence of a court decision which would have sparked this change, such advice, coming from corporate lawyers, became ever more common throughout the 1990s.

There are several possible explanations. First, while there was no explicit verdict calling for internal grievance procedures, Edelman et al. show that "defendants with [grievance] procedures won cases at a greater rate (50 %) than those without (30 %)."[212] Second, contrary to lawyers' initial apprehensions, judges did not fault employers for having a grievance procedure in place as long as the employer could prove that immediate action was initiated after receiving a complaint. Third, even without lawyers' endorsement, grievance procedures among employers had grown enormously popular. Results of a study by Dobbin, in which he surveyed 389 employers, show that "nearly half had a sexual harassment grievance procedure by 1990."[213] Hence, as grievance procedures were increasingly sought after by employers, employment lawyers began to offer their en-

---

209 Ibid., p. 202.
210 Bassen, Ned: Let's Ask the Lawyers, 1992; Ecabert: An Employer's Guide.
211 Bassen: Let's Ask the Lawyers.
212 Edelman: When Organizations Rule, p. 908; Edelman: Endogeneity of Legal Regulation, pp. 409, 413, 416, 440; Dobbin: Equal Opportunity, p. 214.
213 Cited in: Dobbin: Equal Opportunity, p. 213.

dorsement. By doing so, lawyers' advice for employers began resembling that of management consultants.

When the Supreme Court in 1998 allowed employers to mount an affirmative defense by providing proof of a policy, training, and grievance procedure, these strategies had already been adopted by the great majority of American corporations. Dobbin et al. provide data from their quantitative study showing that "95 percent of corporations had grievance procedures and 70 percent had training."[214] The Hill-Thomas hearings and the passing of the 1991 Civil Rights Act, acted as a catalyst for the implementation of these measures. An HR executive of a liquor company emphasized the importance of the hearings:

> We've had sexual harassment training. That goes back a little bit, three or four years ago. I think everybody jumped on that bandwagon – with Clarence Thomas and Anita Hill scenarios – that made them say: "We really ought to do something here."[215]

Action sparked by the increased public attention and the new law in 1991 was not limited to one HR executive. *Glamour magazine*, presented a study showing that the percentage of Fortune 500 companies with anti-sexual harassment training increased by 50 points (from 35% to 85%) in the period from 1990 to 1992.[216]

In addition, employers were aware of how their direct competitors were handling the issue and what their respective industry standard was. Management in various companies exchanged information or advice. Dobbin quotes the head of HR at a department store stated the following:

> 'I would get calls from firms...' Harry over at [a competing retailer] said to give you a call because I got this situation, and he said you guys really have the setup [to handle a harassment complaint]. How do you do it?[217]

My own archival research also suggests communication between companies within the same industry about their sexual harassment policies. In folders dedicated to the establishment of a policy and grievance procedure at Columbia University and Northwestern respectively, I discovered policy statements from various other universities around the country.[218] Similarly, while consulting a collection of Dig-

---

214 Dobbin: Equal Opportunity, p. 191.
215 Ibid., pp. 210f.
216 Ibid., p. 213.
217 Ibid., p. 199.
218 E. g. Found at Northwestern: Project on the Status and Education of Women: Harvard Issues Statement about Sexual Harassment and Related Issues, January 1984, NUA, School of Law Records of the Dean, 1955–1998, Box 12, Folder 307.1; University of Minnesota: Sexual Harassment

ital Equipment Corporation files, I came across existing policies by Apple, Inc. and Microsoft, Inc. This suggests that as policies, training, and grievance procedures grew in popularity, these strategies turned into industry standards worthy of emulation.

In summary, CEOs and boards of directors preferred management consultants' straight-forward, solution-based approach to corporate lawyers' stern references to the ambiguous legal situation. There was neither proof that management consultants' solutions truly curtailed instances of sexual harassment within an organization, nor was there explicit encouragement from judges to follow this advice. Thus, Dobbin maintains and my research further confirms his argument that management consultants' strategies "did not become popular because they were lawful, but rather they became lawful because they were popular."[219] By the time the Supreme Court ruled on employer liability in 1998, 95% of companies had already instituted sexual harassment grievance procedures. They were considered best practices and even though confirmation on their success in limiting discrimination was lacking,[220] the Court accepted them as a means for limiting employers' liability.[221]

The success of personnel departments in defining compliance strategies regarding sexual harassment regulations considerably changed Americans' understanding of the issue. It is important to remember that personnel experts, in contrast to lawyers or even accountants, were not vetted by the state. Management consultants were not bound to uphold the law, nor were they elected to represent the interests of the people. They had no ethical commitment to society at large, and had no interest in shaping gender relationships. Instead, their profession existed to protect employers from legal charges. As such, the policies, training, information material, and grievance procedures consultants conceived and sold to employers did not follow the feminist or social conservative framing of sexual harassment. Instead, personnel experts reconceptualized sexual harassment trough a management lens.

Policy, NUA, School of Law records of the Dean, 1955–1998, Box 12, Folder 307.1; Freedman, James O. (University of Iowa President): University of Iowa Policy on Sexual Harassment and Consensual Relationships, July 28th, 1986, NUA, School of Law Records of the Dean, 1955–1998, Box 12, Folder 307.1.

219 Dobbin: Equal Opportunity, p. 191.
220 Phillips: Employer Sexual Harassment, pp. 1267f., 191.
221 *Faragher v. City of Boca Raton*, 524 U.S. 775 (1998); *Burlington Industries, Inc. v. Ellerth*, 524 U.S. 742 (1998).

5.2 Personnels' New Understanding: The Management Frame

As early as 1980, handbooks, model policies, and training material devised by management consultants appeared on the market. National and local business magazines were publishing articles advising employers on how best to handle the issue. By the late 1980s, videos produced for employee training were so popular that legal scholar Elizabeth Tippett, discusses them as "a genre."[222] This material, especially the audio-visual variety, was costly both in its production and acquisition. Due to the uncertainty of the legal landscape, informational material had to be updated after every potentially influential court decision. Written materials appeared in various editions, while new films were continuously released.[223]

Despite varying in format and genre, and despite the regular modifications, material produced by management consultants was, early on, mostly uniform in content. This was undoubtedly due to the high levels of communication between personnel professionals. In the 1970s, HR teams at companies with government contracts had begun regularly exchanging information with consultants across the country. After 1980, when private businesses without government contracts grew concerned about sexual harassment, this network expanded. Professional associations, such as the Society for Human Resources and the Conference Board, formed to facilitate an easy exchange of information.[224]

The analysis presented here is based on a multitude of works written by personnel experts. Articles, training videos, workshop materials, and handbooks on the topic were all considered. For the sake of clarity, the following pages shall demonstrate the results of this analysis by focusing on two examples: the book *Sexual Harassment* (1981), and a pair of training videos produced by Cordua Training Videos. The argument and conclusions drawn hold strong for the other material reviewed as shall be referenced in the footnotes.

Meyer et al.'s *Sexual Harassment* is a particularly telling source because despite its early publication the management frame is already clearly distinguishable from a social conservative and a feminist framework. Later works, such as the Cordua Training Videos, follow the same understanding of sexual harassment suggesting that the management frame,[225] once established in the early 1980s, did

---

222 Tippett, Elizabeth C.: Harassment Trainings. A Case Analysis, in: Berkeley Journal of Employment & Labor Law 39/2 (January 2018), p. 486.
223 Ibid., p. 502.
224 Dobbin: Equal Opportunity, pp. 2, 10.
225 Cordua Training Videos: A Manager's Responsibility; Cordua Training Videos: An Employee's Responsibility.

not change meaningfully. Rather than portraying sexual harassment as a trivial and natural occurrence (social conservative frame) or depicting it as a gendered and systemic problem (feminist frame), management consultants presented the issue as a non-gendered, individual concern, which harbored high financial risks to the company. Here a point of caution is advised: The categorization of understandings into frames as an analytical device is imposed by the author. It is unclear how apparent this reconceptualization was to contemporaries and impossible to determine to what degree this change was intentional.

Sexual Harassment, published in 1981, was written in response to increased media attention for the issue, feminist pressure, and EEOC action. Mary Coeli Meyer recounts that after Mac McDaniel, president of Management Resources International, "planted the seed" for this book, she enlisted the help of three co-authors: Inge M. Berchtold, Jeannenne L. Oestreich and Frederick J. Collins.[226] All four authors were personnel experts and travelled the country for various speaking engagements. They belonged to the first generation of management consultants specializing on the issue of sexual harassment.

The authors present their book as an "unbiased," expert analysis of the phenomenon, which targeted an audience consisting of interested "individuals, managers and organizations."[227] Within the first few pages, they highlight their intention to make their work "meaningful to a variety of readers without purposely alienating any specific group,"[228] and proclaim that "[t]hroughout the book a sincere effort will be made to provide a balanced perspective – men and women, individual and organization, liberated and traditional."[229] The implied audience varies throughout the book. At times the authors give advice to the "harassee" other times they speak directly to the ("accidental") harasser. In most instances, however, the authors provide information for supervisors, personnel department staff, and employers. As such, the book is an early example representing the management frame.

In addition to Meyer et al.'s work, I highlight two videos in this analysis: "Sexual Harassment – Awareness, Perception and Prevention: An Employee's Responsibility" and its counterpart varying only in the subtitle "A Manager's Responsibility." Neither video provides the viewer with a release date. However, based on actors' clothing, the computer models visible in the background, and the content presented, a release in the late 1990s seems plausible. In both videos the management consultant, Minny Deol, and the attorney, Joe Backer, face two (supervisory)

---

226 Meyer et al.: Sexual Harassment, p. ix.
227 Ibid., p. 16.
228 Ibid., p. vii.
229 Ibid., p. 16.

employees in what resembles a talk show format. At regular intervals, brief and dramatized video clips showing instances of sexually harassing behavior are shown on the screen behind the talk show participants. Both films work with identical examples. After every clip, Deol, Backer, and the two employees discuss the footage. The consultant and the lawyer speak with one voice, adding on to each other's points and at times finishing each other's sentences. Backer, the attorney, takes Deol's lead and seldom recounts recent legal decisions. Instead, he too, focuses on internal corporate solutions.[230] This confirms Frank Dobbin's argument that by the late 1990s lawyers had accepted consultants' strategies and no longer diverged in the advice they gave.[231]

As is clarified in the videos' titles, they differ in their target audience. The first addresses employees and gives advice on how an individual may handle instances of sexual harassment, whether this be in the role of the victim, the bystander, or the harasser. The latter educates supervisors on their responsibility to respond to complaints, investigate them, and discipline perpetrators. Despite this variation in target audience, the message in both videos is based on the management frame. The videos were produced as material for employee and management training. Most likely they were part of a set of materials including workshop materials and model policies and procedures, which employers could purchase. As such, the videos themselves do not mention a specific organization, nor do they go into detail regarding individual company policies. They do, however, assure the viewer that "your organization" has a policy against sexual harassment.[232]

5.2.1 A New Economic Concern

Is sexual harassment a problem? The reader will remember from Chapter One that feminists answered this question with a resounding yes. They argued that first, harassing behavior was widespread; second, it had tremendous consequences for victims in regard to their health and economic situation; and third, such conduct constituted an intentional expression of power on behalf of the harasser. Social conservatives, on the other hand, explained the high numbers with biased surveys, overreactions, and false accusations. They deemed consequences for victims were minimal, because their narrative did not recognize a women's economic need to work. As such, social conservatives viewed resigning a job not only as a reasonable action but a desirable outcome. Additionally, they denied

---

230 Cordua Training Videos: A Manager's Responsibility; Cordua Training Videos: An Employee's Responsibility.
231 Dobbin: Equal Opportunity, pp. 208 f.
232 Cordua Training Videos: An Employee's Responsibility.

the malintent of a harasser by equating sexual harassment with sexual desire which was a natural consequence of men and women working together. In short, contrary to feminists, social conservatives portrayed sexual harassment as a triviality.

In the early years, disregarding claims of sexual harassment as inconsequential was appealing to many employers. As Herman Mapelli, president of a Denver liquor distribution company told *Business Week* in the fall of 1979, "we don't have a policy because we don't have sexual harassment."[233] However, as has been highlighted extensively above, in the 1980s and 1990s, the risk of high costs resulting from court rulings and out-of-court settlements made it impossible for employers to evade the issue. Fittingly, management consultants implored employers not to ignore such conduct, but rather to regard it as a "personnel issue" of great concern.[234] Within the material they produced, consultants often educated their audience that in the past, sexual harassment was "virtually hidden," "regarded as a non-issue," and "acceptable."[235] "Now," however, "we know better" and such behavior "is no longer acceptable." Thus, "[s]exual harassment is a problem in the world of work."[236]

As evidence for the problematic nature of sexual harassment, consultants, not unlike feminists, often referenced statistics which "suggest it is a widespread problem," affecting "all types of organizations" and "impacting millions of employees."[237] Many management handbooks and articles, as well as employer policies cited various Merit System Protection Board surveys.[238] The results of the first MSPB survey had not been published by the release of *Sexual Harassment* in 1980. As such, Meyer et al. relied on some of the less representative surveys discussed in Chapter One. Despite criticizing the broad definitions and the respondent selection process, the authors urge their readers not to "become [...] trapped in a statistical discussion and losing sight of the issue," but instead to acknowledge that "there is enough data now to say that there is a problem."[239]

While the management and the feminist frame agree that "there is a problem," the nuances of how this problem was perceived and who it impacted varied within the two frames. The management frame recognized that victims' "dignity,

---

233 Cited in: Dobbin: Equal Opportunity, p. 198.
234 Find actual quote Dessler: Human Resources Management, p. 497.
235 Meyer et al.: Sexual Harassment, p. 3.
236 Ibid., p. xiii.
237 Ibid., xiii.
238 E.g.: Atana: Sexual Harassment Prevention Training; Digital Electronics Corporation: Addressing Sexual Harassment, p. 12.
239 Meyer et al.: Sexual Harassment, p. 7.

self-respect, and financial security"[240] could be affected, but nevertheless focused on sexual harassment as an economic concern for the organization. Accompanied by ominous music, the Cordua Training Video informs supervisors that "[t]he average harassment defense cost is $300,000" and that "the average harassment verdict is $273,661."[241] Additionally, viewers learn that "[e]ven if the claim isn't successful it can cost a great deal of time and money to defend."[242] Similarly, Meyer and colleagues proclaim that "sexual harassment is expensive" and list a number of settlement agreements in which corporations paid several hundred thousand dollars in the aftermath of sexual harassment allegations.[243]

In addition to the expenses related to litigation, consultants warned employers of hidden costs related to sexual harassment. Several training videos establish the relevance of the topic by referencing headlines and tv reports.[244] Meyer et al., too, explain that the heightened "public visibility" of the issue, influenced their decision to write about the issue. They go on to explain:

> The organization's reputation is now added to the boiling pot and the potential for front page news becomes inviting. [...] Millions are spent annually for advertising to promote the company and the organizational image. One news item which has great and diverse appeal is sexual harassment, but is that the news that the organization wants? No, it wants to sell its product. How much money will be required to reestablish its image once it has been tarnished by such a controversial news story?[245]

Thus, sexual harassment, by the early 1980's, had gained enough mainstream attention and criticism that news about such behavior had the potential to damage a business's public image.[246] By referencing the high media attention, consultants implicitly focused on sexual harassment as an economic concern. More media attention, after all, did not increase the actual instances of sexual harassment. Instead, it could lead to a blemished reputation, which could prove intricate and costly to repair.

---

240 Ibid., p. 9.
241 Cordua Training Videos: A Manager's Responsibility; adjusted for inflation $300 000 in 1997 would be approx. $600 000 in 2025.
242 Cordua Training Videos: A Manager's Responsibility.
243 Meyer et al.: Sexual Harassment, p. 10.
244 Cordua training Videos: An Employee's Responsibility; See also the parody: Spiers, Tyler and Joe Davidson: Sexual Harassment – What Employees Need to Know (Blue Ribbon Panel), [no date].
245 Meyer et al.: Sexual Harassment, p. 78.
246 Ibid.; cf. Zippel: Politics, p. 186.

Moreover, consultants highlighted that sexual harassment cost employers on a day-to-day basis. Employees' discomfort in the workplace lead to a decline in workers' performance, increased sick leave, and the organization's loss of skilled labor. Sexual harassment had the potential of affecting the entire office atmosphere by inducing distrust, low morale, and inhibiting teamwork.[247] According to Meyer and colleagues, in a sexual harassment situation, "the focus is on human interaction rather than production. Hence, productivity is affected." Consultants linked the combination of turnover, absenteeism, and low morale to inefficiency in the workplace and thereby argued that sexual harassment endangered the "organization['s] success."[248]

5.2.2 Gender-Non-Specific Behavior

Meyer et al.'s book and the two videos were released approximately two decades apart. Despite this, the content of the material underwent few changes. All the more noteworthy is their inclusion (or lack thereof) of feminist fore-thinkers on the issue. The training videos, much like other material produced in the 1990s, avoided any mention of feminist groups or individuals. In contrast, early consultants, such as Meyer et al., stylized themselves in a tradition with feminist experts. Meyer and colleagues repeatedly quote from feminist scholars, such as Lin Farley and Catharine MacKinnon.[249] They acknowledge the "strong effort made by feminists" to fight sexual harassment and in Chapter Eight even recommend training material composed by feminist organizations.[250]

Simultaneously, the authors distanced themselves from the feminist movement. In the introduction, they contemplate whether the recent attention given to sexual harassment was "simply" a feminist "fad."[251] Regarding the feminist training material mentioned above, they warn the reader these groups may take a "militant approach which strongly favors women and fails to consider other aspects of sexual harassment."[252] Meyer and colleagues warn that:

> [I]t's important that sexual harassment not become an anti-male cause of a few women who see this issue as another example of the oppression of women. And it is also important that

---

247 Meyer et al.: Sexual Harassment, p. 86. Cordua Training Videos: A Manager's Responsibility.
248 Meyer et al.: Sexual Harassment, p. 77; cf. Althuler Edward A.: The Training Approach... A Recommendation for Center Financial Group, June 4th, 1979, p. 37, AHC, Edward A. Altshuler Papers, Box 8.
249 Ibid., pp. 4 f.
250 Ibid., pp. 147 f.
251 Meyer et al.: Sexual Harassment, pp. vii, 12.
252 Ibid., pp. 147 f.

men consider sexual harassment as a bona fide issue of human dignity and not a feminist attempt 'to get them again.'[253]

While feminist opinions and actions are portrayed as potentially confrontational and radical, the overall feminist analysis and the individual feminist experts mentioned are presented in a positive light. In fact, other than explicitly emphasizing male inclusion as a new approach, the authors do not contrast their analysis of sexual harassment against those feminist works already published.[254]

The lack of explicit criticism of feminist experts and their research is noteworthy. On the one hand, it is feasible that early consultants saw themselves as adopting the feminist topic and narrative and simply adjusting it to make it more inclusive. On the other hand, at this time feminists associated with single-issue organizations were widely accepted as experts.[255] Implying a lineage from feminist research to their own works may have been a strategy of profiting from feminists' authority of expertise. Either way, a reader new to the subject may not have realized that Meyer et al. as well as several other management consultants in the 1980s, had (consciously or not) developed a new understanding of sexual harassment, which significantly differed from the feminist frame.

I posit that by the 1990s, the topic had garnered so much attention – both in the public as well as in the law profession and consulting circles – that there was no need to pay homage to early feminist experts. The topic by then had successfully been submerged into the legal and personnel professions. Thus, contrary to early works, material such as the Cordua Training Videos made no mention of feminist material, experts, or organizations.

The management frame differed considerably from its counterparts in regard to the significance of gender attributed as a factor for sexual harassment. Within both the feminist and the social conservative frameworks, men were the initiators of and women were subject to sexual advances.[256] Within the management frame, a clear stance was taken that sexualized behavior, whether welcome or unwelcome, was not necessarily gendered and could occur between any two individuals.[257] In the foreword of *Sexual Harassment*, Meyer et al. identify the fact that

---

253 Ibid., p. 69.
254 See also Dobbin: Equal Opportunity, pp. 2, 213.
255 Turn to Chapter Two and Three. Feminist activists acted as authors, consultants, expert witnesses etc.
256 Whether these advances were considered coercive or welcomed depended on the framing.
257 The author acknowledges the current rejection of gender as a binary concept; however, contemporaries' understanding of gender would not have included a non-binary approach. Thus, historically speaking, "both genders" is more accurate than the alternative "all genders."

not only one gender was affected by sexual harassment as "the most important" point of their book.[258] Meyer et al., the Cordua Training Videos, and a multitude of other consultants explained that both men and women harassed and that both sexes could become "harassees."[259] The consultants' pronoun usage also highlighted this gender-neutral approach. While feminist texts and even some language within government agencies presented perpetrators as "he" and targets as "she" or "she/he,"[260] within the management frame, the harasser and "harassee" were both strictly referred to as "he/she." [261]

Workshop material, videos, and handbooks often presented fictional examples to help the audience understand the intricacies of the issue.[262] These examples routinely depicted women harassing men as often as vice versa. Both the book and the videos epitomize this pattern. One scenario presented in *Sexual Harassment* shows a female boss excluding the only male employee in her department. The authors analyze the situation as follows:

> The woman who cannot tolerate a man in her department of ladies is as much a threat to a sexually safe environment as the men in the boardroom. Her jokes and asides are as guilty as the men's. [263]

This interpretation leaves the audience under the impression that gender is not, and should not be, a factor in evaluating sexual harassment.

Despite their insistence on sexual harassment as a non-gendered phenomenon, consultants were nevertheless a product of their time. Thus, in early works, ideas about gender differences and traditional gender roles were evident in the choice of examples and general examination of the issue. In Meyer et al.'s analysis the motives, circumstances, and responsibilities for male and female

---

258 Meyer et al.: Sexual Harassment, p. xv.
259 Guteck, Barbara: Sex and the Workplace, London – San Francisco 1985, p. 62; National Education Association Broadcast Services: Sexual Harassment Video, October 3rd, 1990; Kmart: Respect in the Workplace, [no date]. Meyer: Sexual Harassment, p. 88; Cordua Training Videos: An Employee's Responsibility; Cordua Training Videos: A Supervisor's Responsibility.
260 E. g.: WWI: Legal Back-Up Center. Final Report, 1981; WWI: How and Why to Document a Case, BCA, Research on Women Records, Box 97, Folder Working Women's Institute Sexual Harassment Information; OPM: Policy Statement and Definition of Sexual Harassment, 1979; Coal Employment Project: Sexual Harassment in the Mines.
261 Cordua Training Videos: An Employee's Responsibility.
262 Meyer et al.: Sexual Harassment, p. 77; Cordua Training Videos: An Employee's Responsibility; Cordua Training Videos: A Supervisor's Responsibility.
263 Meyer et al.: Sexual Harassment, p. 106.

harassers and victims differed considerably, precisely because the authors included gendered presuppositions in their analysis.

Meyer et al. differentiate between the motives of male and female harassers. They assume that men harassed either by accident or because they felt threatened by women entering the job market.[264] The motivation of using sexual harassment as an instrument of power appears very seldom in regard to male harassers. Female harassers, on the other hand, are often presented in examples in which they are testing "their prowess as conquerors," wishing to show dominance or are purposefully "emulat[ing] what they perceive as successful traits in men." By doing so, they act "tough, aggressive and ruthless," which could sometimes go as far as them asking for "sexual favors and control." Meyer and colleagues accept that sexual harassment might be a tool to exhibit control and even conclude that it is part of socialized male behavior.[265] However, by giving more examples of women purposefully taking on this male gender role, than men exhibiting it, the authors present this behavior as a stereotype and deny its justification in reality.

While Meyer et al. regarded gender dynamics as irrelevant to the issue of sexual harassment on an organizational level, the authors' commentary on individual situations was repeatedly tied to the gender of those involved. The authors argue that societal gender norms and expectations may motivate individuals to sexually harass their coworkers. These gender norms, however, do not lead to the systemic harassment of women by men, but instead may sporadically affect individual males and females in their actions. "Some women" are said to have the wish of "rectify[ing] every injustice wrought by males."[266] In contrast, "some men" perceive women as "invader[s]" into "male territory."[267] Imperative in their analysis of harassers' motivations is that they only affect *some* individuals, and that this is not behavior exhibited by all men or all women as a group. Gendered dynamics, according to the authors, played no further role within the organization beyond motivating *some* individuals in their actions. By describing moments in which men were sexually harassed as often as instances in which women were victimized by harassment,[268] these situations appeared to be balanced. Therefore, in Meyer et al.'s analysis, the wider problem of sexual harassment within an organization became a gender-neutral phenomenon which required a gender-neutral policy, procedure, and management action.

---

264 Ibid., pp. 55, 100.
265 Ibid., pp. 66, 77, 127.
266 Ibid., p. 64.
267 Ibid., p. 55.
268 Baker: Women's Movement, p. 143.

The Cordua Training Videos, as well, present an array of examples with women appearing as harassers as often as men. In contrast to Meyer and colleagues work, however, the individual examples presented and the explanations offered are decidedly gender-neutral. Both the male and female employee participating in the discussion admit to possibly having made a colleague feel uncomfortable; the examples portray both women and men in supervisory as well as subordinate positions; the language throughout the videos is consistently gender non-specific. Even when the discussion turns to individual sensibilities and perspective, gender is not considered a factor. It appears that while management consultants consistently portrayed the issue at large as gender neutral, assumptions about individual behavior being motivated by societal gender roles are less common in later works.[269]

Closely linked to management's non-gendered understanding of the phenomenon is the recognition of same-sex sexual harassment. Both in feminist circles as well as in the mainstream press, this phenomenon accrued very little attention. In the rare cases it was considered, it was examined on a theoretical level and infrequently included a debate of a non-fictional case. Feminists conceded that there was a potential for same-sex harassment among men, but they treated the idea of a woman cast in the role of the harasser as a possible but highly unlikely anomaly.[270] Nevertheless, I have come across a multitude of examples portraying same-sex harassment within corporate material.

Homosexuality and the possibility of same-sex harassment was discussed in the very early court rulings in which judges had argued that gender was not a factor in sexualized behavior. The verdict in *Corne v. Bausch and Lomb* (1977) read:

> in this instance the supervisor was male and the employee was female. But no immutable principle of psychology compels this alignment of parties. The gender lines might as easily have been reversed, or not even crossed at all. Although sexual desire animated the parties, or at least one of them, the gender of each is incidental to the claim of abuse.[271]

As shown here, tying same-sex sexual harassment to an argument which proclaimed that sexual harassment was a gender-neutral phenomenon was not

---

269 Cordua Training Videos: An Employee's Responsibility; Cordua Training Videos: A Supervisor's Responsibility.

270 Farley: Sexual Shakedown; San Francisco Commission on the Status of Women: How to Create a Workplace Free of Sexual Harassment. Employee & Employer Handbook on Sexual Harassment, 1986, at: California Historical Association, American Civil Liberties Union of Northern California Records, Caton 124, Folder: Women's Rights/ Sex Discrimination. Employment – Sexual Harassment 1980–1998.

271 *Tomkins v. Public Service Elec.* **(1976).**

new. However, after the prevalent legal opinion had accepted sexual harassment as a violation of the Civil Rights Act, the legal discussion of same-sex harassment subsided.

It was not until 1998 in *Oncale vs. Sundowner Offshore Services, Inc.* that the Supreme Court ruled to include same-sex sexual harassment under the sex discrimination clause of the Civil Rights Act. Joseph Oncale, an oil-rig worker, had been working on an oil-platform in the Gulf of Mexico, where he was sexually assaulted and verbally harassed by the eight-person, all-male crew. When Oncale filed a lawsuit against his employer, the District Court in a summary judgement held that "Oncale, a male, had no Title VII cause of action for harassment by male co-workers."[272] The 5th Circuit confirmed this ruling, leading Oncale to seek judgment by the Supreme Court. The justices, citing from the racial discrimination suit *Castaneda v. Partida*, argued that "it would be unwise to presume [...] that human beings of one definable group will not discriminate against other members of their group."[273] Therefore, the Court rejected "a categorical rule excluding same-sex harassment claims from coverage of Title VII," and ruled to overturn the original summary judgment.[274] *Oncale v. Sundowner (1998)* set a precedent making legal action against same-sex harassment possible and led to the inclusion of same-sex sexual harassment in the public discourse.[275]

The lack of a public debate as well as the dearth of legal recourse before 1998 makes the wide inclusion of same-sex harassment in consultants' material particularly notable. One training video, for instance, portrayed one woman cat-calling another and then explaining to the camera "she asks for it."[276] Another film shows a male employee asking a male co-worker: "So Pauli, what kind of boys do you like, little ones, like Stevie here, or big boys like me and Earl."[277] This inclusion of same-sex sexual harassment should not be read as a company's progressive and inclusive attitude towards homosexuality. Rather, emphasizing these types of scenarios strengthened the consultants' argument that sexual harassment was not based on gender dynamics and as such was a non-gendered issue. Additionally, as discussed above, management consultants did not rely on current

---

272 *Oncale v. Sundowner Offshore Services, Inc.*, 523 U.S. 75 (1998), p. 75.
273 *Castaneda v. Partida*, 430 U.S. 482 (1977), p. 430.
274 *Oncale v. Sundowner Offshore Services*, p. 79.
275 E.g.: Felsenthal, Edward: U.S. Urges Court to Hear Same-Sex Harassment Case, in: The Wall Street Journal (May 27th, 1997), p. B8; Goodman, Ellen: It's Not About Sex, but Power: Sexual Harassment: A Male vs. Male Case Forces Us to the Heart of the Matter, in: Los Angeles Times (December 7th, 1997), p. M5.
276 Kmart: Respect in the Workplace.
277 Cordua Training Video: An Employee's Responsibility.

precedent but instead sought to anticipate likely future expansion of the law. For management consultants there was no drawback to including same-sex harassment. As such, by the time the Supreme Court ruled it a violation of the Civil Rights Act in 1998, most American employees were already subject to a company policy explicitly forbidding the practice.[278]

In conclusion, contrary to both the feminist and the social conservative frame, in the management frame, sexual harassment is not primarily related to the gender of those involved. Early works, such as Meyer and colleagues' *Sexual Harassment*, included gendered assumptions in their analysis of individual cases but rejected the idea that men as a whole were guiltier of harassing behavior than women. Later works were cautious to remain completely gender-nonspecific in their language and choice of examples. This was in line with legal texts provided by the EEOC, the Civil Rights Act, and the Supreme Court and allowed employers and their consultants to avoid accusations of political bias and gender stereotyping. At the same time the exclusion of gender as a factor also ignored statistical data and removed the examples presented from the lived experiences of those victimized by sexual harassment.

5.2.3 A Personal and Private Issue

If not gender, what factors, according to the management frame, influenced sexual harassment? The answer to this question changed gradually within the two decades analyzed here. While early works acknowledged the influence of systemic power dynamics based on socioeconomic status, sexual orientation, race, and – to a limited extent – gender, later material entirely omitted a discussion of systemic factors. Again, Meyer and colleagues' book and the Cordua training videos are excellent examples for this shift. Meyer et al., briefly discuss gender, race and sexual orientation as possible factors to consider in sexual harassment scenarios. Gender and/or race as determinant factors for sexual harassment are considered a relic of the past, bound to rapidly diminish now that these groups are "integrated into the workplace."[279]

Socio-economic status as a risk factor, however, is highlighted. In the context of economic dependence, the authors acknowledge systemic power dynamics as a cause for potential harassment situations. According to Meyer and colleagues sexual harassment "occur[s] with the greatest frequency" in "jobs which are low level and low paid [...]." These jobs which "carry no power" and in which "success is almost entirely dependent upon the opinion of the supervisor," are held by

---

278 Dobbin: Equal Opportunity, p. 213.

279 Meyer et al.: Sexual Harassment, p. 68.

"lower educated males and females." The authors argue, not unlike feminist groups, that individuals with "few options for economic security" are particularly vulnerable to sexual harassment, especially if their work structure makes them heavily dependent on one supervisor.[280] Unlike feminist groups, Meyer and colleagues describe these individuals as both male and female.

Despite the acknowledgment that systemic circumstances may heighten certain individuals' likelihood of falling victim to harassment, Meyer and colleagues focused on the financial well-being of the business. In Chapter Six of their book, they compare the advantages and disadvantages of a "hierarchical" and a "matrix" organizational form. The authors conclude that sexual harassment was less likely to happen in a matrix system due to the reduced dependence on only one superior and the existence of more horizontal relations. Such a system fostered "communication" and "openness among a greater number of employees." Thus, it would allow for "concerns [to] rise quickly." Nevertheless, the authors did not characterize it as the superior structure. The increased communication between employees in this system made it "difficult" to "[keep] sexual harassment in a low visibility position." Therefore, in comparison to a hierarchal structure, sexual harassment in a matrix structure lead "people to take sides on the issue" and thus heighten "the potential for disruption and the diminishment of productivity."[281]

The authors acknowledged that sexual harassment was facilitated and intensified by systemic factors, but nevertheless insisted on individual solutions. Their advice did not include changing organizations structures to shield individuals from harassment. Economic considerations for the organization outweighed the necessity for the protection of individual employees. Therefore, Meyer et al. cautioned management to prioritize employee morale (and thus, higher productivity) over the elimination of sexual harassment. Despite the acknowledgment of systemic factors influencing relationships, Meyer et al. assert that sexual harassment was most heavily influenced by individual actions and personal relationships. As such, proposed action and solutions in the book differ considerably from the feminist works which preceded them.

The Cordua Training Videos, in line with other material from the 1990s, refrain from discussing systemic factors or the structure of the organization. While people differing in race, gender, and socioeconomic class are represented in the examples, these differences are not treated as factors relevant to the harassment. Scenarios are depicted as interpersonal disputes or misunderstandings.

---

280 Ibid., pp. 92 f.
281 Ibid., p. 92.

The gradual lack of inclusion of systemic power discrepancies in the portrayal of sexual harassment by management consultants over the years coincides with a distancing from feminist groups and feminist rhetoric and material. It is reasonable to assume that the (partial) inclusion of systemic factors in early works was influenced by, if not wholly due to, the feminist dominance within the available reference works.

Resembling the Cordua Training Videos two decades later, Meyer et al.'s proposed action and solutions focus on efforts by individuals rather than institutional changes. Only because this individual behavior had "implications for others as well,"[282] do the authors advise organizations to impose countermeasures and thereby acknowledge the issue on an organizational level. Similarly, the Cordua Training Videos insist on company involvement in facilitating solutions not because they assume the company structures caused the harassment but rather due to the economic risk involved when a conflict remained unresolved.

When discussing sexual harassment, management consultants, similar to judges in early cases, emphasized the personal nature of sexual relationships, no matter whether these were consensual or not. Meyer et al. repeatedly draw their readers' attention to the fact that men and women working together would inevitably prompt friendships and romantic relationships and that a "sexually charged atmosphere" was to be expected.[283] According to Meyer et al., sex integration at work and changing ideas about sexuality put men in a difficult position, since some women now openly sought sexual relations and others maintained a traditional disinclination towards casual sexual relationships. A man meeting a woman in the "present climate" could not easily identify "what species" he was dealing with.[284] The Cordua Training Videos, similarly, acknowledged that romantic and sexual relationships between employees "happen all the time."[285] Sexual harassment, according to management consultants, was most often a result of misinterpreted signs and flirting gone wrong.

Thus, in respect to the harasser's motivation, consultants rarely highlighted intentional power abuse but instead portrayed sexual harassment as an unfortunate but often "accidental" occurrence. Meyer and colleagues explain:

> The magnitude is underestimated, which is something we discovered, as is the pain experienced by the victim. There is another pain as well, the pain suffered by the individual accused of harassing another person when there was no such intent. [...] The harasser may

---

282 Meyer et al.: Sexual Harassment, p. 46.
283 Ibid., pp. xiv, 64, 176.
284 Ibid., p. 64.
285 Cordua Training Videos: An Employee's Responsibility.

> not know they are harassing. Well intended gestures or remarks of friendship and affection may be received as harassment. Imagined harassment, however, can be as destructive as intended harassment. [...] [A minority of bosses] see as one of their life goals success as a sexual harasser. For the most part, it just happens.[286]

Striking, in this citation, is the distinction between "harassment" and "imagined harassment." This distinction did not become crucial in the further analysis both within this quote and the book in question. However, in this instance, Meyer et al. imply that the lack of malicious intent altered the quality of the harassment, transforming it from real to "imagined." Furthermore, "imagined harassment" was "destructive" not only due to the negative experience felt by the victim but also the "pain" ailing an unwitting employee accused of harassment.

Meyer and colleagues as well as the Cordua Training Videos argued that because every employee had the potential of harassing and of becoming a victim of harassment, everyone had a "responsibility" to stop harassment. Meyer et al. instruct the reader to "analyze your feelings and behavior to see if there is anything of the sexual harasser in you."[287] Both Meyer and colleagues as well as Backer explain that an employee's conduct or dress may influence whether they will receive sexual propositions from colleagues. Take, for instance these two statements; the first is a quote by Meyer et al., the second is taken from the Cordua Training Videos:

> How you accept an invitation for a drink can lead a person on or set the record straight. What you wear also send messages; clothes which are too tight for comfort suggest that there is more than business to discuss. [...] The main problem is that most people do not analyze their behavior and then are surprised to find themselves in a distasteful situation.[288]

> All of us have a responsibility not to leave ourselves open to comments or behavior of a sexual nature. Dressing in a short skirt or a seductive outfit can very well indicate to someone, that behavior of a sexual nature may be welcomed.[289]

Both works place the responsibility for sexual harassment with the harasser and the "harassee." The emphasis on clothing and dress may well remind the reader of Phyllis Schlafly's congressional testimony when she asserted that women inviting sexual advances "walk across the room with a certain body language men intui-

---

286 Meyer et al.: Sexual Harassment, pp. xiii., 126.
287 Ibid., p. 127.
288 Ibid., p. 114.
289 Cordua Training Videos: An Employee's Responsibility.

tively understand."[290] Contrary to the conservative framing of the issue, the management frame does not solely make the target of the harassment responsible. In contrast to the feminist framing, it does not absolve the "harassee" of all responsibility.

Working off the assumption that the harassment is purely a misunderstanding both Meyer et al. and Becker emphasize the importance of communication. They agree that the "first thing to do when you feel you are being harassed is to tell the person to stop." When giving such feedback to the ("imagined") harasser, targets are advised to do so in "a respectful way,"[291] and to "deliver the remarks with a pleasant smile" as this "takes some of the sting out of them."[292] Targets are advised to openly assume some responsibility. To initiate a conversation with one's harasser, Meyer et al. suggest the example phrase "perhaps, I've misled you, but [...]." Additionally, the authors encourage targets to focus on the harasser's behavior rather than "him as a person." Both sets of material focus on "leav[ing] the door open for a continuing relationship," and giving the harasser the "opportunity to emerge from the confrontation with dignity."[293]

The implication that sexual harassment could happen without any malicious intent, blurred the line between coerced and consensual behavior. Despite Becker's insistence throughout both Cordua Training Videos that harassment constituted "unwelcome" behavior, he and his consultant colleague clarify that "[a]nything of a sexual nature is not appropriate in the work environment, no matter whether it is welcome or not." While maintaining that a person asking for a date "is most likely not sexual harassment," he insists that such a request "can potentially destroy an otherwise excellent working relationship."[294] In the videos, employees are discouraged from pursuing romantic relationships in the workplace. Managers and supervisors, especially, are cautioned about "crossing personal boundaries with an employee" and are warned of the "great risk" of such behavior for "the employee, the manager, and the organization."[295]

Meyer et al. too, discourage any romantic or sexual relationships in the workplace and clearly specify "businesslike" and "androgynous" behavior to be the ideal.[296] Sexual harassment and consensual sexual relationships are both con-

---

290 Phillis Schlafly's Testimony at the Committee on Labor: Hearings on Sex Discrimination, p. 400.
291 Cordua Training Videos: An Employee's Responsibility.
292 Meyer: Sexual Harassment, p. 116.
293 Ibid., pp. 116 f.
294 Cordua Training Videos: An Employee's Responsibility.
295 Cordua Training Videos: A Manager's Responsibility.
296 Meyer et al.: Sexual Harassment, p. 109.

sidered harmful for the success of the company. Not only could a consensual relationship sour, but such a relationship could cause discord in the wider team, affect employee morale, and consequently induce lower productivity. Meyer and colleagues drew on Margaret Mead's 1978 article "taboos on sex at work,"[297] which drew an analogy between a family and a company both representing an "economic unit." Meyer et al., quoting from Mead proclaimed that "the incest taboo [...] directly relates to sexual harassment." Just like a taboo on sex within the family, a taboo on sex in the workplace would allow for "the betterment of both the organization and the individual."[298]

According to Meyer et al., a taboo on sex at work would "establish different thinking within our minds and express the willingness to take personal responsibility for our actions."[299] In instances in which individual self-monitoring failed, a taboo could be enforced on an organizational level. In the event of a broken taboo, termination and disciplinary action within the workplace would substitute for "ostracism or murder" within the family. Following this analysis, the authors implore employers to "seriously consider" limiting or disallowing sexual relationships between employees.[300]

Most feminists focusing on sexual harassment considered a ban on all sexual relations as detrimental, because such a policy did not distinguish between coerced and consensual behavior. Many feared, that broad restrictions on sexuality would shift the focus of the discussion towards sex and sexuality rather than discrimination and violence against women. Such restrictions were reminiscent of social conservative ideas of morality and chastity and, according to feminists, restricted women's sexual self-determination.[301]

From a management perspective, a ban on sex had a significant upside: it was an unambiguous rule. Consultants often stated that the issue of sexual harassment was not "clear cut" and lamented the lack of a clear definition.[302] Meyer et al. argued that, since a "compliment," "lewd remark," and "sexual assault" "seem to be in the same broad category," sincere confusion in discussions of sexual harassment was to be expected.[303] With a taboo on sex in the workplace such confusion

297 Mead: We Need Taboos.
298 Meyer et al.: Sexual Harassment, p. 86.
299 Ibid., p. 86.
300 Ibid., p. 70.
301 Farley: Sexual Shakedown; MacKinnon: Sexual Harassment of Working Women; Wehrli: Sexual Harassment at the Workplace; Cohen: The Secret Oppression.
302 Cordua Training Videos: Sexual Harassment – Awareness, Perception and Prevention: An Employee's Responsibility.
303 Meyer et al.: Sexual Harassment, p. 4.

could easily be eliminated. Regarding limitations on sexual relationships at work, consultants' advice differed in intensity. Some, like Meyer and colleagues proposed a zero-tolerance approach for sexual relations between employees. Others advised employers and employees alike to monitor their own behavior and keep relationships professional.[304] Despite these differences, a staple of the management frame is a general skepticism towards any sexual, romantic, or generally "unprofessional" behavior between colleagues.[305]

When harassment did occur or was "imagined," consultants in general advised unmediated communication between the harasser and the harassee. Material from the early to mid-1980s was often particularly adamant about this point. Meyer et al., for instance, advise directly telling the harasser to stop "a couple of times, to make sure your message really got through." If the harassment still did not cease "it is time to get additional help." Rather than make a report to the HR office or a superior, however, the authors suggest to "turn to your peers." The harasser, according to the authors, "will get the message if he receives it from a variety of people."[306]

Meyer et al. explain that abstaining from official complaints benefits the harassee for three reasons:

> [First,] she is more likely to retain a working relationship with the harasser and his peers if she can do this without calling in the Marines. Second, she will be respected by her superiors if she does not need to run to them for help. And third, the skills necessary to diminish and stop this type of behavior are excellent ones to develop and to transfer to other areas of work relationships. The woman manager, or the woman eager to enter management, must concentrate on these skills. Managers handle people's problems. So, learn to handle this one. [307]

Sexual harassment is portrayed like any other inter-personal conflict which could be readily resolved when those involved communicate. For a target to enlist the HR department's or a supervisor's assistance would be tantamount to them admitting that they lacked the skill set to handle personnel issues.

This tendency to discourage official complaints, even within the company, is typical for very early consultant works.[308] Interestingly, these same consultants strongly encouraged employers to institute internal policies and procedures. Meyer et al. recognized that "there are many benefits to organizations that have

---

304 Cordua Training Videos: A Manager's Responsibility; Kmart: Respect in the Workplace.
305 Meyer et al.: Sexual Harassment, p. 109.
306 Ibid., p. 118.
307 Ibid., p. 120.
308 Cf. Gutek: Sex and the Workplace, pp. 153 f.

clearly defined policies and procedures,"[309] and warn employers that "if [...] you do not have a policy that includes sexual harassment, then you leave yourself vulnerable to problems." Thus, early consultants discouraged employees from seeking their organizations' assistance while at the same time lobbying employers to institute an official process of employee complaints. These two pieces of advice did not contradict but rather complimented each other. The authors recognize a company's vulnerability resulting from the lack of policies and grievance procedures. As most companies in the 1980s had not yet instituted such policies, consultants advised companies to close this gap and at the same time led employees away from discovering this vulnerability in the first place.

Training material and workshops more confidently directed employees to file official complaints as companies increasingly took consultants' advice and implemented policies and grievance procedures. The Cordua Training Videos, like much of the material produced in the 1990s, elucidates the importance of seeking "help from your employer." Becker emphasizes that if the harassment does not cease after a direct conversation with the harasser, or if such a conversation is not possible, the aggrieved employee should "follow [their] organization's grievance procedure" and/or "talk to [their] supervisor."[310] This was also in line with the trend of legal decisions focusing increasingly on company action and often rejecting employers' claims of ignorance.

On a practical level, consultants made their clients aware of legal requirements. Education on the legal situation and the classification of sexual harassment as a civil rights violation were indispensable in any management consultant's work. Often, the legal situation was depicted as stricter and more clearly defined than was actually the case. Sexual harassment was in most, if not all cases, referred to as "illegal."[311] On a theoretical level, however, consultants understood sexual harassment as an individual issue and rejected feminists' assertions that the phenomenon necessitated political action and government involvement. Meyer et al., for instance, argue that "[s]exual harassment is basically a moral issue and therefore the overall responsibility for its elimination lies within the individual rather than with the law."[312] Ideologically, this rejection of state intervention coincides with a business friendly, laissez-faire world view, in which govern-

---

309 Meyer et al.: Sexual Harassment, pp. 85 f.

310 Cordua Training Videos: An Employee's Responsibility.

311 Guteck, Barbara: Sex and the Workplace, London – San Francisco 1985, p. 62; National Education Association Broadcast Services: Sexual Harassment Video, October 3rd, 1990; Kmart: Respect in the Workplace. Meyer: Sexual Harassment, p. 88; Cordua Training Videos: An Employee's Responsibility; Cordua Training Videos: A Supervisor's Responsibility.

312 Meyer et al.: Sexual Harassment, p. 79.

ment involvement was seen with great skepticism.[313] At the same time, conceptualizing sexual harassment as a moral rather than a legal issue supported consultant's strategy of handling the problem internally.

In this chapter, I have outlined the differing strategies of corporate lawyers and management consultants. Lawyers insisted that precedent was not settled and advocated for litigation on a case-by-case basis. Therefore, the profession endorsed clear policies and training in order to discourage harassers but warned employers against implementing grievance procedures which had the potential of endangering their legal claim of plausible deniability. Management consultants, on the other hand, had accepted sexual harassment as a civil rights violation with strict employer liability before the Supreme Court ruled on either issue. Policies, training, and grievance procedures were presented as compliance strategies for employers to resolve complaints internally and avoid litigation. Despite a lack of proof that internal measures decreased either instances of sexual harassment or the number of lawsuits filed against the company, many employers chose consultants advice over that offered by corporate lawyers.

As employers increasingly sought personnel experts' services, management consultants increasingly specialized in the issue and devised material for use within a company. Within their handbooks, pamphlets, training, and counseling, consultants created a new understanding of sexual harassment: the management frame. The core objective of this frame was not the perpetuation of a wider narrative, nor the intention to influence societal structures and gender norms. Instead, sexual harassment was seen as individual, gender-non-specific behavior, which could negatively affect the organization's productivity and financials. Sexual harassment, in this frame, became primarily an economic concern.

By emphasizing the individual nature of the problem, consultants denied that the structure of the organization facilitated or encouraged sexual misconduct, while at the same time stressing their clients' organization's institutional power for prevention and discipline. Due to employers' efforts to limit sexual harassment within their organization, many Americans' first contact with the subject matter was mediated by the policy and procedure of their place of work. This gave employers' much influence on the public perception of sexual harassment.

By following management consultants' advice employers attempted to remain one step ahead of the courts. For almost two decades the business community attempted to anticipate the next precedent setting judgement.[314] While strategies varied and were negotiated throughout this time period, it was clear that employ-

---

313 Cf. Klatch: Women, pp. 4–12.
314 Dobbin: Equal Opportunity, p. 192.

ers were playing defense. This state of limbo was concluded when the Supreme Court in 1998 made a broad decision on the matter of employment liability in its twin decision *Burlington Industries, Inc. v. Ellerth* and *Faragher v. City of Boca Raton*. These decisions again severely influenced both the government's and the private sector's approach to sexual harassment.

In Part II sexual harassment was acknowledged by the federal government as a civil rights violation. Additionally, I identified a move away from activist groups handling the issue, and instead a professionalization in this regard of lawyers and management consultants. Similarly, instead of feminist organizations being the first port-of-call for affected employees, institutionalized paths for complaints both through the EEOC as well as internally in many places of work were made available. Through these developments a new framework of sexual harassment emerged. The phenomenon was represented, not as a systemic, gendered concern based on power relations, but instead as a problem between two individuals, independent of structural or gender relationships, which could prove to be very costly for the employer.

Part III
Privatization

"Court rulings force businesses to visit sexual harassment issues."[1]
"Court cases alter sexual harassment law."[2]
"Employers take steps to avoid charges of sexual harassment."[3]

In the fall of 1998, headlines, like the ones quoted above, were splashed across business magazines throughout the country. On June 26th, 1998, the Supreme Court had handed down its twin-decision on the cases of *Faragher v. Boca Raton* and *Burlington Industries Inc. v. Ellerth*, and the business community was responding. Article after article informed employers that the Supreme Court had "fundamentally changed the law of sexual harassment." Employers could now mount an affirmative defense: If the employer could prove in court, that the organization had a policy and grievance procedure in place, and that "appropriate action" had been taken immediately after having been given notice about the harassment, they would not be held liable for their employees' actions. Now more than ever, lawyers and management consultants were encouraging employers to be "proactive,"[4] and to "review and, if necessary, revise [their] anti-harassment policy."[5] Indeed, the *Faragher* and *Ellerth* cases mark a shift in sexual harassment law and in employers' response to the issue.

The former of the two cases, *Faragher v. Boca Raton*, was initially brought by Beth Ann Faragher, a female lifeguard formerly employed by the City of Boca Raton. Faragher alleged that two of her immediate supervisors Bill Terry and David Silverman had "among other things [...] created a 'sexually hostile atmosphere' at work by repeatedly subjecting [her] and other female lifeguards to 'uninvited and offensive touching,' by making lewd remarks and by speaking of women in offensive terms [...]."[6] The complaint included "specific allegations that Terry once said that he would never promote a woman to the rank of lieu-

---

1 Rutledge-Jones, Dawn: Court Rulings Force Businesses to Visit Sexual Harassment Issues, in: Nashville Business Journal (September 13th, 1998).
2 Anonymous: Court Cases Alter Sexual Harassment Law, in: Triangle Business Journal (October 26th, 1998).
3 Anonymous: Employers Take Steps to Avoid Charges of Sexual Harassment, in: Houston Business Journal (September 13th, 1998).
4 Rutledge-Jones, Dawn: Court Rulings Force Businesses to Visit Sexual Harassment Issues, in: Nashville Business Journal (September 13th, 1998).
5 Anonymous: Court Cases Alter Sexual Harassment Law.
6 *Faragher v. City of Boca Raton*, p. 775.

tenant, and that Silverman had said to Faragher, '[d]ate me or clean the toilets for a year.'"[7]

Faragher was unaware of the City's official grievance procedure as it had never been distributed among the employees of the Marine Safety Section. She complained informally to a member of higher management, but when no action followed, Faragher resigned her position. In her lawsuit, Faragher claimed that the "hostile atmosphere" had altered her working conditions, as it was "severe and pervasive." Therefore, she sought "nominal damages and other relief" from her employer.[8]

When distilled, the core question put before the courts in *Faragher v. City of Boca Raton* concerned employer liability: Was the City to be held accountable for Terry's and Silverman's actions? The District Court held that Terry and Silverman, in their supervisory position, were acting as agents of the employer. Further, the Court considered the harassment "severe and pervasive" enough that the defendant should have known about the misconduct, especially since Faragher had informed management of the situation. The Eleventh Circuit Appeals Court overturned this ruling, stating that Terry and Silverman "were not acting within the scope of their employment when they engaged in the harassing conduct."[9] Thus, the City, according to the Appeals Court, could not be held liable for their offences. In 1998 the case was heard by the Supreme Court.

In spring of the same year another, similar case came before the Supreme Court. *Burlington Industries v. Ellerth*, concerned Kimberly Ellerth, a salesperson at Burlington Industries, who accused her supervisor Ted Slowik of sexually harassing her. Besides his "alleged repeated boorish and offensive remarks and gestures [towards her]," Ellerth charged him of making "threats to deny her tangible job benefits." She had refused her supervisor's advances and although he did not follow through on his threats, she felt the working environment had become intolerable. Like Faragher, Ellerth did not make use of her employer's internal grievance procedure before resigning her position.[10]

The District Court did not let the case proceed to trial, instead granting Burlington Industries a summary judgement. Upon appeal, the Seventh Circuit Appeals Court reversed this decision. On the appeals level *Burlington Industries v. Faragher*, like *Ellerth v. City of Boca Raton*, was heard *en banc*. This meant that not only one judge but all eleven circuit judges resided over the hearings. The judg-

---

7 Ibid.
8 Ibid., p. 776.
9 Ibid., p. 775.
10 *Burlington Industries, Inc. v. Ellerth*, p. 743.

es found no accord and issued eight separate opinions. Points of disagreement were the usefulness of the categorization of *quid pro quo* and hostile work environment sexual harassment as well as the issue of employer liability. Due to the lack of consensus among the judges in the Appeals Court, the case was heard by the Supreme Court.[11]

As Justice Kennedy later wrote in the majority opinion of *Burlington v. Faragher*, "[t]he disagreement revealed in the careful opinions of the judges of the Court of Appeals reflects the fact that Congress has left it to the courts to determine controlling agency law principles in a new and difficult area of federal law [...]."[12] The Supreme Court had been hesitant to make a broad decision in 1986, but now after near two decades of legislative inaction the justices were ready to settle the law regarding employer liability in cases involving hostile work environment sexual harassment perpetrated by a supervisor.[13]

Both Ellerth and Faragher alleged that their respective supervisors regularly engaged in harassing behavior but had never taken tangible employment actions. Thus, in these cases, the Court considered the following: Were the harassers, Terry, Silverman, and Slowik, acting as agents of their respective organizations, even without invoking the concrete authorities endowed to them by their employer? Should the employers have been given formal notice by Ellerth or Faragher? Or was an employer automatically liable for the conduct of their supervisory staff?

The Court agreed with Ellerth and Faragher that "there are good reasons" to distinguish between hostile work environment cases, depending on whether the harasser had supervisory authority. While a target could "walk away or tell the offender where to go" when the harasser was a fellow employee, the Court acknowledged that "it may be difficult to offer such responses to a supervisor, whose 'power to supervise, [...] to hire and fire, and to set work schedules and pay rates – does not disappear [...] when he chooses to harass through insults and offensive gestures rather than directly with threats of firing or promises of promotion.'"[14] Therefore, even though the supervisors' harassing conduct did not further the goals of the organization and even though the supervisors did not explicitly use the organizations' authority to facilitate their misconduct, the

11 Ibid.
12 Ibid., p. 752.
13 As has been explained in previous chapters, employer liability was established in cases comprised of *quid pro quo* sexual harassment. Additionally, most courts agreed that a knowledge standard applied in hostile-work environment cases involving coworkers. For a closer analysis refer to Chapters Three and Four.
14 Estrich, Susan: Sex at Work, 43 Stanford Law Review (1991), pp. 813, 854, cited in *Faragher v. City of Boca Raton* (1998), p. 804.

Court recognized that the "conduct of a supervisor" was "made possible by the abuse of his supervisory authority." The justices applied the "aided-by-agency-relation" principle, holding the employers vicariously liable for the actions of their supervisors.[15]

However, citing Title VII's "basic polic[y] of encouraging forethought by employers,"[16] the Court opted against absolute, automatic liability and included a provision allowing the employer to present an affirmative defense.

> When no tangible employment action is taken, a defending employer may raise an affirmative defense to liability or damages, [...]. The defense comprises two necessary elements: (a) that the employer exercised reasonable care to prevent and correct promptly any sexually harassing behavior, and (b) that the plaintiff employee unreasonably failed to take advantage of any preventive or corrective opportunities provided by the employer or to avoid harm otherwise.[17]

What had been implied in *Meritor Savings Bank v. Vinson* in 1986 was now made explicit: Preventative measures, such as internal policies, grievance procedures, training, as well as a rapid response by the organization when a problem occurred, could insulate an employer from liability in hostile work environment cases.

Furthermore, the Court upheld the notice requirement and specified that an employee "unreasonably" foregoing internal procedures gave the employer grounds for an affirmative defense. Thus, although the justices did not make "anti-harassment polic[ies] or complaint procedures [...] necessary in every instance as a matter of law,"[18] they did unequivocally present these measures as safeguards against legal liability in hostile work environment cases. An employer without a policy or procedure was not breaking the law but would have a hard time protecting himself in the case of a sexual harassment suit.

Based on these legal developments, action against sexual harassment shifted from the government to the private sector. I argue that employers gained significant control over the subject matter and that this led to changes not only pertaining to responses to sexual harassment but also regarding the understanding of the phenomenon. In Chapter Six, I discuss how, regarding sexual harassment, the private sector took on authorities previously held by the federal government. Due to the judiciary's insistence that victims use internal measures, companies – while working within the given legal limits – functioned as state-like, self-contained en-

---

15 *Faragher v. City of Boca Raton* (1998), p. 776.
16 *Burlington Industries, Inc. v. Ellerth* (1998), p. 765.
17 Ibid., p. 764.
18 Ibid., p. 765.

tities. Employers published definitions of sexual harassment (legislative), implemented programs and material regarding employee education, proposed grievance procedures, investigated complaints (executive), assessed whether an accusation had merit, and decided on disciplinary action (judicative). All the while, employers, at large, subscribed to the management framework of sexual harassment. Therefore, the increase of employers' discursive power, which accompanied the shift of authority from the federal government to the private sector, entrenched the management frame as a dominant understanding of sexual harassment.

Employers' best efforts notwithstanding, not all sexual harassment complaints could be resolved internally. In Chapter Seven, I turn my focus outside of the company to various methods of alternative dispute resolution. For employers, resolving matters through mediation or arbitration had the significant benefit of avoiding public attention and judicial involvement. Therefore, employers increasingly implemented mandatory arbitration as a tool to settle employer-employee conflicts. I will demonstrate that both the practice of binding arbitration, and the confidentiality and non-disclosure agreements often associated with alternative dispute resolution heavily influenced the handling and conceptualization of sexual harassment.

For the historian, internal grievance procedures, alternative dispute resolution, and confidentiality agreements present a considerable challenge; access to sources is extremely restricted. For instance, I can assess written grievance procedures, which on paper promise confidentiality but I have no knowledge of what transpired during a confidential internal investigation. Similarly, I have access to the specifics of a non-disclosure agreement only when it failed its purpose and the information has been made public. Nevertheless, internal measures to prevent sexual harassment as well as binding arbitration are widely discussed topics in the social sciences, which often rely on anonymized survey data. This data will be a cornerstone of my analysis.

Additionally, in Chapter Six and Seven, I will rely on examples which have been made public. Some of these instances, occurred pre-1998, when confidentiality agreements were not as common. While outside of the time period analyzed here, they exemplify dynamics which, according to social scientists, continued throughout the decades. Other instances were made public during the #MeToo movement.[19]

---

19 The hashtag #MeToo was first used in 2007 by activist Tarana Burke in the context of sexual assault of women and girls of color. The movement went viral in 2017 after Minlano's tweet. For

On October 15th, 2017, actor Alyssa Milano tweeted:

> If all the women who have been sexually harassed or assaulted wrote "Me too." as a status, we might give people a sense of the magnitude of the problem. If you've been sexually harassed or assaulted write 'me too' as a reply to this tweet.[20]

Within 48 hours, the hashtag was tweeted nearly one million times.[21] A year later this number had risen to nineteen million.[22] On- and offline, women and men recounted their stories of sexual violence and sexual harassment. In doing so, an increasing number of survivors violated the non-disclosure agreements they had signed. Others made very public non-statements about being prohibited from commenting due to such agreements. While these stories were told in and after 2017, most of the incidences discussed occurred within the period analyzed in Part III. As such, they prove to be a valuable source for the following chapters.

6 Judge, Jury, and Executioner: Keeping Complaints Internal

The *Ellerth* and *Faragher* decisions had a significant impact on legal and corporate responses to sexual harassment. As demonstrated in Part II, company internal action on sexual harassment was already extremely common by 1998. In light of the Supreme Court's decisions even those employers who had held back earlier instituted anti-harassment policies and grievance procedures. The significance of such policies and procedures grew because they were more widely spread than ever before and because the judiciary now accepted them as a shield against liability. Additionally, their relevance increased because employees wishing to complain about sexual harassment *had* to make use of them. Therefore, I hypothesize that these rulings presented the final straw in a process that shifted state authority on sexual harassment to the private sector.

Before the *Faragher* and *Ellerth* decisions, employers' procedure had been one of several options complainants had available. Such a grievance procedure could offer what many complainants sought: a chance to make the harassment stop. On the other hand, if the employee's complaint was directed at the employ-

―――
more information see: Burke, Tarana: Unbound. My Story of Liberation and the Birth of the MeToo Movement, London 2021.

20 Milano, Alyssa: Tweet. October 15th, 2017. 10:21pm.

21 Anonymous: More than 12M 'MeToo' Facebook posts, comments, reactions in 24 hours, in: CBS News, (October 17th, 2017).

22 Anderson, Monica and Skye Toor: How social media users have discussed sexual harassment since #MeToo went viral, in: Pew Research Center (October 11th, 2018).

er's handling of the situation or the complainant did not trust the employer to take sexual harassment allegations seriously and launch a fair investigation, targets had been free to circumvent company grievance procedures and remedies. They could file a complaint with the EEOC and pursue litigation.

After the Supreme Court's decisions in 1998, this choice no longer existed. In a great majority of cases summary judgments were granted to the employer, if the complainant had not utilized the internal procedure. Even when a plaintiff had made use of the internal procedure but found the result unsatisfactory, the mere existence of preventative and punitive measures within the company was often enough to persuade a judge to rule in favor of the employer. The quality and effectiveness of these measures were seldom seriously examined. Therefore, most victims of harassment were precluded from the possibility of pursuing the matter in the judicial system.[23]

6.1 Legislative: Establishing Definitions

As has been discussed in earlier chapters, the U.S. legislature did not play a great role in shaping sexual harassment law. While it is true that Congress devised the Civil Rights Act, which of course, presented the basis for all further judicial and executive action, the law lacked a definition of "discrimination," and never even mentioned the term "sexual harassment." Discrimination and more specifically sexual harassment were contentious topics, and thus, clearer definitions were not agreed upon within Congress.[24]

As Richard Hasen, Professor of Law and Political Science, explained, "[w]hen polarization leads to gridlock in Congress or between Congress and the president, it can empower other political actors, including the courts."[25] In this case, the ambiguity in discrimination law induced the executive and the judiciary branch to further define sexual harassment and effectively shape legislation. Nevertheless, the writing of laws and definitions of the concepts regulated within these laws must continue to be seen as legislative functions. When comparing a company with a state, written policies could be seen as analogous to governmental legislation. American employers provided explicit definitions of sexual harassment

---

23 Edelman, Lauren and Jessica Cabrera: Sex-Based Harassment and Symbolic Compliance, in: Annual Review of Law and Social Science (June 2020), pp. 363, 373 f., 376 f.
24 Dobbin: Equal Opportunity, pp. 3, 7, 198, 200.
25 Hasen, Richard: Polarization and the Judiciary, in: Annual Review of Political Science 22 (2019), p. 272.

within their respective policies. These policies followed the management frame and differed from the EEOC definition in small, yet significant, ways.

The analysis of company policies from the early 1980s, in Chapter Three, revealed that most company policies took their lead from the EEOC guidelines. This trend persisted throughout the decades and holds true for policies from the late 1990s and the early 21st century. For instance, a 1996 policy by Reed and Barton Corporation forbid any "unwelcome sexual advances" and "requests for sexual favors [...] implicitly or explicitly linked to terms of employment."[26]

Contrary to early policies and the EEOC guidelines, Reed and Barton further specified the conduct covered. Rather than using the overarching, more generalized EEOC phrasing in which "conduct [...] creating an intimidating, hostile, or offensive working environment" was prohibited,[27] the policy emphasized the ban of distinct behavior. Examples included "[suggestive] visual displays," "jokes [...] that promote stereotypes," or "directing communication with an individual to matters involving his or her [...] gender."[28] While such behavior could rise to the legal standard of hostile-work-environment sexual harassment, individually and in isolation the instances described would not have met the legal threshold of sexual harassment. Nevertheless, according to the policy, any of the actions listed "may [be] subject to [...] disciplinary action, including termination."[29] The Reed and Barton Corporation was not alone in broadening the scope of their sexual harassment policy to include behavior which went beyond the extent of the law.[30] Such policies allowed employers to act before the level of illegal conduct was reached.

These policies also had implications for Americans' understanding of sexual harassment. The EEOC forbade the creation of a hostile work environment due to its discriminatory character. The individual acts mentioned above, however, were forbidden in their own rights. Suggestive visual displays or conversations revolving around one's gender were not necessarily discriminatory. Nevertheless, they were termed "sexual harassment" and forbidden without the policy having offered any further qualifiers. This aligned with the management frame as it

---

26 Reed and Barton Corporation Policy, 1996, p. 1, HBL, Kenneth H. Olson Collection, 1940–2011, Carton 18, Folder Diversity File 1996; cf. Household International Human Resources – Guidelines and Procedures, Sexual Harassment, December 1991, HSBC, 7-NA0078/002 Human Resources Guidelines and Procedures.

27 EEOC guidelines 1980.

28 Reed and Barton Corporation Policy, 1996, pp. 1f.

29 Ibid., p. 2.

30 E.g. Wal-Mart refer to: *State v. Wal-Mart Stores*, 207 A.D.2d 150, 152 (N.Y. App. Div. 1995); McDonald's refer to: Dobbin, Ben: Voice-Mail Romance Brings Legal Test of Worker Privacy Rights, in: San Francisco Chronicle (January 23rd, 1995), p. A6; cf. Schultz: The Sanitized Workplace, pp. 2099–2101.

has been portrayed in Chapter Five. Policies, like the one implemented by the Reed and Barton Corporation, emphasized individual bad action over a pattern of behavior and the interplay of various factors.

Closely linked to this was the company's understanding of the examples of misconduct as "both inappropriate and unprofessional [...]."[31] Thus, sexual harassment was presented as an individual issue with the potential of disturbing a professional environment rather than an illegal and discriminatory practice. The focus on professionality also conflated instances of coercive and consensual sexual behavior. While the EEOC definition forbids "unwelcome" behavior, company policies often did not highlight this distinction. Instead, many company policies banned, limited, or monitored intimate relationships between employees. This is a trend that began with the specialization of management consultants on sexual harassment, but seems to have gotten more prominent in the beginning of the 21st century.[32]

Sociologist Frank Dobbin estimates that in the late 2000s, roughly 40% of American companies with over fifteen employees implemented, so called, "zero-tolerance policies," which forbade any sexual or romantic contact between employees.[33] Other companies adopted, what Vicki Schultz termed, a "cultural sensitivity approach." Although it was not as strict as the zero-tolerance approach, it forbade intimate relations between individuals in a hierarchical relationship and monitored those between coworkers. Colleagues involved in a romantic and/or sexual relationship – no matter how fleeting – were required to disclose their relationship to the human resources department in what colloquially became known as a "love contract." Failure to do so was a violation of the company's sexual harassment policy and could be penalized accordingly.[34]

Many critics have attributed employers' bans – or disapproval – of voluntary sexual and/or romantic relationships in the workplace to social conservative calls for the preservation of "morality" at work.[35] The social conservative disapproval of sexuality in the public sphere was in line with employers forbidding and/or

---

31 Reed and Barton Corporation Policy, 1996, p. 2.
32 E.g. Wal-Mart refer to: *State v. Wal-Mart Stores*, 207 A.D.2d 150, 152 (N.Y. App. Div. 1995); McDonald's refer to: Dobbin, Ben: Voice-Mail Romance, p. A6; cf. Schultz: The Sanitized Workplace, pp. 2099–2101.
33 Schultz: The Sanitized Workplace, pp. 2101–2103; Cannada, Lisa: Zero-Tolerance for Hospital Romance, in: AMA Journal of Ethics (January 2010); Kohn, Arthur et al.: Companies' Anti-Fraternization Policies: Key Considerations, in: Harvard Law School Forum on Corporate Governance (January 26th, 2020).
34 Schultz: The Sanitized Workplace, pp. 2101–2103.
35 Ibid., p. 2064; Kohn: Companies' Anti-Fraternization Policies.

limiting the sexual expression of their employees. However, while the result may be the same, employers' motives, with the notable exception of some decidedly conservative Christian corporations, such as Chick-Fil-A or In-N-Out Burger,[36] seem not to be linked to social conservative ideas.

Instead, legal scholar Vicki Schultz explained that employers drew their disapproval of sexuality from a different ideological spring.

> It wasn't Victorian churchwomen, but twentieth-century organization men who took the lead in creating the asexual imperative: men like Frederick Winslow Taylor, who saw managers as rational 'heads' who would control the unruly 'hands' and irrational 'hearts' of those who assumed their places as workers in the modem organization.[37]

Taylorist standards and theories on effective bureaucracy suggested that for maximum productivity a worker had to shed their 'humanness.'[38] Max Weber, while himself critical of the effect a bureaucracy could have on the individuals involved, theorized that a business' success would increase significantly "the more perfectly the [...] bureaucracy is 'dehumanized [...].'" In fact, he considered the elimination of "love, hatred, and all purely personal, irrational, and emotional elements which escape calculation [from official business]" as the "special virtue" of bureaucracy.[39] Upon entering the workplace, rationality and productivity rather than emotion and individuality, were expected from employees. Romance and sexuality were at the center of the "personal" and "irrational," and therefore were subject to oversight by "rational" managers.

These theories found footing in the reality of the 20th century American business world.[40] Employers had been suspicious of sexuality in the workplace long before a discussion of sexual harassment appeared on the horizon. R.R. Donnelley

---

36 Chatelain, Marcia: The Conservative and Christian Roots of Many Beloved Fast Food Chains. It's Not Just Chick-fil-A, in: The Washington Post (August 9th, 2021).
37 Schultz: Sanitizing the Workplace, p. 2064; cf. Taylor, Frederick Winslow: The Principles of Scientific Management, (Akasha Classics Series), 2008; Uhl, Karsten: Humane Rationalisierung? Die Raumordnung der Fabrik im Fordistischen Jahrhundert, Bielefeld 2014, pp. 134f.; Derksen, Maarten: Turning Men into Machines? Scientific Management, Industrial Psychology, and the "Human Facor," in: Journal of the History of the Behavioral Sciences, 50/2 (Spring 2014), pp. 148–165; Rabin-Margalioth: Love at Work, in: Duke Journal of Gender Law and Policy 13 (2006), p. 237.
38 Cf. Schultz: Sanitizing the Workplace, p. 2064; Greenspan, Alan and Adrian Wooldrige: Capitalism in America. A History, 2018, p. 147.
39 Weber, Max: From Max Weber. Essays in Sociology, transl. by H.H. Gerth and C. Wright Mills, London 1991, p. 216; cf. Berebitsky: Sex and the Office, p. 6.
40 Cf. Nicholas, Michael: The Little Black Book of Decision Making. Making Complex Decisions in a Fast-Moving World, Chinchester 2017; Head, Simon: The New Ruthless Economy. Work and Power in the Digital Age, New York 2003.

and Sons Company, for instance, published a section entitled "Talking Between Men and Women" in their pamphlet *Plant Rules You Should Know* before the term sexual harassment was even coined. The section stated:

> Business Only During Working Hours. Your private affairs should not follow you to work. On the job, the good employee sticks strictly to business – and avoids personal conversation particularly between men and women.[41]

The inclusion of such rules in employee code of conduct material was not uncommon throughout the 20th century. In her excellent monograph *Sex in the Office*, historian Julie Berebitsky discusses American behavior and attitudes regarding sexuality in the white- and pink-collar workplace throughout 20th century. Berebitsky depicts that sexual conduct in the office was no anomaly and that women bore the "lion's share" of the moral responsibility. However, the author highlights that when employees' actions put "productivity […] at risk," such policies were invoked against both male and female employees.[42]

An important distinction between these early non-fraternization policies and the later sexual harassment policies was their scope. As quoted above, Donnelley and Son's policy from the early 1970s explicitly stated "[y]our private affairs should not follow you to work." Conversely, this policy did not apply to employees' private lives. As long as the relationship was kept private and did not impact the employees' performance in the workplace, the company took no interest in a relationship between coworkers. In contrast, sexual harassment policies forbidding or monitoring intimate relationships between coworkers extended into employees' off-hours.

An early example of such a policy is Wal-Mart's 1989 policy on "fraternization," which forbade a "dating relationship" between coworkers. In 1993, this policy cost Samuel Johnson and Laural Allen their jobs. The couple had met when employed in the sporting goods department in a New York based Wal-Mart and had gotten to know each other at "informal gatherings with other coworkers." Despite Allen's assertions that she and Johnson "at no time […] show[ed] affection at the store," the couple was let go when management became aware of the relationship. In response to her termination Allen proclaimed, "I felt it was my personal life. It

---

41 R.R. Donnelley and Sons Company: Plant Rules You Should Know, 1975, UCL, R.R. Donnelley & Sons Company Archive, Box 1953.
42 Berebitsky: Sex and the Office, pp. 157, 190.

wasn't interfering with my job. [...] I don't think it was right that they could dictate to me that way [...]."[43]

Allen was not alone in thinking that one's private life should not be regulated by one's employer. The American Civil Liberties Union (ACLU) was, at this time, already heavily involved in a fight against employer overreach. Referring to a company with a policy forbidding "its managers from riding motorcycles," and cases in which employers "excluded people with high cholesterol levels, or high blood pressure," the ACLU argued that employers should not be allowed to discriminate against their employees "on the basis of employees' lifestyles."[44] The debate on how much leeway employers had, and should have, in regulating their employees actions outside of work, was particularly vigorous on the issue of smoking. Beginning as early as the 1980s, and increasing significantly in the 1990s and 2000s,[45] there existed employer policies forbidding employees from smoking in their leisure time; effectively precluding individuals from smoking in their own homes.[46]

The debate escalated, after Weyco, a Michigan-based insurance benefits administrator, in 2005, implemented a policy which was "the first of its kind." Rather than relying on employee pledges, as had been the norm in companies with no-smoking policies, Weyco tested all 200 employees for smoking and announced future random breathalyzer tests. Failure or refusal of the test resulted in immediate termination. When explaining the reasoning behind the policy, Weyco's president, Howard Weyers, cited the high medical costs associated with smoking and the higher productivity of healthy workers.[47] Kary Moss, the executive director of the Michigan ACLU, indignantly responded to Weyco's policy by rhetorically asking what other leisure activities employers would soon be regulating; "[w]hat's next? Sitting in the sun?"[48] Lewis Maltby, president of the National Workers Rights Institute expressed the same sentiment, albeit more productively: "[o]nce you cross the line and allow employers to control any type of behavior that's not re-

---

43 Steinberg, Jacques: At Walmart, Workers Who Dated Lose Jobs, in: The New York Times, New York, (14th July, 1993).

44 American Civil Liberties Union: Briefing Paper. The Rights of Employees Number 12, no date (estimated 1991), p. 1, CHA, American Civil Liberties Union of Northern California Records, Carton 120, Folder: Public Information Subject Files, Employment/Labor/Worker's Rights, Discrimination/ Affirmative Action/ALU Policy, 1984–1993.

45 Anonymous: None of an Employer's Business, in: The New York Times (July 7th, 1991).

46 Anonymous: Protecting Employee Privacy Too Far, in: The New York Times (August 6th, 1991); ACLU: Briefing Paper, p. 1.

47 Peters: Jeremy: Company's Smoking Ban Means Off-Hours, Too, in: The New York Times (February 8th, 2005).

48 Ibid.

lated to job performance, there's no limit to the harm that can and will be done." The fact, however, was that in Michigan, this line had long since been crossed.

Most states in the United States operated on an at-will employment basis.[49] At-will employment, in its pure form, allowed both the employer and the employee to terminate their employment relationship at any point for any (or no) reason. Thus, in Michigan, an at-will employment state, Mr. Weyers was fully within his rights to require breathalyzer tests as a condition for continued employment. By 2005, however, there were several states that had implemented varying degrees of limitations on the at-will employment relationship. Thirty states enacted legislation making employers' off-duty smoking bans illegal, and thirteen states disallowed similar policies regarding the consumption of alcohol.[50]

Four states, California, Colorado, New York, and North Dakota took broader steps and declared it illegal for employers to dismiss or take other negative employment action against an employee on the basis of "legal recreational activities outside of work hours and off of the employer's premises."[51] Residents of these states were free to go to sports games or movie theaters, frequent gay bars, or publicly participate in political activities without fearing for their jobs. None of these states, however, included specific mentions of whether these laws precluded companies from regulating their employees' private relationships in the name of sexual harassment prevention. In all four cases, this question was later addressed in the judiciary and in all states, judges allowed, at least some, employer-imposed limitations on relationships.

New York enacted Section 201-D of its Labor Law in 1992; only months before Samuel Johnson and Laural Allen's love story began in the sporting goods department of Johnstown's Wal-Mart. Based on this law, Allen and Johnson filed lawsuits claiming wrongful termination. They found support in the State of New York, which filed a lawsuit of its own. Before the New York Supreme Court, New York State argued that Allen and Johnson's romance did not interfere with their working hours. Their dating, according to the State, should be considered a legal "recreational activity." The New York Supreme Court in *State v. Wal-Mart Stores* (1995) disagreed with this assessment arguing that "personal relationships fall outside of the scope of legislative intent" and that "'dating' is entirely distinct from and, in fact, bears little resemblance to 'recreational activity.'"[52]

---

49 ACLU: Briefing Paper, p. 1.

50 Peters: Company's Smoking Ban.

51 New York. Labor Law. § 102-D. 1992; near identical wording in: California. Labor Code. §96(k). 2000.

52 *State v. Wal-Mart Stores*, 207 A.D.2d 150, 152 (N.Y. App. Div. 1995).

Allen and Johnson lost their case and employers with non-fraternization policies in New York could again rest easy.

Almost a decade later, in California, Robert Barbee, similarly to Allen and Johnson, argued that his state's labor laws protected his relationship with Melanie Tomita. Both Barbee and Tomita worked at the Household Automotive Finance Corporation (HAFC). In contrast to the New York-based couple, however, Barbee and Tomita were not equal coworkers, instead Barbee was Tomita's supervisor. HAFC's code of conduct explicitly forbade a "consensual intimate relationship between a supervisor and any employee within that supervisor's direct or indirect area of responsibility" and required any such relationship to be "[brought] to management's attention for appropriate action." After confirming suspicions of a romance, the company gave the couple the choice to either end their "special relationship" or for either of them to resign. When the couple continued dating, and neither party left the company, HAFC terminated Barbee's employment.[53]

Barbee, like Allen and Johnson in New York, argued that his relationship was part of his private life and therefore, was covered by California's Labor Code Section 96. As had been the case in New York, this argument did not sway the California Appeals Court. However, the judges' reasoning in California differed from that in the New York Supreme Court. In *Barbee v. Household Automotive Finance Corp* (2003), the Court ruled that "managerial-subordinate relationships present issues of potential sexual harassment" leading employers to be "legitimately concerned with [...] possible claims of sexual harassment [...] created by romantic relationships between management and nonmanagement employees."[54] Thus, rather than excluding a "dating relationship" from the scope of "recreational activity," as was done in New York, in California the judges contended that the relationship in question presented a risk for the company and was, therefore, within the sphere of the employer's authority.

This decision was kept relatively narrow and applied only to supervisor-subordinate relationships. Legal experts commented that the Court had not remarked upon the different but related, issue of consensual relationships between coworkers. Were California privacy and labor laws going to insulate such romances from employer scrutiny, or would judges again contend that employers' "legitimate concern [regarding] possible claims of harassment" made these protections obsolete?[55] This question has thus far been left unanswered.

---

53 *Barbee v. Household Automotive Finance Corp.*, 113 Cal.App.4th 525, 529 (Cal. Ct. App. 2003).
54 Ibid., p. 532.
55 Anonymous: What are the Implications of an Anti-Fraternization Policy as applied to Non-Supervising Coworkers? in: Yadegar, Minoofar & Soleymani, LLP Website (January 2023).

It has become apparent that in most states, employment at-will regulations allowed for employers to insist on non-fraternization policies or require employees to register relationships with their company's HR department. As such, by allowing at-will employment, the states in question gave employers considerable leeway regarding the scope of corporate policies and procedures. However, even in states in which state labor codes limited employers' reach into their employees' private lives, these relationships were not, or were only to a limited extent, protected by the law. Thus, in the name of sexual harassment prevention, American employers were within their rights to forbid or require disclosure of any consensual relationships.

Again, this aligned with the management frame presented in Chapter Five. Policies that forbid fraternization in the name of sexual harassment prevention, blurred the line between coerced and consensual behavior. The equation of sexual harassment with sexuality as well as the focus on individual instances, framed the phenomenon along concepts of professionalism and productivity, while minimizing concerns regarding discrimination. Therefore, definitions promulgated in the private sector differed considerably from the U.S. federal government's definition. This was the case, despite relatively small variances in wording. These differences were – and are – not immediately obvious to contemporaries. The conflation of both these interpretations within the public discourse has led to serious confusion and misunderstandings. An individual publicly labeled a 'sexual harasser' may have engaged in discriminatory and, per chance, even sexually violent behavior, or they may have fallen in love on the job.

6.2 Executive: Enforcing Policies

As was stated by feminists, management consultants, and government representatives, without enforcement, company policies were entirely ineffective. All three groups had long since advertised the importance of a written and widely published grievance procedure outlining the complaint and investigation process. By devising grievance procedures, investigating complaints, and monitoring employees, the HR department took over executive functions. In an analogy in which a company resembled a state, the HR department, in addition to writing 'legislation,' was also responsible for 'law enforcement.'

An internal investigation in most companies could be triggered by a complaint, analogous to how a victim of a crime might file charges at a police station. Additionally, comparable to the police investigating a potential crime after an anonymous 911 call or an officer witnessing suspicious behavior, the HR department could themselves initiate an inquiry.[56] In contrast to the government's executive branch, employers had great leeway in monitoring their employees. When enforcing internal policies, employers did not have to pay heed to employees' freedom of speech, privacy, or due process rights. Contrary to the government-citizen relationship, the employer-employee relationship was not protected by the Constitution and the Bill of Rights. Information about policy breaches could be obtained by means of monitoring employees' communications, video surveillance, and/or searching of personal items brought onto the company premises.[57] Therefore, a discussion of a company's effort to enforce their policy necessarily includes two aspects: the internal grievance and investigation process as well as the practice of employee monitoring.

6.2.1 Grievance and Investigation Procedures

By the time the Supreme Court issued their ruling in *Faragher* and *Ellerth*, internal grievance procedures were already common and widely considered good business practice.[58] In this regard, the decisions did not significantly alter the way most employers handled sexual harassment complaints. However, the Court's second stipulation, requiring the "plaintiff employee [...] to take advantage of [the employer's] preventive or corrective opportunities,"[59] considerably increased the significance of such internal procedures.

John Marks, professor of law, shows in his essay "Smoke, Mirrors, and the Disappearance of 'Vicarious' Liability," that summary judgements benefiting the employer increased significantly post-*Ellerth/Faragher*. Marks argues that due to the inherent lack of a trial and a jury in a summary judgement, "reviewing scholars and courts cannot know whether compensation was unjustly denied." However, Marks inferred from the drastic increase in summary judgements benefitting employers that judges were easily convinced by companies' affirmative defense in

56 See for instance Wilkinson and Partners advice on establishing policies and grievance procedures, AHC, Edward A. Altshuler Papers, Box 13.

57 Maltby, Lewis L. et al.: National Task Force on Civil Liberties in the Workplace. American Civil Liberties Union. Progress Report 1994, pp. 6 f., CHA, American Civil Liberties Union of Northern California Records, Carton 120, Folder Public Information Subject Files, Employment/Labor/ Worker's Rights, Discrimination/Affirmative Action/ACLU Policy, 1984–1993.

58 E. g. Cukjati, Curt and Marlene Martin: Company Holiday Parties Offer Fun – and Possible Lawsuits, in: South Florida Business Journal (November 3rd, 1997); Anonymous: Mitsubishi U.S. Unit Vows Strong Policy Against Harassment, in: A Wall Street Journal (May 2nd, 1996), p. C12.

59 *Burlington Industries, Inc. v. Ellerth* (1998), p. 745.

preliminary phases of litigation.[60] In the wake of the *Ellerth/Faragher* decisions, avenues of action discussed in Chapter Four, such as the EEOC and the judiciary, were effectively closed to complainants, if they had not utilized their employer's internal grievance procedure.

Additionally, complainants often had difficulty pursuing their case in court, even after they had followed the now obligatory steps of a company internal procedure. Edelman posited that "plaintiffs often lose their lawsuits [...] because judges defer to organizations' symbolic structures [...] even in cases where those structures are clearly ineffective."[61] In a series of essays, Edelman explained this dynamic by invoking her concept of "judicial deference,"[62] which she applies to corporate anti-discrimination procedures. She argued that the law is not only a bottom-down process but that "law acquires meaning from [...] the social arenas that it seeks to regulate."[63] Therefore, as internal grievance and investigation procedures often mimicked legal proceedings and used terminology associated with the legal system, corporate defense attorneys increasingly succeeded in convincing judges of the "rationality and legality" of management's internal measures.[64] This, Edelman argued, resulted in rulings beneficial to the employer and forwent an analysis of whether the "internalized structures actually promote legal ideals," such as due process or adherence to anti-discrimination law.[65]

Edelman's concept of judicial deference and her application of this concept to workplace grievance procedures is not only persuasive but also widely ac-

---

60 Marks, John H.: Smoke, Mirrors, and the Disappearance of 'Vicarious' Liability: The Emergence of a Dubious Summary-Judgement Safe Harbor for Employers Whose Supervisory Personnel Commit Hostile Workplace Harassment, in: Houston Law Review 38 (2002), p. 1405; cf. Drobac: Sexual Harassment Law, pp. 251f.
61 Edelman: Sex Based Harassment, p. 376.
62 Edelman: When Organizations Rule; Edelman, Lauren: The Legal Lives of Private Organizations, in: The Blackwell Companion to Law and Society (2004), pp. 231–252; Edelman: Sex Based Harassment; Edelman, Lauren: Legal Ambiguity and Symbolic Structures: Organizational Mediation of Civil Rights Law, in: American Journal of Sociology, 97/6 (May 1992), pp. 1531–1575; Edelman, Lauren: Legal Environments and Organizational Governance: The Expansion of Due Process in the American Workplace, in: American Journal of Sociology, 95/6 (May 1990), pp. 1401–1440; Edelman: The Endogeneity of Legal Regulation.
63 Edelman: When Organizations Rule, p. 888.
64 Dobbin, Frank et al.: The Expansion of Due Process in Organizations, in: Institutional Patterns and Organizations: Culture and Environment, ed. by Lynne G. Zucker, Cambridge 1988; Edelman: When Organizations Rule, p. 900; Edelman, Lauren: Legal Environments; Edelman: Legal Ambiguity; Bisom-Rapp, Susan: Bulletproofing the workplace. Symbol and substance in Employment Discrimination Law Practice, in: Florida State University Law Review 26/4 (1999), pp. 959–1047.
65 Edelman: When Organizations Rule, p. 900.

knowledged within sociological texts regarding workplace discrimination.[66] Nevertheless, Edelman, herself, curtailed her own hypothesis by stating that, in the case of workplace discrimination procedures, the process of judicial deference was not yet completed. While courts widely accepted the mere existence of grievance procedures as proof of compliance, Edelman acknowledged that the content of the internal procedures is not altogether irrelevant.[67] In cases in which the procedure was not well advertised or in which the process did not allow the plaintiff to bypass the accused harasser when filing the complaint, judges held employers liable for sex discrimination.[68] Edelman was, however, correct in claiming that internal procedures had to be obviously and egregiously flawed for them to be rejected as an affirmative defense in court.[69]

Following the Supreme Courts' insistence that internal grievance procedures must be used prior to bringing a claim and the judiciary's overall acceptance of internal measures as compliance, employers and their human resources departments became the first and only port-of-call for most sexual harassment complainants. While consultants proclaimed that quick and internal resolution of disputes was advantageous to all involved, the limitations on litigation as an option made targets of harassment wholly dependent on company procedures.

All the more unfortunate then, are the findings of social science research on the validity of such procedures. The literature suggests that grievance procedures as well as internal anti-harassment training seminars have been generally ineffective in reducing illegal sexual harassment within an organization.[70] A study of 805 American companies, conducted in 2019 by Frank Dobbin and Alexandra Kalev analyzed anti-harassment programs from 1971 to 2002. The authors, not only

66 E.g. Dobbin: Equal Opportunity; Bisom-Rapp: Bulletproofing; Foote, William E. and Jane Goodman-Delahunty: Understanding Sexual Harassment. Evidence-Based Forensic Practice, Washington DC 2021.
67 Edelman: When Organizations Rule, p. 908.
68 Boshak, Heather R: The Affirmative Defense to a Vicarious Liability Sexual Harassment Claim, in: The New Jersey Law Journal (April 7th, 2008).
69 Edelman: When Organizations Rule, p. 908.
70 Edelman: Sex Based Harassment, p. 374; cf. Baron, James M. et al.: Targets of Opportunity: Organizational and Environmental Determinants of Gender Integration within the California Civil Service, 1979–1985, in: American Journal of Sociology 96 (1991), pp. 1362–1402; Kelly, Erin et al.: Best Practices or Best Guesses? Assessing the Efficacy of Corporate Affirmative Action and Diversity Policies, in: American Sociological Review 71 (2006), pp. 589–617.

deemed a majority of programs ineffective, they also observed that internal complaint procedures often "incite retaliation without satisfying complainants."[71]

When considering the flaws of such procedures, I propose that there are two aspects to consider. First, the written instructions for the procedure itself must be analyzed. Inconsistencies and undemocratic command structures allow for managerial and personal bias in the process. This could hamper any attempt at curbing sexual harassment in the workplace. Second, the implementation of the grievance procedure must be evaluated. When complaints were not taken seriously and/or the corporate culture was discriminatory, targets justly feared retaliation when making a complaint. The resulting lack of trust in a formal grievance procedure could render it ineffective.

When inspecting written, internal grievance procedures, it is striking how similar they are across sectors and company sizes. As with the affinities between various company policies, this was, most likely, due to the network of management consultants whose advice became increasingly unified.[72] Thus, the largest difference between various grievance procedures was the amount of detail they exhibited. Some companies briefly named a contact person, assured complainants that a "thorough investigation" would follow any complaint, and declared that if the complaint was found to have merit, the accused would face "disciplinary action, up to and including termination of employment."[73] In contrast, other companies, published several pages, highlighting all steps of the complaint process, and the following investigation.

Internal grievance and investigation procedures in many ways mimicked governmental procedures. The Reed and Barton Corporation procedure proves to be an excellent example. First, the language used, both pertaining to register and terminology, resembled that of a legal text. Article 3c, for instance determined that "the alleged offender shall have the right to make a written submission to the Investigators and to suggest witnesses for interview by the Investigators." Notable

---

71 Dobbin, Frank and Alexandra Kalev: The Promise and Peril of Sexual Harassment Programs, in: Proceedings of the National Academy of Sciences of the United States of America, 116/25 (June 2019), p. 12255.

72 Turn to Chapter Five for a discussion of management networks; cf. Dobbin: Equal Opportunity, pp. 2, 10.

73 AIRCO. Inc: Sexual Harassment Policy, 1981, p. 19; Universal Manufacturing Corporation: Personnel Policy Procedure, 1981; Ross Systems, Inc.: Policy Regarding Sexual Harassment, 1982; Water, Terry Vande: Expectations, Appeals, Sexual Harassment Issues Addressed in New Participative Owner's Notebook, in: Herman Miller Connections (November 19th, 1986), p. 2, HMCA; Anonymous: Sexual Harassment: Review of Herman Miller's Position, in: Herman Miller Connections (December 1991), p. 5, HMCA; Herman Miller, Inc.: Sexual Harassment, in: Participative Owner's Notebook, 1986, p. 22, HMCA.

here is the allocation of "right[s]" to individuals under investigation. Somewhat less striking but nevertheless redolent of the criminal justice system is the use of terminology such as "witness" and "investigator."

Second, this and many other procedures, promised aspects associated with due process. Reed and Barton assured its employees that "all complaints are responded to promptly, fairly, and in a professional and objective manner." To this end, companies commonly implemented safeguards against unfair treatment for both the complainant and the alleged harasser. Usually procedures determined, by office or by name, individuals responsible for receiving harassment complaints. In order to allow the complainant some flexibility, more than one individual was appointed. Reed and Barton Corporation, for instance, instructed targets of harassment to report the conduct to their supervisor, the Director of Personnel, or to the Chair of the Diversity Committee.[74]

Additionally, employers regularly cautioned investigators within the written procedure, that "[r]etaliation against any individual for reporting violations of the policy [...] will not be tolerated and will be subject to strict discipline."[75] Less frequently but nevertheless prevalent, investigators were also advised that "false accusations have serious effects on innocent persons." In order to be fair to both the complainant and the accused, the Reed and Barton procedure explicitly stated that "the Company recognizes that the inquiry of whether a particular course of conduct constitutes a violation of the Policy requires a factual determination." In the event that either the complainant or the accused disagreed with the handling or the results of the investigation, some companies inscribed in their procedures an "appeals process."[76] The Reed and Barton Corporation promised that a decision by the Chair of the Diversity Committee or the Director of Personnel "may be appealed [...] to the President [or] the Board of Directors."[77]

However, despite promises of fairness and objectiveness, company internal procedures held an inherent bias. The safeguards described, resembled due process regulations in the government context, but I suggest, company hierarchies prevented a truly "fair" and "objective" process. In the example presented above, the Chair of the Diversity Committee and the Director of Personnel were presented as two separate points of contact targets of harassment could address. Both, however, were appointed by and answered to the company's president. Sim-

---

74 Reed and Barton Corporation Policy, 1996.
75 Ibid.
76 E.g.: Herman Miller: Sexual Harassment.
77 Reed and Barton Corporation: Guidelines for Conducting Investigations of Complaints of Violations of the Diversity Vision and Policy Statement of Reed and Barton Corporation, 1996, HBL, Kenneth H. Olson Collection, 1940–2011, Carton 18, Folder Diversity File 1996.

ilarly, "actions by the president could be appealed to the Board of Directors," which was the very body giving the president the authority to act in the first place. Within a company the principle of checks and balances did not apply. The company was not a democracy. Therefore, investigations of complaints and decisions about guilt or innocence could easily be swayed by managerial interests and were only as "fair" and "objective" as the executive suite wanted them to be.

Alongside the lack of objectivity within a corporate investigation, many company policies involved another aspect, which had the potential to considerably hamper a "full and fair" investigation:[78] Most procedures included promises of confidentiality within internal investigations.[79] The Reed and Barton Corporation was no exception. Within their investigation procedure, the company mandated that "all actions taken in response to complaints will be undertaken with the maximum possible confidentiality." The written procedure further specified that:

> Upon conclusion of the proceedings, including any appeal, the President shall retain one copy of the single written report prepared by the Investigator(s) in a separate confidential file. All other copies of the report, notes, any written complaint and any written submission by the alleged offender shall be destroyed to preserve confidentiality for all parties. The Co-Chairs and Investigators shall <u>not</u> retain any originally or copies of documents or notes relating to a complaint.[80]

The confidentiality regulations included in various companies' grievance procedures differed in their specificity and their scope. No matter their form, however, provisions, as the one quoted above, could severely hamstring the collection of evidence and the tracing of behavioral patterns. When investigations were kept confidential, witnesses did not know to come forward, serial harassers remained undiscovered, and complainants were unable to attain the documentation necessary for future litigation.

While confidentiality could severely impede the effectiveness of an investigation, it brought significant benefits for the employer. Employers often explained the confidential handling of sexual harassment complaints with a desire to protect the privacy of both the complainant and the accused. Considering the massive encroachments on employee privacy in the context of employee monitoring, which shall be discussed later in this chapter, this concern seems slightly disingenuous. Confidentiality surrounding investigations, however, limited the possibility of libel

---

78 Ibid.
79 E.g. AIRCO. Inc: Sexual Harassment Policy, 1981, p. 19; Bell Laboratories: Policy on Sexual Harassment, pre-1980; Herman Miller promises "discretion": Herman Miller: Sexual Harassment; Resorts International Hotel Casino: Sexual Harassment Inter Office Correspondence, 1981.
80 Reed and Barton Corporation: Guidelines for Conducting Investigations.

suits against the company, shielded employees from the knowledge of sexual harassment in their midst, thus protecting morale, and buffered the company from public scrutiny.

It has become apparent that internal, written procedures had significant flaws when it came to eradicating sexual harassment. While on their face they resembled legal proceedings, they lacked necessary accountability. These flaws left significant room for the mishandling of complaints and the prioritization of the company's interests. Fairness and objectivity towards both the complainant and the accused were of secondary importance when these elements did not overlap with managerial interests. However, by reviewing the written documents alone, there is little I can surmise about their practical implication. Thus, for information on the reception and impact of internal grievance procedures, I turn, again, to the social science literature.

The research concurs: While employers extensively implemented grievance procedures, targets of harassment often did not take advantage of them. Herzog et al. in a 2008 study analyzing the "impact of organizational practices on sexual harassment reporting," emphasized that contrary to "commonsense [which] may suggest that fewer reports are analogous with low incidents of sexual harassment, [...] lower rates of reporting may actually indicate [increased tolerance of harassment]."[81] Thus, a small number of complaints did not indicate that policies and procedures were functional, but rather that they were ineffective. The underreporting of sexual harassment, within and outside of the company, was a grave issue.[82] In a report published by the EEOC's Select Task Force on the Study of Harassment in the Workplace in 2016, the agency revealed that:

> [t]he least common response of either men or women to harassment is to take some formal action – either to report the harassment internally or file a formal legal complaint. [...] approximately 70 % of individuals who experienced harassment never even talked with a supervisor, manager, or union representative about the harassing conduct.

---

81 Hertzog, Jodie et al.: There's a Policy for that; A comparison of the organizational culture of workplaces reporting incidents of sexual harassment, in: Behavior and Social Issues 17/2 (2008), p. 177.
82 Bumiller, Kristin: The Civil Rights Society: The Social Construction of Victims, in: Political Science Quarterly, 103/4 (Winter 1988), pp. 751f.; Edelman, Lauren: Working Law: Courts, Corporations, and Symbolic Compliance, Chicago 2016; Fitzgerald Louise et al.: But Was It Really Sexual Harassment? Legal, Behavioral, and Psychological Definitions of the Workplace Victimization of Women, in: Sexual Harassment: Theory, Research, and Treatment, ed. by W. O'Donohue, Needham Heights 1997, pp. 5–28; Edelman: Symbolic Compliance, p. 374.

In the report the agency further specified that only an estimated 6 % to 13 % of harassed individuals filed a formal complaint with their employer, their union, or the EEOC.[83]

The type of harassment significantly influenced reporting rates. According to the EEOC survey, only 0.9 % of participants who had experienced non-sexualized gender harassment formally or informally reported the incidents.[84] 8 % of self-reported targets indicated that they had taken action against "unwanted physical touching," and 30 % did so when the harassment involved "sexually coercive behavior."[85] A survey conducted in 2016 by the Merit Systems Protection Board confirmed that most reports followed physical threats or coercion and that harassment often remained unreported "the first few incidents."[86]

Victims of harassment had a multitude of reasons not to report misconduct. Many had little faith that management would respond to a complaint. Several studies indicated that such skepticism was justified. Legal scholar Anna-Maria Marshall found that HR professionals "frequently discourage women who inquire about filing a complaint from framing their complaint as sexual harassment." Instead, complainants were encouraged to report "an instance of poor management," or disclose an "interpersonal conflict."[87] By removing the phrase "sexual

83 Feldblum, Chai R. and Victoria A. Lipnic: EEOC Report by the Select Task Force on the Study of Harassment in the Workplace, June 2016; Similar studies have been done specifically for the public sector. A 1995 survey of the Department of Defense uncovered that only 14 % of harassed participants reported the harassment to a supervisor; Bastian, L.D. et al.: Department of Defense 1995 Sexual Harassment Survey (DMDC Report No. 96 – 014), December 1996; cf. Foote: Understanding Sexual Harassment; For more research on reporting rates see Green, Michael: A New #MeToo Result: Rejecting Notions of Romantic Consent with Executives, in: Employee Rights and Employment Policy Journal 23/1 (2019), pp. 116 – 164.
84 For a definition and discussion of non-sexualized sexual harassment see Chapter Three.
85 Feldblum: EEOC Report 2016.
86 U.S. Merit Systems Protection Board, Sexual Harassment in Federal Workplaces: Understanding and Addressing the Problem. A Report to the President and the Congress of the United States, December 2022, p. 32; see also: Foote: Understanding Sexual Harassment, p. 167; Benavides Espinoza, Claudia and George Cunningham: Observers' Reporting of Sexual Harassment: The Influence of Harassment Type, Organizational Culture, and Political Orientation, in: Public Organization Review 10/4 (2010), p. 323 – 333; Lee, J. Y. et al.: Blowing the Whistle on Sexual Harassment: Test of a Model of Predicators and Outcomes, in: Human Relations 57/3 (2004), pp. 297 – 322.
87 Edelman: Sex-Based Harassment and Symbolic Compliance, p. 374; Marshall Anna-Maria: Injustice frames, legality, and the everyday construction of sexual harassment, in: Law and Social Inquiry 28/3 (Summer 2003), pp. 659 – 689; Marshall, Anna-Maria: Idle rights: employees' rights consciousness and the construction of sexual harassment policies, in: Law and Society Review 39/1 (2005), pp. 83 – 124.

harassment" from the complaint, the complainant's possible future legal case was severely weakened. In such instances, the employer was, nevertheless, advised of a problem and could take further steps to avoid liability. Sexual harassment was explicitly and intentionally reframed as a workplace conflict rather than an instance of sexual violence or a violation of the Civil Rights Act.

When conflict arising from instances of sexual harassment were viewed as managerial differences, then seeking assistance from the human resources department or from a supervisor could be seen as an inability to resolve interpersonal disputes independently. Many targets were aware that filing a sexual harassment complaint could impede their career advancement in the long run. According to two separate studies, one published by Beth Quinn in 2000, the other by Anna-Maria Marshall in 2005, female victims in particular were cognizant of the importance of "being a good team player" for professional success.[88] Finding oneself in the middle of a dispute, especially regarding an issue as contentious as sexual harassment, could be detrimental for one's professional image.

In addition to worries about lasting reputational damages, targets often feared immediate retaliation and hostility from their employer, their supervisor, and/or their colleagues.[89] Again, these fears were not unwarranted. According to law professor and director of the Texas A&M University Workplace Law Program, Michael Green, three out of four employees who filed a formal complaint with their employer, faced "some form of retaliation."[90] Green estimates that the true numbers were even higher, because many retaliatory acts could not be easily traced or proven.[91]

Take for instance Mira Sorvino's experience after rejecting Harvey Weinstein's sexual advances. In September 1995, Sorvino and Weinstein found themselves at the Toronto International Film Festival, promoting the movie *Mighty Afrodite*, which Sorvino had starred in and Weinstein had directed. In 2017, in the midst of various accusations of sexual assault and coercion against Weinstein, Sorvino told her story in an interview with the *New York Times*. In it, she revealed that Weinstein had asked for a meeting, the evening before the festival. When they were alone, he began "massaging my shoulders, which made me very uncom-

88 Edelman: Sex-Based Harassment and Symbolic Compliance, p. 374; Marshall: Idle Rights; Quinn, Beth: The Parody of Complaining: Law, Humor, and Harassment in the Everyday Work World, in: Law and Social Inquiry 25/4 (2000), pp. 1151–1185.
89 Edelman: Sex-Based Harassment and Symbolic Compliance, p. 374; Bumiller: The Civil Rights Society; Dessler: Human Resources Management, p. 69; Foote: Understanding Sexual Harassment, p. 136.
90 Green: A New #MeToo Result, p. 128.
91 Ibid., p. 150.

fortable and then tried to get more physical, sort of chasing me around." Sorvino left the hotel room, but Weinstein persisted. Several weeks after the festival he went to Sorvino's home "after midnight," under the pretext of discussing the marketing strategy for the movie. "Harvey had managed to bypass my doorman. [...] I opened the door terrified, brandishing my twenty-pound Chihuahua mix in front of me, as though that would do any good." Weinstein only left when Sorvino informed him that her "new boyfriend was on his way."[92]

As was the case with others who had rejected Weinstein's advances, Sorvino suspected that Weinstein in response to her disinterest "had [her] removed from projects or dissuaded people from hiring [her]." In her interview she explained that she "felt iced out and that my rejection of Harvey had something to do with it." At the time, Sorvino did not file a complaint, nor could she confirm that Weinstein was responsible for her slowed career advancement. However, in the wake of the #MeToo movement, after her allegations were made public, movie producer Peter Jackson confirmed Sorvino's decade-old suspicions. In an interview Jackson recounted that he had considered both Mira Sorvino and Ashley Judd, another actor who had refused Weinstein's advances, for parts in the Lord of the Rings series.

> I recall Miramax [Weinsteins production company] telling us they were a nightmare to work with and we should avoid them at all costs. [...] At the time, we had no reason to question what these guys were telling us. But in hindsight, I realize that this was very likely the Miramax smear campaign in full swing. I now suspect we were fed false information about both of these talented women.[93]

The actors' blacklisting by the production company Miramax was a direct result of their refusal to engage in sexual conduct with Harvey Weinstein. However, even if the actors had decided to file a complaint against Weinstein with the EEOC at the time, they would not have been able to prove their suspicions of retaliation.

Although retaliation claims had a better chance than other sexual harassment complaints to be heard by the judiciary, they, nevertheless, had a high failure rate.[94] Due to limited recourses and protections, many victims decided on delaying or abstaining from filing an internal complaint for fear of retaliation. This was especially true since the Supreme Court in *Clark County School District v. Breeden* (2001) drastically limited the scope of retaliatory action.

---

92 Farrow, Ronan: From Aggressive Overtures to Sexual Assault: Harvey Weinstein's Accusers Tell Their Stories, in: The New Yorker (October 10th, 2017).
93 Redden, Molly: Peter Jackson. I blacklisted Ashley Judd and Mira Sorvino under pressure from Weinstein, in: The Guardian (December 16th, 2017).
94 Green: A New #MeToo Result, p. 147.

In the case, the courts deliberated whether Shirley Breeden had a right to protection from retaliation, even though the behavior she complained about did not constitute illegal sexual harassment. Breeden, an employee of the Clark County School District, complained to her supervisor, Assistant Superintendent George Ann Rice, about sexualized comments two of her coworkers had made during a meeting. According to Breeden, this was the first and only incidence of sexualized behavior she had experienced within the School District. Shortly after making this complaint, Rice transferred Breeden to a less desirable position.[95] Upon her transfer, Breeden filed a retaliation suit against her employer, Clark County School District.

The Appeals Court had reversed the Districts Court's summary judgment, arguing that the Civil Rights Act protected employees, not only from retaliation after discriminatory conduct had occurred but also "if [the plaintive] had a reasonable, good faith belief that the incident [...] constituted unlawful sexual harassment."[96] Thus, according to the 9th Circuit Appeals Court, a complainant was protected against retaliation, if she complained about conduct she believed to be harassment, even when said conduct did not amount to the legal definition.

The Supreme Court, in 2001, disagreed. The Justices argued that Breeden's colleague's behavior was to be interpreted as an "isolated incident" and that "[n]o reasonable person could have believed that the single incident [...] violated Title VII's standard." The Supreme Court reinstated the District Court's decision for summary judgment and, thereby, set a precedent, that the Civil Rights Act's protection against retaliation only applied when the original conduct constituted illegal discrimination.[97]

With this precedent in place, it made strategic sense for a target to abstain from filing an internal complaint until the harassment became severe and pervasive, lest they risk a defenseless position in case of retaliation by their employer. At the same time, the precedent set by *Faragher/Ellerth* required an internal grievance procedure to be utilized within a "reasonable period of time." Lower courts had since determined this period to be as short as two weeks after the initial harassing behavior occurred.[98] In combination, the *Breeden* and *Faragher/Ellerth* de-

95 *Clark County School District v. Breeden.* 532 U.S. 268, 2001.
96 Ibid., Appeals Court is quoted by Supreme Court opinion.
97 *Clark County School District v. Breeden (2001)*; for an in-depth interpretation see: Green: A New #MeToo Result, p. 148.
98 *Phillips v. Taco Bell Corp.*, 83 F. Supp. 2d 1029 (E.D. Mo 2000); *Conatzer v. Medical Professional Building Services Corp.* 03–5074 (N.D. Okla. 2004); *Malvia v. Bald Head Island Management, Inc.* 259 F. 3d 261 (4th Cir. 2001); cf. White, Evan: A Hostile Environment: How the 'severe or Pervasive' Requirement and the Employer's Affirmative Defense Trap Sexual Harassment Plaintiffs in a

cisions created a catch-22: If an employee notified their employer of possible harassment too early, they could risk losing protection against retaliation, but if the
complaint was filed too late, a court could fault them for the delay.[99] This quan-
dary influenced the skepticism towards and the resulting inefficiency of internal
grievance procedures. Rather than navigate this conflict or risk retaliation, for
many targets of sexual harassment the "most reasonable" course of action was
"work withdrawal." Some employees resigned their job outright, others lost motivation, were increasingly absent, and overall disengaged from their jobs.[100]

Despite the similarity between various written policies and grievance procedures, depending on the company culture, rates of sexual harassment differed extensively from workplace to workplace.[101] This indicates that in some companies
the procedures put in place were more effective than in others. In some, employees trusted that their complaints would be acted upon, while others feared retaliation or disinterest. In this context, two trends are discernable: First, the sector or
industry and second, the attitude and actions of the company's high-level executives played a vital role in shaping a company's responses to sexual harassment.

Company culture was heavily influenced by the industry in which the workplace was positioned. In Chapter Four, I have highlighted the wide-spread sexual
harassment in America's mines and other blue-collar jobs. Several studies have
found that the level of sex-segregation in the workplace was directly correlated
to the pervasiveness of sexual harassment.[102] Thus, in jobs in which women
were viewed as intruders and had few female allies within the command structure, official anti-harassment measures were often ineffective.[103]

Catch-22, in: Boston College Law Review 47 (2006), pp. 869 f.; Henry, Ann: Employer and Employee
Reasonableness Regarding Retaliation under the Ellerth/Faragher Affirmative Defense, in: University of Chicago Legal Forum 1 (1999), pp. 563 f.

99 White: A Hostile Environment, p. 854; Foote: Understanding Sexual Harassment, p. 69.

100 White: A Hostile Environment, p. 887; Foote: Understanding Sexual Harassment, p. 182; cf.
Sims, Carra et al.: The Effects of Sexual Harassment Turnover in the Military: Time-Dependent
Modeling, in: Journal of Applied Psychology, 90/6 (2005), pp. 1141–1152.

101 Gruber, James: An Epidemiology of Sexual Harassment: Evidence from North America and
Europe, in: W. O'Donohue (ed.): Sexual Harassment: Theory, Research, and Treatment, 1997,
pp. 84–98; Foote: Understanding Sexual Harassment, p. 132.

102 Schultz 2139; Edelman: Sex-Based Harassment and Symbolic Compliance, p. 369; Maass, Anne
et al.: Sexual harassment Under Social Identity Threat: The Computer Harassment Paradigm, in:
Journal of Personality and Social Psychology 85/5 (2003), pp. 853–870.

103 E.g.: Anonymous: Many Doctors Tell of Sexual Harassment in Training, in: The New York
Times (February 4th, 1993); Anonymous: Women 'Hard-Hats' Tell of Harassment, in: San Francisco
Chronicle (February 18th, 1982); Anonymous: Sexual Harassment on the Assembly Line, in: Los
Angeles Times (December 14th, 1981).

Vulnerabilities other than gender also played a significant role in shaping work cultures conducive to sexual harassment. Industries which relied heavily on minimum wage workers and/or offered few opportunities for upward mobility often found sexual harassment to be prevalent. The food, hospitality, and tourism industry as well as the domestic care economy are prominent examples. Not only was a great majority of employees in these industries part of the low-income working class, but people of color and undocumented immigrants were overrepresented in these workforces. Class, race, language barriers, and immigration status accounted for higher economic dependency and increased vulnerability of workers in these industries and prevented targets of harassment from utilizing official complaint processes.[104]

In addition to the type of industry, a second major factor in shaping workplace culture was the mindset and demeanor of company executives. These attitudes often extended to supervisors on all levels. One supervisor summarized succinctly, "[w]ithout ever putting pen to paper supervisors have a way of signaling what level of behavior is demanded or tolerated."[105] Therefore, levels of trust in a company's grievance procedure were closely tied to managements' perceived commitment to eradicating the phenomenon. Feminists, social science research, and management consultants agreed that supervisors' conduct and attitude greatly influenced the company culture regarding harassment and discrimination.[106] When high level executives condoned a culture rife with harassment or engaged in harassing behavior themselves, such behavior overrode all official measures, including written policies and procedures. Fittingly, in an interview with *the New Yorker*, employees working at Harvey Weinstein's production companies spoke of "a culture of silence about sexual assault at Miramax and Weinstein Company."[107] Edel-

---

104 Schuster, Karolyn: Sexual Harassment. The Most Sensitive Subject in Foodservice, in: Food Management (February 1981), pp. 35–60, BCA, Research on Women Records, Box 95, Folder Equal Rights Advocate, Mountain Life and Fork, Food Services; Semuels, Alana: Low-Wage workers Aren't Getting Justice for Sexual Harassment. Despite the #MeToo Movement, Poor Women Often Find That Speaking Out About Abuse At Work is Too Costly, in: The Atlantic (December 17th, 2017); Barreto, Milagros et al.: Workplace Sexual Harassment and Vulnerabilities Among Low-Wage Hispanic Women, in: Occupational Health Science, 5/3 (2021), pp. 391–414; Lewis, Elaine: Who Is at High Risk of Sexual Harassment, in: ACLU News and Commentary, January 18th, 2018; Schultz: Sanitizing the Workplace, pp. 2138 f.

105 Survey participant quoted in: U.S. Merit Systems Protection Board: Sexual Harassment in the Federal Workplace. Trends, Progress, Continuing Challenges, 1994, p. 36.

106 Dessler: Human Resources Management, p. 83; Foote: Understanding Sexual Harassment, p. 32; De Coster, S. et al.: Routine Activities and Sexual Harassment in the Workplace, in: Work and Occupations 26/1 (1999), pp. 21–49.

107 Farrow: From Aggressive Overtures.

man and Cabrera explain, "[w]here leaders fail to set a strong example or to make clear that the anti-harassment rules are to be taken seriously, anti-harassment policies and procedures can become merely symbolic and exist alongside a culture in which harassment is common."[108]

Conversely, a survey of 6,500 employees at a company in the telephone industry indicated that employees experienced notably less harassment compared to their colleagues when their direct supervisor actively spoke out against sexual harassment.[109] Many companies devised programs in which supervisors were explicitly made responsible for eliminating sexual harassment in their teams. Policies from the early 1980s onwards instructed supervisors to distribute the policy and procedure among their employees.[110] Several companies encompassed equal opportunity goals in supervisors' performance reviews and used this data as one metric for decisions on pay raises and promotions. A further step, which gained in popularity over the time period discussed here, was the establishment of an "ethics office" or an "ethics officer" within the company. Lockheed Martin Corporation, for instance, appointed several ethics officers who, alongside the human resources department, addressed issues such as conflicts of interests, access to company information, and employee discrimination.[111]

Both supervisor training as well as employee workshops on sexual harassment were additional methods of involving supervisors. In the former, supervisors themselves learned about the issue, how to monitor their own behavior, and how to mediate and resolve complaints. The latter served not only to inform employees of the issue and the company policy but was also intended as an avenue in which supervisors and upper management could demonstrate their commitment. It was no coincidence that multiple organizations began or ended their anti-harassment training by showing a recording of the CEO addressing all employees.[112]

As with grievance procedures, the effectiveness of anti-sexual harassment training was rarely questioned by employers or judges. Over the years, however, social scientists have shown that such training often created a backlash. In an interview-based study conducted by Sociologist Justine Tinkler in 2012, anti-harassment training sessions were proven to "activate gender stereotypes and polarize

---

108 Edelman: Sex-Based Harassment and Symbolic Compliance, p. 373.

109 De Coster: Routine Activities; Foote: Understanding Sexual Harassment, p. 32.

110 E.g.: Universal Manufacturing Corporation: Personnel Policy Procedure, 1981; AIRCO. Inc: Sexual Harassment Policy, 1981; cf. Schultz: Sanitizing the Workplace, p. 2112.

111 Dessler: Human Resources Management, p. 491.

112 Tippett: Harassment Trainings, p. 486; cf. Employment Issues Sexual Harassment, KIC Document, NMSU, Frances F. Williams Papers, Ms 0284 Box 16 Folder 4.

men and women [...]."[113] In line with these findings, Dobbin and Kalev in 2017 found that male colleagues often blamed "the burden of mandatory training" on the women they worked with.[114] According to these studies, male employees were more likely than before the training to blame the target of the harassment and harbor misgivings towards their female colleagues.[115] Thus, in many cases anti-harassment training was unsuccessful and had the potential of fueling distrust along the gender line, thereby intensifying the problem of sex discrimination.[116]

6.2.2 Employee Monitoring

By holding managers responsible for sexual harassment within their departments, employers encouraged action even when no complaint had been filed. Supervisors were instructed to be alert for employee conduct which violated the company's sexual harassment policy.[117] No complaint was needed to initiate company action. An article published in the *New York Times* in 1994 highlights just such an incident. "A male middle-level manager" at a "consumer products corporation," was accused of violating the company's policy which forbade any "behavior which might be construed as sexual harassment." Upon hearing that his secretary's mother had passed away, he hugged her in an attempt to console her. He and his secretary were spotted in this position by a third employee who reported the incident to the company's HR department. An investigation was conducted in which both the manager as well as his secretary explained the situation and insisted that there had been no sexual harassment, or for that matter, sexual con-

113 Tinkler, Justine: Resisting the Enforcement of Sexual Harassment Law, in: Law and Social Inquiry 37/1 (Winter 2012), p. 20; cf. Edelman: Sex-Based Harassment and Symbolic Compliance, p. 375.

114 Dobbin: The Promise and Peril; Edelman: Sex-Based Harassment and Symbolic Compliance, p. 375.

115 Edelman: Sex-Based Harassment and Symbolic Compliance, p. 375; cf. Bingham, Shereen and Scherer, Lisa: The Unexpected Effects of a Sexual Harassment Educational Program, in: Journal of Applied Behavioral Science 37/2 (2001), pp. 125–153; Baynard, Victoria et al.: Multiple Sexual Violence Prevention Tools: Doses and Boosters, in: Journal Aggression, Conflict and Peace Research, 10 (December 2017), pp. 145–155; Potter, Sharyn: Using a Multimedia Social Marketing Campaign to Increase Active Bystanders on the College Campus, in: Journal of American College Health 60 (2012), pp. 282–295.

116 Edelman: Sex-Based Harassment and Symbolic Compliance, p. 375; cf. Bingham: The Unexpected Effects; Baynard: Multiple Sexual Violence Prevention Tools; Potter: Using a Multimedia Social Marketing Campaign.

117 E.g.: AIRCO. Inc: Sexual Harassment Policy, 1981, p. 17, Becton Dickinson and Company: Equal Employment Handbook, pre-1983.

tact, of any kind. Nevertheless, based on this incident alone, the internal investigation concluded that the manager in question disregarded the company's sexual harassment policy which prohibited "sexual touching." The manager was suspended for a week, a write-up was permanently placed in his personnel file, and he was placed on probation for a year.[118]

In this case, the information was given to the HR department by a third employee. However, employers could gain such information through monitoring employees' phone and email communications, conducting searches of personal property on company premises, as well as surveillance via security cameras and headsets.[119] In the context of the government's executive branch, the surveillance of citizens was (and is) strictly regulated. A wiretap on a phone or a search through an email account by a police officer, for instance, required a judges' approval. This check of the executive by the judicial branch was implemented in the democratic system in order to protect citizens from "unreasonable searches and seizures," as declared by the 4th Amendment to the U.S. Constitution.[120]

However, the Constitution and more specifically the Bill of Rights only regulated the relationship between citizens and the government. They had no impact on employer-employee relationships. In a leaflet on employee monitoring, the ACLU explained the situation as follows:

> The Founders could not have imagined back then that, one day concentrations of corporate power would exist on a scale rivaling, and in some cases exceeding governmental power. Today, most Americans are more vulnerable to having their rights violated by their employers than the early Americans were to having their rights violated by the government. Yet because the Constitution does not limit their authority, private employers are free to violate the civil liberties of their employees. Nationwide, the American Civil Liberties Union receives more complaints about abuses by employers than about abuses by the government.[121]

The ACLU strategically omitted the fact that employers' most severe course of action was the termination of the employment relationship. Employers, could not, as could the state, imprison or even execute their employees. Nevertheless, within the bounds of the employment agreement, the ACLU was correct in stating that

---

118 Slade, Margot: Sexual Harassment: Stories from the Field, in: The New York Times (March 27th, 1994), p. 124, cf. Young, Cathy: Ceasefire. Why Women and Men Must Join Forces to Achieve True Equality, 1999, p. 178.
119 Anonymous: Guide to Employee Monitoring Laws of the U.S., in: Workstatus Workforce Management, 2021; Bush, John et al.: Monitoring Employees Makes Them More Likely to Break Rules, in: Harvard Business Review (June 27th, 2022).
120 U.S. Constitution, Amendment IV.
121 Maltby: National Task Force on Civil Liberties in the Workplace, pp. 6 f.

"private sector employees [...] [had few] protection[s] against even the most intrusive practices."[122]

While some states enacted privacy laws,[123] which influenced employee monitoring, federally there existed only one statute regulating electronic surveillance: The Electronic Communications Privacy Act (ECPA) of 1986, which was an extension of the earlier Wiretap Act of 1968. Although it was not specifically written to regulate actions in the private sector, it was invoked by several plaintiffs who had sued against what they considered unwarranted surveillance by their employers. Employers, however, argued that the risk of sexual harassment within their company threatened their business. Therefore, their surveillance of employees was a necessary business practice, and should be excluded from the ECPA.

The earliest case applying the ECPA to workplace monitoring, *Huffcut v. McDonald's Corporation*, was filed in 1995. The San Francisco Chronicle reported the story of a "short-lived, middle-distance love affair" between two McDonald's employees working in two separate restaurants. Michael Huffcut and Rose Hasset "left messages for each other on their voice mail at work." These "lovey-dovey whisperings" were then recorded by Huffcut's boss, who not only fired Huffcut but played the recordings to his wife, Lisa.[124] Huffcut filed a lawsuit against McDonald's Corporation for "invasion of privacy,"[125] claiming that his employer had violated the ECPA. The case was ultimately settled out of court, but prompted both liberal and libertarian organizations to question "[h]ow private is the American workplace?"[126]

Robert Ellis Smith, publisher of the *Privacy Journal*, commented on the *Huffcut* case in the *Los Angeles Times*, stating that employers should not have "the right to listen further when it's clearly private and personal."[127] In the same article, Milind Shah, a spokesperson for the American Civil Liberty Union's National

---

122 Ibid.

123 These laws differ in their scope. Connecticut and Delaware, for instance, forbid employers from monitoring email communication and internet in the workplace without prior consent from the employee. Illinois, Texas, and Washington strictly regulate the circumstances under which employers may collect biometric information. 26 states limit an employer's access to employees' social media accounts. As of this writing, Missouri is the only state to forbid an employer from requiring an employee implant a personal identification microchip. For more information see Willkie Compliance: State Employee Privacy Laws.

124 Dobbin: Voice-Mail Romance, p. A6.

125 Hatoff, Howard and Robert West: Law Office Policy & Procedures Manual, ⁵2006, p. 259.

126 Dobbin, Ben: Federal Suit Questions Worker Privacy Rights: Courts: Case will weigh what protections employees are entitled to, as well as how far employers can go in monitoring staff, in: Los Angeles Times (January 25ᵗʰ, 1995).

127 Dobbin: Federal Suit Questions Worker Privacy Rights.

Task Force on Civil Liberties in the Workplace, argued that employees "should be told how [and when] they're going to be monitored." He went on to caution that as the law stood, this was no requisite:

> You'd be amazed at how many different ways your privacy can be violated when you walk into the workplace – video cameras, sound bugging, keyboard and e-mail monitoring. According to the law, you effectively check your privacy rights at the door.[128]

Shah's certainty that the ECPA did not prevent employers from surveilling their employees was based on two exceptions the law specified. First, if one of the participants of the communication had given prior permission, the surveillance did not violate the ECPA. This condition was easily fulfilled. Many companies had provisions in employment contracts in which new hires agreed to surveillance by the employer. As this was a non-negotiable condition of employment, most applicants agreed to sign.

Second, an employer was authorized to intercept and monitor communications of employees "in the normal course of [their] employment while engaged in any activity which is a necessary incident to the rendition of [their] service[s]."[129] This was the provision Huffcut attempted to challenge in court. According to his lawyer, the recorded message was to be considered "private" and therefore was not relevant to Huffcut's "rendition of services."[130] However, when Huffcut and McDonald's Corporation settled out of court, this legal question was left open.

In 2001, the 6th Circuit Appeals Court in *Adams v. City of Battle Creek* settled the question brought up in *Huffcut v. McDonald's*. The court ruled that all communication occurring on equipment provided by the company was property of the employer and could be monitored without restrictions. This also included any communication outside of office hours, when it involved the use of a company computer or phone. Communication between employees, even when discussing private matters were, thus, subject to surveillance. The content of such private conversations could trigger disciplinary action for employees using company equipment to sustain their workplace romances. In one curious case, an AT&T em-

---

128 Ibid.

129 Electronic Communications Privacy Act. Pub. L. No. 99–508, 100 Stat. 1848, 1986.

130 Dobbin: Federal Suit Questions Worker Privacy Rights.

ployee was even "upbraided for exchanging affectionate e-mail notes with his wife, who also work[ed] for the company."[131]

Employers' legal victories were not the only factor leading to the increased installation of monitoring software.[132] A *New York Times* article from 1999 illustrated that although employers were not restricted in "monitor[ing] their employees, including videotaping them on the job or monitoring their telephone and computer use [...] few did so in the past because of the cost and technological challenge."[133] As monitoring software became more accessible and affordable, more companies implemented it. According to the American Management Association, by 1999, "about 20 percent of Fortune 1000 companies and half a dozen federal agencies" used "monitoring software to watch over their office PCs."[134] Numbers provided by the National Workrights Institute show, that by 2017 this number had risen to 67 percent.[135]

In the same article, *The New York Times* reported that "employees are grumbling that, in an era when they often take their work home, it is unfair for companies to monitor their personal time at work."[136] As technology advanced, remote work became more feasible, and personal laptops and cell phones became increasingly common. Both of these developments contributed to the blurring of the line between the personal and the professional throughout the 2000s, 2010s, and beyond. For instance, video monitoring through the camera of a company owned computer or phone was legal during working hours, even if the laptop was in the employee's home rather than an office. Similarly, employers could rightfully access the devices GPS location.

Employees' privacy rights were bolstered but not completely ensured when they owned the equipment they were using. The legal waters were murky concerning privately owned devices for which the employer paid some portion of upkeep or service. Personal cellphones, for instance, were often used to make work-related calls and it was not uncommon for an employer to pay for a part or all of the monthly plan. However, depending on their employment contracts, even when

---

131 Shiver, Jube Jr.: Workers Upset Over Y2K Monitoring, in: New York Times (October 12th, 1999), pp. 2K, A6; Sexual Harassment Training Video advising employees of email surveillance: Gunter, Peter: Harassment in the Workplace Part 2, [no date, early 2000s].

132 American Civil Liberties Union: Briefing Paper. The Rights of Employees Number 12, no date (estimated 1991), p. 1.

133 Shiver: Workers Upset Over Y2K Monitoring, pp. 2K, A6.

134 Anonymous: Davis Vetoes Bill to Warn Workers About Monitoring. E-Mail Oversight Deemed Legal, in: The Oakland Tribune (October 12th, 1999), p. 5.

135 Rains, Parker: To Monitor Your Employees (Or Not): Pros vs. Cons, in: Nashville Business Journal (January 13th, 2017).

136 Shiver: Workers Upset Over Y2K Monitoring, pp. 2K, A6.

the employer was not financially involved in the purchase or upkeep of a device, an employee could still be subject to digital surveillance by their employer. New hires often signed, as part of their contracts, a "Bring Your Own Device" (BYOD) Policy.[137] If the job required the use of one's personal computer, an employment contract could specify that the employer was authorized to install monitoring software on the machine. Similarly, a job requiring the use of a personal car may have had as a condition of employment that the employee provide the employer with access to the car's GPS system. Depending on the company's BYOD policy, during workhours, the employer was privy to "web browsing, personal email, messenger interactions, social media, workday errands," and more.[138]

Additionally, at-will employment dynamics left the employer with leverage when investigating alleged misconduct. When inquiring about a possible data leak, ethics violation, or accusations of sexual harassment the employer could ask to review private messages on a personal cellphone or computer. Refusal to comply with this request could be interpreted by the company appointed investigator as "lack of full cooperation" and be followed by termination.[139] While employers, legally speaking, had no right to compel access to the personal devise and information, federal law did not explicitly preclude them from ending the employment relationship when an employee denied such a request.

Employee surveillance became popular and was implemented in the name of quality assurance and discrimination prevention.[140] As has been explained throughout, major corporate goals of discrimination prevention, and specifically anti-sexual harassment prevention were the avoidance of lawsuits and the preservation of high morale and productivity among the staff. Employee monitoring brought new risks of litigation and could have a devastating effect on workers' disposition toward their workplace.

In 2015, an article in the *Nashville Business Journal* warned that "HR experts predict that this will become a source of litigation in the coming years, so employers should proceed with caution when monitoring any personal devices in the workplace." Additionally, the article encouraged employers to ask themselves "to what extent [...] the monitoring [will] prove disruptive" and whether "employee morale [will] suffer as a result of a monitoring and inspection policy."[141] An article published in 2017 expanded on the issue of employee morale.

---

137 Rains: To Monitor Your Employees (Or Not).
138 Ibid.
139 Ibid.
140 Dobbin: Federal Suit Questions Worker Privacy Rights.
141 Starkman, Jay: What to Consider Before Monitoring Employee Smartphones, in: Nashville Business Journal (May 27th, 2015).

The article described a boss "Tim" who "watches his employees on the security cameras from home and has been known to listen into their conversations via the voice detectors that are part of the store's security system." The article explained that Tim's behavior, which was portrayed by his employees as "creepy" and "just weird," caused "a self-inflicted problem [...] of trust." The employees felt "disrespected, under-appreciated and untrusted" leading to low morale and, thus, low productivity.[142]

This raises the following questions: Is employee monitoring counterproductive to its original goals? And if so, why is the practice so popular to this day? I leave these questions to be answered by researchers specializing in privacy law and policies. However, I maintain that employers' claims of concern about sexual harassment, some of them in good faith, others not, have given employers a cover for the increase of employee monitoring. This is especially true for the expansion of permissible monitoring "in the ordinary course of business" to include the viewing of private messages, social media, and webcam footage. As of yet, the current academic landscape lacks sufficient exploration and analysis on whether employee surveillance has actually aided in the prevention of unlawful sexual harassment. Here is a pressing need for comprehensive academic investigation and scholarly attention. Undebatable is the fact that in the name of preventing sexual harassment employers have exponentially increased the scope of managerial oversight and control.

Encouraged by the *Faragher* and *Ellerth* decisions in 1998, employers erected an enormous apparatus devised to put into effect their anti-harassment policies. Neither employee monitoring, nor the existence of grievance procedures, however, have been proven to be effective in limiting sexual harassment and sex discrimination. Nevertheless, because judges accepted these internal "preventative measures" and "immediate disciplinary action" as proof of compliance of the Civil Rights Act, targets of harassment, in many cases, could no longer count on the assistance of the EEOC. Thus, the government's enforcement mechanism remained functional only in the most egregious cases. To a large extent, executive functions have been shifted from the government to the private sector.

---

142 English, Bill: Owner's Creepy Surveillance Disrespects Employees, in: Nashville Business Journal (July 17th, 2017).

6.3 Judicative: Deciding Upon Disciplinary Action

As was the case with legislative and executive functions, managerial interests were present as a steady undercurrent during internal adjudication regarding a complaint's merit and/or the extent of disciplinary actions. Legally speaking, the safest action an employer could take after an accusation of sexual harassment had been made, involved the termination of the alleged harasser. For an affirmative defense under *Ellerth* and *Faragher* to be effective, the employer was required to demonstrate that "immediate remedial action" had been taken after the harassment had become known.[143] As Vicki Schultz, explained in her essay "Sanitizing the Workplace," the Supreme Court rulings gave "employers an incentive to censor individual employee's conduct well before the legal threshold is met."[144] An employee, who had been complained against in the past, presented an enormous legal risk, even if disciplinary action such as suspension or mandatory counseling had been taken. The first complaint established that the employer knew about the employee's conduct. Any further misconduct by the employee in question constituted a pattern of harassment, which weakened the employer's affirmative defense should the case advance to litigation.

By acting on infractions before they amounted to illegal sexual harassment, employers could avoid litigation. I argue that in such situations the process of adjudication shifted into the organization. The judicial functions of evaluating a complaint's merit and the level of disciplinary action fell to the employer rather than the state. In the following pages I will deliberate on the consequences of a dynamic, which induced employers to terminate employment contracts after unconfirmed allegations or seemingly inconsequential infractions. Additionally, I will examine how sexual harassment policies were applied differently depending on the status and value to the company an alleged harasser held.

In Chapter Four, I discussed union members filing grievances against their current or former employer when disciplined or terminated on the grounds of sexual harassment allegations. Similarly, employers could find themselves caught in between the alleged target and harasser. Beginning in the late 1980s, employees fired for violating sexual harassment policies, at times, resorted to filing libel suits against their former employers. These lawsuits, however, only had limited success.[145] As discussed previously, a policy going beyond the extent of the law was legal and so too, was termination of an employee for violating a company pol-

---

143 Burlington Industries, *Inc. v. Ellerth* (1998).
144 Schultz: Sanitizing the Workplace, pp. 2086, 2104.
145 Baker: Women's Movement, pp. 140–143.

icy. With these protections in place, employment lawyers, and management consultants alike encouraged employers not to shy away from termination as a disciplinary action.[146] On this subject, Schultz quotes a partner at Morgan, Lewis & Bockius, a Philadelphia based law firm:

> [Y]ou must be sure the person raising the complaint feels there is an adequate response. Supervisors who make sexual threats should be fired because, if the supervisor sues, it is a lot easier to defend than a sexual harassment case. But even in the troublesome grey area of sexual joking, the use of progressive discipline – reprimand, suspension, and ultimately termination – is warranted.[147]

While advantageous to the company, the strict disciplining in the aftermath of sexual harassment complaints could actually be counterproductive in eliminating instances of unwelcome behavior. Before making their way through the judiciary, a great majority of the cases recounted within this book began with a single seemingly inconsequential inappropriate act. Considering that judges had repeatedly faulted targets of harassment for delaying their reports, it seemed reasonable for an employee targeted by inappropriate conduct by a supervisor or colleague to want such actions on record. That is, of course, if the target trusted their employer not to retaliate against such a complaint. Management consultants and feminists alike encourage employees to act immediately in order to "nip harassment in the bud."[148] At this point, few complainants intended for the offending party to be disciplined, never mind terminated.

The knowledge that an employer was quick to sever employment relations with those accused of harassment could prevent targets from coming forward in early stages of harassment. Additionally, those employees reporting relatively benign incidences of harassment could quickly become the target of resentment, especially from male employees.[149] Thus, a working environment in which employers were quick to discipline and even terminate employees based on harassment allegations could foster distrust along the gender line. Various studies have demonstrated that rather than blaming management for overzealous definitions and actions, a great portion of employees, mostly male, criticize those filing complaints and in extension female employees in general for "overreacting."[150]

---

146 Schultz: Sanitizing the Workplace, p. 2086.
147 Cited in: Schultz: Sanitizing the Workplace, p. 2093.
148 E.g. AASC: Advocacy Handbook 1979; Women Organized Against Sexual Harassment: What it is; Cordua Training Videos: An Employee's Responsibility.
149 Tinkler: Resisting the Enforcement of Sexual Harassment Law, p. 375.
150 Schultz: Sanitizing the Workplace, p. 2103; Tinkler: Resisting the Enforcement.

Knowing that employers did not offer due process and fearing false or frivolous accusations, many male employees adjusted their interactions with female
colleagues and subordinates. Beginning in the late 1990s in many companies it became common practice for male coworkers to take precautions, such as only meeting on company premises instead of going out for a working lunch, leaving doors
open during meetings, and avoiding socialization with female colleagues outside
of work. Many companies explicitly encouraged such behavior. An article published in *Working Woman* as early as 1995 reported "several personnel directors"
advising male employees to "'play it safe' and not even have lunch or drinks with
a female subordinate alone." In one extreme case, a lawyer, in all seriousness, advised male employees of a university business school not to "talk to any female
employee without a witness or a tape recorder." The school in question had recently lost a sexual harassment lawsuit.[151]

This avoidance of the opposite sex, considerably limited opportunities for female workers to network and to further mentor-mentee relationships; especially
considering that higher-ups were (and in many cases still are) likely male.[152] A hu-
man-resources director at a Washington, D.C. based computer firm commented
that "[s]afety in numbers isn't just a cliché […]." According to him it was "more
prudent" and "just as easy" to "mentor or share information" in a group setting.[153]
Vicki Schultz countered this assessment. In her essay she eloquently outlines a
pattern of male employees avoiding female colleagues in both individual and
group settings in order to avoid frivolous complaints. According to Schultz, this
had a grave effect on the training and career advancement of young women.

In this context, Schultz demonstrated that employers often reacted quickly to
violations of the sexual harassment policy but ignored other forms of gendered
discrimination. According to Schutz, this was due to the common equivalence of
sexuality with unprofessionalism and unproductivity. I fully agree with this assessment, but propose to take it one step further. Within the management framework, the rejection of sexual harassment was conflated with the denigration of
sexuality in the workplace. This new framing divorced sexual harassment from
ideas of discrimination and focused on issues of professionalism and productivity.
Other discrimination issues, such as unequal pay or a lack of training opportuni-

151 Kruger, Pamela: When Companies Turn a Blind Eye to sexual Harassment, They Set Themselves Up for Megadollar Lawsuits and PR Nightmares. Here's What Employers Can do To Protect
Themselves – And Their Employees, in: Working Woman (June 1995), p. 34.
152 Swoboda, Frank: Most Senior-Level Managers Still White, Male, Panel Finds. Commission's
Last Report Puts Blame on 'Glass Ceiling,' in: San Francisco Examiner (November 26th, 1995), p. A9;
U.S. Bureau of Labor Statistics: Women in the Labor Force: A Databook. Report 1097, March 2022.
153 Kruger: When Companies Turn a Blind Eye, p. 34.

ties for women and racial minorities, did not undergo such a reconceptualization. Thus, sexual harassment was not only viewed as unprofessional but as a distinctly separate issue from discrimination. Additionally, instances of sexual harassment were often portrayed as either sexual violence or as a "sex scandal" in the press.[154] As such, sexual harassment, compared to other forms of sex discrimination, had a more sensationalist quality, which could significantly damage a company's reputation.

Despite the advantages for employers in firing those accused of sexual harassment immediately, sometimes the legal risks of keeping them on were superseded by other managerial interests. When a member of an organization, be it an employee, partner, or executive, was particularly valuable to the institution, organizations were known to be more lenient towards possible misconduct. Green argues in an article examining sexual harassment by executives that "companies try to keep the victim quiet" when the harasser is a "top-level executive," because the company "becomes [...] concerned about losing their star and how that loss will affect the company's prospects."[155] Rather than part ways with these individuals, companies regularly agreed to settlements, paying large sums in exchange for the complainant's silence.[156] To illustrate this point, there is hardly a more fitting example, than Bill O'Reilly's "downfall" from Fox News.[157]

In the summer of 2016, "a tidal wave of harassment claims" came crashing down on Bill O'Reilly, Fox News' "founding father" and "number one host." O'Reilly left the network in 2016, claiming that he had been "subjected to a brutal campaign of character assassination [...] unprecedented in post-McCarthyist America." However, when the scandal broke, various news outlets unveiled that accusations against O'Reilly had gone back decades and that he and Fox News had "repeatedly settled complaints of harassment, to the tune of $13 [million]."[158] Fox News had been aware of O'Reilly's sexual misconduct, but his value to the network had exceeded the financial cost of settlements and risk of litigation. Only when the company's reputation was damaged to the point that a majority of businesses can-

---

154 McDonald: Framing Sexual Harassment, pp. 95–103; cf. Heriksen, Ellen Emilie: #MeToo Has Changes How the Media Portrays Rape, in: Kilden (March 14th, 2023).
155 Green: A New #MeToo Result, p. 147.
156 For an in-depth discussion on settlements, alternative dispute resolution, and non-disclosure & confidentiality agreements, see Chapter Seven.
157 Redden, Molly and Dominic Rushe: A Timeline of Bill O'Reilly's Downfall: Another Fox News Founding Father Exits, in: The Guardian (April 20th, 2017).
158 Redden: A Timeline of Bill O'Reilly's Downfall; cf. Levinson, Marsha: Mandatory Arbitration: How the current System Perpetuates Sexual Harassment Cultures in the Workplace, Santa Clara Law Review, 59 (2019), p. 506.

celled their advertisement contracts with the network did Fox News part ways with O'Reilly.[159]

This example demonstrates that when an individual was indispensable to a company, that person was endowed with authority by the organization. Even if this authority was not officially given by means of a supervisory position or a seat in the C-suite the employee's value to the business placed them high up in the company hierarchy. Oftentimes their position, in status and influence, exceeded that of individual members of the human resources department. Edelman and Cabrera showed that human resources staff in charge of a complaint were often reluctant to "challenge management" for fear of being "viewed skeptically by those in control of their future employment prospects."[160]

Employees were often aware that their complaint against a valued member of the organization would fall on deaf ears. Quoted in a 1994 Merit System Protection Board survey, one survey participant lamented:

> The higher the position of the man, the less is done to him – if anything at all. Complaints can be brought against the high-ranking person but at worst he gets a slap on the hand and that is the example that is set. [161]

Another employee expanded on this problem and declared:

> Each agency needs a management team that truly does punish the harasser and allows the victim to know how and to what extent the harasser was punished. [162]

These quotes indicate that, generally speaking, employees knew of the dynamics protecting individuals important to the organization. Not only were victims more reluctant to come forward, because they feared the harassers' personal retaliatory action, many also knew that they could rely neither on the assistance of the human resources department, nor on the protection of internal policies and grievance procedures.

---

159 Steel, Emily and Michael Schmidt: Fox Losing More Advertisers After Sexual Harassment Claims Against O'Reilly, in: The New York Times, (April 4th, 2017); Wrigth, Robert: Advertisers Continue to Drop Fox News' 'O'Reilley Factor.' At Least 52 Companies Have Withdrawn Advertisements from the Show, in: ABC News (April 7th, 2017); Berg, Madeline: Here Are All the Advertisers Who Have Dropped Bill O'Reilly, in: Forbes (April 4th, 2017).
160 Edelman: Sex-Based Harassment and Symbolic Compliance, p. 374.
161 MSPB: Sexual Harassment in the Federal Workplace 1994, p. 38; cf. Schultz: Sanitizing the Workplace, p. 2109.
162 MSPB: Sexual Harassment in the Federal Workplace 1994, p. 38; cf. Schultz: Sanitizing the Workplace, p. 2109.

Protecting high-value employees from credible allegations perpetuated sexual harassment within the company. First, by settling and concealing multiple accusations against a single person the company obscured a pattern of misconduct. If valuable to the company, serial harassers, such as Harvey Weinstein or Bill O'Reilly, were allowed free reign. Second, because such employees were influential in their organizations, their behavior greatly affected the general company culture. As discussed above, executives led by example. The more leeway upper management gave in regard to sexual harassment, the freer middle-level supervisors and employees felt to discount written policies and procedure.

If high valued harassers could escape discipline based on their status in the company, it seems prudent to examine how, conversely, anti-sexual harassment policies affected workers who had fallen out of grace with their employer; especially, when those employees were protected from at-will employment conditions by their employment contract, their union contract, or anti-discrimination laws. Vicki Schultz contended that all-encompassing internal sexual harassment policies and arbitrary enforcement gave employers a way to circumvent worker protection laws. She highlighted cases in which African American men, gay men, union men, and men holding seniority or awaiting large bonuses filed for wrongful termination after having been accused of sexual harassment. Schultz argued that these groups were particularly vulnerable to being fired after violating internal policies as "management appears to seize on a sexual harassment complaint as a subterfuge for less benign motives for getting rid of an employee."[163]

More scholarly attention and especially the collection of quantitative data will be necessary to determine whether Schultz is correct in asserting that sexual harassment policies were (and are) *routinely* used to circumvent workers' protections. Whether by design or serendipity, broad anti-sexual harassment policies effectively provided employers with an escape hatch for situations in which they were barred from legally terminating employment without cause.

In conclusion, with the shift of the first response regarding allegations of sexual harassment into individual organizations, employers gained much power over the issue. As long as action regarding sexual harassment was contained within the organization, the company could operate as a state-like micro-system. In contrast to the United States, however, a company was not conceived as a democracy. The employer was not an elected body; the company's interests did not always align with and in fact, often contradicted those of the employees; and the system of checks and balances was eliminated, giving reign to arbitrary decision making. It was the employer or their respective human resources department, not the

---

163 Schultz: Sanitizing the Workplace, p. 2107.

state, who decided on how to respond to complaints; They choose the depth of inquiry; It was them who decreed whether an allegation had merit; And they determined what consequences a perpetrator should face. It was the employer or their respective human resources department, not the state, who decided on how to respond to complaints. They chose the depth of inquiry, they decreed whether an allegation had merit, and they determined what consequences a perpetrator should face.

Following the management framework, employers implemented policies and grievance procedures which defined sexual harassment much more broadly than the law. These written documents highlighted individual instances, focused on language of professionalism rather than discrimination, and blurred the line between consensual and coercive behavior. By doing so, they covered many instances which would neither amount to sexual harassment under the law, nor under the feminist definition of the term.

The enforcement of these policies was dependent on various managerial interests. If the alleged harasser was valuable to the organization, employers were more likely to overlook a pattern of sexual misconduct. If, on the other hand, the accused was expendable, employers were quick to discipline minor violations in order to minimize legal risks. By terminating employees without determining whether the misconduct had been of a discriminatory nature, employers encouraged an atmosphere of distrust and fear among their employees. Male employees often dreaded that unfounded allegations and a lack of due process within the organization could cost them their jobs and reputation.[164] Therefore, it was not unusual for male employees to take precautions and avoid close contact with female colleagues and subordinates.

Rather than having the issue of sexual harassment forced onto the employer's agenda as an overreach of the government, as it as was often seen in earlier years, by keeping the issue internal, many companies managed to reduce the threat the issue presented to them, and, in some instances, even turn it to their advantage. Allegations of sexual harassment could provide cause for terminating an employment relationship that was otherwise protected. Additionally, in the name of anti-harassment and anti-discrimination measures, employers not only increased the quantity of employee monitoring but also expanded the scope. Employee's private conversations, their relationships, and even their sex lives were now, quite literally, the employer's business.

---

164 Ibid., p. 22.

7 Forced Arbitration and Non-Disclosure Agreements

Despite the legal systems' encouragement and employers' high motivation to re-solve issues internally, complainants continued to seek redress outside of the or-ganizational context. Instead of working themselves through the judiciary, howev-er, these cases were often resolved through alternative dispute resolution (ADR). ADR became increasingly used as precursor to or substitute for legal action.[165] In its origin, ADR was a voluntary process in which both parties attempted to find a solution without involving a judge or jury. Increasingly, however, arbitra-tion was mandated as a condition of employment in many private organizations. Employment contracts included "pre-dispute arbitration agreements," which ob-liged both parties to submit to binding arbitration, also known as mandatory or forced arbitration.

Similarly, to company internal grievance procedures and resolutions, ADR procedures kept the complaint out of court. In the following, I shall briefly present the three most common methods of alternative dispute resolutions: conciliation, mediation, and arbitration. Close attention will be paid to mandatory arbitration, which played a significant role in the handling of sexual harassment cases. Its per-vasiveness and obligatory nature, coupled with the increased use of confidential-ity and non-disclosure agreements, created an environment in which the manage-ment frame could flourish.

7.1 Strictly Voluntary Forms of ADR: Conciliation, Mediation, and Voluntary Arbitration

To this day, the most common forms of alternative dispute resolution are concil-iation, mediation, and arbitration.[166] Concerning the latter, a sharp distinction be-tween voluntary and binding arbitration must be made. Conciliation, mediation, and voluntary arbitration could be initiated at any point in the complaint process. Employee and employer could choose to enter into negotiations as soon as the ag-grieved filed an internal complaint with the HR department, or the parties could seek an extralegal solution as late as seconds before a judge or jury gave a verdict

---

165 Foote: Understanding Sexual Harassment, p. 255; Green: A New #MeToo Result, p. 154; Levinson: Mandatory Arbitration, p. 486.
166 Foote: Understanding Sexual Harassment, p. 238.

on the case.[167] In most cases, the EEOC attempted to facilitate mediation before pursuing litigation.[168]

The first variant mentioned – conciliation – consisted of negotiations without a neutral third-party present. If the conciliation process was successful, the parties agreed upon a settlement agreement. At the minimum such an agreement involved a payment by the employer in exchange for the complainant's waiver of future litigation in the matter. In 1997, for instance, Rose McGowan, "signed away her right to sue [Harvey] Weinstein" after he allegedly raped her. In exchange she was paid a sum of one hundred thousand dollars.[169] In most cases settlement agreements included further stipulations. McGowan's settlement agreement was unusual, because it did not include a non-disclosure agreement (NDA). NDAs were a common element of settlement agreements, including those signed by Harvey Weinstein after the incident in 1997.[170]

Additional elements which could be included such an agreement were changes to company policy, counseling for the harasser, the implementation of anti-harassment training, and any other form of disciplinary or preventative action. Zelda Perkins, a former assistant to Harvey Weinstein, who "from the very first time left alone with Harvey, [...] had to deal with him being present either in his underpants or totally naked," and who described the "barrage of advances" Weinstein subjected her to as "exhausting," initiated legal action against the production company Miramax in 1998. Besides a payment of $125.000, in exchange for abandoning future litigation and signing an NDA, the resulting settlement agreement had several additional stipulations. It mandated that Miramax make changes to their internal grievance procedure and human-resources department. Additionally, the company was obliged to "provide proof that Weinstein was receiving counseling for three years or 'as long as his therapist deems necessary.'" Lastly, the settlement determined that Miramax was to fire Weinstein and report his behavior to Disney, who at the time owned Miramax, "if a subsequent sexual-harassment settlement was reached in the following two years." [171]

---

167 Ibid., p. 241.
168 Ibid., p. 240.
169 Farrow, Ronan: Harvey Weinstein's Secret Settlements. The Mogul Used Money from His Brother and Elaborate Legal Agreements to Hide Allegations of Predation for Decades, in: The New Yorker (November 21st, 2017).
170 Farrow, Ronan: Harvey Weinstein's Secret Settlements. The Mogul Used Money from His Brother and Elaborate Legal Agreements to Hide Allegations of Predation for Decades, in: The New Yorker (November 21st, 2017).
171 Ibid.

Perkins initially rejected the idea of a settlement but felt she had no alternative to address her complaints. In an interview with *The New Yorker* in 2017, she explained that she "felt trapped:"

> I was, like, 'Right. O.K. So, we can't go to police because it's too late. We can't go to Disney 'cause they don't give a shit. So who do we tell? [...] I was a twenty-three or twenty-four-year-old girl sitting in a room with often up to six men telling me I had no options. [172]

Generally speaking, the power differential and the extensive discrepancy in available resources between employers and employees put the employee at a disadvantage throughout the conciliation process. This asymmetry could make an employee hesitant to participate in such a proceeding. Forensic psychologists William Foote and Jane Goodman-Delahunty explained that this hesitation could be further intensified, if the accused held a position of authority within the company. "Trust," they determined, was a vital component of "meaningful informal negotiations." If the alleged harasser was highly valued by the company, there was little basis for such trust and therefore increased skepticism towards a conciliation proceeding.[173]

Despite this power discrepancy, complainants often engaged in conciliation efforts. In fact, Foote and Goodman-Delahunty estimate that roughly 80% of cases are resolved by means of a settlement (agreed upon through conciliation or mediation) before reaching the court room.[174] Importantly, the EEOC in a majority of cases did not issue a right to sue letter before the complainant had engaged in an attempt to resolve the issue.[175] Hence, engagement in conciliation or mediation became a semi-mandatory step in pursing litigation. However, even without EEOC intervention both parties could have an incentive to seek out conciliation. This was particularly true when a case was either very weak or very strong.

For an employer it often proved more cost effective to offer a small settlement payment than to mount an expensive defense before a third party – even if the complainant's case was weak and a judge or jury would in all likelihood rule in the employer's favor. For a complainant with a weak case, the expediated process

---

172 Ibid.
173 Foote: Understanding Sexual Harassment, p. 248.
174 Ibid., p. 247; Berrey et al. show that 58% of cases filed in court are resolved through settlement. This, however, does not include the cases which settled before they were officially filed. For more quantitative data on civil rights litigation see: Berrey, Ellen et al.: Rights on Trial. How Workplace Discrimination Law Perpetuates Inequality, Chicago – London 2017, p. 61.
175 Ibid.

a settlement offered could be tempting, especially when weighed against the high risk of receiving nothing in litigation. Similarly, when it was obvious to both parties that a complaint had merit and held great potential of swaying a neutral party, the employer would often offer a significant settlement rather than risking a verdict. Accepting such terms and thereby, finding a speedy resolution, could be appealing to a complainant when compared to an arbitration process or a trial, which harbored some risk.[176]

When cases were murkier or when parties lacked trust in the conciliation process, it was often beneficial to enlist a third-party to guide the negotiations in order to include a more distanced, neutral perspective.[177] Both mediation and arbitration involved a neutral third party.[178] Although arbitrators and mediators had distinct roles and functions, their training was remarkably similar. Neither was required to go through extensive legal or psychological training and neither was specially trained regarding sexual harassment. While various states differed in their educational requirements, conditions for accreditation in the United States were lax; courses offered by universities as well as private consulting firms usually did not exceed forty hours.[179]

Mediation and arbitration offered different benefits and drawbacks when used to resolve a sexual harassment complaint. Mediation most closely resembled the conciliation process. Here the mediator acted as a neutral third party in charge of structuring the process, ensuring that both parties voiced their concerns while remaining respectful and non-threatening.[180] Contrary to a judge or arbitrator, a mediator had no control over the outcome of the process. It was their job to facilitate the negotiations, usually over the span of one or two sessions. The decision on whether a final resolution was reached, however, purely resided with the conflicting parties.[181] As parties retained control over the outcome, there was little risk in attempting mediation.[182] In fact, Foote and Goodman-Delahunty's argue that there was a benefit to mediation, even when no agreement was reached: the process was often "still useful in narrowing issues, educating the parties, and advancing the case in a more cost-effective and less adversarial fashion

---

176 Ibid., p. 253.
177 Ibid., p. 249.
178 Ibid., p. 241.
179 Ibid., p. 255.
180 Dessler: Human Resources Management, p. 79.
181 Foote: Understanding Sexual Harassment, pp. 252f.
182 Dessler: Human Resources Management, p. 79.

than formal discovery."[183] When mediation was successful, it resulted in a settlement agreement as described above.

Obtaining a resolution through the court system could take years. Thus, the potential of a speedy conclusion of the matter was often the main driver for the mediation process. The quick process was made possible not only by the informality of the process itself but also by the variety of possible solutions. As with a settlement reached through conciliation, the employer could agree to discipline the harasser,[184] transfer either the harasser or the complainant, offer an apology to the victim,[185] implement company-wide training, offer a letter of recommendation, and/or modify the job to benefit the complainant. These non-monetary solutions were not available in a court room. Additionally, while an employment relationship was often irreparably damaged throughout a court proceeding, mediation could preserve the employer-employee relationship, allowing the complainant to retain her position in the company.[186] For many targets, the sole motivation for filing a complaint was to make the harassment stop. For this, mediation was often a promising avenue.

Nevertheless, there were significant drawbacks which could deter either party from participating in mediation. On the one hand, depending on the strength of a case, the employer could fear that their "willingness to mediate" would be seen as a "concession of weakness." On the other hand, a complainant could reevaluate their readiness to participate in mediation, depending on the end-goal of their complaint. As shall be further explained, out-of-court resolutions did not have precedential value. A settlement agreement, especially when it included a non-disclosure agreement, could not be cited by other targets when seeking similar relief or attempting to establish a pattern of discrimination.[187] If the ideal outcome for the defendant was to gain public recognition or even aid in transforming the law, mediation was not a suitable strategy.

There were additional drawbacks to mediation, which were specific to civil rights violations. Mediation was devised for situations in which two parties could meet on equal footing. Therefore, as Foote and Goodman-Delahunty explained, mediation "assumes that a compromise exists between the two perspectives." They continue that in sexual harassment cases, the process "risks losing sight of the fact that a wrong has been committed and that one of the parties

---

183 Foote: Understanding Sexual Harassment, p. 252.
184 Ibid., p. 253.
185 Shuman, D: The Role of Apology in Tort Law, in: Judicature 83/4 (2000), pp. 180–190; Foote: Understanding Sexual Harassment, p. 253.
186 Foote: Understanding Sexual Harassment, p. 253.
187 Ibid.

has to bear blame for that wrong." The focus on equality and compromise could be very valuable in other types of disagreements, such as divorce negotiations or neighborhood conflicts. In sexual harassment cases, however, it shifted the focus away from the illegal conduct by one party. Instead, it reframed the issue as an employee or management conflict and implied the (partial) guilt of both parties.[188]

Arbitration, in contrast to mediation, sought adjudication instead of compromise. Of the three methods of extralegal dispute resolution, arbitration was the most "adversarial" and most closely resembled a court proceeding. Throughout the process both parties presented their case to a neutral third party, the arbitrator. After hearing the facts, the arbitrator made a ruling. By agreeing to enter into arbitration both parties consented to abide by the arbitrator's decision. Arbitration was a suitable method of dispute resolution, when negotiations were not likely to yield a compromise, but neither party wished to pursue the matter in court. Compared to litigation, the three major advantages of arbitration were the informality and thus, the potential for a speedy resolution, the discretion the process offered, and the flexibility in available solutions.[189]

Despite the perceived similarity between a judge and an arbitrator, arbitration was not bound by the same regulations that applied in the legal sphere. The structure and rules of an arbitration proceeding were agreed upon by both parties before beginning the process.[190] This meant that if the parties to the arbitration had not specified to honor the same laws of evidence and procedure that are essential to a court proceeding in their arbitration agreement, these regulations did not apply in the arbitration process.[191] For instance, statements considered "hearsay" and inadmissible in court were often admitted in arbitration; rape shield laws seldom applied; and neither side was required to be represented by a lawyer. Furthermore, unless otherwise stipulated by the parties before beginning arbitration, the process did not include a mechanism for appeal.[192] The arbitrator's decision was final.

---

188 Ibid., p. 254.
189 Ibid., p. 255.
190 While this was true for voluntary arbitration, the following section will show, that an equal influence over the specific format of arbitration proceedings was nearly impossible in binding arbitration; Colvin, Alexander J.S.: The Growing Use of Mandatory Arbitration. Access to the Courts is Now Barred for More Than 60 Million American Workers, in: Economic Policy Institute (September 2017), p. 2.
191 Foote: Understanding Sexual Harassment, p. 239.
192 Seymour, R.: More Arbitration; Understanding Sexual Harassment, p. 239.

Legal battles were lengthy and expensive, even when they were not slowed down by "an overburdened civil justice system."[193] An arbitration could be concluded within weeks and seldom took longer than a few months.[194] Additionally, although the fee for the arbitrator could be quite high, the process was much less costly than pursuing litigation.[195] Its cost-effective nature was the main reason arbitration became increasingly popular among employers.[196] However, this also benefited many victims of harassment. According to an assessment by the ACLU:

> These private justice systems could be either a blessing or a curse, depending on the form they take. If they are truly voluntary arrangements which provide due process, they could provide needed justice for rank and file employees for whom the civil justice system is an unaffordable luxury.[197]

The possibility of filing a complaint and participating in the proceeding without legal counsel made arbitration, in contrast to the civil justice system, accessible to low-income individuals.[198] Due to its speed and low cost (compared to litigation), voluntary arbitration could be a tempting alternative to the legal system for both employers and employees.

This rings particularly true in light of the research of Ellen Berrey, Robert Nelson, and Laura Beth Nielson, which is based on interviews conducted with civil rights plaintiffs who had been successful in their legal suits. The study, published in 2017, highlighted that despite winning their case, many plaintiffs were unsatisfied with the outcome. Not only did they expend time and money, plaintiffs also had to testify to personal and sensitive experiences. Their family life may have suffered, they risked being branded as a 'trouble maker' within their industry, and in most cases they had no job to which to return.[199] In contrast, arbitration was often combined with confidentiality agreements and thus offered privacy as part as the

---

193 Dana, Anne et al.: The 'Ending Forced Arbitration of Sexual Assault and Sexual Harassment Act of 2021' Brings Significant Change to Employers with Mandatory Pre-Dispute Arbitration Agreements, in: Employee Relations Law Journal 48/2 (Autumn 2022), p. 15.

194 Levinson: Mandatory Arbitration, pp. 487 f.

195 Ibid., pp. 490, 523.

196 Ibid., p. 499; Hippensteele, Susan: Mediation Ideology: Navigating Space from Myth to Reality in Sexual harassment Dispute Resolution, in: Journal of Gender, Social Policy and the Law 15/1(2006), p. 45.

197 Maltby: National Task Force on Civil Liberties in the Workplace, p. 6.

198 Levinson: Mandatory Arbitration, p. 491.

199 Berrey, Ellen et al.: Workers Wronged, in: American Bar Association Journal 103/11 (November 2017), p. 38.

process.[200] In many cases, targets of harassment welcomed that their statements would not be part of the public record, where it was easily accessible to their friends, family, future employers, and the press. In 2018, using the hashtag #WhyI-DidntReport, victims of sexual harassment and assault spoke out about why they did not pursue their cases. A common theme was the fear that "people will find out."[201] One twitter user, @girlsreallyrule, recounted:

> I was humiliated. I knew everyone would find out. I was afraid it would ruin my professional reputation before I had even started.[202]

Considering this common fear among victims, the promise of a confidential proceeding could be an encouraging factor for raising a complaint.[203]

Employers, too, were cautious about their companies' reputations. As discussed at length throughout the preceding chapters, even rumors of sexual harassment within a business could affect employee morale and productivity and damage a company's image. Therefore, arbitration proceedings covered by confidentiality agreements in contrast to public court hearings were preferable to employers. An arbitration process, even without a confidentiality agreement, drew less attention from the press and the public than did a prolonged trial and thereby caused less reputational damage.[204] An employer could be more willing to admit to wrongdoing or issue an apology in private.

The expedience, informality, and privacy of the arbitration process could aid in finding an outcome beneficial to the target of harassment. Most arbitration agreements permitted arbitrators to order both monetary and non-monetary relief. A combination of the two often played a significant role in the complainant's satisfaction regarding the outcome.[205] An apology, the removal of bad performance evaluations, or a promotion could calm the waves and at times even salvage the employment relationship.[206] When arbitration and confidentiality agreements were freely agreed upon by both parties, they could be immensely beneficial in limiting the fallout from the process.

---

200 Levinson: Mandatory Arbitration, p. 490.

201 Willingham, AJ and Christina Maxouris: These Tweets Show Why People Don't Report Sexual Assaults, in: CNN Health (September 21st, 2018).

202 Tweet by Amee Vanderpool (@girlsreallyrule) from September 21st, 2018, cited in: Willingham: These Tweets Show Why People Don't Report.

203 Berrey: Workers Wronged, p. 42.

204 Foote: Understanding Sexual Harassment, p. 253.

205 Berrey: Workers Wronged, p. 39.

206 Levinson: Mandatory Arbitration, p. 490; Shuman: The Role of Apology in Tort Law, p. 79.

7.2 Pre-Dispute Arbitration Agreements

In most cases, however, employees did not enter the arbitration completely voluntarily. Ever since the early 1990s, binding arbitration agreements in employment gained in popularity.[207] In these pre-dispute arbitration agreements employer and employee consented that any future disagreements, whether they be based on violations of the employer policy or the United States legal code, be resolved through arbitration.[208] Over the years, many businesses, including Fox News,[209] Microsoft, AirBnB, and Facebook made binding arbitration a non-negotiable term of employment.[210]

Alexander Colvin, Professor of Conflict Resolution at Cornell University, has done extensive research on the extent of mandatory arbitration agreements. In 2017 Colvin found, in a study of 628 "large private-sector American business establishments," that over half (55%) of American non-union employees in the private sector were bound by mandatory arbitration.[211] In absolute numbers this translated to 60 million American workers who had signed binding arbitration agreements.[212] According to Colvin, "[m]andatory employment arbitration has [...] surpassed court litigation as the most common process through which the rights of American workers are adjudicated and enforced."[213] As such, mandatory arbitration warrants serious consideration when analyzing reactions and conceptualizations of sexual harassment.

The history of mandatory arbitration goes back to the beginning of the 20th century. The judiciary originally refused to enforce such agreements and thus, refused to cede parts of their jurisdiction to private arbitrators. Congress, however, considered arbitration a valuable asset with the potential of expediating resolu-

---

207 Maltby: National Task Force on Civil Liberties in the Workplace, p. 6; Colvin: The Growing Use of Mandatory Arbitration, p. 1; Binding arbitration agreements are also common in consumer contracts, e.g. cellphone contract, nursing homes etc.

208 Levinson: Mandatory Arbitration, p. 489.

209 Elsesser, Kim: Sexual Harassment and Assault Force Arbitration Bill to Get Vote This Week, in: Forbes (February 7th, 2022).

210 Anonymous: Court: Employers May take Away Right to Sue, in: Oakland Tribune (September 15th, 1999), reprinted from Los Angeles Times; In the wake of the #MeToo Movement Microsoft, AirBnB, Facebook alongside Google, and eBay made arbitration voluntary in sexual harassment cases. Moore, Mark H.: The state of the campaign to end mandatory arbitration misconduct claims in employment agreements, in: Westlaw Today (June 2021).

211 Colvin: The Growing Use of Mandatory Arbitration, p. 1; also discussed in Foote: Understanding Sexual Harassment, pp. 256 f.

212 Colvin: The Growing Use of Mandatory Arbitration, p. 2.

213 Ibid., p. 7.

tions and lightening the burden on the court system. Thus, in 1925, Congress enacted the Federal Arbitration Act (FAA) which "required courts to grant motions to compel arbitration pursuant to arbitration agreements."[214]

Over the decades, various Supreme Court decisions expanded the FAA's reach.[215] The most significant decision in the context of sexual harassment law, *Alexander v. Gardner-Denver* (1991), set the precedent for allowing mandatory arbitration agreements to cover Title VII, Age Discrimination, and Family and Disability Leave complaints.[216] While complainant Harrel Alexander argued that arbitration was "inconsistent with the Age Discrimination in Employment Act's purpose," the Supreme Court ruled that "an agreement to arbitrate an [Age Discrimination in Employment Act] claim is not a waiver of substantive rights, but merely an agreement to resolve claims arising from those rights 'in an arbitral, rather than a judicial forum.'"[217] Following this verdict, pre-dispute arbitration agreements could cover discrimination issues, including sexual harassment complaints.

Criticism against mandatory arbitration extending to civil rights violations was extensive and led to some action in the federal government. In 2014, Executive Order 13673 signed by President Obama "bar[red] all federal contractors with contacts of greater than one million dollars from enforcing mandatory arbitration agreements in claims base on Title VII, or tort claims involving sexual assault or harassment."[218] Additionally, there have been repeated attempts to limit the scope of mandatory arbitration through the Arbitration Fairness Bill (AFB). The bill had been introduced in various versions in 2009, 2011, 2013, and 2015 with the newest rendition reading: "no pre-dispute arbitration agreement shall be valid or enforceable if it requires arbitration of an employment, consumer or franchise dispute, or a dispute arising under any statute intended to protect civil rights."[219] However, the bill was rejected and by the beginning of the #MeToo movement in 2017, Congress had not enacted any limitations on the Federal Arbitration Act of 1925.

Colvin's research shows that in 1992, a year after the *Gardner* verdict, employers had not yet broadly implemented mandatory arbitration which covered Title VII complaints. At the time, only two percent of non-union employees in the private sector were bound by such agreements. Although the legal parameters of arbitration developed separately from sexual harassment law, the rise of

214 Levinson: Mandatory Arbitration, p. 496.
215 Ibid., p. 497.
216 Dessler: Human Resources Management, p. 80.
217 Levinson: Mandatory Arbitration, p. 498.
218 Ibid., p. 501.
219 Ibid., p. 502.

mandatory arbitration agreements coincides with the caesuras established in *Bad for Business.* In 1998, mandatory arbitration was appearing as a meaningful phenomenon.

Employers looking to establish such an agreement had to gradually induce their staff to agree. Rockwell International, for instance, sought to protect itself from future litigation by implementing a binding arbitration policy. For new, non-union employees, mandatory arbitration was a condition of employment. For those already employed, signing the agreement was a prerequisite for any transfer or promotion.[220] Thus, for a future at the company, one had to agree to arbitrate any disputes. Other companies went even further and severed employment relations with those individuals not willing to agree to mandatory arbitration.[221] By 2003, nearly a quarter of the non-unionized private workforce in America had agreed to mandatory arbitration in advance of a dispute.[222]

Although it took the Federal Arbitration Act to guide the judiciary to enforce mandatory arbitration agreements, their legal validity was based in contract law. Due to the "freedom of contract" principle, Americans had great leeway in making agreements without government interference. Mandatory arbitration agreements were considered a "bargained-for element" of employment contracts, and as such, were enforced by the judiciary.[223] In 2001, the Supreme Court, in *Circuit City Stores, Inc. v. Adams* (2001), moved from merely enforcing such agreements to actively encouraging them, stating that arbitration was not only permitted, but "favored" over litigation.[224]

Relieving the overburdened justice system was a significant benefit of mandatory arbitration.[225] The numbers of bound arbitration cases were high and thus, had a significant impact on the EEOC's and courts' case load. Proponents had long argued that "mandatory arbitration increases judicial efficiency by reducing the courts' dockets." They explained that eradicating binding arbitration agreements would cause the judicial system to "become severely overloaded."[226] In fact, repeated congressional bills to limit mandatory arbitration failed with key representatives arguing that neither the EEOC nor the U.S. Judiciary would be able to ap-

---

220 Dessler: Human Resource Management, p. 80.
221 Anonymous: Court: Employers May Take Away Right to Sue.
222 Colvin: The Growing Use of Mandatory Arbitration, p. 1.
223 Levinson: Mandatory Arbitration, p. 493.
224 *Circuit City Stores, Inc. v. Adams*, 532 U.S. 105 (2001); discussed in Levinson: Mandatory Arbitration, p. 499.
225 Dana: The Ending Forced Arbitration Act, p. 15.
226 Levinson: Mandatory Arbitration, p. 491.

propriately process the influx of cases presented to them.[227] On an individual level legal expert Marsha Levinson argues, that "in light of the overworked, underfunded, [sic] Equal Employment Opportunity Commission, and backlogged federal courts, both employers and employees may actually be better off with mandatory arbitration."[228]

Despite these benefits, and despite the general approval for mandatory arbitration from the judiciary and Congress, there was (and is) an abundance of critics who oppose the practice, especially when used to resolve civil rights complaints.[229] Criticism ranged from opposition to a discrepancy in bargaining power, to doubts over the neutrality of arbitrators, to resistance against the transfer of judicial jurisdiction to a private process. These factors combined lead to the same conclusion; arbitration, according to critics, was slanted in favor of the employer, and thus made it hard for a complainant to enforce their rights. Most opponents of binding arbitration agreed that "litigation ultimately provides a better forum for sexual harassment targets to secure justice."[230]

The first major component of the criticism is the discrepancy in bargaining power of both parties.[231] As has been explained above, a pre-dispute arbitration agreement was legally valid because it was a bargained-for clause within a contract. In theory both parties negotiated the terms of the contract and agreed to add such a clause. However, in practice, employers increasingly added mandatory arbitration clauses as a non-negotiable term of employment. The larger the company, the higher the likelihood of such an agreement. Thus, the applicant had the choice to either accept the contract, as is, or to turn their back on the job.[232] When presented with limited employment options, financial insecurity, or a narrow career path, combined with the reality that many other employers offered similar terms, an applicant often had limited options. In addition, many prospective employees did not understand the full implications of mandatory arbitration and were unaware that they would not be able to appeal an arbitrator's decision in a court of law. As Levinson explains this may be partially due to "people [being] overly optimistic, and often under-predict[ing] the need they might have to bring a future claim and thus undervalue[ing] what they are losing by giving up the right

---

227 Foote: Understanding Sexual Harassment, pp. 246 f.
228 Levinson: Mandatory Arbitration, p. 487.
229 Ibid., pp. 500 f.; Foote: Understanding Sexual Harassment, p. 242; Bozin, Doris et al: ADR: Championing the (Unjust) Resolution of Bullying Disputes? in: Australasian Dispute Resolution Journal 29/3 (2019), pp. 162–172.
230 Foote: Understanding Sexual Harassment, p. 242.
231 Ibid., p. 256.
232 Levinson: Mandatory Arbitration, p. 490.

to sue." Additionally, empirical studies have shown that a majority of Americans did not read the full agreements before signing the contract. Without fully understanding the agreement and without a real opportunity to negotiate better terms, critics argue, applicants and employees lack the bargaining power which would allow them to make an informed and voluntary decision.[233]

The "take it or leave it" approach allowed employers to dictate the terms of the arbitration procedure. Arbitration processes differed according to the terms of the specific arbitration agreement. Due to the discrepancy in bargaining power, "[m]andatory arbitration clauses are drafted by employers and imposed on employees."[234] Often employers turned to an arbitration agency and relied on their proposed procedure.[235] This, however, was not required. Thus, there was no governmental or industry standard; the rules of arbitration could vary considerably depending on the agreement.

Early on, there were some extra-governmental attempts to set standards for arbitration agreements. In 1994, for instance, the American Bar Association assembled a national taskforce "composed of business and labor leaders, public and private arbitration services [...] and employee rights groups, including the ACLU." In a status report on the negotiations, the ACLU National Task Force on Civil Liberties in the Workplace, reported that the taskforce was divided on whether agreeing to binding arbitration should be a "condition of employment." On the other hand, most participants agreed that there should be "due process standards" within arbitrations and that "these standards should be legally enforceable."[236]

In that same year, the 9th Circuit refused to enforce an arbitration agreement. In the early 1990s, it was not uncommon for employers to include mandatory arbitration agreements in the employee handbook rather than the employment contract itself.[237] The contract then mentioned adherence to the handbook as part of the employment agreement. This practice resulted in conflicting rulings in the lower courts,[238] leading to the 9th circuit to invalidate an existing mandatory arbitration agreement in *Prudential Insurance Co. of America v. Lai* (1994). The court argued that since the appellants did not know about the clause in the handbook, never having been given a copy of said handbook before signing the contract,

---

233 Ibid., pp. 493f., 511.
234 Ibid., p. 513.
235 Agencies, like the American Arbitration Association, offer examples for arbitration clauses, refer arbitrators, and facilitate arbitration proceedings. Levinson: Mandatory Arbitration, p. 489.
236 Maltby: National Task Force on Civil Liberties in the Workplace, p. 7.
237 Levinson: Mandatory Arbitration, p. 489.
238 Foote: Understanding Sexual Harassment, p. 256.

"they were not bound by any valid agreement to arbitrate [...] employment disputes."[239]

Following this ruling and a growing consent on due process in arbitration, management consultants explicitly advised employers to include mandatory arbitration clauses in their contracts rather than in other employment material.[240] Additionally, in order to secure the process against judicial appeal,[241] management handbooks warned personnel experts to conceive of a process which "protect[ed] against arbitrator bias," "allow[ed] the arbitrator to offer a claimant broad relief (including reinstatement)," and "allow[ed] for a reasonable amount of prehearing fact finding." [242]

Nevertheless, critics argued that due to the prevalence of confidentiality agreements, an appeal in court was nearly impossible. Additionally, due to the one-sided process of establishing a procedure the arbitration process "grossly favor[ed]" the employer.[243] The ACLU explained their apprehensions as follows:

> [When] employers shape their private justice systems to their own advantage and condition employment on the use the [sic] company's adjudication system, rather than the courts, in the event that a dispute arises, workplace justice [...] suffer[s] an enormous setback.[244]

Closely related to arguments about unequal bargaining power, critics warned against arbitrator bias. The process of choosing an arbitrator was settled in the arbitration clause. Usually this means that the arbitrator, or the private agency facilitating the arbitration, was chosen and paid for by the employer. While arbitration providers assured that neither they nor their arbitrators were "biased against one party or favorable to another,"[245] critics warned against "the repeat-provider problem."[246] They argued that because the employer, in contrast to the employee, was in a position to rehire the agency and thus provide them with future business, the arbitrator's decision could "consciously or subconsciously" be more favorable to the employer. In addition, detractors warned that employers were usually "repeat players" in arbitration and had much more experience and resources avail-

---

239 *Prudential Insurance Co. of America v. Lai*, 42 F.3d 1299, 1305 (9th Cir. 1994); discussed in Levinson: Mandatory Arbitration, pp. 503, 518.
240 E.g. Dessler: Human Resources Management, p. 80.
241 Arbitrator bias is one of the few reasons for a judge to vacate the outcome of arbitration. (See American Arbitration Association: Ethical Principles.)
242 Dessler: Human Resources Management, p. 80.
243 Levinson: Mandatory Arbitration, p. 492.
244 Maltby: National Task Force on Civil Liberties in the Workplace, pp. 6f.
245 American Arbitration Association: Ethical Principles.
246 Levinson: Mandatory Arbitration, p. 494; Foote: Understanding Sexual Harassment, p. 256.

able to them than an employee. The advantage of being a "repeat player," could be even more significant, if employers repeatedly used the same arbitrator.[247]

Social science research corroborated many of these concerns. A study from 2017 confirmed the "repeat player" effect, finding that "the more frequently an employer used arbitration, the better the employer fared in arbitration."[248] Additionally, various studies have shown that employers won a higher percentage of cases in arbitration than they did in state and federal courts.[249] When an employer did lose their case in arbitration, arbitrators were shown to be more conservative in their assessment of monetary damages than judges or juries.[250] Due to the lower chances of winning the case and the inferior awards, complainants lawyers were reluctant to take arbitration cases, especially when working on commission. Thus, complainants often had trouble finding legal counsel to represent them during arbitration.[251]

Additionally, critics argued that binding arbitration in civil rights cases harmed employees on a systemic level. Title VII was only one example of a "statute designed to further important social policies."[252] In this case the social policy referred to the prevention of discrimination in the workplace. Ever since the 1990s, critics have argued that mandatory arbitration circumvented public policy by "submer[sing] important public law matters into a private process."[253] Critics pointed out that this privatization led to the diminishment of judicial authority, and that it "deprives citizens of a judicial forum provided to them by law." Thus, precluding litigation on a wide scale "insults public policy."[254]

Congressional intent regarding Title VII of the Civil Rights Act was both to remedy and to prevent discrimination. There is, however, mounting evidence that mandatory arbitration did (and does) not have a preventative effect.[255] Arbitration, like any alternative dispute resolution method, did not have precedential

---

247 Levinson: Mandatory Arbitration, p. 494.

248 Ibid., p. 514.

249 Gough, Mark: A Tale of Two Forums: Employment Discrimination Outcomes in Arbitration and Litigation, in: IRL Review 68/5 (2020), pp. 1019–1042; Foote: Understanding Sexual Harassment, pp. 244, 255.

250 Gough: A Tale of Two Forums; Foote: Understanding Sexual Harassment, p. 244.

251 Levinson: Mandatory Arbitration, p. 494.

252 Foote: Understanding Sexual Harassment, p. 255.

253 Levinson: Mandatory Arbitration, p. 490.

254 Ibid., p. 487.

255 Edelman: Sex-Based Harassment and Symbolic Compliance; cf. Berrey: Rights on Trial; Seymour, R.: Trends in Employment Discrimination Law, Arizona State Bar Association Sedona, 2017; Sperino, Sandra and Suja Thomas: Unequal. How America's Courts Undermine Discrimination Law, 2007; Foote: Understanding Sexual Harassment, p. 243.

power. Unlike a court proceeding in which a judge or jury took into consideration previous rulings, arbitrators could disregard rulings in other arbitration proceedings. Similarly, an arbitration verdict had no influence on future court cases.

Throughout this book I have highlighted the importance of legal developments for public and corporate conceptions of sexual harassment. In lieu of congressional action, judiciary decisions expanded the definition of sexual harassment from solely including heterosexual *quid pro quo* harassment, to include hostile work environment harassment, harassment by non-supervisory staff, harassment by clients and contractors, harassment based on uniform requirements, and same-sex harassment. When a federal court determined guilt and liability in one case, this not only affected the defendant in question, but employers nationwide. Knowing that they would be held to the same standard if accused, they were often deterred from discriminatory action and worked to take precautions.[256]

With this in mind, it is particularly relevant to consider Levinson's research. In her essay she indicated that employers offered higher settlements, if a loss in court were to set an unfavorable precedent. At the same time, when a case was likely to yield a beneficial precedent, employers were known to release the complainant from binding arbitration and agreed to take the matter before a judge. By insisting on pre-dispute arbitration agreements, employers were not only securing an advantageous position in their individual cases, they also influenced the interpretation of the law.[257]

7.3 How Mandatory Arbitration and Non-Disclosure Agreements Shaped Sexual Harassment Definitions

The drawbacks of mandatory arbitration, including the lack of judicial oversight, the unavailability of an appeals process, and the missing preventative effect were reinforced by confidentiality and non-disclosure agreements. While in theory, binding arbitration did not have to remain confidential, in practice the majority of pre-dispute arbitration agreements contained a confidentiality provision. Like with the arbitration agreement itself, the confidentiality agreement was often included in the employment contract as a non-negotiable element. Such agreements could cover 'only' possible future arbitration proceedings or could be so broad

---

256 Levinson: Mandatory Arbitration, p. 495.
257 Ibid.

that an employee had to be vigilant about speaking negatively about their employer in any situation.[258]

Confidentiality agreements were also common in other forms of alternative dispute resolution and most settlements contained a non-disclosure agreement (NDA). While confidentiality agreements bound both parties and non-disclosure agreements only prevented one party from divulging the information covered in the agreement, this legal distinction has little bearing on this analysis; the effects of both overlapped to such an extent that a joint discussion is warranted.

Of course, due to the private nature of confidentiality agreements, settlements and arbitration awards covered by such a clause are not readily available as source material. However, throughout and after the #MeToo movement a multitude of targets broke their NDAs and spoke out publicly about their experiences and their employers' reactions. A myriad of cases came to light, proving that NDAs and confidentiality agreements had been used for decades in order to conceal a pattern of sexual harassment in the workplace. Bill O'Reilly's conduct at Fox News and Harvey Weinstein's behavior within and outside of his production company, Miramax, are only two of many examples.[259]

Berrey et al. explained that confidentiality agreements "serve to reinforce social inequalities and buffer the workplace from change."[260] As discussed in Chapter Six, for procedures to function it was vital for targets to trust in the human resources department and upper management. However, due to confidential internal investigations and settlement agreements, victims of harassment could not gauge how widespread the problem was, nor were they assured that their employer would take immediate and strong action.

Additionally, confidentiality agreements ensured that the company faced no public scrutiny for keeping on serial harassers if these individuals were valuable to the business. Thus, employers skirted public responsibility, and serial harassers faced little to no consequences.[261] According to Berrey, "[t]his functions to isolate the discrimination dispute from the workplace and forestall reform. Management maintains control over information about allegations of discrimination."[262] Confidentiality agreements ensured that the employer was pressured neither by the ju-

---

258 Ibid., pp. 514 f.

259 Elsesser, Kim: Five Years After #Metoo, NDAs Are Still Silencing Victims, in: Forbes (March 21st, 2022); McShane, Julianne: She Broke Her NDA with Harvey Weinstein in 2017. Here's How She Wants to Change the System for Others. Zelda Perkins Has Continued to Advocate for Limiting Confidentiality Agreements in Workplace Settings, in: The Washington Post (November 15th, 2021).

260 Berrey: Workers Wronged, p. 40.

261 Foote: Understanding Sexual Harassment, p. 266; Green: A New #MeToo Result, p. 154.

262 Berrey: Workers Wronged, p. 40.

diciary nor by the press into making meaningful adjustments to eradicate sexual harassment in their organization.[263]

Warnings against allowing mandatory arbitration agreements to cover incidences of sexual harassment or more generally discrimination claims were abundant; the arbitration system was considered biased against the complainant and the privatization of the procedure limited both public accountability and the further development of the law. However, the scholarship on the subject matter has given little attention to how mandatory arbitration and confidentiality agreements influenced the definition and conceptualization of sexual harassment. I argue that confidential binding arbitration emphasized key aspects of the management framework. By making space for corporate definitions of sexual harassment and by the individual and private structure of the proceeding, binding arbitration cemented management's reinterpretation of the phenomenon.

As has been explained above, arbitrators only required brief training in order to take on their role. Training programs for arbitration heavily recruited personnel experts and management consultants. Foote and Goodman-Delahunty presented a convincing argument in which she concludes that arbitrators often lacked an understanding of the "intricacies of sexual harassment laws."[264] According to Foote and Goodman-Delahunty arbitrators were seldom aware of the sociological evidence and psychological research on sexual harassment. Judges and juries, while usually not experts themselves, sought testimony from those knowledgeable on the subject matter. In arbitration, this void was not filled by expert witnesses as they were usually excluded from the proceedings.[265]

Bolstering Foot and Goodman-Delahunty's analysis, Susan Hippensteele, in her examination of ADR in sexual harassment cases, found that due to their lack of expertise, arbitrators often relied on their own assumptions about sexual harassment. Therefore, considering the consultant or business background of many arbitrators, it is reasonable to assume that their preconceptions will have been shaped by the management frame. Furthermore, confidentiality agreements ensured that misinterpretations of legal definitions and the prioritization of corporate interpretations by arbitrators could not be appealed by the complainant. It was not only corrupt or biased arbitrators who went unnoticed due to the lack of public accountability but also subtle yet meaningful changes in definitions.[266]

Definitions of sexual harassment in arbitration could vary depending on the arbitrator but also depending on the case in question. If the complainant claimed

---

263 Levinson: Mandatory Arbitration, pp. 511, 514.
264 Foote: Understanding Sexual Harassment, p. 255.
265 Levinson: Mandatory Arbitration, p. 515.
266 Ibid., p. 514.

to be the target of unlawful harassment and the subject of the arbitration was to determine whether a company was to be held liable, then the arbitrator, most likely, leaned on civil rights legislation, EEOC definitions, and recent court rulings. However, if the complainant was an alleged perpetrator fighting disciplinary action or claiming wrongful termination, the arbitrator changed course. In these cases, the question at hand was no longer whether the employee's conduct amounted to illegal sexual harassment, but instead whether or not the complainant broke company policy, giving the employer cause for discipline or termination.

This differentiation was seldom made explicit and the term sexual harassment was used, sometimes to refer to a breach of the Civil Rights Act and sometimes to refer to a violation of company policy. As company policies were often much stricter and regularly encompass consensual sexual and romantic relationships, an arbitrator may agree that the company's sexual harassment policy was broken and label the action as "sexual harassment." In such cases, arbitrators often muddied the waters between legal and corporate definitions of sexual harassment and thereby gave weight to the latter.

The reader will remember the middle-level manager who comforted his secretary after her mother had died and was subsequently disciplined for violating the company's sexual harassment policy.[267] In protest of his suspension, write up, and year-long probation, the manager in question took the matter to arbitration. The arbitrator, however, agreed with the employer that the company policy had been violated and that the disciplinary action was appropriate.[268] In this specific case, there was no confidentiality agreement in place. When asked by his coworkers and supervisors about the note in his personnel file or his suspension, the manager was free to explain the situation. It is easy to imagine that giving a full account would have gained him some sympathy for his plight from his coworkers or even future employers.

In contrast, the majority of arbitration cases were bound by confidentiality agreements. These agreements, however, only went so far in stopping office scuttlebutt. Rumors involving sexual harassment could quickly get out of hand and could prove detrimental to a person's reputation and career. With a confidentiality agreement in place, the disciplined employee could find himself in a position in which he was not permitted to publicly correct exaggerated or misleading rumors. In these situations, bystanders could easily confuse definitions following the management framework with feminist and government understandings of

---

267 For details turn to Chapter Six.
268 Young: Ceasefire, p. 178.

sexual harassment. The accused could be labeled as a "sexual harasser" without having committed any incidence of sex discrimination.

Arbitration did not only emphasize the management framework by relying on the employer's definition of sexual harassment. The process itself perpetuated this understanding. Seemingly obvious but nevertheless important to make explicit is the shift of the dispute from a public to a private forum. Contrary to the social conservative frame, management consultants were clear in their categorization of sexual harassment as a problem. However, from their viewpoint, this problem was of a financial and moral nature and as such, management consultants argued that the "overall responsibility for its elimination [did not lie] with the law. [...] Morality cannot be legislated."[269] Resolving sexual harassment complaints through the private forum of arbitration rather than before a judge or jury, reinforced an understanding, which denied government jurisdiction over the issue.

Additionally, confidentiality agreements mimicked the conditions of an era before the term sexual harassment was coined or discussed. The feminist effort to portray sexual harassment as a public and systemic rather than a private problem has been extensively outlined in Part I. Feminists in the late 1970s argued that victims speaking out was the first step to eradicating the workplace from sexual harassment. Without victims' testimony, whether in or out of court, neither other targets nor the public at large could understand how widespread the problem was; repeat offenders could not be identified; discriminatory patterns within a workplace would go unnoticed; and, no public pressure could be put on employers allowing harassment in their organizations.

With the rise of confidentiality agreements these issues were given a new breath of life. Targets of harassment were barred from speaking about their experiences, repeat offenders remained employed, if their value to the organization superseded the financial damage they caused with their misconduct, and the public was kept in the dark. Silence around the issue made it seem less prevalent. Victims were less willing to issue a complaint when they were unaware of the pervasiveness of larger patterns of misconduct both within their specific place of work as well as in society at large. Similarly, those unaffected by sexual harassment were likely to view the matter as trivial, when unaware of how many colleagues had been victimized. Thus, confidentiality agreements played a significant role in retrivializing discriminatory conduct and transforming sexual harassment back into a private issue.

Furthermore, an arbitrator had no commitment to upholding public policy or protecting citizens' rights. Instead, the objective of arbitration was to resolve the

---

269 Meyer: Sexual Harassment, p. 79.

immediate dispute.[270] Systemic variables such as race or gender usually played only a limited role in arbitration proceedings. Instead, employers often strategically portrayed complainants "as problem employees [...] of questionable judgment and integrity." Additionally, due to arbitration cases being covered by confidentiality agreements, complainants were limited in their ability to prove patterns of discrimination within the organization. They were also unable to rely on prior decisions made in arbitration as the results were usually confidential and the process did not heed precedent. As a result of focusing purely on the dispute at hand, the issue was seldom portrayed as a breach of an employee's civil rights but rather as a disagreement between employer and employee.[271] This neglected systemic factors and power discrepancies based on gender and reinforced the management frame's interpretation of sexual harassment as a problem isolated to the conflicting parties.

In conclusion, when employers did not succeed in resolving issues within their organizations, they often turned to alternative dispute resolution methods. Employees often voluntarily engaged in conciliation and mediation procedures and at times even freely agreed to arbitration. ADR, in comparison to the legal system, offered a much more cost and time effective path to resolve issues. However, because pre-dispute arbitration and confidentiality clauses were increasingly a non-negotiable part of an employment contract, these agreements were, by many critics, not considered voluntary.

Mandatory arbitration presented the privatization of the judiciary. While employers, contrarily to their internal investigations and grievance procedures, were not fully in charge of arbitration, binding arbitration was slanted towards the employer. This had an enormous effect on the definition of sexual harassment itself. In arbitration proceedings the term sexual harassment was often used to include instances of consensual behavior. Additionally, arbitration focused on isolated, individual incidences and thereby obscured the systemic and discriminatory nature of the phenomenon. Thus, mandatory arbitration did not only decrease a complainant's chances for a successful case, but it also aided in reconceptualizing the phenomenon of sexual harassment through a management lens.

In Part III, I demonstrated that the Supreme Court decisions in *Ellerth* and *Faragher* created an environment in which employers gained considerable discursive authority over the concept of sexual harassment. The judicial acceptance of unproven methods as confirmation of Title VII compliance, coupled with employers' prioritization of management interests over employees' rights, and the expan-

270 Levinson: Mandatory Arbitration, p. 514.
271 Berrey: Workers Wronged, pp. 39f.

sion of binding arbitration aided a framing of sexual harassment as a dispute between a pair (or group) of employees rather than systemic discriminatory misconduct. Thus, the discourse on sexual harassment, prominent in and promulgated by the private sector neglected the crucial element of why feminist sought to fight the issue in the first place: Sexual harassment was (and is) a form of sex discrimination.

8 Conclusion and Outlook:
The #MeToo Movement – A Revival of the Feminist Frame?

A pat on the behind, repeated propositions for "a night out," sperm on the fresh clothes in one's locker, or the straight-out demand for sexual intercourse in exchange for not getting laid off: Sexual coercion, exploitation, and bullying of women in the workplace was nothing new, even before the term sexual harassment was coined. *Bad for Business* tells the story of how the term was defined and conceptualized. Beginning in 1975, when sexual harassment had only just been given a name, the feminist and the social conservative were the two frames available within the public discourse. These two approaches clashed over the question of socially acceptable gender relations and proponents of both sides fought to have their views recognized and confirmed in public and all three branches of government.

Feminist theorists and activists like Lin Farley, Karen Sauvigné, Peggy Crull, and Catharine MacKinnon analyzed sexual harassment and developed theories akin to those conceived of in the feminist anti-rape movement. Denoting sexual harassment as an issue based on expressions of power rather than unconstrained sexual desire contributed largely to acknowledging sexual harassment as a serious issue.[272] Moreover, these texts emphasized the consequences faced by those targeted by sexual harassment. These extended far into the victim's life, influencing their health, reputation, finances, and career advancement. Affected women often found themselves in what Farley described as a "submit-or-quit dynamic."[273] The targets' options were reduced to either tolerating or engaging in coerced sexual activity or resigning their position. Similar to many other issues which had long been considered private, individual matters, second-wave feminists linked sexual harassment to systemic conditions which affected women as a group.[274]

---

272 Baker: Women's Movement, p. 94; Boris: Workplace Discrimination, p. 203.
273 Farley: Sexual Shakedown, p. 22.
274 Ibid., pp. 45f., 112; Enke: Taking Over Domestic Space, p. 164; Zippel, Politics, p. 14.

There was no doubt that it constituted a serious concern, worthy of political and legal action.

As more feminist single-issue groups formed and the first judges declared sexual harassment a civil rights violation, there was increased push-back from the social conservative pro-family movement. In these circles sexual harassment was considered a trivial issue. It proved to be a matter of female behavior, easily remedied by a change in female conduct and dress. By proposing the easy solution of a simple change of conduct, this framing denied that the phenomenon had far-reaching consequences for the woman in question. In this line of reasoning, far from causing sexual harassment, the division of labor actually counteracted the phenomenon. By diverging from the established system, the "many more women in the workplace," had provoked the increase of sexual behavior at work.[275] Thus, the social conservative framing conflated ideas of coerced and consensual sexual harassment, presented harassment as a natural gendered interaction, and considered it an individual issue.

A vital turning point for the acceptance of sexual harassment as a systemic and important issue was the publication of the EEOC guidelines in 1980. Although the guidelines were, initially, not legally binding, they had a considerable influence. First, they were an official acknowledgment that sexual harassment was a Civil Rights violation and was now on the EEOC's radar. Second, it gave judges a definition outside of feminist expertise to lean on. Third, the guidelines made many employers pay attention to the issue. Feminist organizations were now no longer the only port-of-call for targets of sexual harassment.

As complaint procedures were available in the executive and the judiciary as well as in various unions, employers increasingly took note. Corporate lawyers and management consultants began professionalizing on the subject matter and soon eclipsed feminists' influence with employers. Management consultants, in particular, capitalized on the newfound market, and produced workshop material, videos, and consultation packets. Like feminists, they argued for companies to implement policies and grievance procedures. Unlike feminists, however, their primary concern was shielding the employer from liability in court. The material they devised and consequently the policies and procedures implemented by employers, increasingly reflected a new understanding of sexual harassment.

The management framework was based not on a political or ideological aspiration to change accepted gender relations but on a pragmatic economic desire to avoid financial losses for a corporation. Sexual harassment was considered a serious issue because it was expensive, not because of the consequences suffered by

---

275 Ibid., p. 401.

the individual victim or by women as a whole. In consultants' and employers' material, inappropriate conduct was represented as an occurrence between two individuals. It was by no means a problem exacerbated by the structures of the company or society at large. It was also not represented as a gendered issue. Although contemporary surveys showed that only a fraction of men fell victim to sexual harassment, fictional examples provided in workshop material, books, and pamphlets described women harassing men as often as vice versa. Additionally, in the management frame sexual harassment was not understood as an expression of power. Instead, it propagated the idea that anyone could accidentally harass without meaning to do so.

When the Supreme Court, in 1998, settled the question of employer liability and allowed for an affirmative defense, action against sexual harassment shifted from the federal government to the private sector. Where internal procedures had previously been one option for targets, it was now the first and often only option. Due to this new dynamic, employers' definitions, procedures, and adjudication process gained in importance. Therefore, regarding the issue of sexual harassment, the employer was now responsible for legislative, executive, and judicative functions. Employer action, most often, followed the management framework; consequently, definitions of sexual harassment taught to American employees portrayed the issue as non-gendered and individual.

Employers' anti-sexual harassment measures were focused on avoiding litigation. Therefore, convincing a court that one's organization was in compliance with the Civil Rights Act was often prioritized over the actual eradication of illegal sexual harassment. Instead of focusing on the issue of discrimination, policies focused on individual actions and conflated coerced and consensual activities. Grievance procedures lacked accountability and were often mistrusted, which rendered them ineffective. Lastly, while adjudication was promised to be "fair" and "objective,"[276] social science research has indicated that those valuable to the company were punished less severely, while others were disciplined for minor infractions.

Moreover, targets of harassment were limited or barred from seeking resolutions through the EEOC or the judiciary by the increased implementation of mandatory arbitration and confidentiality clauses. Non-negotiable, pre-dispute arbitration clauses prevented over half of American, non-unionized, private sector employees from taking their claims to court. While cost and time effective, these arbitration proceedings often were advantageous to employers and were, in a majority of cases, covered by confidentiality agreements. I argue that these

---

276 Reed and Barton Corporation Policy, 1996.

agreements functioned to silence targets and recreated conditions victims faced before the issue was politicized in the 1970s. Victims were prohibited from speaking about their experiences, they could not gauge how widespread the problem was, they could not seek help from the authorities, and if the harasser was valuable enough to a company, they could not prevent him from continuing his behavior.

Under these circumstances, the eruption of the #MeToo movement seems to have been almost inevitable. I am convinced that the #MeToo movement was an attempt to reclaim the feminist frame. The movement, much like the early speak-outs and consciousness raising groups in the 1970s, began with the intent to uncover a pattern of behavior within society and "give people a sense of the magnitude of the problem."[277] The name alone highlighted the belief in the systemic, rather than the individual nature of sexual harassment. By posting their stories, affected individuals raised awareness and often felt less alone in their struggle. Many drew attention to the gendered power dynamics which had both enabled harassers' conduct in the first place and had discouraged victims from reporting their experiences earlier.[278]

Like with the politicizing of the term sexual harassment in 1975, the #MeToo movement did not occur in a vacuum. In 1975, second-wave feminism was well on its way. While sexual harassment was not yet discussed, sexual violence, and sex discrimination in the workplace were prominent topics within the public discourse and inspired a string of activist events. When WWI and AASC took action against sexual harassment they drew on the ideology and infrastructure provided by other feminist organizations.

Similarly, in 2017, the #MeToo Movement was preceded by several highly publicized events and moments of activism. Tarana Burke's work against the sexual abuse of African American women and girls beginning in 2006, and the "campus sexual assault" movement of the 2010s are established forerunners of the viral #MeToo Movement of 2017.[279] Just a year prior to Alyssa Milano's call to tweet #MeToo, Donald Trump's now infamous 2005 Access Hollywood Tape had been

277 Milano: Tweet; cf. North, Anna: The #MeToo Movement and Its Evolution Explained. From Charges Against Harvey Weinstein to the Confirmation of Brett Kavanaugh to the Ongoing Drive for Accountability, Here's Where the Movement Stands Today, in: Vox (October 11th, 2018).
278 Atwater, Leanne et al.: Looking Ahead. How What We Know About Sexual Harassment Now Informs Us of the Future, in: Organizational Dynamics 48/4 (October-December 2019); cf. Boyle, Karen: Of Moguls, Monsters, and Men, in: The Routledge Handbook of the Politics of the #MeToo Movement, ed. by Giti Chandra and Irma Erlingsdóttir, New York 2021, p. 169.
279 MacKinnon, Catharine: Global #MeToo, in: The Routledge Handbook of the Politics of the #MeToo Movement, ed. by Giti Chandra and Irma Erlingsdóttir, New York 2021, p. 43.

leaked. On the recording, then-presidential candidate Donald Trump could be heard bragging about "grabbing [women] by the pussy" because "when you're a star they let you do it. You can do anything."[280] The incident inspired the widely used hashtag #NotOkay.[281] Several months later, when Trump succeeded in his bid for president, roughly four million Americans marked his first day in office by attending Women's Marches across the country. The Women's March in Washington, with 500.000 participants, went down in American history as the largest, single day protest the nation had ever seen.[282] Then, when allegations against Harvey Weinstein surfaced, public outrage hit a new high. It was in this climate, that Milano tweeted #MeToo.

Hashtags and tweets had replaced flyers and press releases.[283] However, while the medium had changed, action against sexual harassment in the aftermath of the #MeToo Movement in many ways resembled that of the 1970s. Women in both the 20th and the 21st century rallied in formal and informal ways. Two striking examples highlighting the parallels are the creation of informal 'whisper networks' devised to warn each other of harassers in their workplace, and the efforts to organize legal assistance for victims.

Whereas women had written lists of harassers on bathroom walls to warn each other in the 1970s, the #MeToo Movement brought with it the rise of 'whisper networks' in the form of digital spreadsheets. One open-source file, entitled "shitty media men," was shared among several women in the publishing industry in October 2017. The document opened with a disclaimer stating that it was "only a collection of allegations and rumors. Take everything with a grain of salt."[284] Within several hours, the document listed roughly seventy men. The alleged misconduct ranged from "inappropriate direct messages to violent sexual assault."[285] Names of men accused of "physical sexual violence by multiple women" were highlighted in red.[286] Although the list did get publicized, leading to media attention and even

---

280 Anonymous: US Election. Full Transcript of Donald Trump's Obscene Videotape, in: BBC NEWS (October 9th, 2016); Corbett, Holly: #MeToo Five Years Later. How the Movement Started and What Needs to Change, in: Forbes (October 27th, 2022).

281 Corbett: #MeToo Five Years Later.

282 Felmlee, Diane et al.: the Geography of Sentiment Towards the Women's March of 2017, in: PLOS One 15/6 (2020).

283 Vogelstein, Rachel and Meighan Stone: Awakening. #MeToo and the Global Fight for Women's Rights, London 2021, p. 229.

284 Shapiro, Lila: Bad Reputation. Moira Donegan Created the 'shitty Media Men' List to Address a Moral Injustice. Stephen Elliott Says He's Suing Her for the Same Reason, in: Intelligencer (October 25th, 2022).

285 Corbett: #Me Too Five Years Later.

286 Shapiro: Bad Reputation.

criminal investigations against some of the men named, the alleged intention was identical of the bathroom lists: Alert colleagues about sexual predators in their workplace.

In January 2018, Hollywood celebrities founded the Time's Up Legal Defense Fund with the goal of securing legal assistance for victims of sexual harassment. As did the Working Women's Institute, Time's Up created a network of lawyers willing to take on such cases, provided legal counseling, and collected donations to finance litigation. When Time's Up put out a call for donations, it raised $20 million in the first month alone, making it the most successful go-fund-me campaign to date.[287] In the years after #MeToo, feminist organizations were again being heard, financially supported, and considered experts on the issue of sexual harassment by many politicians, media outlets, and even some employers seeking advice on their internal policies.[288] The #MeToo movement pushed the issue of sexual harassment back to the forefront of the public discourse. Armed with laptops and pink pussy hats, the #MeToo movement revived the feminist framework of sexual harassment.

While inspiring much activism on the left, the #MeToo Movement has also provoked a conservative backlash, which played its part in the second election of Donald Trump and his administration's vigorous cuts regarding any federally funded diversity-equality-inclusion (DEI) programs. Again, paralleling the developments in the 1970s and 80s, those criticizing the movement often built their understanding of sexual harassment on the social conservative framework. Echoing the sentiments of roughly 20% of the U.S. population,[289] actor Debra Winger stated in an interview with Fox News that the #MeToo Movement had gone "ridiculously too far." Winger did not identify as a social conservative and although she publicly supported democratic Senator Bob Kerrey in the 1990s, she did not consider herself "political."[290] Her self-declared non-partisanship is an indicator on how the various frames have permeated societal understandings of sexual harassment, even outside of their core ideological camps.

In her interview Winger explained:

287 Langone, Alix: #MeTo and Time's Up Founders Explain the Difference Between the Two Movements – And How They're Alike, in: Time (March 8th, 2018).

288 Ibid.; cf. Gilmore, Leigh: the #MeToo Effect: What Happens When We Believe Women, New York 2023.

289 Brown, Anna: More Than Twice as Many Americans Support Than Oppose the #MeToo Movement, in: Pew Research Center (September 29th, 2022).

290 Anonymous: Short Takes. Debra Winger Is Not for Politics, in: Los Angeles times (September 12th, 1990).

I always found my way [...]. I felt like I was in very abusive situations, but it was my responsibility to buck up, get strong.[291]

Winger implicitly dismissed the necessity of a #MeToo movement. Although much less explicit, this quote mirrors many of the aspects Phyllis Schlafly addressed when testifying before Congress four decades ago. Schlafly proposed women change their conduct and dress and thereby solve the issue of harassment. Winger similarly allocated the responsibility to solve "abusive situations" to the target of the behavior. If targets themselves could prevent harassment by changing their conduct and "get[ting] strong," then the issue was unworthy of any collective, political action.

In her interview, Winger showed immense concern for her three sons who had followed her into show business. Again, she was not alone in her worries that the #MeToo Movement would bring with it false and frivolous accusations and endanger innocent men's careers. As one opinion piece, also published by Fox News, explained: "#MeToo has morphed into a career-destroying angry mob."[292] This quote rings eerily reminiscent of now-Supreme Court Justice Clarence Thomas' statement, in the course of his nomination hearings in 1991 in which he accused the proceeding of being a "high-tech lynching." In both instances, although the former lacks the racial component, the loss of a career and reputation were equated with the dangers of physical violence.

I agree that the lack of due process in the court of public opinion is a serious problem in the context of the #MeToo Movement and beyond. Nevertheless, I find it striking that social conservative voices rarely blame corporations for overzealous enforcement of their sexual harassment policies, but instead make individual complainants or feminist rhetoric responsible for this issue. I explain this with the extent of polarization of the public discourse on sexual harassment. Throughout the four decades analyzed within this book mainstream media has presented sexual harassment along the lines of either the feminist or the social conservative framework. There is no, or only limited, awareness of a third frame of sexual harassment. It seems that individuals beholden to a social conservative narrative often blame issues – such as a lack of due process – on feminist activists, while those influenced by a feminist narrative falsely associate the prevalence of non-

291 Roberto, Melissa: Debra Winger Says #MeToo Movement Has 'Gone Ridiculously Too Far,' in: Fox News (August 13th, 2021).
292 Smith, Kyle: #MeToo Has Morphed into a Career-Destroying Angry Mob, in: Fox News (September 23rd, 2018).

disclosure agreements with social conservative trivialization of the issue.[293] Neither group appears to be aware of the extent to which the private sector has influenced the understanding and handling of sexual harassment.

This also explains why proponents of the #MeToo Movement repeatedly called for "more action" from employers but did not specify what that action may look like. In response, many employers tightened their policies and procedures in and after 2017.[294] Dennis Williams vice president of corporate affairs at HBO, for instance, told of added guidelines on office behavior in addition to existing sexual harassment guidelines at Time Warner Inc. Similarly, NBC, in 2017, implemented a new policy requiring all employees to report office relationships.[295] Additionally, fears of scandal and litigation heightened fears among employers and supervisors. A study published in the Harvard Business Review in 2019, showed that, because of #MeToo, 10% of respondents would be less likely to hire attractive women and roughly 30% of male participants admitted that they now avoided one-on-one meetings with female colleagues and subordinates.[296]

Despite these worrying developments, #MeToo also changed employer-employee dynamics in positive ways. First, shareholders in publicly traded companies became intensely interested in sexual harassment accusations when the alleged perpetrator was an executive. Misconduct by a CEO or other high-level manager led to extreme financial losses and thus, a decline in organizations' stock value. Therefore, many executive compensation contracts now contain explicit provisions enabling the board of directors to more easily sever ties with high level executives, if they violate the company's sexual harassment policy.[297] Additionally, so called "Weinstein clauses" became popular in both sale and merger agreements. Such contracts commonly include a provision demanding the "disclosure of any 'allegations of sexual harassment' against officers, directors, or em-

293 Martin, Michel: Perspectives on the 'MeToo' Movement, in: National Public Radio (September 1st, 2019); Smith, Tovia: On #MeToo, Americans More Divided by Party than Gender, in: National Public Radio (October 31st, 2018); Reyes-Menendez, Ana et al.: Exploring Key Indicators of Social Identity in the #MeToo Era: Using Discourse Analysis in UGC, in: International Journal of Information Management 54 (20202), pp. 1-11.
294 Cone, Sydney et al.: Workplace Conduct Still Needs Improvement After #MeToo, in: Bloomberg Law (October 24, 2022); Gaines, Rachel: Why We Are Still Talking About #MeToo at Work, in: Berkeley Law (January 11th, 2023).
295 Cao, Sissi: #MeToo Movement Impels companies to Rethink Sexual Harassment Policies, in: Observer (January 18th, 2018).
296 Bower, Tim: The #MeToo Backlash, in: Harvard Business Review (September-October 2019).
297 Green: A New #MeToo Result, p. 156.

ployees who supervise at least eight other employees.'"[298] WWIs message that "sexual harassment is obviously bad for business" reached the executive suite.[299] The establishment of such contracts brings with it the hope that high-level managers will be held accountable for sexual misconduct.

Second, the #MeToo Movement encouraged legal changes both on the state and on the federal level. In 2018, California, New York, and New Jersey banned non-disclosure agreements in cases of sexual assault, harassment, or sex discrimination. In 2020, Texas was the most recent state to enhance employee protections in the workplace, lengthening the statute of limitation on sexual harassment claims, and extending employer liability to smaller companies formerly not covered by the federal Civil Rights Act.[300] Then, in 2021, President Joe Biden signed the "Ending Forced Arbitration of Sexual Assault and Sexual Harassment Act" and the "Speak Out Act." The former released all employees from binding arbitration agreements in the context of sexual assault and harassment, allowing victims to seek justice through litigation. The latter forbid the use of non-disclosure agreements covering sexual assault and harassment. Therefore, all NDAs signed after December 7th, 2022, cannot and will not be enforced by American courts. As I have explained in Chapter Seven, the use of NDAs and mandatory arbitration has had an enormous effect on the handling and perception of sexual harassment. For many victims of sexual harassment, this development restored access to the EEOC and the judiciary.

In this book, I have made a concerted effort to approach the topic from a neutral, academic standpoint. However, the outcomes of my research have led me to propose several practical political actions aimed at mitigating sexual harassment in the workplace. Thus, in the following sections, I will step beyond my role as a historian to offer these reflections to the reader. It is my assessment that in order to truly make these avenues effective in limiting sexual harassment, the federal government needs to make crucial adjustments. I am not so naïve as to suggest that the following recommendations are easy goals to fulfill within the American gridlocked political system, especially within a polarized society which traditionally limits government influence and spending. This would hold true even with an administration committed to fighting sexual harassment in the workplace, but is decidedly unlikely during the current Trump administration. Nevertheless, these

298 Tippett: Harassment Trainings, p. 486; Green: A New #MeToo Result, p. 156.
299 Sauvigné: Letter to Vice President Bush, p. 2.
300 North, Anna: 7 Positive Changes That Have Come From the #MeToo Movement, in: Vox (October 4th, 2019); Ravitsky, Greta: Texas Expands Employer Liability for Sexual Harassment Claims, Effective September 1st, 2021, in: Epstein Becker Green Website (August 20th, 2021).

policy recommendations may inspire activists, politicians, and administrators both on the federal as well as on the state level.

First, the EEOC budget needs to be increased significantly. Within a year of the release of the EEOC guidelines in 1980, the agency had managed to decrease its backlog and establish a representation as a resource for targets of harassment. When President Reagan cut the agency's funding and made significant staffing changes, the backlog again increased. Complainants could no longer rely on any action by the agency and the government's enforcement agency grew to be ineffective in preventing sexual harassment. Eleanor Norton's tenure proved that when well-staffed, funded, and committed to the cause, the EEOC has the potential of limiting the extent of sexual harassment in the workplace.

Additionally, it is reasonable to assume that a well-funded EEOC could cushion the justice system from an increase of sexual harassment cases, now that mandatory arbitration has been limited. A crucial part of the EEOC process is the investigation of cases which is then followed by the agency attempting to facilitate negotiations between the parties. Mediation, or even arbitration, overseen and governed by the EEOC provide the benefits of voluntary alternative dispute resolution. The process, compared to litigation, is time and cost effective. Moreover, without confidentiality agreements and with a truly neutral third-party, targets of harassment can much more easily trust in the proceedings. Additionally, if the negotiations failed or the arbitrator appeared biased, complainants are not precluded from pursuing litigation. Thus, the agency ensures that the parties meet on an even playing field. Currently, however, the backlog within and funding of the agency allows only a small percentage of complainants to profit from this system. This will not be helped by the wave of litigation pauses, firings, and stop-work orders in both the federal government at large and specifically within the EEOC only days after President Trump's second inauguration.[301]

My second policy suggestion for fighting sexual harassment concerns the judiciary, which must be made accessible to all Americans. Disallowing mandatory arbitration in instances of sexual harassment is a first step. However, with over 60 percent of Americans living paycheck to paycheck,[302] it comes as no surprise that many victims cannot afford legal assistance. According to Berrey et al., roughly 23 percent of plaintiffs pursue litigation without legal representation leading to "far

301 Goldstein, Matthey and Jessica Silver-Greenberg: Deregulation by Firings: Breaking Down the Cuts to Financial Oversight, in: The New York Times (13th February, 2025).
302 Becker, Joshua: 61% of Americans Live Paycheck-to-Paycheck: Here's the Simple Solution We're Overlooking, in: Forbes (August 18th, 2023); Dickler, Jessica: 60% of Americans Are Still Living Paycheck to Paycheck as Inflation Hits Workers' Wages, in: CNBC (September 27th, 2023).

worse litigation outcomes than plaintiffs with lawyers."[303] This number does not include the many Americans abstaining from pursuing their claims in the judiciary, because they lack financial resources. The problem of inaccessibility to the justice system due to financial restraints goes far beyond the single issue of sexual harassment. However, as is the case with a multitude of social and political issues, in order to truly limit sexual harassment, targets must have secure access to the judiciary. Here again, a well-funded EEOC, committed to eradicate sexual harassment may cushion the effect of financial disparities by bringing suit on behalf of victims.

Last, I repeat here a recommendation made by Vicki Schultz in 2003. Schultz argued that the judiciary should consider the level of sex-segregation within an organization in their decision-making process. In this reasoning, if a sexual harassment claim is found to have merit, a judge would penalize organizations with high levels of sex-segregation more harshly than those with a more integrated workforce. This, according to Schultz would encourage employers to focus on systemic sex discrimination issues, such as unequal pay, limited job mobility for women, and the exclusion of female workers from high-status jobs and training opportunities. Individual instances of sexualized behavior would become important only when part of a larger, discriminatory pattern. As study after study has shown a link between sex-segregation and work cultures promoting sexual harassment, I believe this is a legal approach that could shift the focus back on the systemic and gendered nature of sexual harassment.

By declaring that sexual harassment was "obviously bad for business," the Working Women's Institute succeeded in drawing politicians' and businesses' interest. Inadvertently, however, the use of this narrative led the Institute to yield discursive authority to the private sector. By focusing on the economic risks and damages of sexual harassment, employers reconceptualized the term and lost sight of the original reasoning. This framing of sexual harassment was and is pervasive in American society and has been counterproductive to eliminating what feminists had conceived of as sexual harassment. Therefore, four decades after Carmita Wood and the Working Women's Institute defined sexual harassment, a new generation of "silence breakers" spoke out and demanded change. It now remains to be seen, whether decades from now, this silence will again need breaking.

---

303 Berrey: Workers Wronged, p. 42.

Acknowledgements

The quality of this book was immeasurably enhanced through the involvement of many incredibly talented, generous, and kind colleagues, friends, and family. The mistakes are wholly mine; the successes are shared.

First and foremost, I am deeply grateful to Prof. Dr. Manfred Berg, who encouraged me early in my studies and has remained the best teacher and mentor I could have hoped for. His confidence in me made this work possible. I also want to thank Prof. Dr. Welf Werner, my second supervisor, for his thoughtful feedback – particularly in helping me engage with the economic dimensions of this topic, an area I had to grow into as a historian.

This research was carried out with the generous support of the Deutsche Forschungsgemeinschaft (DFG), which funded the Graduate Research Group *Authority and Trust*, within which I wrote my dissertation. I am grateful to the group for its intellectually stimulating environment and the insightful feedback that helped shape this project in meaningful ways. I also thank the Heidelberg Center for American Studies, which hosted the research group and continues to be an important institution in my academic life. Furthermore, I am thankful to the History Department at the University of Heidelberg for providing both a scholarly home and a place of return. Finally, I owe my gratitude to the Open Access Monograph Fund of the University Library of Heidelberg University, whose support made it possible for this book to be published online and freely accessible to anyone interested.

I am especially grateful to my colleagues and friends at the Curt-Engelhorn Chair for American History. I was fortunate to have the daily support, camaraderie, and encouragement of Michaela Neidig, Richard Lange, Winand Tremmel, Amaya Gandy, Alina Marotta, and Zoé Ferreira Custodio. Their good humor, kindness, and shared breaks were an essential source of balance and motivation throughout this process.

A number of friends went above and beyond discussing ideas, meticulously proofreading chapters and rescuing me from more than a few embarrassing mistakes. Your advice, feedback, corrections, and time were invaluable: Gerti and John McQueen, Albert Loran, Kenny Gaona, Mark Wieder, Shauna Haines, Don Macleay, and Richard Lange.

I appreciate the kindness, encouragement, and support of my family and friends in the United States who welcomed me during my archival research and have, over the years, made the San Francisco Bay feel like a second home. For that and so much more, thank you, Don and René Macleay, Shauna Heines, Mark Wieder, Casey, Kyra, and Colaine.

To the incredibly strong women who have inspired me and my work through years of conversation, laughter, and shared conviction – Grace Feakes, Linda Lammensalo, and Salla Sigvart – thank you. I owe a special debt of thanks to Grace Feakes for creating the cover art for this book – her talent is matched only by her generosity.

I am especially grateful from the bottom of my heart to my partner, Jonas Osnabrügge, whose steady support, thoughtful advice, last-minute proofreading, and strategic deployment of ice cream made all the difference in turning this project into a book.

Finally, and most importantly, I want to thank my parents, Christa Walter and Ed Colaianni, whose unwavering and loving support has profoundly shaped who I am today. I also wish to acknowledge my stepfather, Klaus Jochims, whose intellectual curiosity, genuine interest in my work, and warm presence in our family have meant a great deal to me. To my mother, Christa Walter – a strong working woman who has always led by example and continues to give selflessly to her community, to her friends, and to her family – this book is dedicated to you.

Bibliography

Archival Material

American Heritage Center University of Wyoming (AHC)
Edward A. Altshuler Papers
Barnard College Archives (BCA)
Barnard Center for Research on Women Feminist Ephemera Collection
Barnard Center for Research on Women Records
California Historical Association (CHA)
American Civil Liberties Union of Northern California Records
Computer History Museum (Mountain View, CA) (CHM)
Digital Equipment Corporation Records
Information Technology Corporate Histories Collection
Harvard Baker Library (HBL)
Kenneth H. Olson Collection
Harvard Schlesinger Library (HSL)
Cambridge Women's Center Records
Feminist Ephemera Collection
Kristen R. Yount Papers, 1980–2004
Herman Miller Corporate Archive Zeeland, MI (HMCA)
HBSC Archive
Human Resources Guidelines and Procedures
The George Washington University, Washington DC (GWU)
National Education Association Records
New Mexico State University Archive (NMSU)
Frances F. Williams Papers
Northwestern University Archives (NUA)
School of Law Records of the Dean, 1955–1998
St. Louis Washington University Archive
Monsanto Company Records
The New York Public Library Humanities and Social Sciences Library Manuscripts and Archives Division (NYPL)
Women's Action Coalition Records
University of California, Davis Campus Archive
Martha West Papers
University of Chicago Library (UCL)
R.R. Donnelley & Sons Company Archive
University of Miami Archive (UoMA)
Pan American World Airways, Inc. Records

Court Rulings, Legal Statutes, Congressional Hearings

Barbee v. Household Automotive Finance Corp., 113 Cal.App.4th 525, 529 (Cal. Ct. App. 2003).

Barnes v. Costle, 561 F.2d 983 (D.C. Cir. 1977), Court of Appeals, District of Columbia Circuit.

Bohen v. City of East Chicago, 799 F.2d 1180 (7th Cir. 1986).

Bundy v. Jackson, 641 F.2d 934 (1981), United States Court of Appeals, District of Columbia.

Burlington Industries, Inc. v. Ellerth, 524 U.S. 742 (1998).

Castaneda v. Partida, 430 U.S. 482, 499 (1977).

Circuit City Stores, Inc. v. Adams, 532 U.S. 105 (2001).

Clark County School District v. Breeden. 532 U.S. 268, 2001.

Conatzer v. Medical Professional Building Services Corp. 03 – 5074 (N.D. Okla. 2004).

Continental Can Company v. Minnesota, 297 N.W.2d 241, 1980.

Corne v. Bausch and Lomb, Inc., 390 F. Supp. 161 (1975), United States District Court, District of
    Arizona.

Downes v. Federal Aviation Administration, 775 F. 2d 288 (1985).

EEOC v. Sage Realty. Corp., 507 F. Supp. 599 (S.D.N.Y. 1981).

Faragher v. City of Boca Raton, 524 U.S. 775 (1998).

Garber v. Saxon Business Prods., Inc., 552 F.2d 1032 (4th Cir. 1977).

Henson v. City of Dundee 682 F. 2d 897 (11th Cir. 1982).

Horn v. Duke Homes, 755 F.2d 599 (7th Cir. 1985).

Howard University v. Best, 547 A.2d 144 (1988).

Jenson v. Eveleth Taconite Co., 130 F.3d 1287 (8th Cir. 1997).

Jerold J. Mackenzie v. Miller Brewing Company and Robert L. Smith, Patricia G. Best, 2001 WI App 48.

Kyriazi v. Western Electric Co., 476 F. Supp. 335 (D.N.J. 1979).

Malvia v. Bald Head Island management, Inc. 259 F. 3d 261 (4th Cir. 2001).

Meritor Savings Bank v. Vinson, 477 U.S. 57 (1986).

Miller v. Bank of America, 418 F. Supp. 233 (1976).

Nelson v. Cyprus Bagdad Copper Corp., 119 F.3d 756 (1997).

Oncale v. Sundowner Offshore Services, Inc.,523 U.S. 75 (1998).

Phillips v. Taco Bell Corp., 83 F. Supp. 2d 1029 (E.D. Mo 2000).

Prudential Insurance Co. of America v. Lai, 42 F.3d 1299, 1305 (9th Cir. 1994).

State v. Wal-Mart Stores, 207 A.D.2d 150, 152 (N.Y. App. Div. 1995).

Tomkins v. Public Service Elec. and Gas Co., 422 F. Supp. 553 (1976).

Vaca v. Sies, 386 U.S. 171 (1967).

Vinson v. Taylor, 753 F. 2d 141 (D.C. Cir. 1985).

Weeks v. Baker & McKenzie, No. A068499, Court of Appeal First District, Division 1, California (1998).

Williams v. Saxbe, 413 F. Supp. 654 (1976), United States District Court, District of Columbia.

California. Labor Code. § 96(k). 2000.

Civil Rights Act of 1964. 42 U.S.C. § 2000e-2.

Civil Rights Act of 1991. Pub. L. No. 102 – 166, 105 Stat. 1071, 1991.

Electronic Communications Privacy Act. Pub. L. No. 99 – 508, 100 Stat. 1848, 1986.

Equal Employment Opportunity Commission: Guidelines on Sexual Harassment, 45 Federal Register
    74676, November 10th, 1980.

National Labor Relations Act of 1935. Public Law No. 74 – 198, 49 Stat.449, 1935.

New York. Labor Law. § 102-D. 1992.

U.S. Constitution, Amendment IV.

Committee on Labor and Human Resources, United States Senate: Hearings on Sex Discrimination in the Workplace. Examination of Issues Affecting Women in Our Nation's Labor Force. 97th Congress. First Session. April 21st, 1981, Washington 1981.

Committee on the Judiciary, United States Senate: Nomination of Judge Clarence Thomas to be Associate Justice of the Supreme Court of the United States. 102nd Congress. First Session. October 11th-13th, 1991, Washington 1993.

Subcommittee on Investigations of the Committee on Post Office and Civil Service, United States House of Representatives: Hearings on Sexual Harassment in the Federal government. 96th Congress. First Session. October 23rd, November 1st, 13th, 1979.

Published Sources

9 to 5: The 9 to 5 Bill of Rights, November 17th, 1983, available at: <https://www.csmonitor.com/1983/1117/111716.html> (last accessed December 27th, 2023).

Alliance Against Sexual Coercion: "Organizing Against Sexual Harassment," in: Worker's Struggles Past and Present. A 'Radical America' Reader, ed. by James Green, Philadelphia 1983, pp. 234–248.

Alliance Against Sexual Coercion: "Sexual Harassment and Coercion. Violence Against Women," in: Aegis (July/August 1978), pp. 28 f, accessible at: <https://documents.alexanderstreet.com/d/1000682399>, last viewed: December 24th, 2023.

Alliance Against Sexual Coercion: "Sexual Harassment at the Workplace," Boston 1977, accessible at: <https://documents.alexanderstreet.com/d/1000689709>, last viewed: Jun 25, 2020.

American Arbitration Association: Ethical Principles at: https://www.adr.org/StatementofEthicalPrinciples (last viewed on January 18th, 2024).

Anderson, Katherine S.: Employer Liability under Title VII for Sexual Harassment after Meritor Savings Bank v. Vinson, in: Columbia Law Review 87/6 (October 1987), pp. 1258–1279.

Anderson, Monica and Skye Toor: "How social media users have discussed sexual harassment since #MeToo went viral," in: Pew Research Center, (October 11th, 2018), at: https://www.pewresearch.org/fact-tank/2018/10/11/how-social-media-users-have-discussed-sexual-harassment-since-metoo-went-viral/ (last accessed on January 16th, 2024).

Anonymous: Court Cases Alter Sexual Harassment Law, in: Triangle Business Journal (October 26th, 1998).

Anonymous: Court: Employers May take Away Right to Sue, in: Oakland Tribune (September 15th, 1999), reprinted from Los Angeles Times.

Anonymous: Davis Vetoes Bill to Warn Workers About Monitoring. E-Mail Oversight Deemed Legal, in: The Oakland Tribune (October 12th, 1999), p. 5.

Anonymous: DEI Dead at Revamped EEOC: EEOC Enforcement Priorities after Trump Administration Makeover, in: Epstein Becker Green Workforce Bulletin, February 5th, 2025, available at: https://www.workforcebulletin.com/dei-dead-at-the-eeoc-whats-next-for-eeoc-enforcement-priorities-after-trump-administration-actions#:~:text=These%20sweeping%20changes%20initiated%20by%20President%20Trump,Orders%20targeting%20Diversity%2C%20Equity%2C%20and%20Inclusion%20(DEI) (last accessed: May 20th, 2025).

Anonymous: Don't 'Reach Ourt and Touch Them.' Opinion, in: Ithaca Journal (Apr. 24th, 1975), p. 13.

Anonymous: EEOC Continues Operations Amid Leadership Changes and New Executive Orders, in: Thomson Reuters Tax & Accounting, February 6th, 2025, available at: https://tax.thomsonreuters.com/news/eeoc-continues-operations-amid-leadership-changes-and-new-executive-orders/ (last accessed: May 20th, 2025).

Anonymous: Employers Take Steps to Avoid Charges of Sexual Harassment, in: Houston Business Journal (September 13th, 1998).

Anonymous: Executive Sweet: Many Office Romeos Are Really Juliets, in: Time Magazine (October 8th, 1979), p. 76.

Anonymous: Guide to Employee Monitoring Laws of the U.S., in: Workstatus Workforce Management, 2021, available at: https://www.workstatus.io/blog/workforce-management/guide-to-employee-monitoring-laws-of-the-u-s/ (last accessed, March 3rd, 2022).

Anonymous: Homicide Is Top Cause of Death from On-Job Injury for Women, in: The New York Times (August 18th, 1990), p. 8.

Anonymous: How Do You Handle Sex on the Job? in: Redbook (January 1976), pp. 149, 217–221.

Anonymous: Increase Predicted in Sexual Harassment Cases. Human Relations Official Says New Federal Law Will Encourage Seeking of Redress, in: The Washington Post (November 19th, 1991), p. C7.

Anonymous: Just When are Passes Harassing? in: The Atlanta Constitution (August 4th, 1978), p. 1B.

Anonymous: Many Doctors Tell of Sexual Harassment in Training, in: The New York Times (February 4th, 1993).

Anonymous: Mitsubishi U.S. Unit Vows Strong Policy Against Harassment, in: A Wall Street Journal (May 2nd, 1996), p. C12.

Anonymous: More than 12M 'MeToo' Facebook posts, comments, reactions in 24 hours, in: CBS News, (October 17th, 2017), at: https://www.cbsnews.com/news/metoo-more-than-12-million-facebook-posts-comments-reactions-24-hours/ (last accessed on January 16th, 2024).

Anonymous: None of an Employer's Business, in: The New York Times (July 7th, 1991).

Anonymous: Protecting Employee Privacy Too Far, in: The New York Times (August 6th, 1991).

Anonymous: Sexual Harassment on the Assembly Line, in: Los Angeles Times (December 14th, 1981).

Anonymous: Sexual Harassment. Working Women's Dilemma, in: Quest 3/3 (1976), p. 15–24.

Anonymous: Short Takes. Debra Winger Is Not for Politics, in: Los Angeles Times (September 12th, 1990).

Anonymous: Speak Out Draws Tears and Anger, in: Labor Pains 1/1 (1975), p. 1.

Anonymous: Stewardesses Protest Suggestive Airline Ads, in: New York Times, N.Y. (June 30th, 1974), p. 33.

Anonymous: The high Cost of Sex Harassment, in: The New York Times (December 12th, 1994), p. A14.

Anonymous: The Law and Threats to Virtue, in: The Wall Street Journal (April 27th, 1976), p. 22.

Anonymous: The Mess at EEOC, in: The Washington Post (April 28th, 1976), p. A12.

Anonymous: US Election. Full Transcript of Donald Trump's Obscene Videotape, in: BBC NEWS (October 9th, 2016), available at: https://www.bbc.co.uk/news/election-us-2016–37595321 (last viewed on January 18th, 2024).

Anonymous: What are the Implications of an Anti-Fraternization Policy as applied to Non-Supervising Coworkers? in: Yadegar, Minoofar &Soleymani, LLP Website (January 2023), available at: https://www.ymsllp.com/blog/2014/august/what-are-the-implications-of-an-anti-fraternizat/ (last accessed on January 16th, 2024).

Anonymous: Why Working Women United, in: Labor Pains 1/1 (1975), p. 3.

Anonymous: Women 'Hard-Hats' Tell of Harassment, in: San Francisco Chronicle (February 18th, 1982).

Asner, Edward et al.: The Workplace Hustle: A Film About Sexual Harassment of Working Women, 1980.

Atana: Sexual Harassment Prevention Training – Once and For All: Stopping Sexual Harassment at Work, 2021, available at: https://www.youtube.com/watch?v=SjAh-FBDFjg, (last accessed March 27th, 2021).

Bailey, Morris: Sexual Harassment is a Valid Grievance, in: The Boston Globe (April 27th, 1980), p. C5.

Baker, Donald P.: Proving Sexual Harassment Is a Struggle, in: The Washington Post (October 24th, 1979), p. A7.

Baker, Russell: The Court of First Resort, in: The New York Times (July 26th, 1977), p. L29.

Barrier, Michael: Lawsuits Gone Wild, in: Nation's Business: A General Magazine for Businessmen, 1 (1998), pp. 1, 15–18.

Bassen, Ned: Let's Ask the Lawyers – What Can an Employer Do to Help Protect Against Sexual Harassment Lawsuits? in: Public Relations Quarterly 37/2 (1992), p. 26.

Bastian, L.D. et al.: Department of Defense 1995 Sexual Harassment Survey (DMDC Report No. 96–014), December 1996.

Becker, Joshua: 61% of Americans Live Paycheck-to-Paycheck: Here's the Simple Solution We're Overlooking, in: Forbes (August 18th, 2023), available at: https://www.forbes.com/sites/joshuabecker/2023/08/18/61-of-americans-live-paycheck-to-paycheck-heres-the-simple-solution-were-overlooking/ (last viewed on January 18th 2024).

Berg, Madeline: Here Are All the Advertisers Who Have Dropped Bill O'Reilly, in: Forbes (April 4th, 2017).

Berns, Walter: Terms of Endearment, in: Harper's Weekly (October 1st, 1980), pp. 14–20.

Blumenthal, Susan K: EEOC Guidelines. Comments and Analysis, Model Policies for the Office, June 10th, 1980, Files of the Equal Employment Opportunity Commission, Washington D.C., available at: https://documents.alexanderstreet.com/d/1000678706 (last accessed on January 18th, 2024).

Bower, Tim: The #MeToo Backlash, in: Harvard Business Review (September-October 2019).

Bralove, Mary: A Cold Shoulder. Career Women Decry Sexual Harassment by Bosses and Clients, in: The Wall Street Journal (January 29th, 1976), p. 1.

Bralove, Mary: Women Give Gate to Career 'Advances' by Wolves, in: Chicago Tribune (February 4th, 1976), p. B1.

Brenner, Elizabeth: Sexual Harassment: Hard to Define, Harder to Fight. Sex Harassment Hits Women's Self-Respect, in: Chicago Tribue (May 30, 1979), p. B1.

Brown, Anna: More Than Twice as many Americans Support Than Oppose the #MeToo Movement, in: Pew Research Center (September 29th, 2022), available at: Americans' Views of the #MeToo Movement | Pew Research Center (last accessed on January 19th, 2024).

Brown, Helen Gurley: Sex and the Single Girl, New York [2]2003.

Brown, Laura: Sex Harassment Killed Our Daughter. Parents: Job Abuse Led to Murder, in: Sun Herald (November 17th, 1994), pp. 88f.

Brownmiller, Susan and Dolores Alexander: How We Got Here, From Carmita Wood to Anita Hill, in: Ms. The New Magazine for Women (January/February 1992), pp. 70f.

Brownmiller, Susan: Against Our Will. Men, Women and Rape, New York – Toronto 1981.

Bularzik, Mary: Sexual Harassment at the Workplace. Historical Notes, in: Worker's Struggles, Past and Present: A 'Radical America' Reader, ed. by James Green, Philadelphia 1983, p. 89–121.

Bush, John et al.: Monitoring Employees Makes Them More Likely to Break Rules, in: Harvard Business Review (June 27th, 2022), available at: https://hbr.org/2022/06/monitoring-employees-makes-them-more-likely-to-break-rules (last accessed on January 17th, 2024).

Cannada, Lisa: Zero-Tolerance for Hospital Romance, in AMA Journal of Ethics (January 2010), available at: https://journalofethics.ama-assn.org/article/zero-tolerance-hospital-romance-commentary-1/2010–01 (last accessed on January 18th, 2024).

Cao, Sissi: #MeToo Movement Impels companies to Rethink Sexual Harassment Policies, in: Observer (January 18th, 2018), available at: https://observer.com/2018/01/metoo-movement-companies-rethink-sexual-harassment-policies/ (last viewed on January 18th, 2024).

Carlson, Walter: Advertising. Feminist Mystique under Fire, in: The New York Times (June 30th, 1965), p. 46.

Carton, Barbara: An Unsolved Slaying of an Airline Worker Stirs Family to Action, in: Wall Street Journal (June 20th, 1995), p. A1.

Cauterucci, Christina: Sexual Harassment Claims Spiked After Clarence Thomas Hearings. They're Spiking Again Now, in: Slate (October 2018), available at: https://slate.com/news-and-politics/2018/10/eeoc-2018-sexual-harassment-metoo-clarence-thomas-anita-hill.html (last accessed: December 27th, 2023).

Cawthon, Frances: Danger! Curves Ahead Driving Harassed Worker off his Track, in: The Atlanta Constitution (January 4th, 1881), p. 3F.

Chatelain, Marcia: The Conservative and Christian Roots of Many Beloved Fast Food Chains. It's Not Just Chick-fil-A, in: The Washington Post (August 9th, 2021), available at: https://www.washingtonpost.com/outlook/2021/08/09/conservative-christian-roots-many-beloved-fast-food-chains/ (last accessed on January 16th, 2024).

Churchman, Deborah: Sexual Harassment a Continuing Employment Challenge, in: Mountain Life and Work. The Magazine of the Appalachian South, July/August 1984, p. 10.

Cohen, Leah and Constance Backhouse: The Secret Oppression. Sexual Harassment of Working Women, Toronto 1978.

Collins, Eliza G. C. and Timothy B. Blodgett: Sexual Harassment…Some See It…Some Won't, in: Harvard Business Review (March 1981), available at: https://hbr.org/1981/03/sexual-harassmentsome-see-itsome-wont (last accessed on January 14th, 2023).

Cone, Sydney et al.: Workplace Conduct Still Needs Improvement After #MeToo, in: Bloomberg Law (October 24, 2022), available at: https://news.bloomberglaw.com/daily-labor-report/workplace-conduct-still-needs-improvement-after-metoo (last viewed on January 19th, 2024).

Connaught, Marshner: "Who is the New Traditional Woman?" (1982), in: Reaction to the Modern Women's Movement. 1963 to the Present (Antifeminism in America. A Collection of Readings from the Literature of the Opponents to U.S. Feminism. 1848 to the Present 3), ed. by Angela Howard and Sasha Ranaé Adams Tarrant, New York – London 1997, pp. 161–165.

Corbett, Holly: #MeToo Five Years Later. How the Movement Started and What Needs to Change, in: Forbes (October 27th, 2022).

Cordua Training Videos: Sexual Harassment – Awareness, Perception and Prevention: A Manager's Responsibility, [no date], available at: https://www.youtube.com/watch?v=R3FbwZTs1TA (last viewed: December 27th, 2023).

Cordua Training Videos: Sexual Harassment – Awareness, Perception and Prevention: An Employee's Responsibility, [no date], available at: https://www.youtube.com/watch?v=o3FhoCz-FbA (last viewed: December 27th, 2023).

Crain, Marion: Women, Labor Unions, and Hostile Work Environment Sexual Harassment: The Untold Story, in: Texas Journal of Women and the Law 4/9 (1995), p. 44.

Crittenden, Ann: Women Tell of Sexual Harassment at Work, in: The New York Times (October 25th, 1977), p. 60.

Cukjati, Curt and Marlene Martin: Company Holiday Parties Offer Fun – and Possible Lawsuits, in: South Florida Business Journal (November 3rd, 1997).

Dickler, Jessica: 60 % of Americans Are Still Living Paycheck to Paycheck as Inflation Hits Workers' Wages, in: CNBC (September 27th, 2023), available at: https://www.cnbc.com/2023/09/27/60percent-of-americans-are-still-living-paycheck-to-paycheck.html (last accessed on January 18th, 2024).

Dienstag, Eleanor: Women's Lib for Boys and Girls, The New York Times (May 7th, 1972), p. BRA3.

Dobbin, Ben: Federal Suit Questions Worker Privacy Rights: Courts: Case will weigh what protections employees are entitled to, as well as how far employers can go in monitoring staff, in: Los Angeles Times (January 25th, 1995).

Dobbin, Ben: Voice-Mail Romance Brings Legal Test of Worker Privacy Rights, in: San Francisco Chronicle (January 23rd, 1995), p. A6.

Ecabert, Gayle: An Employer's Guide to Understanding Liability for Sexual Harassment Under Title VII: Meritor Savings Bank v. Vinson, in: University of Cincinnati Law Review 55 (1986), pp. 1258–1279.

EEOC: Fiscal Year 2025 Congressional Budget Justification, March 11th, 2024.

EEOC: The State of the EEOC: Frequently Asked Questions, no date, accessible at: https://www.eeoc.gov/wysk/state-eeoc-frequently-asked-questions (last accessed: May 20th, 2025).

Ellis, Judy Trent: Sexual Harassment and Race: A Legal Analysis of Discrimination, in: Journal of Legislation 8/1 (1981), pp. 30–45.

Elsesser, Kim: Five Years After #Metoo, NDAs Are Still Silencing Victims, in: Forbes (March 21st, 2022).

Elsesser, Kim: Sexual Harassment and Assault Force Arbitration Bill to Get Vote This Week, in: Forbes (February 7th, 2022).

Elshtain, Jean Bethke: Feminists Against the Family, in: The Nation (November 17th, 1979) pp. 1, 497–500.

English, Bill: Owner's Creepy Surveillance Disrespects Employees, in: Nashville Business Journal (July 17th, 2017).

Estrich, Susan: Sex at Work, in: 43 Stanford Law Review (1991), pp. 813–861.

Farley, Lin: Response to Sexual Shakedown Review, in: Aegis (January/February 1979), pp. 24–26.

Farley, Lin: Sexual Shakedown. The Sexual Harassment of Women on the Job, New York 1978.

Farrow, Ronan: From Aggressive Overtures to Sexual Assault: Harvey Weinstein's Accusers Tell Their Stories, in: The New Yorker (October 10th, 2017).

Farrow, Ronan: Harvey Weinstein's Secret Settlements. The Mogul Used Money from His Brother and Elaborate Legal Agreements to Hide Allegations of Predation for Decades, in: The New Yorker (November 21st, 2017).

Feldblum, Chai R. and Victoria A. Lipnic: EEOC Report by the Select Task Force on the Study of Harassment in the Workplace, June 1016, available at: https://www.eeoc.gov/select-task-force-study-harassment-workplace (last viewed on January 17th, 2024).

Felsenthal, Edward: U.S. Urges Court to Hear Same-Sex Harassment Case, in: The Wall Street Journal (May 27th, 1997), p. B8.

Finkel, Lynn: Sexual Harassment, in: The Daily Californian, no date, pp. 20–22. Cited in full at: https://berkeleysexualassault.wordpress.com/1980s/ (last accessed: December 27th, 2023).

Furgurson, Pat: The Women at Work, in: The Atlanta Constitution (August 29th, 1975), p. 4 A.

Gaines, Rachel: Why We Are Still Talking About #MeToo at Work, in: Berkeley Law (January 11th, 2023), available at: https://sites.law.berkeley.edu/thenetwork/2023/01/11/why-we-are-still-talking-about-metoo-at-work/ (last accessed on January 13th, 2024).

Gingras, Abbey: 28 Companies Invested in the Success of Women at Work, in: Ripplematch (March 8th, 2021), available at: https://ripplematch.com/career-advice/companies-invested-in-the-success-of-women-at-work-d819cb0b/ (last accessed on January 13th, 2024).

Goldstein, Matthey and Jessica Silver-Greenberg: "Deregulation by Firings": Breaking Down the Cuts to Financial Oversight, in: The New York Times (13th February, 2025).

Goldstein, Morris and Robert Smith: The Estimated Impact of Anti-Discrimination Laws Aimed at Federal Contractors, in: Industrial and Labor Relations Review 29 (1976), pp. 523–543.

Goleman, Daniel: Sexual Harassment: It's About Power, Not Lust: What looks like Lechery May Be an Attempt to Keep a Woman 'in her place.' Sexual Harassment: A Matter of Power, in: The New York Times (October 22nd, 1991), p. C1.

Goodman, Ellen: It's Not About Sex, but Power: Sexual Harassment: A Male vs. Male Case Forces Us to the Heart of the Matter, in: Los Angeles Times (December 7th, 1997), p. M5.

Gross, Terry: Anita Hill Started a Conversation About Sexual Harassment. She's Not Done Yet, in: NPR (September 28th, 2021).

Gunter, Peter: Harassment in the Workplace Part 2, [no date, early 2000s], available at: https://www.youtube.com/watch?v=9rgAj1gDQIE (last viewed on January 18th, 2024).

Hatoff, Howard and Robert West: Law Office Policy & Procedures Manual, ⁵2006.

Head, Simon: The New Ruthless Economy. Work and Power in the Digital Age, New York 2003.

Heriksen, Ellen Emilie: #MeToo Has Changed How the Media Portrays Rape, in: Kilden (March 14th, 2023), available at: https://kjonnsforskning.no/en/2023/03/metoo-has-changed-how-media-portrays-rape, (last viewed on January 17th, 2024).

High, Tracey et al.: President Trump Acts to Roll Back DEI Initiatives, in: Harvard Law School Forum on Corporate Governance, February 10th, 2025, https://corpgov.law.harvard.edu/2025/02/10/president-trump-acts-to-roll-back-dei-initiatives/ (last accessed: May 19th, 2025).

hooks, bell: Ain't I a Woman? Black Women and Feminism, New York ²2015.

Hooven, Martha and Nancy McDonald: The Role of Capitalism: Understanding Sexual Harassment, in: Aegis (November/December 1978), p. 33.

Hudspeth, Ron: It's Men Not Women Who Are Harassed, in: The Atlanta Constitution (April 4th, 1981), p. 1B.

Igasaki, Paul: Doing the Best with What We Had: Building a More Effective Equal Employment Opportunity Commission During the Clinton-Gore Administration, in: The Labor Lawyer 1/2 (2001), pp. 261–284.

Johnston, Laurie: Airlines Assailed by Stewardesses: 'sexism' of Employers and Flying Public Is Scored, in: The New York Times, N.Y. (December 13th, 1972), p. 21.

Kallev, Alexandra et al.: Enforcement of Civil Rights Law in Private Workplaces: The Effects of Compliance Reviews and Lawsuits Over Time, in: Law and Social Inquiry 31/4 (2006), pp. 855–903.

Karwoski, Susan Anne: Women Miners Show Strength at Annual Conference, in: Mountain Life and Work. The Magazine of the Appalachian South (July/August 1984), p. 6.

Klein, Freada: Book Review of Sexual Shakedown: The Sexual Harassment of Women on the Job, by Lin Farley, in: Aegis (November/December 1978), pp. 34 f.

Kmart: Respect in the Workplace, [no date], available at: https://www.youtube.com/watch?v=qps5bA NuBFs (last accessed on September 4th, 2025).

Kohn, Arthur et al.: Companies' Anti-Fraternization Policies: Key Considerations, in: Harvard Law School Gorum on Corporate Governance (January 26th, 2020), available at: https://corpgov.law. harvard.edu/2020/01/26/companies-anti-fraternization-policies-key-considerations/ (last viewed on January 18th, 2024).

Kruger, Pamela: When Companies Turn a Blind Eye to sexual Harassment, They Set Themselves Up for Megadollar Lawsuits and PR Nightmares. Here's What Employers Can do To Protect Themselves – And Their Employees, in: Working Woman (June 1995), p. 34.

Kurita, Shari: The Status of Berkeley's Title IX Compliance, in: Daily Californian, no date, no page. Cited in full at: https://berkeleysexualassault.wordpress.com/1980s/ (last accessed on December 27th, 2023).

Langone, Alix: #MeTo and TIme's Up Founders Explain the Difference Between the Two Movements – And How They're Alike, in: Time (March 8th, 2018).

Leonard, Jonathan: Employment and Occupational Advance under Affirmative Action, in: Review of Economics and Statistics 66 (1984), pp. 377 – 385.

Lewis, Elaine: Who Is at High Risk of Sexual Harassment, in: ACLU News and Commentary, January 18th, 2018, available at: https://www.aclu.org/news/womens-rights/who-highest-risk-sexual-harassment, (last accessed on January 2nd, 2024).

Lublin, Joann: Guideline-Happy at the EEOC? in: The Wall Street Journal (August 28th, 1980), p. 18.

Lublin, Joann: Resisting Advances: Employers Act to Curb Sex Harassing on the Job; Lawsuits, Fines Feared. Formal Policies Are Issued. Training Sessions Held. But Policing Is Difficult," in: The Wall Street Journal (April 24th, 1981), p. 1.

MacKinnon, Catharine: Sexual Harassment of Working Women. A Case of Sex Discrimination, New Haven et al. 1979.

Martin, Michel: Perspectives on the 'MeToo' Movement, in: National Public Radio (September 1st, 2019), available at: https://www.npr.org/2019/09/01/756564705/perspectives-on-the-metoo-movement, (last viewed on January 19th, 2024).

Mathis, Patricia and Ruth Prokop with the Merit Systems Protection Board: Sexual Harassment in the Federal Workplace. Is It a Problem? A Report of the U.S. Merit Systems Protection Board Office of Merit Systems Review and Studies, March 1981, available at: https://www.mspb.gove/ studies/studies/Sexual _Harassment_in_the_Federal_Workplace_Is_it_a_Problem_240744.pdf (last accessed 24.12.2023).

McShane, Julianne: She Broke Her NDA with Harvey Weinstein in 2017. Here's How She Wants to Change the System for Others. Zelda Perkins Has Continued to Advocate for Limiting Confidentiality Agreements in Workplace Settings, in: The Washington Post (November 15th, 2021).

Mead, Margaret: A Proposal: We Need Taboos on Sex at Work, in: Redbook 150 (April 1978), pp. 31, 33, 38.

Merit Systems Protection Board: About MSPB, 2024, available at: https://www.mspb.gov/about/ about.htm (last accessed on January 12th, 2024).

Meyer, Coeli Mary et al.: Sexual Harassment, New York – Princeton 1981.

Milano, Alyssa: Tweet. October 15th, 2017. 10:21pm. Available at: https://twitter.com/Alyssa_Milano/status/919659438700670976?lang=de (last accessed on January 18th, 2024).

Moore, Mark: The State of the Campaign to End Mandatory Arbitration Misconduct Claims in Employment Agreements, in: Westlaw Today (June 2021), available at: https://today.westlaw.com/Document/I56668b01ce2e11ebbea4f0dc9fb69570/View/FullText.html?transitionType=Default&contextData=(sc.Default)&firstPage=true, (last viewed on January 2nd, 2024).

Nemy, End: Women Begin to Speak Out Against Sexual Harassment at Work, in: The New York Times (August 19th, 1975), p. 38.

Nicholas, Michael: The Little Black Book of Decision Making. Making Complex Decisions in a Fast-Moving World, Chinchester 2017.

North, Anna: 7 Positive Changes That Have Come From the #MeToo Movement, in: Vox (October 4th, 2019), available at: https://www.vox.com/identities/2019/10/4/20852639/me-too-movement-sexual-harassment-law-2019 (last accessed on January 18th, 2024).

North, Anna: The #MeToo Movement and Its Evolution Explained. From Charges Against Harvey Weinstein to the Confirmation of Brett Kavanaugh to the Ongoing Drive for Accountability, Here's Where the Movement Stands Today, in: Vox (October 11th, 2018), available at: https://www.vox.com/identities/2018/10/9/17933746/me-too-movement-metoo-brett-kavanaugh-weinstein (last accessed on January 18th, 2024).

Pasztor, Andy: Dozens of U.S. Regulations are Targeted for Review, Probable Easing, Bush Says, in: The Wall Street Journal (August 13th, 1981), p. 5.

Peters: Jeremy: Company's Smoking Ban Means Off-Hours, Too, in: The New York Times, (Feb 8th, 2005).

Phillips, Michael: Employer Sexual Harassment Liability Under Agency Principles: A Second Look at Meritor Savings Bank, FSB v. Vinson, in: Vanderbilt Law Review 44/6 (1991), p. 1229 – 1272.

Rains, Parker: To Monitor Your Employees (Or Not): Pros vs. Cons, in: Nashville Business Journal (January 13th, 2017).

Rattner, Steven: National Airlines Shutdown is Nearing Four Months, in: The New York Times, N.Y. (December 29th, 1975), pp. 43 f.

Ravitsky, Greta: Texas Expands Employer Liability for Sexual Harassment Claims, Effective September 1, 2021, in: Epstein Becker Green Website (August 20th, 2021), available at: https://www.ebglaw.com/insights/publications/texas-expands-employer-liability-for-sexual-harassment-claims-effective-september-1 – 2021 (last accessed on January 18th, 2024).

Redden, Molly and Dominic Rushe: A Timeline of Bill O'Reilly's Downfall: Another Fox News Founding Father Exits, in: The Guardian (April 20th, 2017).

Redden, Molly: Peter Jackson. I blacklisted Ashley Judd and Mira Sorvino under pressure from Weinstein, in: The Guardian (December 16th, 2017).

Reuben, Carol: CRC Plans South's 1st Institute to Fight Sexual Harassment, in: The Atlanta Constitution (February 26th, 1981), p. 1E.

Roberto, Melissa: Debra Winger Says #MeToo Movement Has 'Gone Ridiculously Too Far,' in: Fox News (August 13th, 2021), available at: https://www.foxnews.com/entertainment/debra-winger-metoo-movement-gone-ridiculously-too-far (last accessed on January 18th, 2024).

Rosenthal, Andrew: Theater of Pain. A Terrible Wrong Has Been Done, But to Whom? in: The New York Times (October 13th, 1991), p. E1.

Rucinski, Dianne: The Polls – A Review. Rush to Judgment? Fast Reaction Polls in the Anita Hill-Clarence Thomas Controversy, in: The Public Opinion Quarterly 57/4 (Winter 1993), pp. 575 – 592.

Rutledge-Jones, Dawn: Court Rulings Force Businesses to Visit Sexual Harassment Issues, in: Nashville Business Journal (September 13th, 1998).

Schlafly, Phyllis: Feminism Falls on its Face, in: Phyllis Schlafly Report (November 1991), pp. 1f.

Schlafly, Phyllis: A Choice Not an Echo, Alton, IL 1964.

Schlafly, Phyllis: The Power of the Positive Woman, New Rochelle, NY 1977.

Seligman, David: Sex in the Office, in: Fortune (April 7th, 1980), p. 42.

Semuels, Alana: Low-Wage workers Aren't Getting Justice for Sexual Harassment. Despite the #MeToo Movement, Poor Women Often Find That Speaking Out About Abuse at Work is Too Costly, in: The Atlantic (December 17th, 2017).

Sexual Assault Kit Initiative: Victim or Survivor. Terminology from Investigation Through Prosecution, available at: https://sakitta.org/toolkit/docs/Victim-or-Survivor-Terminology-from-Investigation-Through-Prosecution.pdf (last accessed on January 13th, 2024).

Shapiro, Lila: Bad Reputation. Moira Donegan Created the 'shitty Media Men' List to Address a Moral Injustice. Stephen Elliott Says He's Suing Her for the Same Reason, in: Intelligencer (October 25th, 2022), available at: https://nymag.com/intelligencer/article/shitty-media-men-lawsuit-moira-donegan-stephen-elliott.html (last accessed on January 18th, 2024).

Sherman, Carter: Sexual Assault Allegations Seem to be a Badge of Honor in Trump's America. Was #Metoo an Epic Failure? In: The Guardian (Mar. 30th, 2025).

Shiver, Jube Jr.: Workers Upset Over Y2K Monitoring, in: New York Times (October 12th, 1999), pp. 2K, A6.

Slade, Margot: Sexual Harassment: Stories from the Field, in: The New York Times (March 27th, 1994), p. 124.

Smith, Kyle: #MeToo Has Morphed into a Career-Destroying Angry Mob, in: Fox News (September 23rd, 2018), available at: https://www.foxnews.com/opinion/metoo-has-morphed-into-a-career-destroying-angry-mob (last accessed on January 18th, 2024).

Smith, Tovia: On #MeToo, Americans more Divided by Party than Gender, in: National Public Radio (October 31st, 2018), available at: https://www.npr.org/2018/10/31/662178315/on-metoo-americans-more-divided-by-party-than-gender (last accessed on January 19th, 2024).

Smolowe, Jill et al.: Anita Hill's Legacy, in: Time U.S. (October 1992), available at: https://content.time.com/time/magazine/article/0,9171,976770,00.html, (last accessed on December 27th, 2023).

Spiers, Tyler and Joe Davidson: Sexual Harassment-What Employees Need to Know (Blue Ribbon Panel), [no date], available at: https://www.youtube.com/watch?v=iMgl7G_Z62o (last viewed: December 27th, 2023).

Starkman, Jay: What to Consider Before Monitoring Employee Smartphones, in: Nashville Business Journal (May 27th, 2015).

Steel, Emily and Michael Schmidt: Fox Losing More Advertisers After Sexual Harassment Claims Against O'Reilly, in: The New York Times (April 4th, 2017).

Steinberg, Jacques: At Walmart, Workers Who Dated Lose Jobs, in: The New York Times, New York, (14th July, 1993).

Strom, Stephanie: Harassment Cases Can Go Unnoticed: Many Companies Are Assailed as Not Being Aggressive Sexual Harassment Policies Are Often Not Pushed Hard, in: The New York Times (October 20th, 1991), p. 1.

Swoboda, Frank: Most Senior-Level Managers Still White, Male, Panel Finds. Commission's Last Report Puts Blame on 'Glass Ceiling,' in: San Francisco Examiner (November 26th, 1995), p. A-9.

Taub, Nadine: Plaintiff-Appellant's Appeal Brief, *Tomkins v. Public Service Electric and Gas Company*, 568 F. 2d 1044.

Taylor, Frederick Winslow: The Principles of Scientific Management, (Akasha Classics Series), 2008.

Trump, Donald J.: Executive Order 14151: Ending Radical and Wasteful Government DEI Programs and Preferencing, January 20th 2025, available at: https://www.whitehouse.gov/presidential-actions/2025/01/ending-radical-and-wasteful-government-dei-programs-and-preferencing/ (last accessed May 20th, 2025).

Trump, Donald J.: Executive Order 14168: Defending Women from Gender Ideology Extremism and Restoring Biological Truth to the Federal Government, January 20th, 2025, available at: https://www.whitehouse.gov/presidential-actions/2025/01/defending-women-from-gender-ideology-extremism-and-restoring-biological-truth-to-the-federal-government/ (last accessed: May 20th, 2025).

Trump, Donald J.: Executive Order 14173: Ending Illegal Discrimination and Restoring Meri-Based Opportunity, January 21st, 2025, available at: https://www.whitehouse.gov/presidential-actions/2025/01/ending-illegal-discrimination-and-restoring-merit-based-opportunity/, (last accessed on May 20th, 2025).

Trump, Donald J.: Remarks by President Trump at the World Economic Forum, January 23rd, 2025, available at: https://www.whitehouse.gov/remarks/2025/01/remarks-by-president-trump-at-the-world-economic-forum/, (last accessed on May 19th, 2025).

U.S. Bureau of Labor Statistics: Women in the Labor Force: A Databook. Report 1097, March 2022, available at: https://www.bls.gov/opub/reports/womens-databook/2021/home.htm, (last viewed on January 17th, 2024).

U.S. Department of Labor, Women's Bureau: Occupations of Women in the Labor Force Since 1920, 2021, available at: Occupations of Women in the Labor Force Since 1920 | U.S. Department of Labor (dol.gov) (last viewed on January 19th, 2024).

U.S. Merit Systems Protection Board, Sexual Harassment in Federal Workplaces: Understanding and Addressing the Problem. A Report to the President and the Congress of the United States, December 2022, available at: https://www.mspb.gov/studies/studies/Sexual_Harassment_in_Federal_Workplaces_Understanding_and_Addressing_the_Problem_1987037.pdf, (last viewed on January 17th, 2024).

U.S. Merit Systems Protection Board: Sexual Harassment in the Federal Workplace. Trends, Progress, Continuing Challenges, 1994.

Valinsky, Jordan: How Chick-fil-A Became a Target for Going 'Woke,' in: CNN Business (June 2nd, 2023), available at: https://edition.cnn.com/2023/06/02/business/chick-fil-a-fake-controversy/index.html (last accessed January 13th, 2024).

Vermuelen, Joan: Comments on the Equal Employment Opportunity Commission's Proposed Amendment Adding Section 1604.11, Sexual Harassment, to Its Guidelines on Sexual Discrimination, in: Women's Rights Law Reporter, 6/4 (1980), pp. 285–294.

Weber, Max: From Max Weber. Essays in Sociology, transl. by H.H. Gerth and C. Wright Mills, London 1991.

Wehrli, Lynn: Sexual Harassment at the Workplace. A Feminist Analysis and Strategy for Social Change. Master's Thesis, Massachusetts Institute of Technology, 1976.

White House: Fact Sheet: President Donald J. Trump Removes DEI From the Foreign Service, March 18th, 2025, accessible at: https://www.whitehouse.gov/fact-sheets/2025/03/fact-sheet-president-donald-j-trump-removes-dei-from-the-foreign-service/, (last accessed: May 19th, 2025).

White, Jane See: Sexual Harassment. A Pivotal Issue, in: The Washington Post (August 15th, 1978), p. E10.

Wicker, Tom: Blaming Anita Hill, in: The New York Times (October 10th, 1991), p. A27.

Wilkins, David Brian: Presumed Crazy. The Structure of Argument in Hill/Thomas Hearings, Southern California Law Review 65/3 (1992), pp. 1145–1220.

Willingham, AJ and Christina Maxouris: These Tweets Show Why People Don't Report Sexual Assaults, in: CNN Health (September 21st, 2018), at: https://edition.conn.con/2018/09/21/health/why-i-didnt-report-tweets-trnd/index.html, (last accessed: December 24th, 2023).

Willkie Compliance: State Employee Privacy Laws; at: https://complianceconcourse.willkie.com/resources/privacy-and-cybersecurity-us-state-employee-privacy-laws/ (last accessed November 20th 2024).

Wood, Camita: Woman Alone, in: Labor Pains, 1/1 (Aug. 1975), p. 5.

Wrigth, Robert: Advertisers Continue to Drop Fox News' 'O'Reilley Factor.' At Least 52 Companies Have Withdrawn advertisements from the Show, in: ABC News (April 7th, 2017).

Secondary Literature

Aberbach, Joel D.: Transforming the Presidency. The Administration of Ronald Reagan, in: Ronald Reagan and the 1980s. Receptions, Policies, Legacies (Studies of the Americas), ed. by Cheryl Hudson and Gareth Davies, New York 2008, pp. 197–201.

Adamson, Machael R.: Reagan and the Economy. Business and Labor. Deregulation and Regulation, in: A Companion to Ronald Reagan (Wiley Blackwell Companions to History), ed. by Andrew L. Johns, Chichester et al. 2015, pp. 149–166.

Alleyne, Reginald: Arbitrating Sexual Harassment Grievances: A Representation Dilemma for Unions, in: University of Pennsylvania Journal of Labor and Employment Law, 2/1 (Spring 1999), pp. 1–17.

Arnold, Gretchen: U.S. Women's Movements to End Violence Against Women, Domestic Abuse, and Rape, in: The Oxford Handbook of U.S. Women's Social Movement Activism (Oxford Handbooks), New York 2017, pp. 270–290.

Aronson, Pamela: The Dynamics and Causes of Gender and Feminist Consciousness and Feminist Identities, in: The Oxford Handbook of U.S. Women's Social Movement Activism, ed. by McCammon et al., New York 2017.

Arriola, Elvia R.: 'What's the Big Deal?' Women in the New York City Construction Industry and Sexual Harassment Law. 1970–1985, in: Columbia Human Rights Law Review 22/1 (1990), pp. 21–71.

Atwater, Leanne et al.: Looking Ahead. How What We Know About Sexual Harassment Now Informs Us of the Future, in: Organizational Dynamics 48/4 (October-December 2019).

Autor, David H. et al.: Does Employment Protection Reduce Productivity? Evidence From US States, in: The Economic Journal 117 (June 2007), pp. 189–217.

Avendano, Ana: Sexual Harassment in the Workplace: Where Were the Unions? In: Labor Studies Journal 43/4 (2018), pp. 245–262.

Avrahm, Ronen: An Empirical Study of the Impact of Tort Reforms on Medical Malpractice Settlement Payments, in: The Journal of Legal Studies 36/2 (June 2007), pp. 183–229.

Baker, Carrie N.: He Said, She Said. Popular Representation of Sexual Harassment in Second-Wave Feminism, in: Disco Divas. Women and Popular Culture in the 1970s, ed. by Sherrie A. Inness, Philadelphia 2003, pp. 39 – 53.

Baker, Carrie N.: Sexual Extortion. Criminalizing Quid Pro Quo Sexual Harassment, in: Law and Inequality: A Journal of Theory and Practice 13/1 (1994), pp. 213 – 250.

Baker, Carrie N.: The Emergence of Organized Feminist Resistance to Sexual Harassment in the United States in the 1970s, in: Journal of Women's History 19/3 (2007), pp. 161 – 184.

Baker, Carrie N.: The Women's Movement Against Sexual Harassment, New York 2008.

Baker: Race, Class, and Sexual Harassment in the 1970s, in: Feminist Studies 30/1 (2004), pp. 7 – 27.

Baron, James M. et al.: Targets of Opportunity: Organizational and Environmental Determinants of Gender Integration within the California Civil Service, 1979 – 1985, in: American Journal of Sociology 96 (1991), pp. 1362 – 1402

Barreto, Milagros et. al.: Workplace Sexual Harassment and Vulnerabilities Among Low-Wage Hispanic Women, in: Occupational Health Science, 5/3 (2021), pp. 391 – 414.

Baxandall, Rosalyn and Linda Gordon: Second-Wave Feminism, in: A Companion to American Women's History, ed. by Nancy A. Hewitt, Oxford 2002, pp. 414 – 432.

Baynard, Victoria et al.: Multiple Sexual Violence Prevention Tools: Doses and Boosters, in: Journal Aggression, Conflict and Peace Research 10 (December 2017), pp. 145 – 155.

Benavides Espinoza, Claudia and George Cunningham: Observers' Reporting of Sexual Harassment: The Influence of Harassment Type, Organizational Culture, and Political Orientation, in: Public Organization Review 10/4 (2010), p. 323 – 333.

Berebitsky, Julie: Sex and the Office. A History of Gender, Power, and Desire (Society and the Sexes in Modern World), New Haven – London 2012.

Berrey, Ellen et al.: Rights on Trial. How Workplace Discrimination Law Perpetuates Inequality, Chicago – London 2017.

Berrey, Ellen et al.: Workers Wronged, in: American Bar Association Journal 103/11 (November 2017), p. 36 – 45.

Bingham, Shereen and Lisa Scherer: The Unexpected Effects of a Sexual Harassment Educational Program, in: Journal of Applied Behavioral Science 37/2 (2001), pp. 125 – 153.

Bisom-Rapp, Susan: Bulletproofing the workplace. Symbol and substance in Employment Discrimination Law Practice, in: Florida state University Law Review 26/4 (1999), pp. 959 – 1047.

Boris, Eileen and Allison Louise Elias: Workplace Discrimination, Equal Pay, and Sexual Harassment. An Intersectional Approach, in: The Oxford Handbook of U.S. Women's Social Movement Activism (Oxford Handbooks), New York 2017, pp. 193 – 213.

Boris, Eileen and Lara Vapnek: Women's Labors in Industrial and Postindustrial America, in: The Oxford Handbook of American Women's and Gender History (Oxford Handbooks), New York 2018, pp. 171 – 194.

Born, Patricia and W. Kip Viscusi: Insurance Market Response to the 1990s Liability Reforms: An Analysis of Firm-Level Data, in: The Journal of Risk and Insurance 61/2 (June 1994), pp. 192 – 218.

Boshak, Heather R: The Affirmative Defense to a Vicarious Liability Sexual Harassment Claim, in: The New Jersey Law Journal (April 7th, 2008), available at: https://www.foxrothschild.com/publications/the-affirmative-defense-to-a-vicarious-liability-sexual-harassment-claim, (last viewed on January 16th, 2024).

Boyle, Karen: Of Monguls, Monsters, and Men, in: The Routledge Handbook of the Politics of the #MeToo Movement, ed. by Giti Chandra and Irma Erlingsdóttir, New York 2021, pp. 186–198.

Bozin, Doris et al.: ADR: Championing the (Unjust) Resolution of Bullying Disputes? in: Australasian Dispute Resolution Journal 29/3 (2019), pp. 162–172.

Bradford, Beverly: Women's Lib Comes to Suburbs, in: The Washington Post (Aug 6th, 1970), p. H1.

Brocker, Manfred: Protest – Anpassung – Etablierung. Die Christliche Rechte im Politischen System der USA, Frankfurt 2004.

Bularzik, Mary: Sexual Harassment at the Workplace. Historical Notes, in: Workers' Struggles, Past and Present. A 'Radical America' Reader, ed. by James Green., Philadelphia 1983, pp. 117–135.

Bumiller, Kristin: The Civil Rights Society: The Social Construction of Victims, in: Political Science Quarterly 103/4 (Winter 1988), pp. 751f.

Burnham, William and Stephen Reed: Introduction to the Law and Legal System of the United States, St. Paul, MN [7]2021.

Busch, Andrew E.: Reagan and the Evolution of American Politics. 1981–1989, in: A Companion to Ronald Reagan (Wiley Blackwell Companions to History), ed. by Andrew L. Johns, Chichester et al. 2015, pp. 96–116.

Campbell, Jessica: The First Brave Woman Who Alleged 'sexual Harassment,' in: Legacy.com (Dec 7th, 2017), available at: https://www.legacy.com/news/culture-and-history/the-first-brave-woman-who-alleged-sexual-harassment/ (last viewed on January 19th, 2024).

Cohen, Jean-Louis and Maeve Cooke: Regulating Intimacy: A New Legal Paradigm, in: Philosophy and Social Criticism 31/1 (2005), p. 131–143.

Colvin, Alexander J.S.: The Growing Use of Mandatory Arbitration. Access to the Courts is Now Barred for More Than 60 Million American Workers, in: Economic Policy Institute (September 2017).

Craig, Steve: Madison Avenue Versus *The Feminine Mystique*. The Advertising Industry's Response to the Women's Movement, in: Disco Divas. Women and Popular Culture in the 1970s, ed. by Sherrie A. Inness, Philadelphia 2003, pp. 13–24.

Critchlow, Donald T.: Mobilizing Women. The 'social' Issue, in: The Reagan Presidency. Pragmatic Conservatism and its Legacies, ed. by W. Elliot Brownlee and Hugh Davis Graham, Lawrence, KS 2003, pp. 293–326.

Critchlow, Donald T.: Phyllis Schlafly and Grassroots Conservatism. A Woman's Crusade (Politics and Society in Twentieth-Century America), Princeton – Oxford 2005.

Dana, Anne et al.: The 'Ending Forced Arbitration of Sexual Assault and Sexual Harassment Act of 2021' Brings Significant Change to Employers with Mandatory Pre-Dispute Arbitration Agreements, in: Employee Relations Law Journal, 48/2 (Autumn 2022), pp. 15–19.

De Coster, S. et al.: Routine Activities and Sexual Harassment in the Workplace, in: Work and Occupations 26/1 (1999), pp. 21–49.

Derksen, Maarten: Turning Men into Machines? Scientific Management, Industrial Psychology, and the "Human Facor," in: Journal of the History of the Behavioral Sciences 50/2 (Spring 2014), pp. 148–165.

Deslippe, Denise: Whose Equality? Race and Working-Class Feminism in the United States, in: Austalasian Journal of American Studies 17/2 (December 1998), pp. 31–44.

Dobbin, Frank and Alexandra Kalev: The Promise and Peril of Sexual Harassment Programs, in: Proceedings of the National Academy of Sciences of the United States of America 116/25 (June 2019), pp. 12255–12260.

Dobbin, Frank and Erin L. Kelly: How to Stop Sexual Harassment. Professional Construction of Legal Compliance in Organizations, in: American Journal of Sociology 112/4 (2007), pp. 1203–1243.

Dobbin, Frank et al.: The Expansion of Due Process in Organizations, in: Institutional Patterns and Organizations: Culture and Environment, ed. by Lynne G. Zucker, Cambridge 1988.

Dobbin, Frank: Inventing Equal Opportunity, Princeton, NJ et al. 2009.

Draper, Alan: Conflict of Interests. Organized Labor and the Civil Rights Movement in the South:1954–1968, Ithaca 1994.

Drobac, Jennifer Ann et al.: Sexual Harassment Law. History, Cases, and Practice, Durahm 2020.

Dunn, Megan and James Walker: U.S. Bureau of Labor Statistics. Union Membership in the United States, (September 2016), accessible at: <https://www.bls.gov/spotlight/2016/union-membership-in-the-united-states/pdf/union-membership-in-the-united-states.pdf> last viewed: December 27th, 2023.

Dziech, Billie Wright and Michael W. Hawkins: Sexual Harassment in Higher Education. Reflections and New Perspectives, Abington [2]2011.

Edelman, Lauren and Jessica Cabrera: Sex-Based Harassment and Symbolic Compliance: in: Annual Review of Law and Social Science (June 2020), pp. 361–383.

Edelman, Lauren B.: The Endogeneity of Legal Regulation: Grievance Procedures as Rational Myth, in: American Journal of Sociology 105/2 (September 1999), pp. 406–454.

Edelman, Lauren: Legal Ambiguity and Symbolic Structures: Organizational Mediation of Civil Rights Law, in: American Journal of Sociology 97/6 (May 1992), pp. 1531–1575.

Edelman, Lauren: Legal Environments and Organizational Governance: The Expansion of Due Process in the American Workplace, in: American Journal of Sociology 95/6 (May 1990), pp. 1401–1440.

Edelman, Lauren: Working Law: Courts, Corporations, and Symbolic Compliance, Chicago 2016.

Edelman, When Organizations Rule; Edelman, Lauren: The Legal Lives of Private Organizations, in: The Blackwell Companion to Law and Society (2004), pp. 231–252.

Eileen and Allison Louise Elias: Workplace Discrimination, Equal Pay, and Sexual Harassment. An Intersectional Approach, in: The Oxford Handbook of U.S. Women's Social Movement Activism (Oxford Handbooks), New York 2017.

Enke, Anne: Taking Over Domestic Space. The Battered Women's Movement and Public Protest, in: The World the Sixties Made. Politics and Culture in Recent America (Critical Perspectives on the Past), ed. by Van Gosse and Richard Moser, Philadelphia 2003, pp. 162–191.

Federal Judicial Center: Biographical Directory of Article III Federal Judges 1789-Present, Judges appointed by Jimy Carter, available at: https://www.fjc.gov/history/judges/search/advanced-search, (last viewed: May 13th, 2023).

Felmlee, Diane et al.: the Geography of Sentiment Towards the Women's March of 2017, in: PLOS One 15/6 (2020).

Fernandez, Lilia: Ronald Reagan, Race, Civil Rights, and Immigration, in: A Companion to Ronald Reagan (Wiley Blackwell Companions to History), ed. by Andrew L. Johns, Chichester et al. 2015, pp. 185–203.

Fitzgerald Louise et al.: But Was It Really Sexual Harassment? Legal, Behavioral, and Psychological Definitions of the Workplace Victimization of Women, in: Sexual Harassment: Theory, Research, and Treatment, ed. by W. O'Donohue, Needham Heights 1997, pp. 5–28.

Foner, Philip: Organized labor and the black worker, New York 1974.

Foote, William E. and Jane Goodman-Delahunty: Understanding Sexual Harassment. Evidence-Based Forensic Practice, Washington DC 2021.

Foucault, Michel: Archäologie des Wissens, Frankfurt [15]2011.

Frymer, Paul: Black and Blue. African Americans, the Labor Movement, and the Decline of the Democratic Party, Princeton 2008.

Garfinkel, Irwin et al.: The Growth of Families Headed by Women. 1950–1980, in: Demography 27/1 (1990), pp. 19–30.

Geise, Ann L: The Female Role in Middle Class Women's Magazines from 1955 to 1976. A Content Analysis of Nonfiction Selections, in: Sex Roles 5/1 (1979), pp. 51–62.

Geppert, Dominik: Konservative Revolutionen? Thatcher, Reagan und das Feindbild des Consensus Liberalism, in: Liberalismus im 20. Jahrhundert (Stiftung Bundespräsident-Theodor-Heuss-Haus Wissenschaftliche Reihe 12), ed. by Anselm Doering-Manteuffel and Jörn Leonhard, Stuttgart 2015, pp. 271–289.

Gilmore, Leigh: the #MeToo Effect: What Happens when We Believe Women, New York 2023.

Gilson, Erinn Cunniff: Vulnerability and Victimization: Rethinking Key Concepts in Feminist Discourse on Sexual Violence, in: Journal of Women in Culture and Society 42/1 (2024), pp. 71–98.

Gough, Mark: A Tale of Two Forums: Employment Discrimination Outcomes in Arbitration and Litigation, in: IRL Review 68/5 (2020), pp. 1019–1042.

Graham, Hugh Davis: Civil Rights Policy in: The Reagan Presidency. Pragmatic Conservatism and its Legacies, ed. by W. Elliot Brownlee and Hugh Davis Graham, Lawrence, KS 2003, pp. 283–291.

Green, Michael: A New #MeToo Result: Rejecting Notions of Romantic Consent with Executives, in: Employee Rights and Employment Policy Journal 23/1 (2019), pp. 116–164.

Greenspan, Alan and Adrian Wooldrige: Capitalism in America. A History, New York 2018.

Gruber, James: An Epidemiology of Sexual Harassment: Evidence from North America and Europe, in: Sexual Harassment: Theory, Research, and Treatment, ed. by W. O'Donohue, no location 1997, pp. 84–98.

Hasen, Richard: Polarization and the Judiciary, in: Annual Review of Political Science 22 (2019), pp. 261–276.

Heclo, Hugh: Ronald Reagan and the American Public Philosophy, in: The Reagan Presidency. Pragmatic Conservatism and its Legacies, ed. by W. Elliot Brownlee and Hugh Davis Graham, Lawrence, KS 2003, pp. 17–39.

Hellmann, Kai-Uwe: Paradigmen der Bewegungsforschung, in: Paradigmen der Bewegungsforschung. Entstehung und Entwicklung von Neuen Sozialen Bewegungen und Rechtsextremismus, ed. by Kai-Uwe Hellmann and Ruud Koopmans, Wiesbaden 1998, pp. 9–30.

Henry, Ann: Employer and Employee Reasonableness Regarding Retaliation under the Ellerth/Faragher Affirmative Defense, in: University of Chicago Legal Forum 1 (1999), pp. 553–586.

Hertzog, Jodie et al.: There's a Policy for that; A comparison of the organizational culture of workplaces reporting incidents of sexual harassment, in: Behavior and Social Issues 17/2 (2008), pp. 169–181.

Herzog, Ulrich: Sexuelle Belästigung am Arbeitsplatz (Abhandlungen zum Arbeits- und Wirtschaftsrecht 76), Heidelberg 1997.

Hilson, Christopher J.: New Social Movements. The Role of Legal Opportunity, in: Social Movements. Transformative Shifts and Turning Points, ed. by Savyasaachi and Ravi Kumar, New Delhi 2014, pp. 304–325.

Hippensteele, Susan: Mediation Ideology: Navigating Space from Myth to Reality in Sexual harassment Dispute Resolution, in: Journal of Gender, Social Policy and the Law 15/1 (2006), pp. 43–68.

Howard, Angela: Series Introduction, in: Reaction to the Modern Women's Movement. 1963 to the Present (Antifeminism in America. A Collection of Readings from the Literature of the Opponents to U.S. Feminism. 1848 to the Present 3), ed. by Angela Howard and Sasha Ranaé Adams Tarrant, New York – London 1997.

Hurwitz, Heather McKee: From Ink to Web and Beyond. U.S. Women's Activism Using Traditional and New Social Media, in: The Oxford Handbook of U.S. Women's Social Movement Activism (Oxford Handbooks), New York 2017, pp. 462–487.

Inness, Sherrie A.: 'strange Feverish Years.' The 1970s and Women's Changing Roles, in: Disco Divas. Women and Popular Culture in the 1970s, ed. by Sherrie A. Innes, Philadelphia 2003, pp. 1–12.

Kelly, Erin et al.: Best Practices or Best Guesses? Assessing the Efficacy of Corporate Affirmative Action and Diversity Policies, in: American Sociological Review 71 (2006), pp. 589–617.

Kessler, Daniel et al.: Effects of the Medial Liability System in Australia, the UK, and the USA, in: Lancet (2006), pp. 240–246.

Klatch, Rebecca E.: Women of the New Right, Philadelphia 1987.

Koopmans, Ruud: Konkurrierende Paradigmen oder Friedlich Ko-Existierende Komplemente? in: Paradigmen der Bewegungsforschung. Entstehung und Entwicklung von Neuen Sozialen Bewegungen und Rechtsextremismus, ed. by Kai-Uwe Hellmann and Ruud Koopmans, Wiesbaden 1998, pp. 216–231.

Korstad, Robert Rodgers: Civil rights unionism: Tobacco workers and the struggle for democracy in the mid-twentieth century South. Chapel Hill 2003.

Landwehr, Achim: Historische Diskursanalyse, New York – Frankfurt ²2009.

Lareau, Craig R.: 'Because of … Sex.' The Historical Development of Workplace Sexual Harassment Law in the USA, in: Psychological Injury and Law 9/3 (2016), pp. 206–215.

Lee, J. Y. et al.: Blowing the Whistle on Sexual Harassment: Test of a Model of Predicators and Outcomes, in: Human Relations 57/3 (2004), pp. 297–322.

Levin, Yuval: The Fractured Republic. Renewing America's Social Contract in the Age of Individualism, New York 2016.

Levinson, Marsha: Mandatory Arbitration: How the current System Perpetuates Sexual Harassment Cultures in the Workplace, Santa Clara Law Review 59 (2019), pp. 485–523.

Lutner, Rachel: Employer Liability for Sexual Harassment: The Morass of Agency principles and Respondeat Superior, in: University of Illinois Law Review 3 (1993), pp. 589–628.

Maass, Anne et al.: Sexual harassment Under Social Identity Threat: The Computer Harassment Paradigm, in: Journal of Personality and Social Psychology 85/5 (2003), pp. 853–870.

MacKinnon, Catharine: Global #MeToo, in: The Routledge Handbook of the Politics of the #MeToo Movement, ed. by Giti Chandra and Irma Erlingsdóttir, New York 2021, pp. 42–54.

MacKinnon, Catharine: The Logic of Experience. Reflections on the Development of Sexual Harassment Law, in: Georgetown Law Journal 90/3 (2002), pp. 813–833.

Marks, John H.: Smoke, Mirrors, and the Disappearance of 'Vicarious' Liability: The Emergence of a Dubious Summary-Judgement Safe Harbor for Employers Whose Supervisory Personnel Commit Hostile Workplace Harassment, in: Houston Law Review 38 (2002), pp. 401–1462.

Marshall Anna-Maria: Injustice frames, legality, and the everyday construction of sexual harassment, in: Law and Social Inquiry 28/3 (Summer 2003), pp. 659–689.

Marshall, Anna-Maria: Idle rights: employees' rights consciousness and the construction of sexual harassment policies, in: Law and Society Review 39/1 (2005), pp. 83–124.

McAllister, Ted V.: Reagan and the Transformation of American Conservatism, in: The Reagan Presidency. Pragmatic Conservatism and its Legacies, ed. by W. Elliot Brownlee and Hugh Davis Graham, Lawrence, KS 2003, pp. 40–60.

McCammon, Holly J. and Brittany N. Hearne: U.S. Women's Legal Activism in the Judicial Arena, in: The Oxford Handbook of U.S. Women's Social Movement Activism, ed. by McCammon et al., New York 2017.

McDonald, Paula and Sara Charlesworth: Framing Sexual Harassment through Media Representation, in: Women's Studies International Forum 37 (2013), pp. 95–103.

McWilliams, Mike and Margaret Smith: An Overview of the Legal Standard Regarding Product Liability Design Defect Claims and a Fifty State Survey on the Applicable Law in Each Jurisdiction, in: Defense Counsel Journal (January 2015), pp. 80–90.

Mellor, Steven and Lisa Kath: Union Revitalization: How Women and Men Officers See the Relationship between Union Size and Union Tolerance for Sexual Harassment, in: Employee Response Rights Journal 28/1 (2016), pp. 45–59.

Modleski, Tania: Breaking Silence, or an Old Wives' Tale. Sexual Harassment and the Legitimation Crisis, in: Mass Culture and Everyday Life, ed. by Peter Gibian, New York – London 1997, pp. 219–232.

Moser, Richard: Was It the End or Just a Beginning? American Storytelling and the History of the Sixties, in: The World the Sixties Made. Politics and Culture in Recent America (Critical Perspectives on the Past), ed. by Van Gosse and Richard Moser, Philadelphia 2003, pp. 37–52.

Nickerson, Michelle: Mothers of Conservatism. Women and the Postwar Right, Princeton, N.J. 2012.

Nissen, Bruce: The Legacy of Racism. A Case Study of Continuing Racial Impediments to Union Effectiveness, in: Labor Studies Journal 33/4 (December 2008), pp. 349–370.

Olofsson, Gunnar: From the Working-Class Movement to the New Social Movements, in: Social Movements. Transformative Shifts and Turning Points, ed. by Savyasaachi and Ravi Kumar, New Delhi 2014.

Opp, Karl-Dieter: Die Perspektive der Ressourcenmobilisierung und die Theorie Kollektiven Handelns, in: Paradigmen der Bewegungsforschung. Entstehung und Entwicklung von Neuen Sozialen Bewegungen und Rechtsextremismus, ed. by Kai-Uwe Hellmann and Ruud Koopmans, Wiesbaden 1998, pp. 90–108.

Potter, Sharyn: Using a Multimedia Social Marketing Campaign to Increase Active Bystanders on the College Campus, in: Joual of American College Health 60 (2012), pp. 282–295.

Quinn, Beth: The Parody of Complaining: Law, Humor, and Harassment in the Everyday Work World, in: Law and Social Inquiry 25/4 (2000), pp. 1151–1185.

Rabin-Margalioth: Love at Work, in: Duke Journal of Gender Law and Policy 13 (2006), pp. 237–253.

Reyes-Menendez, Ana et al.: Exploring Key Indicators of Social Identity in the #MeToo Era: Using Discourse Analysis in UGC, in: International Journal of Information Management 54 (2020), pp. 1–11.

Roth, Roland: Kollektive Identitäten Neuer Sozialer Bewegungen, in: Paradigmen der Bewegungsforschung. Entstehung und Entwicklung von Neuen Sozialen Bewegungen und Rechtsextremismus, ed. by Kai-Uwe Hellmann and Ruud Koopmans, Wiesbaden 1998, pp. 52–56.

Ryan, Barbara: Feminism and the Women's Movement. Dynamics of Change in Social Movement Ideology and Activism, New York 1992.

Ryan, Charlotte: Prime Time Activism. Media Strategies for Grassroot Organizing, Boston 1991.

Rymph, Catherine E.: Republican Women. Feminism and Conservatism from Suffrage through the Rise of the New Right, Chapel Hill, NC 2006.

Schoenbaum, Thomas: Liability for Damages in Oil Spill Accidents: Evaluating the SA and International Law Regimes in the Light of Deepwater Horizon, in: Journal of Environmental Law 24/3 (2012), pp. 365–416.

Schreiber, Ronnee: Anti-Feminist, Pro-Life, and Anti-Era Women, in: The Oxford Handbook of U.S. Women's Social Movement Activism, ed. by McCammon et al., New York 2017, pp. 315–334.

Schreiber, Ronnee: Righting Feminism. Conservative Women and American Politics, Oxford, NY 2011.

Schultz, Vicki: The Sanitized Workplace, in: The Yale Law Journal 112/8 (2003), pp. 2001–2193.

Seymour, R.: More Arbitration, at: https://www.seymouradr.com/arbitration/more-on-arbitration (last accessed on May 2nd, 2021).

Seymour, R.: Trends in Employment Discrimination Law, Arizona State Bar Association Sedona, 2017, available at: https://rickseymourlaw.com/files/2012/10/Arizona-2017-Seymour.pdf (last viewed on September 6th, 2022).

Shuman, Daniel: The Role of Apology in Tort Law, in: Judicature 83/4 (2000), pp. 180–190.

Sims, Carra et al.: The Effects of Sexual Harassment Turnover in the Military: Time-Dependent Modeling, in: Journal of Applied Psychology 90/6 (2005), pp. 1141–1152.

Skaine, Rosemarie: Power and Gender. Issues in Sexual Dominance and Harassment, Jefferson, NC – London 1996.

Sowerwine, Charles and Patricia Grimshaw: Equality and Difference in the Twentieth-Century West. North America, Western Europe, Australia, and New Zealand, in: A Companion to Gender History (Blackwell Companions to History), Malden, MA – Oxford – Victoria [2]2006, pp. 586–610.

Sperino, Sandra and Suja Thomas: Unequal. How America's Courts Undermine Discrimination Law, New York 2007.

Strüver, Anke: Grundlagen und Zentrale Begriffe der Foucault'schen Diskurstheorie, in: Handbuch Diskurs und Raum. Theorien und Methoden für die Humangeographie sowie die Sozial- und Kulturwissenschaftliche Raumforschung, ed. by Georg Glasze and Annika, Bielefeld [2]2005, pp. 61–82.

Sutton, Matthew Avery: Reagan, Religion, and the Culture Wars of the 1980s, in: A Companion to Ronald Reagan (Wiley Blackwell Companions to History), ed. by Andrew L. Johns, Chichester et al. 2015, pp. 205–220.

Tinkler, Justine: Resisting the Enforcement of Sexual Harassment Law, in: Law and Social Inquiry 37/1 (Winter 2012), pp. 1–24.

Tippett: Elizabeth C.: Harassment Trainings. A Case Analysis, in: Berkeley Journal of Employment & Labor Law 39/2 (January 2018), pp. 481–526.

Tuck, Stephen: African American Protest during the Reagan Years. Forging New Agendas, Defending Old Victories, in: Ronald Reagan and the 1980s. Receptions, Policies, Legacies (Studies of the Americas), ed. by Cheryl Hudson and Gareth Davies, New York 2008, pp. 119–134.

Uhl, Karsten: Humane Rationalisierung? Die Raumordnung der Fabrik im Fordistischen Jahrhundert, Bielefeld 2014.

Vogelstein, Rachel and Meighan Stone: Awakening. #MeToo and the Global Fight for Women's Rights, London 2021.

White, Evan: A Hostile Environment: How the 'severe or Pervasive' Requirement and the Employer's Affirmative Defense Trap Sexual Harassment Plaintiffs in a Catch-22, in: Boston College Law Review 47 (2006), p. 853–890.

Whittier, Nancy: Identity Politics, Consciousness-Raising, and Visibility Politics, in: The Oxford Handbook of U.S. Women's Social Movement Activism, ed. by McCammon et al., New York 2017, pp. 376–397.

Williams, Daniel K.: Reagan's Religious Right. The Unlikely Alliance between Southern Evangelicals and a California Conservative, in: Ronald Reagan and the 1980s. Receptions, Policies, Legacies (Studies of the Americas), ed. by Cheryl Hudson and Gareth Davies, New York 2008, pp. 135–149.

Young, Cathy: Ceasefire. Why Women and Men Must Join Forces to Achieve True Equality, 1999.

Zippel, Katharin: The Politics of Sexual Harassment. A Comparative Study of the United States, the European Union, and Germany, New York et al. 2006.

List of Abbreviations

AA	Affirmative Action
AASC	Alliance Against Sexual Coercion
ACLU	American Civil Liberties Union
ADR	Alternative Dispute Resolution
AFB	Arbitration Fairness Bill
BLS	Bureau of Labor Statistics
BYOD	Bring Your Own Device Policy
CDC	Center for Disease Control
DEC	Digital Equipment Corporation
ECPA	Electronic Communication Privacy Act
EEO	Equal Employment Opportunity
EEOC	Equal Employment Opportunity Commission
FAA	Federal Arbitration Act
HAFC	Household Automotive Finance Corporation
MSHA	Mine Safety and Health Administration
MSPB	Merit Systems Protection Board
NDA	Non-Disclosure Agreements
NOW	National Organization for Women
OPM	Office of Personnel Management
OSHA	Health and Safety Administration
UAW	United Automobile, Aerospace and Agricultural Implement Workers of America
UMWA	United Mine Workers of America
WOASH	Women Organized Against Sexual Harassment
WOW	Women Office Workers
WWI	Working Women's Institute

Index

www.ingramcontent.com/pod-product-compliance
Lightning Source LLC
Chambersburg PA
CBHW050632280326
41932CB00015B/2616